Catholic Source Book

*A Collection of Prayers and Information
to Help Learn, Renew, Teach and Live the
Risen Life of Jesus Christ in the Catholic Church*

**Edited by
Rev. Peter Klein**

BROWN **ROA**
Publishing Media
Dubuque, Iowa

Unless otherwise noted, Scripture texts used in this work are taken from the *New American Bible,* copyright © 1970 by the Confraternity of Christian Doctrine, Washington, D.C. Used by permission of the copyright owner. All rights reserved.

Occasionally (where noted) Scripture texts are taken from *The Jerusalem Bible,* copyright © 1966 by Darton, Longman, and Todd, Ltd. and Doubleday and Company, Inc. Used by permission of the publisher.

Most of the pictures in this book are from St. Adrian's Church, Adrian, Minnesota, and St. Mary's Church, Ellsworth, Minnesota. All of these were taken by Kevin and Brenda Gisolf (Future Photography, Adrian, Minnesota).

These are some church window sketches taken from St. Mary's Church, Worthington, Minnesota. They were originally created by Mr. Robert Leader, Notre Dame University, and are rendered herein with his permission by Ilene Becker.

All maps are drawn and lettered by Karen Lorenz.

Sincere effort was made to comply with copyrights where material was not ours originally or not in the public domain. If we have been unsuccessful on any point in this regard and any party finds their copyright violated please inform the editor so credit can be given and settlement made.

Dedicated to **Helen**

". . . qui laetificat iuventutem meam."

(*". . . who gives joy to my youth."* Ps 43.4,
formerly used in the prayers at the foot of the
altar.)

Contents

Introduction

Often, families have photo albums. Some have scrapbooks for their keepsakes. The *Catholic Source Book* is one person's collection of catholic keepsakes. It has pictures, graphic ones as well as the kind stories paint. It records information and customs of the disciples of Christ that depict the way we were, and the way we are. Its purpose is to provide information, but also to evoke from within others the memories and experiences, the teachings and traditions that have played a part in shaping lives and making faith so catholic, so rich and varied. The *Catholic Source Book* is another sign of a renewing Church who, like the Gospel scribe, brings forth things both old and new.

Prayers

Traditional

Sign of the Cross

In the name of the Father, and the Son, and the Holy Spirit. Amen.

Our Father *(Pater Noster)*

Mt 6.9–13; Lk 11.2–4. The seven petitions of the Lord's Prayer are a synthesis of faith and true hierarchy of values. The doxology "for thine is the kingdom . . ." was added in the sixteenth century. Originally a liturgical ending, it was used during Mass with the embolism (insertion) "Deliver us, O Lord. . . ." "Fiat voluntas Tua" is the familiar prayer from the Our Father in Latin, "Thy will be done".

Our Father, who art in heaven, hallowed be your name; your Kingdom come; your will be done on earth as it is in heaven. Give us this day our daily bread; and forgive us our trespasses as we forgive those who trespass against us; and lead us not into temptation, but deliver us from evil.* Amen.

Hail, Mary *(Ave, Maria)*

The Hail Mary is a composite of the angel Gabriel's greeting (Lk 1.25) and Elizabeth's greeting (Lk 1.42). It has been a popular prayer since the eleventh century. The word "Jesus" was added in the thirteenth century. Various versions of the "Holy Mary . . ." emerged in the fourteenth century and were in general use by the sixteenth century.

Hail, Mary, full of grace! The Lord is with thee; blessed art thou among women, and blessed is the fruit of thy womb, Jesus. Holy Mary, Mother of God, pray for us sinners, now and at the hour of our death. Amen.

The Lady of the Lake

In 1825, Franz Schubert set to music some of Sir Walter Scott's verses in "The Lady of the Lake." It was later discovered that the Latin text of The Hail Mary, "Ave, Maria . . .", could be sung to the same music. There are those who believe that it was this prayer, and the Blessed Lady herself, who originally inspired Schubert to compose one of the greatest pieces of devotional music ever: the "Ave Maria."

---

*This verse has known many translations; the petition is always the same, however, whatever the translation: strength from God to protect us against evil.

Glory Be to the Father *(Gloria Patri)*

This is the "Lesser Doxology" (Lt: doxa, glory), the "Greater" being the Gloria of the Mass. It is said at the end of psalms in the Liturgy of the Hours. The first-verse wording is ascribed to St. Basil, the second to Telesphorus (A.D. 139) (See doxology.) Probably adapted from Jewish blessings, it was influenced by the Trinitarian baptism formula (Mt 28.19). It was forbidden by English Puritans as unscriptural.

Glory be to the Father, and to the Son, and to the Holy Spirit. As it was in the beginning, is now, and ever shall be, world without end. Amen.

Gloria *(in excelsis Deo)* (Glory to God in the highest)

This is the "Greater Doxology" (Lt: doxa, glory), the lesser being the "Glory Be" prayer. It echoes the song of the angels at Bethlehem, (Lk 2.14), hence, it is called "The Angelic Hymn."

Glory to God in the highest, and peace to his people on earth. Lord God, heavenly King, almighty God and Father, we worship you, we give you thanks, we praise you for your glory. Lord Jesus Christ, only son of the Father, Lord God, Lamb of God, you take away the sin of the world: have mercy on us; you are seated at the right hand of the Father: receive our prayer. For you alone the Holy One, you alone are the Lord, you alone are the Most High, Jesus Christ, with the Holy Spirit, in the glory of God the Father. Amen.

Apostles' Creed

The Apostles' Creed is the epitome of Christian doctrine. In twelve articles, it was taught by the apostles. It existed essentially since the second century, was precisioned by early Church councils, and adopted in its present form in the eleventh century. Since the early years of the Western Church, catechumens were required to learn and recite it before baptism.

I believe in God, the Father Almighty, Creator of heaven and earth; and in Jesus Christ, his only Son, our Lord, who was conceived by the Holy Spirit, born of the Virgin Mary, suffered under Pontius Pilate, was crucified, died, and was buried. He descended into hell; the third day he rose again from the dead. He ascended into heaven and sits at the right hand of God, the Father Almighty. From thence he shall come to judge the living and the dead. I believe in the Holy Spirit, the Holy Catholic Church, the communion of saints, the forgiveness of sins, the resurrection of the body and life everlasting. Amen.

Nicene Creed

The Nicene Creed takes its name from Nicea, city of the Ecumenical Council that formulated the Creed, in A.D 325. It is common ground for the Catholic, Orthodox, and Anglican Churches.

We believe in one God, the Father, the Almighty, maker of heaven and earth of all that is seen and unseen. We believe in one Lord, Jesus Christ, the only Son of God, eternally begotten of the Father, God from God, Light from Light, true God from true God, begotten, not made, one in Being with the Father. Through him all things were made. For us men and for our salvation he came down from heaven: by the power of the Holy Spirit he was born of the Virgin Mary, and became man. For our sake he was crucified under Pontius Pilate; he suffered, died, and was buried. On the third day he rose again in fulfillment of the Scriptures; he ascended into heaven and is seated at the right hand of the Father. He will come again in glory to judge the living and the dead, and his kingdom will have no end. We believe in the Holy Spirit, the Lord, the giver of life, who proceeds from the Father and the Son. With the Father and the Son he is worshipped and glorified. He has spoken through the Prophets. We believe in one holy catholic and apostolic Church. We acknowledge one baptism for the forgiveness of sins. We look for the resurrection of the dead, and the life of the world to come. Amen.

Athanasian Creed

This creed is so-called because it embodies Athanasius' theology of the Trinity. Composed by Hilary, bishop of Arles (fifth century), it is common doctrinal ground (along with the Apostles' and Nicene creeds) for Catholics and Anglicans. It is also characterized by its extraordinary length and its anathemas against any who would deny the doctrines it professes. Its Latin title is its opening word, "Quicumque": "If anyone wishes to be saved, before everything else he must hold the Catholic faith."

A Profession of Catholic Christianity

I, N., enlightened by divine grace, profess the Christian faith as it is taught and practiced in the Catholic Church.

I believe in God, the father Almighty, creator of heaven and earth; and in Jesus Christ, his only Son, our Lord, who was conceived by the Holy spirit, born of the Virgin Mary, suffered under Pontius Pilate, was crucified, died, and was buried. He descended into hell; the third day he rose again from the dead; he ascended into heaven, sits at the right hand of God, the Father Almighty; from thence he shall come to judge the living and the dead. I believe in the Holy Spirit, the holy Catholic Church, the communion of saints, the forgiveness of sins, the resurrection of the body, and life everlasting.

I believe that this Church is the Church in which the fullness of God's revelation through his Son, Jesus Christ, abides. I believe that her college

4

of bishops, with the Pope, the bishop of Rome, presiding at its center, continues to exercise in the world the authority for teaching and moral guidance given by Jesus Christ to his apostles for the salvation of men.

I further believe in seven sacraments, signs of worship through which the grace of the death, resurrection and ascension of Jesus Christ is communicated. They are: baptism, confirmation, holy Eucharist, penance, anointing of the sick, holy orders, and matrimony.

I promise, through prayer, participation in Church life and worship, and continued efforts to understand the tenets of my faith, to form my conscience in such a way as to live according to the doctrines and practices which the Roman Catholic Church prescribes for the individual and common good of her faithful.

Act of Faith

O my God, I firmly believe that You are one God in three Divine Persons, Father, Son, and Holy Spirit; I believe that Your Divine Son became man and died for our sins, and that He will come to judge the living and the dead. I believe these and all the truths which the Holy Catholic Church teaches, because You revealed them, who can neither deceive nor be deceived.

Act of Hope

O my God, relying on Your infinite goodness and promises, I hope to obtain pardon of my sins, the help of your grace, and life everlasting, through the merits of Jesus Christ, my Lord and Redeemer.

Anchor, cross, and heart—signs of faith, hope, and love

Act of Love

O my God, I love You above all things, with my whole heart and soul, because You are all-good and worthy of all love. I love my neighbor as myself for the love of You. I forgive all who have injured me, and I ask pardon of all whom I have injured.

Act of Contrition (*Traditional*)

O my God, I am heartily sorry for having offended You, and I detest all my sins, because of Your just punishments, but most of all because they offend You, my God, who are all-good and deserving of all my love. I firmly resolve, with the help of Your grace, to sin no more and to avoid the near occasion of sin.

Act of Contrition *(Contemporary)*

O my God, I am sorry I have sinned. Please forgive me. I know you love me. I want to love you and to be good to everyone. Help me make up for my sins. I will try to do better from now on. Amen.

Confiteor *("I Confess")*

Mea culpa, *"through my fault,"* (or *"It's my fault"*) *is a phrase in any* Confiteor, *particularly the one sometimes used during the penitential rite of the Mass. (The* maxima culpa *is "grevous" fault.)*

I confess to almighty God, and to you, my brothers and sisters, that I have sinned through my own fault, in my thoughts and in my words, in what I have done, and in what I have failed to do; and I ask blessed Mary, ever virgin, all the angels and saints, and you, my brothers and sisters, to pray for me to the Lord our God.

Leonine Prayers *("Prayers after Mass")*

These prayers were formerly said after Mass, ordered universally by Pope Leo XIII: three Hail Marys, the Hail Holy Queen and the prayer to St. Michael the Archangel. The prayers ended with a three-fold invocation to the Sacred Heart (added by Pope St. Pius X). The Leonine Prayers were formally abrogated in 1964.

St. Michael the Archangel

O God, our refuge and our strength, look down in mercy on Your people who cry to You; and by the intercession of the glorious and Immaculate Virgin Mary, Mother of God, of Saint Joseph her spouse, of Your Blessed Apostles Peter and Paul, and all the Saints, in mercy and goodness hear our prayers for the conversion of sinners, and for the liberty and exaltation of our holy mother the Church. Through the same Christ our Lord. Amen.

Holy Michael, the Archangel, defend us in battle; be our safeguard against the wickedness and snares of the devil. May God rebuke him, we humbly pray; and you, Prince of the heavenly host, by the power of God, cast into hell Satan and all the evil spirits, who wander through the world seeking the ruin of souls. Amen.

Angelus ("The Angel")

Honoring the incarnation, the Angelus is named for its first Latin word (Angelus Domini, the angel of the Lord . . .). Since the sixteenth century, the church bells (one of the community's clocks) called the Angelus, at six A.M., twelve noon, and six P.M. The evening call probably began as a curfew bell, a call for evening prayer. The six A.M. call was originally a prayer for peace. The noon prayer was said formerly only on Friday. In Easter season, the Angelus was replaced by Regina Caeli Laetare (Queen of Heaven Rejoice.)

The angel of the Lord declared unto Mary.
And she conceived of the Holy Spirit.
Hail Mary, full of grace . . .
Holy Mary, Mother of God . . .
Behold the handmaid of the Lord.
Be it done to me according to your word.
Hail Mary, full of grace . . .
Holy Mary, Mother of God . . .
And the Word was made flesh.
And dwelt among us.
Hail Mary, full of grace . . .
Holy Mary, Mother of God . . .

Pray for us, O holy Mother of God.
That we may be made worthy of the promises of Christ.

Let us pray. Pour forth, we beseech you, O Lord, your grace into our hearts, that we to whom the incarnation of Christ, your Son, was made known by the message of an angel, may, by his passion and cross, be brought to the glory of his resurrection, through the same Christ our Lord. Amen.

Queen of Heaven *(Regina Caeli)*

This prayer replaces the Angelus during Eastertime.

Queen of heaven, rejoice, alleluia.
For he whom you were chosen to bear, alleluia.
Has risen as he said, alleluia.
Pray to God for us, alleluia.
Rejoice and be glad, Virgin Mary, alleluia.
For the Lord is truly risen, alleluia.

Let us pray. Father, you were pleased to give joy to the world through the resurrection of your Son, our Lord Jesus Christ. Grant, we beseech you, that through the mediation of the Virgin Mary, His mother, we may come

Christ the King crowning Mary

to possess the joys of life everlasting. Through the same Christ our Lord. Amen.

Latin Version *(Regina Caeli)*
Regina caeli, laetare, alleluia
Quia quem meruisti portare, alleluia
Resurrexit sicut dixit, alleluia
Oro pro nobis Deum, alleluia.

Te Deum

This is an ancient (fourth-century) hymn, called by its first two words, ascribed by some to St. Ambrose, who, it is said, prayed it while baptizing Augustine (386), hence "Ambrosian Hymn." The traditional and popular hymn "Holy God, We Praise Thy Name" is an English translation of a free translation into German of the Te Deum.

You are God: we praise you;
You are the Lord: we acclaim you;
You are the eternal Father;
All creation worships you.

To you all angels, all the powers of heaven,
Cherubim and Seraphim, sing in endless praise:
    Holy, holy, holy, Lord, God of power and might,
    heaven and earth are full of your glory.

The glorious company of apostles praise you.
The noble fellowship of prophets praise you.
The white-robed army of martyrs praise you.

Throughout the world the holy Church acclaims you:
    Father, of majesty unbounded,
    your true and only Son, worthy of all worship,
    and the Holy Spirit, advocate and guide.

You, Christ, are the king of glory,
the eternal Son of the Father.

When you became man to set us free
you did not spurn the Virgin's womb.

You overcame the sting of death,
and opened the kingdom of heaven to all believers.

You are seated at God's right hand in glory.
We believe that you will come, and be our judge.

Come then, Lord, and help your people,
bought with the price of your own blood,
and bring us with your saints
to glory everlasting.

Save your people, Lord, and bless your inheritance.
Govern and uphold them now and always.
Day by day we bless you.
We praise your name for ever.
Keep us today, Lord, from all sin.
Have mercy on us, Lord, have mercy.
Lord, show us your love and mercy;
for we put our trust in you.
In you, Lord, is our hope;
and we shall never hope in vain.

The Jesus Prayer

The Jesus Prayer is an ancient Eastern Christian contemplative prayer. It invokes the name of Jesus, the only name in the world given us by which we are to be saved (Act 4.12; also 2.21; 9.14,21 e.g.). Developed by the Desert Fathers, it consists of short phrases from the Scriptures repeated interiorly with attention to God's presence until prayer becomes one with breathing and the Lord makes a house within (Jn. 14.23; Rv 3.20). The most popular phrase was the prayer of the gospel publican (Lk 18.13). God has given Jesus a name to be exalted (Phil 2.9–11) with a saving power that is sign and source of the Spirit within (1 Cor 12.3).

Traditionally
1. positioning, posturing physically
2. centering mentally
3. breathing deeply, rhythmically
4. thinking:
   LORD JESUS CHRIST—breathing in,
   SON OF GOD—breathing out,
   HAVE MERCY—breathing in,
   ON ME A SINNER —breathing out.

Morning Offering

The Morning offering is the dedication of the day to the Sacred Heart, and is said by members of the Apostleship of Prayer (League of the Sacred Heart)

O Jesus, through the Immaculate Heart of Mary, I offer You all my prayers, works, joys and sufferings of this day, for all the intentions of Your Sacred Heart, in union with the Holy Sacrifice of the Mass throughout the world, in reparation for my sins, for the intentions of all our associates, and for the general intention recommended this month.

Prayer Before Meals

Bless us, O Lord, and these Your gifts, which we are about to receive from Your bounty, through Christ our Lord. Amen.

Prayer After Meals

We give You thanks for all Your benefits, O almighty God, who lives and reigns forever; and may the souls of the faithful departed, through the mercy of God, rest in peace. Amen.

Angel of God

Angel of God, my Guardian dear, to whom His love commits me here, ever this day be at my side, to light and guard, to rule and guide. Amen.

Watch Thou, Dear Lord *(St. Augustine)*

Watch Thou, dear Lord, with those who wake, or watch, or weep tonight, and give Thine angels charge over those who sleep. Tend Thy sick ones, O Lord Christ. Rest Thy weary ones. Bless They dying ones. Soothe Thy suffering ones. Pity Thine afflicted ones. Shield Thy joyous ones. And all, for Thy Love's sake. Amen.

Eternal Rest

Eternal rest grant to them, O Lord,
and let perpetual light shine upon them.
May they rest in peace.
Amen.

Prayer Before a Crucifix

Behold, my beloved and good Jesus, I cast myself upon my knees in Your sight, and with the most fervent desire of my soul I pray and beseech You to impress upon my heart lively sentiments of faith, hope and charity, with true repentance for my sins and a most firm desire of amendment; while with deep affection and grief of soul I consider within myself and mentally contemplate Your five most precious wounds, having before my eyes that which David the prophet, long ago spoke about You, my Jesus:
"They have pierced my hands and my feet; I can count all my bones."
Ps 22.17–18.

Why the Robin's Breast Is Red

This is a story from the life of the Irish saint Columbkille. One morning he woke from sleep in his little hermitage to find a robin perched on the window sill. "Have you a song for me?" he asked, and in reply the robin sang a song of Good Friday, and how its breast was reddened: From its nest among the moss the robin saw the Lord of all upon a cross, and the Lord saw the brown, yellow beaked bird. Christ called, and the robin lighted upon him. As the crowds taunted, the robin sang "Holy, holy, holy," with its breast against Christ's bloody brow. Mary's voice then was heard, "Christ's own bird thou shalt be!" And so the robin's proudest story, of its red breast from the day it saw Christ die.

The Divine Praises

The Divine Praises were traditionally recited after the Benediction of the Blessed Sacrament. They were composed possibly about 1800 in reparation for profanity and blasphemy. Invocations 5, 6, 10, 11 and 13 are post mid-nineteenth century additions.

Blessed be God.
Blessed be His Holy Name.
Blessed be Jesus Christ, true God and true man.
Blessed be the Name of Jesus.
Blessed be His Most Sacred Heart.
Blessed be His Most Precious Blood.
Blessed be Jesus in the Most Holy Sacrament of the Altar.
Blessed be the Holy Spirit, the Paraclete.
Blessed be the great Mother of God, Mary most holy.
Blessed be her holy and Immaculate Conception.
Blessed be her glorious Assumption.
Blessed be the name of Mary, Virgin and Mother.
Blessed be St. Joseph, her most chaste spouse.
Blessed be God in His angels and in His saints.

Come, Holy Spirit

Come, Holy Spirit, fill the hearts of your faithful and enkindle in them the fire of your divine love.

V. Send forth your Spirit and they shall be created.
R. And You shall renew the face of the earth.

Let us pray. O God, who by the light of the Holy Spirit, did instruct the hearts of your faithful, grant that by that same Holy Spirit, we may be truly wise, and ever rejoice in your consolation. Through Christ our Lord. Amen.

Veni, Sancte Spiritus *("Come, Creator Spirit")*

The "Golden Sequence" of Pentecost was probably written by Rabanus Maurus (776–856). This translation is by Edward Caswell (1814–78). Long a part of the Liturgy of the Hours, and called "the most popular of all hymns," it is used at papal elections, bishop consecrations, priestly ordinations, counciliar/synodal gatherings and church dedications.

Come, thou Holy Spirit, come!
And from they celestial home
Shed a ray of light divine!

Come, thou Father of the poor!
Come, thou source of all our store!
Come, within our bosoms shine!

Thou, of comforters the best;
Thou, the soul's most welcome guest;
Sweet refreshment here below.

In our labor, rest most sweet;
Grateful coolness in the heat;
Solace in the midst of woe.

O most blessed Light divine,
Shine within these hearts of thine,
And our inmost being fill!

Where thou art not, we have naught,
Nothing good in deed or thought,
Nothing free from taint of ill.

Heal our wounds, our strength renew;
On our dryness pour thy dew;
Wash the stains of guilt away.

Bend the stubborn heart and will;
Melt the frozen, warm the chill;
Guide the steps that go astray.

On the faithful, who adore
And confess thee, evermore
In thy sev'nfold gift descend.

Give them virtue's sure reward;
Give them thy salvation, Lord;
Give them joys that never end.

St. Augustine as a bishop, with the inspiring Spirit at his ear and the fruit of his writing in hand. At his foot sits Adeodatus ("Gift of God"), a child from his "former life."

Holy Spirit Prayer of St. Augustine

Breathe in me, O Holy Spirit,
That my thoughts may all be holy;
Act in me, O Holy Spirit,
That my work, too, may be holy;
Draw my heart, O Holy Spirit,
That I love but what is holy.
Strengthen me, O Holy Spirit,
To defend all that is holy;
Guard me, then, O Holy Spirit,
That I always may be holy.

The Rosary

The Rosary is called the "Psalter of Mary" because its 150 Aves (all fifteen decades, the "Dominican Rosary") correspond to the number of the psalms. It is the most well-known and used form of "chaplet," a devotion said using beads, from a French word meaning crown, or wreath. There are other chaplets, such as those in honor of St. Bridget of Sweden and in honor of the Immaculate Conception.

12

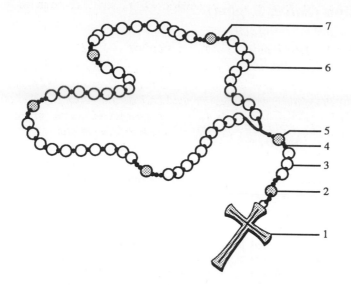

1. Sign of the Cross and Apostles' Creed
2. Our Father
3. Three Hail Marys
4. Glory be to the Father
5. Announce first mystery; Our Father
6. Ten Hail Marys
7. Glory be to the Father

Repeat last three steps, meditating on the other mysteries of the rosary.

Sometimes the Fatima invocation is recited between decades:

"O my Jesus, forgive us our sins. Save us from the fires of hell, and bring all souls to heaven, especially those who most need your mercy."
—recommended by Mary to the children at Fatima (1917)

Hail, Holy Queen *(Salve, Regina)*

One of the most ancient Marian antiphons in Western Christendom, the Hail Holy Queen was used for centuries in the Liturgy of the Hours. It is most often regarded as anonymous (though probably it was composed by Hermannus Contractus, d. 1054). Its finale, "O clement . . .", though attributed to St. Bernard, is found in manuscripts that pre-date him. Traditionally, it is sung as the last prayer of Compline, the Church's liturgical Night Prayer.

Hail, holy Queen, Mother of mercy! Hail, our life, our sweetness, and our hope! To you do we cry, poor banished children of Eve. To you do we send up our sighs, mourning, and weeping in this valley of tears. Turn then, most gracious advocate, your eyes of mercy toward us; and after this, our exile, show unto us the blessed fruit of your womb, Jesus. O clement, O loving, O sweet Virgin Mary! Amen.

Latin Version *(Salve, Regina)*

Salve, Regina, mater misericordiae,
Vita, dulcedo et spes nostra salve.
Ad te clamamus exsules filii Evae
Ad te suspiramus, gementes et flentes
in hac lacrimarum vala.
Eia ergo, advocata nostra
illos tuos misericordes oculos ad nos converte.
Et Jesum, benedictum fructum ventris tui,
nobis post hoc exsilium ostende.
O clemens, O pia, O dulcis, Virgo Maria.

The Mysteries of the Rosary

Including recommended Scriptural meditations.

Joyful Mysteries—Mondays and Thursdays
1. The Annunciation (Humility)
   Is 7.10–14; Lk 1.26–38
2. The Visitation (Charity)
   Is 40.1–10; Lk 1.39–45; Jn 1.19–23
3. The Nativity (Poverty)
   Mi 5.1–5; Mt 2.1–12; Lk 2.1–20; Gal 4.1–7
4. The Presentation (Obedience)
   Lk 2.22–35; Heb 9.6–14
5. The Finding of Jesus in the Temple (Piety)
   Lk 2.41–50; Jn 12.44–50; 1 Cor 2.6–16

Sorrowful Mysteries—Tuesdays and Fridays
1. The Agony in the Garden (Repentance)
   Mt 26.36–46; Mk 14.26–42; Lk 22.39–53; Jn 18.1–12
2. The Scourging at the Pillar (Purity)
   Is 50.5–9; Mt 27.15–26; Mk 15.1–16
3. The Crowning with Thorns (Courage)
   Is 52.13–53.10, Mt 16.24–28; Mt 27.27–31; Mk 15.16–19; Lk 23.6–11; Jn 19.1–7
4. The Carrying of the Cross (Patience)
   Mk 8.31–38; Mk 16.20–25; Lk 22.20–32; Jn 19.17–22; Phil 2.6–11
5. The Crucifixion (Self-renunciation)
   Mk 15.33–39; Lk 23.33–46; Jn 19.17–37; Acts 22.22–24; Heb 9.11–14

Glorious Mysteries—Sundays, Wednesdays, and Saturdays
1. The Resurrection (Faith)
   Mt 28.1–10; Mk 16.1–18; Mk 24.1–11; Jn 20.1–10; Rom 6.1–14; 1 Cor 15.1–11
2. The Ascension (Hope)
   Mt 28.16–20; Lk 24.44–53; Acts 1.1–11; Eph 2.4–7

3. The Descent of the Holy Spirit Upon the Apostles (Love)
   Jn 14.15–21; Acts 2.1–11; 4.23–31; 11.44–48
4. The Assumption (Eternal Happiness)
   Jn 11.17–27; 1 Cor 15.20–28, 42–50, 51–57; Rv 21.1–6
5. The Coronation of Mary (Marian Devotion)
   Mt 5.1–12; 2 Pt 3.10; Rv 7.1–4, 9–12; Rv 21.1–6

"Franciscan Crown" (or "Seraphic Rosary")

The "Franciscan Crown" is a *rosary of seven decades commemorating the seven joys of Mary:* (1) Annunciation, (2) Visitation, (3) Nativity, (4) Adoration of the Magi, (5) Finding in the Temple, (6) Appearance of the risen Christ to his mother, and (7) Assumption and Coronation. It was introduced among the Franciscans in 1422. Two Hail Marys were added since, to total seventy-two, the traditional age of Mary at her assumption.

Memorare (Lt: to call to mind)

The Memorare is ascribed to St. Bernard of Clairvaux (1090–1153), probably because it was popularized by Claude Bernard, the "Poor Priest" (1588–1641).

Remember, most gracious Virgin Mary, that never was it known that anyone who fled to your protection, implored your help, or sought your intercession was left unaided. Inspired by this confidence, I fly to you, O Virgin of virgins, my mother. To you I come; before you I stand, sinful and sorrowful. O Mother of the Word Incarnate, despise not my petitions, but in your mercy, hear and answer me. Amen.

LITANIES

Since Vatican II, these are the formally indulgenced litanies: Holy Name, Precious Blood, St. Joseph, Sacred Heart, Blessed Vigin, The Saints. Other litanies not indulgenced but approved for the faithful number over a hundred. Each begins with an invocation of the Trinity.

Litanies and Rogation Days

Although a "litany" has come to mean an untiring repetition, its deeper—and literal—meaning is "petition." "Rogation" is the Latin translation, a word that gave a title to three days of prayer for the Lord's blessing of a successful harvest on fields and gardens. These are the annual triduum of Monday, Tuesday and Wednesday before Ascension Thursday. They are penitential days, including a mass and procession. Because the Litany ("rogation") of the Saints is invoked, Rogation Days were also called "The Lesser Litanies." (They're "Lesser" because the tradition is younger than the ancient "Greater Litanies," a similar observance but originating as a Christian replacement for a pagan procession on April 25 that propitiated Robigus, the god of frost.) Rogation Days' origin is interesting:

Believers have always given thanks to God for sun and soil, water and air. In the beginning, these believers knew themselves as stewards, not consumers, and had constant reminders of their dependence on the merciful Lord who creates and provides, and who owns the earth. At times, it seems the very elements conspire against a regular harvest, sometimes even causing prolonged periods of fruitlessness and hopelessness. It is particularly at these times that the call goes out to a provident Lord to restore the earth's bounty.

That is what happened in France, some 1500 years ago, around the city of Vienne. Earthquake, fire and inclement weather combined to cause crop failure and widespread hunger. Mamertus, the Bishop of Veinne, called for penance and prayer on the three days preceding Ascension Thursday. The people responded to the call, and the Lord responded to the prayer.

Throughout France, and ultimately beyond, word of this "litany," this "rogation," spread, finding a readiness in the hearts of believers. As the years went by, the same three days of penitential prayer were observed annually, and by the eighth century, universally.

The gratitude, the awareness of God's power and earth's bounty, and human dependence on both—these are no less real today. Now week-long, the penitential prayer is a part of "Soil and Water Stewardship Week." It is still the spirit and style of prayer called forth by St. Mamertus, while, at the same time, we take responsibility for creative conservation and considerate management.

Litany of the Sacred Heart

The Litany was authorized for recitation in the universal Church by Pope Leo XIII in 1889.

Lord, have mercy. *Christ, have mercy.*

Lord, have mercy.

Christ, hear us. *Christ, graciously hear us.*

God, the Father of Heaven, *have mercy on us (after each invocation).*

God the Son, Redeemer of the world,

God, the Holy Spirit,

Holy Trinity, One God,

Heart of Jesus, Son of the Eternal Father,

Heart of Jesus, formed by the Holy Spirit in the womb of the Virgin
  Mother,

Heart of Jesus, substantially united to the Word of God,

Heart of Jesus, of Infinite Majesty,

Heart of Jesus, Sacred Temple of God,

Heart of Jesus, Tabernacle of the Most High,

Heart of Jesus, House of God and Gate of Heaven,

Heart of Jesus, burning furnace of charity,

Heart of Jesus, abode of justice and love,

Heart of Jesus, full of goodness and love,

Heart of Jesus, abyss of all virtues,

Heart of Jesus, most worthy of all praise,

Heart of Jesus, king and center of all hearts,

Heart of Jesus, in whom dwells the fullness of divinity,

Heart of Jesus, in whom the Father was well pleased,

Heart of Jesus, desire of the everlasting hills,

Heart of Jesus, patient and most merciful,

Heart of Jesus, enriching all who invoke you,

Heart of Jesus, fountain of life and holiness,

Heart of Jesus, propitiation for our sins,

Heart of Jesus, loaded down with opprobrium,

Heart of Jesus, bruised for our offenses,

Heart of Jesus, obedient to death,

Heart of Jesus, pierced with a lance,

Heart of Jesus, source of consolation,

Heart of Jesus, our life and resurrection,

Heart of Jesus, victim for our sins,

Heart of Jesus, salvation of those who trust in you,

Heart of Jesus, hope of those who die in you,

Heart of Jesus, delight of all the saints,

Lamb of God, who takes away the sins of the world, *spare us, O Lord.*

Lamb of god, who takes away the sins of the world,
  graciously hear us, O Lord.

Lamb of God, who takes away the sins of the world, *have mercy on us.*

V. Jesus, meek and humble of heart,

R. Make our hearts like to yours.

Let us pray. Almighty and eternal God, look upon the heart of Your most beloved Son and upon the praises and satisfaction which he offers You in the name of sinners; and to those who implore Your mercy, in Your great goodness, grant forgiveness in the name of the same Jesus Christ, Your Son, who lives and reigns with You forever and ever. Amen.

IHS—The first three letters of "Jesus" in Greek

Litany of the Most Holy Name of Jesus

This litany is of unknown origin, though ascribed to St. Bernardine of Siena and St. John Capistran. It was given papal attention as early as 1588 and universal recommendation by Pope Leo XIII in 1886. A Holy Name Society was founded as early as the thirteenth century, by a Dominican, to promote reverence for Jesus' name.

Lord, have mercy on us. *Christ, have mercy on us.*
Lord, have mercy on us. Jesus, hear us. *Jesus, graciously hear us.*

God the Father of heaven, *have mercy on us (after each invocation).*
God the Son, Redeemer of the world,
God the Holy Spirit,
Holy Trinity, one God,

Jesus, Son of the Living God,
Jesus, splendor of the Father,
Jesus, brightness of eternal light,
Jesus, King of glory,
Jesus, Sun of justice,
Jesus, Son of the Virgin Mary,
Jesus most amiable,
Jesus most admirable,
Jesus, mighty God,
Jesus, father of the world to come,
Jesus, angel of the great counsel,
Jesus most powerful,
Jesus most patient,
Jesus most obedient,
Jesus meek and humble of heart,
Jesus, lover of chastity,
Jesus, lover of us,
Jesus, God of peace,
Jesus, Author of life,

Jesus, example of virtues,
Jesus, zealous lover of souls,
Jesus, our God,
Jesus, our refuge,
Jesus, father of the poor,
Jesus, treasure of the faithful,
Jesus, good Shepherd,
Jesus, true light,
Jesus, eternal wisdom,
Jesus, infinite goodness,
Jesus, our way and our life,
Jesus, joy of Angels,
Jesus, King of patriarchs,
Jesus, teacher of the evangelists,
Jesus, strength of martyrs,
Jesus, light of the confessors,
Jesus, purity of virgins,
Jesus, crown of all saints,

Be merciful unto us, *Jesus, spare us.*

Be merciful unto us, *Jesus, hear us.*

From all evil, *Jesus deliver us* (after each invocation).

From all sin,

From your wrath,

From the snares of the devil,

From the spirit of uncleanness,

From everlasting death,

From the neglect of thy inspirations,

Through the mystery of your holy incarnation,

Through your nativity,

Through your infancy,

Through your most divine life,

Through your labors,

Through your agony and passion,

Through your cross and dereliction,

Through your faintness and weariness,

Through your death and burial,

Through your resurrection,

Through your ascension,

Through your institution of the most holy Eucharist,

Through your joys,

Through your glory,

Lamb of God, who takes away the sins of the world, *spare us, O Jesus.*

Lamb of God, who takes away the sins of the world, *graciously hear us, O Jesus.*

Lamb of God, who takes away the sins of the world, *have mercy on us, O Jesus.*

Jesus, hear us. *Jesus, graciously hear us.*

Let us pray. O Lord Christ, who said: "Ask and you shall receive, seek and you shall find, knock and it shall be opened unto you;" grant we beseech you to us your supplicants, the gift of your most divine love, that we may love you with our whole heart, in all our words and works, and never cease from praising you. O Lord, give us a perpetual fear as well as love of your holy Name, for you never cease to govern those you found upon the strength of your love, Who live and reign world without end. Amen.

Litany of the Most Precious Blood of Jesus

Lord, have mercy. *Christ have mercy.*

Lord, have mercy. Christ hear us.
    Christ graciously hear us.

God, the Father of heaven, *have mercy on us (after each invocation).*

God the son, Redeemer of the world,

God the Holy Spirit,

Holy Trinity, one God,

Blood of Christ, only-begotten Son of the eternal Father, *save us (after each invocation).*

Blood of Christ, incarnate Word of God,
Blood of Christ, of the new and eternal Testament,
Blood of Christ, falling upon the earth in the agony,
Blood of Christ, shed profusely in the scourging,
Blood of Christ, flowing forth in the crowning with thorns,
Blood of Christ, poured out on the cross,
Blood of Christ, price of our salvation,
Blood of Christ, without which there is no forgiveness,
Blood of Christ, Eucharistic drink and refreshment of souls,
Blood of Christ, stream of mercy,
Blood of Christ, victor over demons,
Blood of Christ, courage of martyrs,
Blood of Christ, strength of confessors,
Blood of Christ, bringing forth virgins,
Blood of Christ, help of those in peril,
Blood of Christ, relief of the burdened,
Blood of Christ, solace in sorrow,
Blood of Christ, hope of the penitent,
Blood of Christ, consolation of the dying,
Blood of Christ, peace and tenderness of hearts,
Blood of Christ, pledge of eternal life,
Blood of Christ, freeing souls from purgatory,
Blood of Christ, most worthy of all glory and honor,

Lamb of God, you take away the sins of the world,
   spare us, O Lord.
Lamb of God, you take away the sins of the world,
   graciously hear us, O Lord.
Lamb of God, you take away the sins of the world,
   have mercy on us.
V. You have redeemed us, O Lord, in your Blood,
R. *and made us, for our God, a kingdom.*

Let us pray. Almighty and eternal God, you have appointed your only-begotten Son the Redeemer of the world and willed to be appeased by his Blood. Grant, we beg you, that we may worthily adore the price of our salvation, and through its power be safeguarded from the evils of the present life, so that we may rejoice in its fruits forever in heaven. Through the same Christ our Lord. Amen.

Litany of the Blessed Virgin ("Our Lady of Loreto")

This Litany was approved and indulgenced in 1587 by Pope Sixtus V. It is a simplified version of more ancient Marian litanies common even in the twelfth century. Several of the current invocations are additions by popes since Sixtus.

Lord, have mercy. *Christ, have mercy.*
Lord, have mercy, Christ, hear us. *Christ graciously hear us.*

God, the Father of Heaven, *have mercy on us.*

God, the Son, Redeemer of the world, *have mercy on us.*

God, the Holy Spirit, *have mercy on us.*

Holy Trinity, one God, *have mercy on us.*

Holy Mary, *pray for us (after each invocation).*

Holy Mother of God,
Holy Virgin of virgins,
Mother of divine grace,
Mother most pure,
Mother most chaste,
Mother inviolate,
Mother undefiled,
Mother most amiable,
Mother most admirable,
Mother of good counsel,
Mother of our Savior,
Virgin most prudent,
Virgin most venerable,
Virgin most renowned,
Virgin most powerful,
Virgin most merciful,
Virgin most faithful,
Mirror of justice,
Seat of wisdom,
Cause of our joy,
Spiritual vessel,
Vessel of honor,
Singular vessel of devotion,
Mystical rose,
Tower of David,
Tower of ivory,
House of gold,
Ark of the covenant,
Gate of heaven,
Morning star,
Health of the sick,
Refuge of sinners,
Comforter of the afflicted,
Help of Christians,
Queen of Angels,
Queen of Patriarchs,
Queen of Prophets,
Queen of Apostles,
Queen of Martyrs,
Queen of Confessors,
Queen of Virgins,
Queen of all Saints,
Queen conceived without sin,
Queen assumed into heaven,
Queen of the most holy Rosary,
Queen of Peace,

Lamb of God, who takes away the sins of the world, *spare us, O Lord.*

Lamb of God, who takes away the sins of the world, *graciously hear us, O Lord.*

Lamb of God, who takes away the sins of the world,
have mercy on us.
Pray for us, O holy Mother of God,
that we may be made worthy of the promises of Christ.
Let us pray. Grant, we beg you, O Lord God, that we your servants, may enjoy lasting health of mind and body, and by the glorious intercession of the Blessed Mary, ever Virgin, be delivered from present sorrow and enter into the joy of eternal happiness. Through Christ our Lord. Amen.

The Mystical Rose

"I was exalted like the rose plant in Jericho." So says the book of Sirach (24.18). Rendered with five petals, this celebrated symbol signifies Mary's five joys (the five joyful mysteries of the rosary). Also, backed by a five-pointed star, it represents the five major Marian feasts (all pertaining to the divine motherhood): (1) Annunciation, (2) Maternity, (3) Visitation, (4) Nativity, (5) Purification.

Litany of St. Joseph

The Litany of St. Joseph was approved for the universal Church by Pope St. Pius X on March 18, 1909.

Lord, have mercy. *Christ, have mercy.*
Lord, have mercy, Christ, hear us. *Christ, graciously hear us.*
God the Father of Heaven, *have mercy on us.*
God the Son, Redeemer of the world, *have mercy on us.*
God the Holy Spirit, *have mercy on us.*

Holy Trinity, one God, *have mercy on us.*
Holy Mary, *pray for us (after each invocation).*
St. Joseph,
Renowned offspring of David,
Light of Patriarchs,
Spouse of the Mother of God,
Chaste guardian of the Virgin,
Foster father of the Son of God,
Diligent protector of Christ,
Head of the Holy Family,
Joseph most just,
Joseph most chaste,
Joseph most prudent,
Joseph most strong,
Joseph most obedient,

Joseph most faithful,
Mirror of patience,
Lover of poverty,
Model of artisans,
Glory of home life,
Guardian of virgins,

Pillar of families,
Solace of the wretched,
Hope of the sick,
Patron of the dying,
Terror of demons
Protector of Holy Church,

Lamb of God, who takes away the sins of the world, *spare us, O Lord.*

Lamb of God, who takes away the sins of the world, *graciously hear us, O Lord.*

Lamb of God, who takes away the sins of the world, *have mercy on us.*

V. He made him the Lord of his household,

R. *And prince over all his possessions.*

Let us pray. O God, in Your ineffable providence You were pleased to choose Blessed Joseph to be the spouse of Your most holy Mother; grant, we beg You, that we may be worthy to have him for our intercessor in heaven whom on earth we venerate as our protector; You who live and reign forever and ever. Amen.

Litany of the Saints (Traditional)

This is believed to be the most ancient of the Church's litanies. It was mentioned by St. Basil in the fourth century (in a slightly different form) and prescribed by Pope Gregory the Great in 590 for a public procession of thanksgiving after a plague that had ravaged Rome. Traditionally it has been used on Rogation Days, the Feast of St. Mark (April 25), in the Mass of Ordination, before the conferring of major orders, during the Forty Hours' devotion, and during religious profession. (The ''ora pro nobis'' we used to hear so often, of course, is ''pray for us'' in Latin.)

Lord, have mercy. *Christ, have mercy.*

Lord, have mercy, Christ, hear us. *Christ, graciously hear us.*

God, the Father of Heaven, *have mercy on us.*

God, the Son, Redeemer of the world, *have mercy on us.*

God, the Holy Spirit, *have mercy on us.*

Holy Trinity, one God, *have mercy on us.*

Holy Mary, *pray for us (after each invocation).*

Holy Virgin of Virgins,
St. Michael,
St. Gabriel,
St. Raphael,
All holy angels and archangels,
All holy orders of blessed spirits
St. John the Baptist,
St. Joseph,

23

All holy patriarchs and prophets,
St. Peter,
St. Paul,
St. Andrew,
St. James,
St. John,
St. Thomas,
St. James,
St. Philip,
St. Bartholomew,
St. Matthew,
St. Simon,
St. Thaddeus,
St. Matthias,
St. Barnabas,
St. Luke,
St. Mark,
All holy apostles and evangelists,
All holy disciples of the Lord,
All holy Innocents,
St. Stephan,
St. Lawrence,
St. Vincent,
SS. Fabian and Sebastian,
SS. John and Paul

SS. Cosmas and Damian,
SS. Gervase and Protase,
All holy Martyrs,
St. Sylvester,
St. Gregory,
St. Ambrose,
St. Augustine,
St. Jerome,
St. Martin,
St. Nicholas,
All holy bishops and confessors,
All holy doctors,
St. Anthony,
St. Benedict,
St. Bernard,
St. Francis,
All holy priests and Levites,
All holy monks and hermits,
St. Mary Magdalen,
St. Agatha,
St. Lucy,
St. Agnes,
St. Cecelia,
St. Catherine,
St. Anastasia,
All holy virgins and widows,

The angel Raphael and
Tobiah (with fish). The
story is in Tobit 6.

All holy saints of God, *intercede for us.*
Be merciful, *spare us, O Lord.*
Be merciful, *graciously hear us, O Lord.*
From all evil, *deliver us, O Lord (after each
        invocation).*
From all sin,
From your wrath,
From sudden and unprovided death,
From the snares of the devil,
From anger, hatred, and all ill will,
From all lewdness,
From lightning and tempest,
From the scourge of earthquakes,
From plague, famine, and war,
From everlasting death,
By the mystery of your holy incarnation,
By your coming,
By your birth,
By your baptism and holy fasting,

24

By your cross and passion,
By your death and burial,
By your holy resurrection,
By your wondrous ascension,
By the coming of the Holy Spirit, the Advocate,
On the day of judgment.

We sinners, *we beg you to hear us.*
That you spare us,
That you pardon us,
That you bring us to true penance,
That you govern and preserve your holy Church,
That you preserve our Holy Father and all ranks in the Church in holy
     religion,
That you humble the enemies of holy Church,
That you give peace and true concord to all Christian rulers,
That you give peace and unity to the whole Christian world,
That you restore to the unity of the Church all who have strayed from
     the truth, and lead all unbelievers to the light of the Gospel,
That you confirm and preserve us in your holy service,
That you lift up our minds to heavenly desires,
That you grant everlasting blessings to all our benefactors,
That you deliver our souls and the souls of our brethren, relatives, and
     benefactors from everlasting damnation,
That you give and preserve the fruits of the earth.
That you grant eternal rest to all the faithful departed,
That you graciously hear us, Son of God.

Lamb of God, who takes away the sins of the world, *spare us, O Lord.*
Lamb of God, who takes away the sins of the world, *spare us, O Lord.*
Lamb of God, who takes away the sins of the world, *have mercy on us.*
Christ, hear us. *Christ, graciously hear us.*
Lord, have mercy. *Christ, have mercy.* Lord, have mercy.

Let us pray. From You, Lord, come holiness in our desires, right thinking
in our plans, and justice in our actions. Grant Your children that peace
which the world cannot give; then our hearts will be devoted to Your
laws, we shall be delivered from the terrors of war, and under Your
protection we shall be able to live in tranquility. Amen.

Litany of the Saints (Contemporary)

*Today, this is used for solemn intercessions. Sections
marked A and B indicate a choice between one or
the other. Saints' names may be added according to
the occasion (e.g. patron, Church title, founder).
Likewise, petitions may be added according to the
occasion.*

I. Petitions to God

A

Lord, have mercy.
Lord, have mercy.
Christ, have mercy.
Christ, have mercy.
Lord, have mercy.
Lord, have mercy.

B

God our Father in heaven,
have mercy on us (after each invocation).
God the Son, our redeemer,
God the Holy Spirit,
Holy Trinity, one God.

II. Petitions to the Saints

Holy Mary, *pray for us (after each invocation).*
Mother of God,
Most honored of all virgins,
Michael, Gabriel and Raphael,
Angels of God,

Prophets and Fathers of our Faith
Abraham, Moses and Elijah,
St. Joseph,
St. John the Baptist,
Holy patriarchs and prophets,

Apostles and Followers of Christ
St. Peter and St. Paul,
St. Andrew,
St. John and St. James,
St. Thomas,
St. Matthew,
All holy apostles,
St. Luke,
St. Mark,
St. Barnabas,
St. Mary Magdalen,
All disciples of the Lord,

Martyrs
St. Stephen,
St. Ignatius,
St. Polycarp,
St. Justin,
St. Lawrence,
St. Cyprian,
St. Boniface,
St. Thomas Becket,
St. John Fisher and St. Thomas More,
St. Paul Miki,

St. Isaac Jogues and St. John de Brebeuf,
St. Peter Chanel,
St. Charles Lwanga,
St. Perpetua and St. Felicity,
St. Agnes,
St. Maria Goretti,
All holy martyrs for Christ,

Bishops and Doctors
St. Leo and St. Gregory,
St. Ambrose,
St. Jerome,
St. Augustine,
St. Athanasius,
St. Basil and St. Gregory,
St. John Chrysostom,
St. Martin,
St. Patrick,
St. Cyril and St. Methodius,
St. Charles Borromeo,
St. Francis de Sales,
St. Pius,

Priests and Religious
St. Anthony,
St. Benedict,
St. Bernard,
St. Francis and St. Dominic,
St. Thomas Aquinas,
St. Ignatius Loyola,
St. Francis Xavier,
St. Vincent de Paul,
St. John Vianney,
St. John Bosco,
St. Catherine,
St. Theresa,
St. Rose,

Laity

St. Louis,
St. Monica,

St. Elizabeth,
All holy men and women,

III. Petitions to Christ

Lord be merciful. *Lord, save your people.*
OR
Christ, Son of the living God, *have mercy on us.*

From all evil,
From every sin,
From the snares of the devil,
From anger and hatred,
From every evil intention,
From everlasting death,
By your coming as man,
By your birth,
By your baptism and fasting,
By your suffering and cross,
By your death and burial,
By your rising to new life,
By your return in glory to the
    Father,
By your gift of the Holy Spirit,

By your coming again in glory,
You came into this world,
You suffered for us on the cross,
You died to save us,
You lay in the tomb,
You rose from the dead,
Your returned in glory to the
    Father,
You sent the Holy Spirit upon
    your Apostles,
You are seated at the right hand
    of the Father,
You will come again to judge the
    living and the dead.

IV. Petitions for Various Needs

Lord, be merciful to us. *Lord, hear our prayer.*
Give us true repentance,
Strengthen us in your service,
Reward with eternal life all who do good to us,
Bless the fruits of the earth and of man's labor.
OR:
Lord, show us your kindness. *Lord, hear our prayer.*
Raise our thoughts and desires to you,
Save us from final damnation,
Save our friends and all who have helped us,
Grant eternal rest to all who have died in the faith,
Spare us from disease, hunger, and war,
Bring all peoples together in trust and peace.

Guide and protect your holy Church. *Lord, hear our prayer.*
Keep the pope and all the clergy in faithful service to your church,
Bring all Christians together in unity,
Lead all men to the light of the Gospel.

V. Conclusion

Christ, hear us. *Christ graciously hear us.*
Lord Jesus, hear our prayer. *Lord Jesus, hear our prayer.*
OR:

Lamb of God, you take away the sins of the world, *have mercy on us.*
Lamb of God, you take away the sins of the world, *have mercy on us.*
Lamb of God, you take away the sins of the world, *have mercy on us.*

Prayer
God of love, our strength and protection, hear the prayers of your Church.
Grant that when we come to you in faith, our prayers may be answered,
through Christ our Lord.
OR:
Lord God, you know our weakness. In your mercy grant that the example
of your Saints may bring us back to love and serve you through Christ
our Lord.

Peace Prayer of St. Francis

Attributed to St. Francis of Assisi

San Damiano Cross of
St. Francis

Lord, make me an instrument of your peace;
where there is hatred, let me sow love;
where there is injury, pardon;
where there is doubt, faith;
where there is despair, hope;
where there is darkness, light;
and where there is sadness, joy.
Grant that I may not so much seek
to be consoled as to console;
to be understood, as to understand,
to be loved as to love;
for it is in giving that we receive,
it is in pardoning that we are pardoned,
and it is in dying that we are born to eternal life.

The Canticle of Brother Sun

Most high, all powerful, all good, Lord!
   All praise, is yours, all glory, all honor, and all blessing.
To you, alone, Most High, do they belong.
   No mortal lips are worthy to pronounce your name.
All praise be yours, my Lord, through all that you have made.
   And first, my Lord, Brother sun,
   Who brings the day; and light you give to us through him.
How beautiful is he, how radiant in all his splendor!
   Of you, Most High, he bears the likeness.
All praise be yours, my Lord, through sister Moon and Stars;
   In the heavens you have made them, bright and precious and fair.
All praise be yours, my Lord, through Brothers Wind and Air,
   And fair and stormy, all the weather's moods,
   By which you cherish all that you have made.

28

All praise be yours, my Lord, through Sister Water.
So useful, lowly, precious and pure.
All praise be yours, my Lord, through Brother Fire,
Through whom you brighten up the night.
How beautiful is he, how gay! Full of power and strength.
All praise be yours, my Lord, through Sister Earth, our mother.
Who feeds us in her sovereignty and produces
Various fruits with colored flowers and herbs.
All praise be yours, my Lord, through those who grant pardon
For love of you; through those who endure sickness and trial.
Happy those who endure in peace,
By you, Most High, they will be crowned.
All praise be yours, my Lord, through Sister Death,
From whose embrace no mortal can escape.
Woe to those who die in mortal sin!
Happy those she finds doing your will!
The second death can do no harm to them.
Praise and bless my Lord, and give him thanks,
And serve him with great humility.

My Breastplate ("Lorica") St. Patrick

Patrick was not a warrior, except in spiritual terms. In 433 Patrick composed this prayer as a petition for God's help in conquering paganism in Ireland. This prayer, which he offered when he presented himself before the Druids at Tara includes the following verses:

Christ with me, Christ before me,
Christ behind me,
Christ in me, Christ beneath me,
Christ above me,
Christ on my right, Christ on my left,
Christ in breadth,
Christ in length,
Christ in height,
Christ in the mouth of every one who speaks
to me,
Christ in the heart of every one who thinks
of me,
Christ in every eye that sees me,
Christ in every ear that hears me.
I arise today
Through a mighty strength, the invocation of the Trinity,
Through belief in the Threeness,
Through confession of the Oneness,
Of the Creator of Creation.

Too Late Have I Loved You *St. Augustine, Confessions, 10.27*

Too late have I loved you, O Beauty of ancient days, yet ever new! Too late I loved you! And behold, you were within, and I abroad, and there I searched for you; I was deformed, plunging amid those fair forms, which you had made. You were with me, but I was not with you. Things held me far from you—things which, if they were not in you, were not at all. You called, and shouted, and burst my deafness. You flashed and shone, and scattered my blindness. You breathed odors and I drew in breath— and I pant for you. I tasted, and I hunger and thirst. You touched me and I burned for your peace.

Suscipe (Lt: "receive, accept")

Also called "A Prayer of Self-Offering," it may be compared to the Suscipiat *of Mass, "May the Lord receive this sacrifice. . . ." It is the prayer of St. Ignatius Loyola, from the* **Spiritual Exercises.**

Take, O Lord, and receive all my liberty, my memory, my understanding, and all my will, all that I have and possess. You have given all of these to me; to you I restore them. All are yours, dispose of them all according to your will. Give me your love and your grace; having but these I am rich enough and ask for nothing more.

Soul of Christ *(Anima Christi)*

This is a fourteenth-century prayer common at communion and in adoration of the Blessed Sacrament. This translation is by John Henry Cardinal Newman (1801–1890).

Soul of Christ, be my sanctification;
Body of Christ, be my salvation;
Blood of Christ, fill all my veins;
Water of Christ's side, wash out my stains;
Passion of Christ, my comfort be;
O good Jesus, listen to me:
In thy wounds I fain would hide,
Ne'er to be parted from they side;
Guard me, should the foe assail me;
Call me when my life shall fail me;
Bid me come to thee above,
With thy saints to sing thy love
World without end. Amen.

The 150 Psalms: The Prayer Book of the Church

Some Notable Psalms

22 Jesus on the Cross
23 The Lord is my Shepherd
32 A favorite of St. Augustine's
42 Including *abyssus abyssus invocat* "deep calls unto deep," the roaring sea symbolizing affliction
43 The old prayer at the foot of the altar, now a favorite responsorial
45 Christ and his Bride
51 The *Miserere* ("Have Mercy"), David's Prayer of Repentance, has become the name for a Lenten evening service because this psalm is sung, with a sermon following.
66 *Jubilate* ("Jubilate!"); also Ps 100
67 Beginning and entitled *Deus Misereatur,* "May God have mercy," and continuing "and bless us, and cause his countenance to shine upon us."
95 The *Venite Exsultemus* ("Come, let us exalt"), which daily opens the Church's Liturgy of the Hours
130 The *De Profundis* ("Out of the Depths"), a prayer for the faithful departed

Numbering the Psalms

Formerly the Catholic System used the numbering and divisions of the Septuagint (Greek) Translation where Ps 9 was considered two psalms.

Protestant and Jewish (and contemporary Catholic systems) depend on the original Hebrew text.

Star of David

Catholic (formerly)	Protestant and Jewish (contemporary Catholic)
1–9.21	1–9
9.22–112	10–113
113	114–115
114	116.1–9
115	116.10–19
115–145	117–146
146	147.1–11
147	147.12–20
148–150	148–150

The Psalter of Mary

Such is an old name for the rosary, because its fifteen decades—150 Hail Marys with fifteen meditations—is a complete rosary and includes exactly the same number of Hail Marys as there are Psalms in the Psalter (Book of Psalms). It was the laity's desire to share in the Church's daily prayer, the Liturgy of the Hours, that conceived the "rosary" prayer form in the twelfth century. In those days, many of the faithful were unable to read, so praying the Aves from memory took the place of the written prayer texts used by the more educated clergy. The well-known and symbolically powerful beads were adopted simply as a counting aid. Such are the Scriptural, liturgical roots of this symbol of non-Scriptural, non-liturgical prayer: the rosary.

Classification of the Psalms

The psalms can be divided into five "books," possibly in imitation of the five books of the Pentateuch:

Bk. 1:1–41; Bk. 2:42–72; Bk. 3:73–89; Bk. 4:90–106; Bk. 5:107–150

In form and subject matter, however, the psalms vary greatly. Certain similarities and characteristics allow some grouping:

Royal
2, 18, 20, 21, 72, 101, 110, 132, 144
These are for the enthronement of a king, battle hymns, and thanksgiving for victory. With the fall of a monarchy, many took on messianic overtones.

Messianic
2, 8, 16, 22, 45, 69, 72, 89, 110, 118, 132
These are references to David and the future of his line, references which explicitly or implicitly foreshadow Christ, the messianic king in David's family.

Historical
77, 78, 105, 106
The historical psalms record God's constant involvement with Israel.

Penitential
6, 25, 32, 38, 51, 102, 130, 143
(minus 25: "The Seven Penitential Psalms")
These psalms express sorrow for sin and its results.

Traditionally, all were used on Ash Wednesday: the first three at Matins, the 51st at commination, and the last three at Evensong. In the Anglican tradition, commination is an Ash Wednesday penitential office in which divine anger and judgment are proclaimed against sinners.

The Miserere is said. This is Psalm 51, primarily, but referring often to two others also (56 and 57), since all three begin with *Miserere* (Lt: Have mercy).

Imprecatory
35, 52, 58, 59, 69, 109, 137
These are human prayers for vengeance on enemies.

Acrostic
9, 10, 25, 34, 37, 111, 112, 119, 145
These psalms are thus called because of the presence of initial letters of successive verses from Hebrew alphabet, probably a mnemonic device.

Theocratic
95, 96, 97, 98
These psalms reflect upon the sovereignty of God: messianic overtones are present.

Hallel ("Praise")
These are family songs of Passover night: 113, 114 (beginning of meal); 115–118 (end of meal) 136 ("The Great Hallel")

Cross of Triumph

Songs of Ascent
120–134 (Gradual Psalms: Psalms of the Steps)
All fifteen are thus entitled, probably because they formed the "Pilgrim Psalms," i.e., pilgrims' songs as they went up to Jerusalem for the great annual feasts. See significance of the number fifteen.

Protection Prayers
34, 52, 54, 56, 57, 59, 140, 141, 142, 143
Some are of David fleeing Saul

Hallelujah ("Praise the Lord")
146–150
Each begins and ends with this word, common as well in other psalms and a fitting crescendo for the Book of Psalms.

Hymns
e.g. 8, 19, 29, 33, 46, 48, 65, 67, 76, 84, 87, 105, 111
Structurally including:

1. introduction/call to worship
2. reason for worship
3. conclusion which may repeat the introduction, utter a blessing, or vow, or brief petition.

Collective Lamentation
44, 60, 74, 79, 80

These are said on penitential days and for public calamities. Structurally, they have:

1. the memorial of God's past mercy, and an
2. expression of confidence.

Individual Lamentation
3, 5, 6, 7, 13, 22, 26, 31, 35
Structurally, these psalms have the:

1. invocation of God for help
2. description of need
3. petition for deliverance
4. reason for granting petition
5. expression of confidence

Gratitude
34, 66, 67, 103, 124, 136

Praise
7, 19, 29, 47, 93, 96, 97, 98, 99, 104, 146

Meditation
8, 9, 10, 12, 36, 39, 49, 50, 53, 73, 77, 82, 94, 139, 141

Lamentation/Intense Prayer
25, 32, 33, 44, 74, 79, 80, 86, 88

Wisdom
1, 32, 37, 119

Confidence
23, 27, 121, 131

Old Testament Canticles (Lt: *canticulum,* little song)
Sacred chants, apart from the psalms, that are used in the Liturgy of the Hours.

Moses' Song of Deliverance, Ex 15.1–4, 8–13, 17–18
Song of Moses: God's Benefits to His People, Dt 32.1–12
Song of Hannah Offering up Samuel, 1 Sm 2.1–10
David's Song, 1 Chr 29.10–13
Tobit's Song of Praise, Tb 13.1–7
Tobit's Song of Praise (addressed to Jerusalem), Tb 13.8–11, 13–14
Judith's Song of Praise, Jdt 16.13–17
Solomon's Prayer for Wisdom, Wis 9.1–12
Sirach's Prayer for God's People, Sir 36.1–5, 10–13
Isaiah's Song: Zion, City of the Messiah, Is 2.2–5
Thanksgiving Song of the Redeemed, Is 12.1–6
The Divine Vindicator, Is 26.1–4, 7–9, 12
Isaiah's Song: Just Judgment of God, Is 33.13–16
Hezekiah's Song of Thanksgiving, Is 38.10–20
Isaiah's Song: Promise of Salvation, Is 40.10–17

A New Song to the Messiah and Lord, Is 42.10–16
Isaiah's Song to the Hidden God, Is 45.15–25
Israel Renewed, Is 61.11–62.5
Song of Joy to the Holy City, Is 66.10–14
Lament over Zion's Guilt, Jer 14.17–21
God will Gather His People, Jer 31.10–14
Renewal of God's People, Ez 36.24–28
Azariah's Song, Dn 3.26–27, 29, 30, 34–41
The Three Youths Praise of Creation, Dn 3.52–90
Habakkuk's Song of Divine Judgment, Hb 3.2–4, 13, 16–19

The Old Testament Canticles as Prayed by the Church

The Old Testament canticles are arranged by the Church for its Morning Prayer (Lauds) according to their theme. Like the 150 psalms themselves are distributed over a period of time longer than a single week, so in the revised Liturgy of the Hours are the Old Testament canticles spread over FOUR weeks, in four series. (The canticle is prayed between the two psalms of Morning Prayer.)

Week One
Sunday, Dn 3.57–88, 56
Monday, 1 Chr 29.10–13
Tuesday, Tb 13.1–5b, 7–8
Wednesday, Jdt 16.2–3a. 13–15
Thursday, Jer 31.10–14
Friday, Is 45.15–26
Saturday, Ex 15.1–4a, 8–13, 17–18

Week Two
Sunday, Dn. 3.52–57
Monday, Sir 36.1–7, 13–16
Tuesday, Is 38.10–14, 17–20
Wednesday, 1 Sm 2.1–10
Thursday, Is 12.1–6
Friday, Hb 3.2–4, 13a, 15–19
Saturday, Dt 32.1–12

Week Three
Sunday, Dn 3.57–88, 56
Monday, Is 2.2–5
Tuesday, Is 26.1–4, 7–9, 12
Wednesday, Is 33.13–16
Thursday, Is 40.10–17
Friday, Jer 14.17–21
Saturday, Wis 9.1–6, 9–11

Week Four
Sunday, Dn 3.52–57
Monday, Is 42.10–16
Tuesday, Dn 3.26, 27, 29, 34–41
Wednesday, Is 61.10–62.5
Thursday, Is 66.10–14a
Friday, Tb 13.8–11, 13–15
Saturday, Ez 36.24–28

Other Prayers in the Old Testament
Solomon's Personal Prayer, 1 Kgs 3.5–10
Solomon's Public Prayer, 1 Kgs 8.22–61 (2 Chr 6.12–42)
Hezekiah's Temple Prayer, 2 Kgs 19.15–20 (Is 37.14–20)
David's Thanksgiving Prayer, 1 Chr 29.10–19
Tobit's Wedding Night Prayer, Tb 8.5c–7
Rauel's Thanksgiving Prayer, Tb 8.15b–c, 17
Judith's Prayer, Jdt 9.5a, c–6, 11–12, 14
People's Blessing upon Judith, Jdt 15.9–10

Job's Pious Prayer, **Job 1.21**
Job's Pliant, **Job 3.3–26**
Job's Penitential, **Job 42.2–6**
The Sage's Prayer, **Sir 39.16–21, 24–28, 32–35**
Prayer of Praise, Thanksgiving, **Sir 51.1–2, 7–12**
Jeremiah's Complaint, **Jer 15.10–18**
Jeremiah's Vengeance Prayer, **Jer 18.19–23**
Jeremiah's Interior Crisis, **Jer 20.7–18**
Jeremiah's Praise Prayer, **Jer 32.16–24**

Other Poems and Songs in the Old Testament

Deborah's Song, **Jgs. 5.1–31**
David's Lament, **2 Sm 1.17–27**
David's Victory Song, **2 Sm 7.18–29**
David's Deliverance Song, **2 Sm 22**
David's Song, **1 Chr 16.7–36**
Solomon's Love Song, **Sg 2.10–17**

Dayenu

"It would have been enough" is the translation for this Hebrew word. It is the refrain of a traditional Passover Seder hymn. True to the folk tradition, it is cumulative, each verse developing the last (like "The Twelve Days of Christmas" does). It builds a prayer of gratitude for God surprising and wonderful work: "If God had created us and not revealed himself in all his marvelous works, it would have been enough. If God had revealed himself and not made a covenant with his people, it would have been enough. . . ."

The Suffering Servant Poems (Isaiah) "Servant of the Lord Oracles"

Do these describe historical Israel? Ideal Israel? Ideal representative of the People of Israel? An Old Testament historical character before or during the life of the prophet? The prophet himself? The New Testament and Christian tradition: Jesus Christ.

1. 42.1–4
2. 49.1–7
3. 50.4–11
4. 52.13–53.12

Old Testament Blessings

Mizpah Blessing
May the Lord keep watch between you and me when we are out of each other's sight. **Gn 31.49**

Aaron's Blessing
This is also called the "Seraphic Blessing" because it became associated with Francis of Assisi ("the Seraphic Saint") who used a form of it to bless a Brother Leo on Mt. Alverno in 1224.

The Lord said to Moses:
"Speak to Aaron and his sons and tell them: This is how you shall
bless the Israelites. Say to them:
The Lord bless you and keep you!
The Lord let his face shine upon you
and be gracious to you!
The Lord look upon you kindly
and give you peace!
So shall they invoke my name upon the Israelites, and I will bless
them." Nm 6:22–27

The Watchful Ostrich

Being "looked upon kindly" by the Lord, having his face shining upon us, is an image of his constant attention: "Can a mother forget her infant? Even if she could, I would never forget you" (Is 49, 14–15). This watchfulness of God is providence (*providere,* to foresee), and life itself, and is taught in a beautiful fable. It was believed by the ancients that the mother ostrich hatched her eggs by gazing upon them, and that they would addle if she looked away even momentarily. She would know, it was believed, about any bad egg, and surely break it. There was much in this fable to remind believers of God's watchful care, particularly in the East where the ostrich egg would often be suspended in Christian churches as symbol of divine providence.

Moses' Final Blessing of the People
May you be blessed in the city, and blessed in the country!
Blessed be the fruit of your womb,
the produce of your soil and the offspring of your livestock,
the issue of your herds and the young of your flocks!
Blessed be your grain bin and your kneading bowl!
May you be blessed in your coming in,
and blessed in your going out! Dt 28.3–6

Solomon's Blessing
May the Lord, our God, be with us as he was with our fathers
and may he not forsake us nor cast us off.
May he draw our hearts to himself,

that we may follow him in everything
and keep the commands, statutes, and ordinances
which he enjoined on our fathers. **1 Kgs 8.57–58**

New Testament Canticles

The Gospel Canticles

1. The Canticle of Mary (See below.)
2. The Canticle of Zechariah (See next page.)
3. The Canticle of Simeon (See next page.)

Other New Testament Canticles

1. God's Plan Fulfilled in Christ, **Eph 1.3–10**
2. Christ, First-Born from the dead, **Co. 1.12–20**
3. Song of the Paschal Mystery, **Phil 2.6–11**
4. Song of the Mystery of our Faith, **1 Tim 3.16**
5. Song of the Suffering Christ, **1 Pt 2.21–25**
6. Song of the Creator, and the Lamb, **Rv 4.11; 5.9, 10, 12**
7. Song of Divine Judgment, **Rv 11.17–18**
8. Praise of God's Power, **Rv 12.10–12**
9. Song of Moses and the Lamb, **Rv 15.3–4**
10. The Wedding Feast of the Lamb, **Rv 19.1–2, 5–8**

The New Testament Canticles as Prayed by the Church

Like their Old Testament counterparts in Morning Prayer, the New Testament canticles are prayed (following the two psalms) according to theme, in a one week series.

Evening Prayer Canticles

Saturday, **Phil 2.6–11**
Sunday, **Rv 19. 1–2, 5, 7 (1Pt 2. 21–24 in Lent)**
Monday, **Eph 1.3–10**
Tuesday, **Rv 4.11; 5.9–10, 12**

Wednesday, **Col 1.12–20**
Thursday, **Rv 11.17–18; 12.10–12**
Friday, **Rv 15.3–4**

The Three Gospel Canticles

Mary's Canticle *(The Magnificat)* **Lk. 1.46–55**
Mary's Canticle is named after its word in Latin—her response to Elizabeth's greeting at the visitation. It has been prayed each day by the Church as part of its Evening Prayer.

My soul proclaims the greatness of the Lord,
my spirit rejoices in God my Savior
for he has looked with favor on his lowly servant.

From this day all generations will call me blessed:
the Almighty has done great things for me,
and holy is his Name.

He has mercy on those who fear him
in every generation.

He has shown the strength of his arm,
he has scattered the proud in their conceit.

He has cast down the mighty from their thrones,
and has lifted up the lowly.

He has filled the hungry with good things,
and the rich he has sent away empty.

He has come to the help of his servant Israel
for he has remembered his promise of mercy,
the promise he made to our fathers,
to Abraham and his children for ever.

Zechariah's Canticle *(The Benedictus)*
Lk 1.68–79

Zechariah's Canticle is named after its first word in Latin. Zechariah, the father of John the Baptizer, is singing in gratitude after John's birth for God's fidelity to the messianic promise. It is prayed each day by the Church as part of its Morning Prayer.

Blessed be the Lord, the God of Israel;
he has come to his people and set them free.

He has raised up for us a mighty savior,
born of the house of his servant David.

Through his holy prophets he promised of
    old
    that he would save us from our enemies,
    from the hands of all who hate us.

He promised to show mercy to our fathers
and to remember his holy covenant.

This was the oath he swore to our father
    Abraham:
to set us free from the hands of our enemies,
free to worship him without fear,
holy and righteous in his sight
    all the days of our life.

The presentation in the temple: Jesus in the arms of Simeon, Mary with a candle (the Candlemas Day association) and Joseph with "two young pigeons"

You, my child, shall be called the prophet of the Most High,
for you will go before the Lord to prepare his way,
to give his people knowledge of salvation
by the forgiveness of their sins.

In the tender compassion of our God
the dawn from on high shall break upon us,
to shine on those who dwell in darkness and the shadow of death,
and to guide our feet into the way of peace.

39

Simeon's Canticle *(The Nunc Dimittis)* Lk 2.29–32

Simeon's Canticle is named after its first words in Latin. It is the song of the old man in the temple at the Lord's presentation, with his request for permission to die. It is prayed each day by the Church as part of its Night Prayer.

Lord, now you let your servant go in peace;
your word has been fulfilled:

my own eyes have seen the salvation
which you have prepared in the sight of every people:

a light to reveal you to the nations
and the glory of your people Israel.

NEW TESTAMENT PRAYERS

Prayers in the Gospel

The Angel's Greeting Lk 1.28
Rejoice, O highly favored daughter! The Lord is with you. Blessed are you among women.

Mary's Reply Lk 1.38
I am the servant of the Lord. Let it be done to me as you say.

Elizabeth's Greeting Lk 1.42, 45
Blest are you among women and blest is the fruit of your womb . . .
Blest is she who trusted that the Lord's words to her would be fulfilled.

Song of the Angels Lk 2.14
Glory to God in high heaven, peace on earth to those on whom his favor rests.

Temptation of Christ Mt 4.10
Away with you, Satan! Scripture has it: You shall do homage to the Lord your God; him alone shall you adore.

Nathanael Jn 1.49
Rabbi . . . you are the son of God; you are the king of Israel.

The Leper Cured Lk 5.12
Lord, if you will to do so, you can cure me.

The Centurion at Capernaum Mt 8.8
Sir . . . I am not worthy to have you under my roof. Just give an order and my boy will get better.

The Storm on the Lake Mt 8.25
Lord, save us! We are lost!

Two Blind Men Cured Mt 9.27
Son of David, have pity on us!

Peter on Lake Genesareth After the Feeding of the Five Thousand
Mt 14.30
Lord, save me!

Peter at Capernaum Jn 6.68
Lord, to whom shall we go? You have the words of eternal life.

The Canaanite Woman Mt 15.22, 25, 27
Lord, Son of David, have pity on me! Help me, Lord! . . . Please, Lord, even the dogs eat the leavings that fall from the masters' tables.

Peter's Profession Mt 16.16
You are the Messiah . . . the Son of the living God!

Peter at the Transfiguration Mt. 17.4
Lord, how good that we are here! With your permission I will erect three booths here, one for you, one for Moses, and one for Elijah.

The Man Born Blind Jn 9.38
I do believe, Lord.

Praise of Mary Lk 11.27
Blest is the womb that bore you [Lord] and the breasts that nursed you.

The Prodigal Son Lk 15.21
Father, I have sinned against God and against you; I no longer deserve to be called your son.

The Apostle's Petition to the Lord Lk 17.5
Increase our faith.

As Obedient Servants Lk 17.10
We are useless servants. We have done no more than our duty.

The Tax Collector Lk 18.13
O God, be merciful to me, a sinner.

A Rich Man Lk 18.18
Good teacher, what must I do to share in everlasting life?

Martha Jn 11.21, 22, 24, 27
Lord, if you had been here, my brother would never have died. Even now, I am sure that God will give you whatever you ask of him . . . I know he will rise again in the resurrection on the last day. Yes . . . Lord, I have come to believe that you are the Messiah, the Son of God: he who is to come into the world.

The Blind Man Near Jericho Lk 18.38, 39, 41
Jesus, Son of David, have pity on me! . . . Son of David, have pity on me! . . . Lord I want to see.

Zacchaeus the Tax Collector Lk 19.8
I give half my belongings, Lord, to the poor. If I have defrauded anyone in the least, I pay him back fourfold.

Triumphant Entry Into Jerusalem Mt 21.9 (See Mk 11.10; Lk 19.38; Jn 12.13)
Hosanna to the Son of David! Blessed is he who comes in the name of the Lord! Hosanna in the highest!

The Agony in the Garden Mt 26.39 (See Mk 14.36; Lk 22.42)
My Father, if it is possible, let this cup pass me by. Still, let it be as you would have it, not as I.

First Word on the Cross Lk 23.34
Father, forgive them; they do not know what they are doing.

The Good Thief Lk 23.42
Jesus, remember me when you enter upon your reign.

The Death of Jesus Mk 15.34 (See Mt 27.46)
My God, my God, why have you forsaken me?

Passion Cross

42

The Seventh Word on the Cross Lk 23.46
Father, into your hands I commend my spirit.

The Disciples at Emmaus Lk 24.29
Stay with us, (Lord). It is nearly evening—the day is practically over.

Thomas Jn 20.28
My Lord and my God!

Peter, the Shepherd Jn 21.15, 17
Yes, Lord, you know that I love you . . . Yes, Lord, you know everything. You know well that I love you.

Prayers in the Acts of the Apostles

After Peter's Release Acts 4.24, 29–30
Sovereign Lord, who made heaven and earth and sea and all that is in them. . . . Grant to your servants, even as they speak your words, complete assurance by stretching forth your hand in cures and signs and wonders to be worked in the name of Jesus, your holy Servant.

St. Stephen, Protomartyr Acts 7.56, 59, 60
Look! . . . I see an opening in the sky, and the Son of Man standing at God's right hand. . . . Lord Jesus, receive my spirit. . . . Lord, do not hold this sin against them.

The Christians of Caesarea Acts 21.14
The Lord's will be done.

Prayers in the Epistles

Firm Resolution Rom 8.38–39
Yet in all this we are more than conquerors because of him who has loved us. For I am certain that neither death nor life, neither angels nor principalities, neither the present nor the future, nor powers, neither height nor depth nor any other creature, will be able to separate us from the love of God that comes to us in Christ Jesus, our Lord.

Infinite Wisdom See Rom 11.33–36
How deep are the riches and the wisdom and the knowledge of God! How inscrutable his judgments, how unsearchable his ways! For who has known the mind of the Lord? Or, who has been his counselor? Who has given him anything so as to deserve return? For, from him and through him and for him all things are. To you be glory forever. Amen.

Thanksgiving See 1 Cor 1.4–5.8
I continually thank my God for you because of the favor he has bestowed on you in Christ Jesus, in whom you have been richly endowed with every gift of speech and knowledge. He will strengthen you to the end, so that you will be blameless on the day of our Lord Jesus Christ.

Consolation See 2 Cor 1.3–4
Praised be God the Father of our Lord Jesus Christ, the Father of mercies, and the God of all consolation! He comforts us in our afflictions and thus enables us to comfort those who are in trouble, with the same consolation we have received from him.

The Peace of God See Gal 1.3–5
We wish you the favor and peace of God our Father, and of the Lord Jesus Christ, who gave himself for our sins, to rescue us from the present evil age, as our God and Father willed—to him be glory for endless ages. Amen.

Crucified to the World Gal 6.14
May I never boast of anything but the cross of our Lord Jesus Christ! Through it, the world has been crucified to me and I to the world.

The Power of God in Us See Eph 3.20–21
To him, whose power now at work in us can do immeasurably more than we ask or imagine—to him be glory in the church and in Christ Jesus through all generations, world without end. Amen.

Glory to God See Phil 4.20
All glory our God and Father for unending ages! Amen.

The King of Ages 1 Tim 1.17
To the King of ages, the immortal, the invisible, the only God, be honor and glory forever and ever! Amen.

The King of Kings See 1 Tim 6.15–16
He is the blessed and only ruler, the King of kings and Lord of lords who alone has immortality and who dwells in the unapproachable light, whom no human being has ever seen or can see. To him be honor and everlasting rule! Amen.

Birth to Salvation 1 Pt 1.3–5
Praised be the God and Father of our Lord Jesus Christ, he who in his great mercy gave us a new birth; a birth unto hope which draws its life from the resurrection of Jesus Christ from the dead; a birth to an imperishable inheritance, incapable of fading or defilement, which is kept in heaven for you who are guarded by God's power through faith; a birth to a salvation which stands ready to be revealed in the last days.

God Glorified in Us See 1 Pt 4.11
Thus in all of you God is to be glorified through Jesus Christ: to him be glory and dominion throughout the ages. Amen.

Growth in Grace 2 Pt 3.18
Grow rather in grace, and in the knowledge of our Lord and savior Jesus Christ. Glory be to him now and to the day of eternity. Amen.

Prayers in the Book of Revelation

The Four Living Creatures Rv 4.8
Holy, holy, holy, is the Lord God Almighty, He who was, and who is, and who is to come!

All Creatures and The Universe Rv 5.13
To the One seated on the throne, and to the Lamb, be praise and honor, glory and might, forever and ever!

A Huge White-Robed Crowd Rv 7.10
Salvation is from our God, who is seated on the throne, and from the Lamb!

Angels, Elders and Four Living Creatures Rv 7.12
Amen! Praise and glory, wisdom and thanksgiving and honor, power and might, to our God forever and ever. Amen!

One of Seven Angels and the Altar Rv 16.5, 7
You are just, O Holy One, who is and who was . . . Yes, Lord God Almighty, your judgments are true and just!

Prayerful Greetings from the Epistles

Beloved of God and called to holiness, grace and peace (to you) from God our Father and the Lord Jesus Christ. Rom 1.7

May the grace of our Lord Jesus Christ be with you. Rom 16.20; 1 Thes 5.28; Phlm 25

The favor of the Lord Jesus be with you. 1 Cor 16.23

My love to all of you in Christ Jesus. 1 Cor 16.24

The grace of the Lord Jesus Christ, and the love of God, and the fellowship of the Holy Spirit be with you all. 2 Cor 13.13

Brothers, may the favor of our Lord Jesus Christ be with your spirit. Amen. Gal 6.18; Phil 4.23

May God the Father and the Lord Jesus Christ grant (you) peace, love and faith. Eph 6.23

Grace be with all who love our Lord Jesus Christ with unfailing love. Eph 6.24

Grace and peace (be yours) from God our Father and from the Lord Jesus Christ. 1 Cor 1.3; 2 For 1.12; Eph 1.2; Phil 1.2; 2 Thes 1.2; Ti 1.4; Phlm 3

May God our Father give you grace and peace. Col 1.2

The Lord be with you all. 2 Thes 3.16

May the grace of our Lord Jesus Christ be with you all. 2 Thes 3.18

May Grace, mercy, and peace be yours from God the Father and Christ Jesus our Lord. 1 Tim 1.2; 2 Tim 1.2

The Lord be with your Spirit. 2 Tim 4.22

Grace be with you. 2 Tim 4.22

May grace be yours and peace in abundance through your knowledge of God and of Jesus our Lord. 2 Pt 1.2

May mercy, peace, and love be yours in ever greater measure. Jude 2

Paul's Gratitude Prayers for the Church

Romans 1.8–12
First, I thank my God through Jesus Christ for all of you and for the way in which your faith is spoken of all over the world. The God I worship spiritually by preaching the Good News of his Son knows that I never fail to mention you in my prayers, and to ask to be allowed at long last the opportunity to visit you, if he so wills. For I am longing to see you either to strengthen you by sharing a spiritual gift with you, or what is better, to find encouragement among you from our common faith.

Corinthians 1 Cor 1.4–9
I never stop thanking God for all the graces you have received through Jesus Christ. I thank him that you have been enriched in so many ways, especially in your teachers and preachers; the witness to Christ has indeed been strong among you so that you will not be without any of the gifts of the Spirit while you are waiting for our Lord Jesus Christ to be revealed; and he will keep you steady and without blame until the last day, the day of our Lord Jesus Christ, because God by calling you has joined you to his Son, Jesus Christ; and God is faithful.

Ephesians 1.15–19
That will explain why I, having once heard about your faith in the Lord Jesus, and the love that you show towards all the saints, I have never failed to remember you in my prayers and to thank God for you. May the God of our Lord Jesus Christ, the Father of glory, give you a spirit of wisdom and perception of what is revealed, to bring you to full knowledge of him. May he enlighten the eyes of your mind, so that you can see what hope his call holds for you, what rich glories he has promised the saints will inherit and how infinitely great is the power that he has exercised for us believers.

Philippians 1.3–11
I thank my God whenever I think of you; and every time I pray for all of you, I pray with joy, remembering how you have helped to spread the Good News from the day you first heard it right up to the present. I am quite certain that the One who began this good work in you will see that it is finished when the Day of Christ Jesus comes. It is only natural that I should feel like this towards you all, since you have shared the privileges which have been mine: both my chains and my work defending and establishing the gospel. You have a permanent place in my heart, and God knows how much I miss you all, loving you as Christ Jesus loves you. My prayer is that your love for each other may increase more and more

46

and never stop improving your knowledge and deepening your perception so that you can always recognize what is best. This will help you to become pure and blameless and prepare you for the Day of Christ when you will reach the perfect goodness which Jesus Christ produces in us for the glory and praise of God.

Colossians 1.3–4, 9–12
We have never failed to remember you in our prayers and to give thanks for you to God, the Father of our Lord Jesus Christ, ever since we heard about your faith in Christ Jesus and the love that you show towards all the saints because of the hope which is stored up for you in heaven . . . what we ask God is that through perfect wisdom and spiritual understanding you should reach the fullest knowledge of his will. So you will be able to lead the kind of life which the Lord expects of you, a life acceptable to him in all its aspects; showing the results in all the good actions you do and increasing your knowledge of God. You will have in you the strength, based on his own glorious power, never to give in, but to bear anything joyfully, thanking the Father who has made it possible for you to join the saints and with them to inherit the light.

Thessalonians 1 Thes 1.2–3; 2 Thes 1.3–4, 11–12
We always mention you in our prayers and thank God for you all, and constantly remember before God our Father how you have shown your faith in action, worked for love and preserved through hope, in our Lord Jesus Christ. . . . We feel we must be continually thanking God for you, because your faith is growing so wonderfully and the love that you have for one another never stops increasing; we can take special pride in you for your constancy and faith under all the persecutions and troubles you have to bear. . . .. We pray continually that our God will make you worthy of his call, and by his power fulfill all your desires for goodness and complete all that you have been doing through faith; because in this way the name of our Lord Jesus Christ will be glorified in you and you in him, by the grace of our God and the Lord Jesus Christ.

St. Paul Blessings

May God, the source of all patience and encouragement, enable you to live in perfect harmony with one another according to the spirit of Christ Jesus, so that with one heart and voice you may glorify God, the Father of our Lord Jesus Christ. . . . May God, the source of hope, fill you with all joy and peace in believing so that through the power of the Holy Spirit you may have hope in abundance. . . . May the God of peace be with you all. Rom 15.5–6, 13, 33

Now to him who is able to strengthen you in the gospel which I proclaim when I preach Jesus Christ, the gospel which reveals the mystery hidden for many ages but now manifested through the writings of the prophets, and, at the command of the eternal God, made known to all the Gentiles that they may believe and obey—to him, the God who alone is wise, may glory be given through Jesus Christ unto endless ages. Amen. **Rom 16.25–27**

I pray that he will bestow on you gifts in keeping with the riches of his glory. May he strengthen you inwardly through the working of his Spirit. May Christ dwell in your hearts through faith, and may charity be the root and foundation of your life. Thus you will be able to grasp fully, with all the holy ones, the breadth and length and height and depth of Christ's love, and experience this love which surpasses all knowledge, so that you may attain to the fullness of God himself. **Eph 3.16–19**

May God the Father and the Lord Jesus Christ grant the brothers peace and love and faith. Grace be with all who love our Lord Jesus Christ with unfailing love. **Eph 6.23**

Then God's own peace, which is beyond all understanding, will stand guard over your hearts and minds in Christ Jesus. Finally, my brothers, your thoughts should be wholly directed to all that is true, all that deserves respect, all that is honest, pure, admirable, decent, virtuous, or worthy of praise. Live according to what you have learned and accepted, what you have heard me say and seen me do. Then will the God of peace be with you. **Phil 4.7–9**

May the God of peace make you perfect in holiness. May he preserve you whole and entire, spirit, soul, and body, irreproachable at the coming of our Lord Jesus Christ. **1 Thes 5.23**

We pray for you always that our God may make you worthy of his call, and fulfill by his power every honest intention and work of faith. In this way the name of our Lord Jesus may be glorified in you and you in him, in accord with the gracious gift of our God and of the Lord Jesus Christ. **2 Thes 1.11–12**

May he who is the Lord of peace give you continued peace in every possible way. **2 Thes 3.16, 18**

May grace, mercy, and peace be yours from God the Father and Christ Jesus our Lord. **1 Tim 1.2**

Other New Testament Blessings

May the God of peace, who brought up from the dead the great Shepherd of the sheep by the blood of the eternal covenant, Jesus our Lord, furnish you with all that is good, that you may do his will. Through Jesus Christ may he carry out in you all that is pleasing to him. To Christ be glory forever! Amen. **Heb 13.20–21**

The God of all grace, who called you to his everlasting glory in Christ, will himself restore, confirm, strengthen, and establish those who have suffered a little while. Dominion be his throughout the ages. Amen. **1 Pt 5.10–11**

In truth and love, then, we shall have grace, mercy, and peace from God the Father and from Jesus Christ, the Father's son. **2 Jn 3**

May mercy, peace, and love be yours in ever greater measure. **Jude 2**

There is One who can protect you from a fall and make you stand unblemished and exultant in the presence of his glory. Glory be to this only God our savior, through Jesus Christ our Lord. Majesty, too, be his, might and power from ages past, now and for ages to come. Amen. **Jude 24–25**

To the seven churches in the province of Asia: John wishes you grace and peace—from him who is and who was and who is to come, and from the seven spirits before his throne, and from Jesus Christ the faithful witness, the first-born from the dead and ruler of the kings of earth. To him who loves us and freed us from our sins by his own blood, who has made us a royal nation of priests in the service of his God and Father—to him be glory and power forever and ever! Amen. **Rv 1.4–6**

CHURCH BLESSINGS

And the Word Made His Dwelling Among Us

There is an ancient custom among Christians of a house blessing on Epiphany, recalling the visit of the Magi. After the blessing—usually by the pastor—the initials of the traditional names of the Magi, Gaspar (or Caspar), Melchior and Balthasar, are inscribed and connected by crosses, with white chalk on the inside door frame. The numerals of the current year serve as bookends: 19 + G + M + B + __ . In the old Roman ritual, there is even a special blessing for the chalk used. The new (1988) Catholic Household Blessings and Prayers by the United States bishops provide a contemporary version of this, including as Scripture text John 1.1–3, 14.

Order for the Blessing of Homes During the Christmas and Easter Seasons

Introductory Rites
Sign of the Cross

Greeting
Please be with this house and with all who live here.
And also with you.

Introduction
The Word became flesh and made his dwelling place among us. It is Christ who enlightens our hearts and homes with his love. It is Christ, risen from the dead, who is our source of hope, joy, and comfort. May all who enter this home find Christ's light and love.

Reading of the Word of God
For Epiphany: Lk 19. 1–9 (Zacchaeus story)
For Easter: Lk 24.28–32 (end of the Emmaus story)

Responsorial Psalm (or some suitable song) may be sung
For Epiphany: Ps 72
Or Ps 112 or Ps 127.1–6 or Ps 128.1–6 or Ps 118.2–4, 13–15, 22–24

Intercessions
The Son of God made his home among us. With thanks and praise let us call upon him. (Response: Stay with us, Lord.)

Lord, Jesus Christ, with Mary and Joseph, you formed the Holy Family: Remain in our home, that we may know you as our guest and honor you as our head. We pray:

Lord Jesus Christ, though every dwelling is a temple of holiness, build those who live in this house into the dwelling place of God in the Holy Spirit. We pray:

Lord Jesus Christ, you taught your followers to build their houses upon solid rock: grant that the members of this family may live their lives in firm allegiance to your teachings. We pray:

Lord Jesus Christ, you had no place to lay your head, but in the spirit of poverty accepted the hospitality of your friends: grant that through our help the homeless may obtain proper housing. We pray:

(For Christmas) Lord Jesus Christ, you became flesh of the Virgin Mary: grant that your presence may be known always in this home. We pray:

(For Epiphany) Lord Jesus Christ, the three kings presented their gifts to you in praise and adoration: grant that those living in this house may use their talents and abilities to your greater glory. We pray:

(For Easter) Lord Jesus Christ, the disciples recognized you in the break-ing of the bread: grant that the members of this family may be always close to the presence of Christ in word and sacrament. We pray:

(For Easter) Lord Jesus Christ, you appeared to the frightened apostles and said, "Peace be with you": grant that your abiding peace may remain with the members of this family. We pray:

As children of God we confidently pray: Our Father . . .

Prayer of Blessing

(For the Christmas Season) Lord God of heaven and earth, You revealed Your only-begotten Son to every nation by the guidance of a star. Bless this house and all who inhabit it. Fill them with the light of Christ, that their concern for others may reflect Your love. We ask this through Christ our Lord. Amen.

(For the Easter Season) Lord, we rejoice in the victory of Your Son over death: by rising from the tomb to new life he gives us new hope and promise. Bless all the members of this household and surround them with Your protection, that they may find comfort and peace in Jesus Christ, the paschal lamb, who lives and reigns with You and the Holy Spirit, one God, for ever and ever. Amen.

(Sprinkling of those present and of the house may follow) Let this water call to mind our baptism in Christ, who by his death and resurrection has redeemed us.

Concluding Rite

May Christ Jesus dwell with you, keep you from all harm, and make you one in mind and heart, now and forever. Amen.

And may almighty God bless you all, the Father, and the Son, and the Holy Spirit. Amen.

The Old Nuptial Blessing

Look with favor, Lord, upon our prayers and in your kindness assist the institution of marriage which you have planned for the propagation of the human race: may this union, joined by your authority, be blessed by your help. Through our Lord Jesus Christ, your Son, who lives and reigns with you, in the unity of the Holy Spirit, God, forever and ever. Amen.

Let us pray. O God, you created all things out of nothing by your power and your strength: when the foundations of the world were laid and man made to God's image, you then created woman as his inseparable help by forming the woman's body from the man's flesh, to teach that it is never lawful to separate the two whom you had willed to form from one.

O God, you consecrated the marital union by so great a mystery in order to foreshadow in marriage the mystery of Christ and the Church.

O God, you join man to woman and give to this, the first established society, the only blessing that was not taken away by the punishment for original sin or by the condemnation of the flood.

Look with favor upon this your servant who, now to be joined in the common life of marriage, seeks your strength and your protection. May marriage be for her a yoke of love and peace. Faithful and chaste, may she marry in Christ and follow the example of the holy women whose praises are sung in the Scriptures.

May she be the beloved of her husband, as Rachel was; may she be as wise as Rebecca, long of life and faithful as Sarah. May her actions give the author of lies no power over her. May she keep strong in the faith and in the commandments; true to one marriage bed, may she shun unlawful embraces. May she strengthen her weakness by firm discipline, be serious in her modesty, honored for her chastity, learned in the truths of heaven.

May she be rich in children, may she prove virtuous and blameless, and may she come to rest with the blessed in the kingdom of heaven. And let them both see their children's children to the third and the fourth generation, and live to a happy old age. Through the same Jesus Christ, your Son, our Lord, who lives and reigns with you in the unity of the Holy Spirit, God, forever and ever. Amen.

The God of Abraham, the God of Isaac, the God of Jacob be with you and fill you with his blessing, so that you may see your children's children to the third and fourth generation, and afterward have eternal life, life without end: through the help of our Lord Jesus Christ, who with the Father and the Hold Spirit lives and reigns, God, forever and ever. Amen.

Godspeed

"May God prosper you." May God give you good fortune. This was used as a wish to a person starting on a journey, or a new venture, or a new life. An archaic meaning of the word *speed* is prosperity, success (Middle English *spede*, good luck).

Old Blessing of Expectant Mother

Let us pray. Lord God, creator of all things, strong and awesome, just and merciful, you alone are good and loving; you delivered Israel from every evil and made our fathers your beloved children, making them holy by the hand of your Spirit; you prepared the body and soul of the glorious Virgin Mary, by the cooperation of the Holy Spirit, as a worthy dwelling place for your Son you filled John the Baptist with your Holy Spirit and made him leap in his mother's womb: accept the sacrifice of a contrite heart, the fervent desire of your servant N., who humbly asks for the protection of her child which you permitted her to conceive: Guard her work and defend it from every deceit and harm of the bitter enemy, so that at her delivery the child may be brought forth to light by your hand of mercy and kept safe for holy rebirth, may serve you in all things forever and deserve to attain life eternal. Through the same Jesus Christ our Lord, your Son, who lives and reigns with you in the unity of the same Holy Spirit, God, forever and ever. Amen.

Let us pray. Visit, we pray you, Lord, this dwelling place, and drive far from it and from this your servant N., all the deceits of the enemy. May your holy angels dwell here to keep her and her child in peace and may your blessing be with her always. Save them, almighty God, and grant to them light without end. Through Christ our Lord. Amen.

May the blessing of almighty God, Father, Son, and Holy Spirit, descend upon you and upon your child, and remain forever. Amen.

An Old Blessing of Children (partial)

Let us pray. Lord Jesus Christ, when the little children were offered and came to you, you embraced them and placed your hands upon them, blessed them and said: Permit the little children to come to me, and do not forbid them, for theirs is the kingdom of heaven, and their angels always see the face of my Father. Look, we pray, upon the innocence of these children and upon the devotion of their parents and in your kindness bless them this day through our ministry. By your grace and mercy may they always prosper, may they know you, love you, marvel at you, obey your commandments, and happily come to their desired goal: through you, the Savior of the world, who with the Father and the Holy Spirit live and reign, God, forever and ever. Amen.

Let us pray. O Lord, we ask you to defend this family of yours from every adversity, through the intercession of the blessed Virgin Mary. In your grace and mercy protect them, as they kneel devoutly before you, from the attacks of the enemy. Through Christ our Lord. Amen.

Let us pray. O, God, in your generous providence you have sent your holy angels for our protection. Grant that your petitioners may always be defended by the protection of the angels and enjoy their companionship forever. Through Christ our Lord. Amen.

May God bless you and protect your hearts and minds, the Father, the Son, and the Holy Spirit. Amen.

Silver/Golden Wedding Anniversary Blessing

Exhortation before the Mass

Twenty-five (fifty) years have passed since that day when, with the blessing of the Church, you plighted troth before the Altar of God. In the long space of time which has intervened many things have come to pass. You have had your full share of happiness but you have perhaps tasted sorrow as well. There may have been dark days as well as bright ones, and now, by the Providence of God, a very special privilege is granted you, namely, that of celebrating the Silver (Golden) Jubilee of your wedding surrounded by those who love you (your children, your grandchildren, and your friends).

With hearts filled with gratitude you have come to the church today to thank God for His many favors, to renew in His presence the good avowals made long ago and to receive the blessing of the Church on the years that remain to you.

In very truth you have cause to thank God. He has not only showered His blessings on you, but His Fatherly Hand has often protected you from evil, and it is by His mercy that in moments of darkness and discouragement you have been preserved from despair and received courage to persevere. (He has given you children to console and support you as the years come upon you.) I feel sure, however, there is no further need for me to enumerate the many causes of thankfulness which must be well known to yourselves and of which, on a day like this, you must be well aware. The reasons for gratitude must be deeply imprinted on your memory and in your hearts enclosed.

It is for you, then, to remain faithful to God, and in the time that is left, to serve Him with your remaining strength. You have borne the heat and burdens of the day bravely; do not lose now the eternal rest you have earned by your labors. Turn to profit the experience the years have brought you, using such experience to the benefit not only of yourselves but of others. Teach the young people around you how to avoid the shoals and quicksands on which married happiness is so often wrecked; advise them, in particular, how to procure the best interest of their children through Catholic training and education.

Be patient with each other in the weaknesses and failings which sometimes are the accompaniment of advancing years, and let an atmosphere of peace and gentleness increasingly surround you. Should it please God to send one or both of you sickness, do not complain but, uniting your sufferings with those of our Divine Savior, say often as He did humbly and patiently, "Not my will, but Thine be done." In this way your lives will bring forth the fruit of their maturity unto your lasting profit in eternity.

Speaking now to you, children and grandchildren of these happy parents, I charge you to make those lives bright and happy from which you have derived, by the disposition of God, your own being. Anticipate, insofar as you can, their every wish and avoid anything that would sadden or grieve them. Give them that greatest of all consolations, namely, the knowledge that you are leading good Christian lives so that they will understand their labors and pains on your behalf have not been in vain. By doing this you will earn the special blessing promised by God to those who are good to their parents.

OTHER BLESSINGS

Heritage Blessing
May the God of Abraham, Isaac and Jacob,
May the God of Peter, James and John,
May the God of us all bless us
in the name of the Father, Son and Holy
    Spirit

Irish Blessing
May the road rise to meet you,
May the wind always be at your back,
May the sun shine warm upon your face,
May the rains fall soft upon your field,
May God hold you in the palm of his hand.

An Irish Blessing
May Christ give to you at this time and for
    always
His peace in your soul
His presence in your heart
His power in your life.

Harp, Shamrock wreath, honoring the Irish heritage of a parish

The Apache Wedding Benediction
Now you will feel no rain, for each of you
will be shelter for the other.
Now you will feel no cold, for each of you will be warmth to the other.
    Now there is no more loneliness.
Now you are two persons, but there is only one life before you.
Go now to your dwelling to enter into the days of your life together.
May your days be good and long upon the earth.
And may the peace of God go with you always.

Sufi Blessing
May the blessing of God rest upon you.
May his peace abide in you.
May His presence illuminate your heart,
Now and forevermore.

John Ruskin's Blessing
I wish for you
some new love at the lovely things,
and some new forgetfulness at teasing things,
and some higher pride in the praising things,
and some sweeter peace from the hurrying things,
and some closer fence from the worrying things.

God bless your year:
your coming in, your going out;
your rest, your traveling about;
the rough, the smooth, the bright, the dread.
God bless your year.

In your journeys God direct you.
In peril and danger God protect you.
In care, anxiety or trouble, God sustain you.
In your happiness and pleasure God bless you.

Ah-Choo

"God bless you." Thank-you, St. Gregory. During a pestilence in which a sneeze was a mortal symptom, St. Gregory, it is said, originated this blessing by recommending its prayerful use.

Information

General

A Catholic's Faith, Tradition and Practice Known by Heart

According to the Amendments to the National Catechetical Directory, 1977, ". . . elements of Catholic faith, tradition and practice which, through an early, gradual, flexible and never slavish process of memorization, could become lessons learned for a lifetime, contributing to an individual's growth and development in an understanding of the faith."

I. **Prayers**
    A. The Sign of the Cross
    B. The Our Father
    C. The Hail Mary
    D. The Apostles' Creed
    E. The Act of Faith
    F. The Act of Hope
    G. The Act of Charity
    H. The Act of Contrition

II. **Information, formulas, practices**
    A. Scriptural
        1. Key themes of salvation history
        2. Major Old Testament and New Testament personalities
        3. Significant texts expressive of God's love and care
    B. Liturgical-Devotional
        1. The parts of the Mass
        2. The sacraments—names and meaning
        3. The liturgical seasons
        4. The holy days
        5. Major feasts of Our Lord and of Mary
        6. Various Eucharistic devotions
        7. The mysteries of the rosary
        8. The stations of the cross
    C. Moral
        1. The Ten Commandments
        2. The eight Beatitudes
        3. The gifts of the Holy Spirit
        4. The virtues: three theological and four moral
        5. The six laws of the Church
        6. An examination of conscience

GOD

Six Attributes of the Deity
Symbolized in hexagonal chalice base

Power, Majesty, Wisdom, Love, Mercy, Justice

Divine Justice *(Perfect Justice; God's Justice)*
1. Legal, society's claim on individuals for the common good
2. Distributive, individual's claims in society
3. Remunerative, good are rewarded
4. Vindictive, wicked are punished

Four Points of a Soul's Likeness to God
1. Is a spirit, simplicity
2. Is immortal, immortality
3. Can reason, intellect
4. Can choose, free will

Powers of the Soul
1. Memory
2. Understanding
3. Free Will

The Unicorn

The word itself means "one horn" *(unum cornu)*. The creature represents the sinlessness of God's Son, and the incarnation itself: the Son of God whom the heavens could not contain humbled himself and was born of a virgin. The unicorn is a graceful creature of fable with a horse's head, goat's beard, antelope's legs, lion's tail, and, of course, the distinguishing great spiral horn rising from its forehead. According to medieval writers, this great horn is white at the base, black in the middle and red at the tip (which is able to detect poison with one touch). The unicorn has a white body, a red head, and blue eyes. The oldest description we have is one by Ctesias (400 B.C.). The following thirteenth-century account represents well the popular medieval belief (which are voluminous):

It is the only animal that ventures to attack the elephant; and so sharp is the nail of its foot, that with one blow it can rip the belly of that beast. Hunters can catch the unicorn only by placing a young virgin in his haunts. No sooner does he see the damsel than he runs towards her and lies down at her feet, and so suffers himself to be captured by the hunters. The unicorn represents Jesus Christ, who took on him our nature in the virgin's womb, was betrayed, and delivered into the hands of Pontius Pilate. Its one horn signifies the Gospel of truth.

The Devil's Funeral

In medieval England, Ireland, and Scotland it was traditional on Christmas Eve, at 11:00, to solemnly toll the bell, as if for a funeral, and to let them peal come the midnight hour. The legend was that the devil died when Christ was born.

The Four Manifestations of Christ

All are "epiphanies", although the Magi visit has taken the title for itself

1. Nativity
2. Magi visit
3. Baptism
4. Miracle at Cana (first recorded)

The adoration of the Magi

Nativity Scenes

According to tradition, Francis of Assisi began the practice of using managers at Christmas time. Sometimes called the Saint of the Incarnation, Francis believed that of all the ways God has revealed His love, none is more total and tangible than the incarnation of His Son. So, it isn't surprising that for the Midnight Mass, Christmas 1223, Francis presented a living reenactment in a cave in Greccio, Italy. This visual and creative—and apparently first—commemoration of Christ's birth has now become traditional: the nativity scene. (*Creche* is a French word—from Old High German *krippa,* from Italian *presepio,* from the Latin form of the Greek word for manger.)

The Three Nativity Gifts Mt 2.11
1. Gold, for the royalty of Jesus
2. Frankincense, for the divinity of Jesus
3. Myrrh, for the passion and death of Jesus

Three-fold Birth of Christ
1. Eternal, in the bosom of the Father
2. Temporal, in Bethlehem to Mary
3. Spiritual, in liturgy and daily living

Three-fold Office of Christ
1. Priest, sanctifying
2. Prophet, teaching
3. King, pastoring

The Three Kings

Caspar, Melchior, and Balthazar are their names, at least since the eighth century or so. "Magi" *(magoi)* is all Matthew calls them (2.1), and tells of the three gifts they brought. This has given rise to the tradition that there were three. Originally, they were often pictured as astrologers, but since the early Middle Ages, kings became the more common image, what with the various regal Old Testament texts. Because St. Bede (672–735) considered them representatives of the three continents of Europe, Asia, and Africa, we often see them racially as white, yellow and black. According to medieval legend, their bones were deposited in the cathedral of Cologne, the "City of the Three Kings." The famous shrine depository is one of the best examples of medieval metalcraft. These relics were given authenticity as early as the ninth century—brought form Constantinople to Milan and, finally in 1164 to Cologne.

Three-fold Belief in Christ
1. Christ has died, in history
2. Christ is risen, in mystery
3. Christ will come again, in majesty

Pentecost: The Birth of the Church
"Lord, send out Your Spirit, and renew the face of the earth" **Ps 104.30.**
"Each of us hears them in his native tongue" **Acts 2.8.**

Various translations of **Ps 104.30:**

Danish—*Gud, vis dig i Aanden/og genskab Jorden.*
French—*O Seigneur, envoi ton Espirit/qui renouvelle la face de al terre.*
Gaelic—*A Thiarna, cuir amach uait do Spiorad/agus dean aghaidh na talun a athnauchan.*
German—*Sende aus deinen Giest,/usn das Antlitz der Erde wird neu.*
Hungarian—*Araszd szet Lelkedet, Uram,/es meguijjitod a fold szinet.*
Italian—*Manda il tuo spirito, Signore,/a rinnovare la terra.*
Latin—*Emitte Spiritum tuum, Domine,/et renova faciem terrae.*
Lithuanian—*Viespatie siusk savo Dvasiq/ir atnaujink zemes veida.*
Polish—*Niech zstapi Duch Twoj/i odnowi ziemie.*
Portuguese—*Mandai, Senhor o Vosso Espirito/a renoval a terra.*
Spanish—*Envia tu Espiritu, senio,/y repuebla la faz de la tierra.*

Symbols of the Trinity

Trefoil   Equilateral Triangle   Triquetra   Interwoven Circles   Circles of Fish

Symbols explained in the glossary

"That's Impossible!"

Tertullian (3rd century) would have said, "That proves it!" As a matter of fact, he *did* say, in *[De carne Christi]*, *"Certum est quia impossible est"* ("It is certain because it is impossible"). That line may not work every time, but it's still true that the apparent impossibility of a truth of a Christian mystery argues for its acceptance and not its rejection.

Chief Mysteries of Christianity

Trinity, Original Sin, Incarnation have been called "The Three Greater Mysteries."

1. Unity
2. Trinity
3. Incarnation
4. Death of our Savior
5. Resurrection

The Trinity and the Incarnation, intertwined mysteries

Pouring the Ocean Down a Hole

One day Augustine was meditating on the mystery of the Blessed Trinity, strolling along the beach as he pondered. Lost in thought, he encountered a child who had dug a little hole in the sand. With tiny bucket in hand, the youngster had begun making trips to the sea and back, pouring pailfuls of water into the hole in the sand. Observing this for a while, Augustine asked the child what he was doing. "I'm putting the ocean in a hole. Condescendingly, Augustine said, "But you can never do that, whereupon the youngster responded, "And neither can you ever figure out the Holy Trinity." Legend has it that the boy disappeared because in truth he was an angel.

Scriptural Evangelizers

Mary brings Christ to world **Lk 1–2**

John the Baptist points out Jesus (lamb of God) to disciples **Jn 1.35–37**

Andrew introduces Peter to Jesus **Jn 1.40–42**

Andrew introduces boy with bread to Jesus (multiplication) **Jn 6.8–9**

Andrew introduces some Greek believers to Jesus **Jn 12.21–22**

Philip introduces Nathanael to Jesus **Jn 1.44–46**

Samaritan woman tells townspeople about Jesus (at well) **Jn 4.28–30**

Some people bring paralyzed man to Jesus (through roof) **Mk 2.1–12**

Mary Magdalene tells Peter and John of empty tomb **Jn 20.2**

Peter and John, other apostles, Paul and the apostolic Church **Acts**

. . . *and* consider the many "who told" after miracles by Jesus

A Vocation in a Dream

As a boy, St. Patrick was kidnapped and taken from his homeland to Ireland. He later escaped but was destined to return of his own free will to where he had been taken against his will. In his *Confessions* he wrote that he returned to the Emerald Isle after having a recurring dream in which the children of Ireland cried out to him, "Come and walk among us once more."

Stages of Conversion

Using the Scriptures and Peter as a model

1. Under the Law (Before Jesus)
2. Following Jesus (With Jesus)
3. Led by the Spirit (After Pentecost)

The Conversion Process
(Scripturally; radically)

The descending dove represents Pentecost and the gift of the Spirit

1. Hearing the Gospel
Need for preachers of the word **Rom 10.14, 17**

First believers in Corinth **Acts 18.8**

"Everyone who listens to these words of mine . . . ." **Mt 7.24**

"My mother and my brothers are those who hear the Word of God. . . ." **Lk 8.20–21**

2. Believing
"Now it is impossible to please God without faith. . . ."

"If your lips confess that Jesus is Lord and if you believe in your heart that God raised him from the dead, then you will be saved. **Rom 10.9**

"Unless a man is born through water and the Spirit, he cannot enter the Kingdom of God." **Jn 3.5**

3. Repenting sins
Joy over repentance **2 Cor. 7.10**

Paul's discourse to Athenians **Acts 17.30**

Providential calls to penance (e.g. tower of Siloam) **Lk 13.2–3**

Penance for the forgiveness of sins is to be preached **Lk 24.46–47**

Parables of divine mercy **Lk 15.1–32**

4. Confessing Christ
"If anyone declares himself for me. . . ." **Mt 10.32–33**

"If your lips confess. . . ." **see Rom 10.9 above**

Faith leads to justification, confession to salvation **Rom 10.10**

Regarding Timothy's profession of faith. **1 Tim 6.12–14**

"If we disown him then He will disown us." **2 Tim 2.12**

5. Being baptized
The baptism of Cornelius **Acts 10.48**

After Peter's first discourse **Acts 2.38**

Jesus' post-resurrection mandate **Mt 28.19; See Mk 16.16**

"All baptized in Christ, you have all clothed. . . ." **Gal 3.27**

"If we have died with him, we shall also live with him." **2 Tim 2.11**

"No one can enter the kingdom without . . ." **Jn 3.5**

Paul's telling of his own baptism **Acts 22.16**

Noah's ark and its correspondence to baptism **1 Pt 3.20–21**

Three Accounts of Paul's Conversion Experience
Acts 9.1–9   Acts 22.3–16   Acts 26.2–18   See 1 Cor 15.8

Kinds of Unorthodoxy

Agnostic—Denies the knowability of God.

Apostate—Renounces completely one's faith, religion.

Atheist—Denies the existence of God.

Deist—Denies that God revealed any religion.

Heretic (Gk: one who chooses)—Baptized, but denying some of the truths taught by Jesus; one choosing his/her own creed.

Infidel—Formerly, any non-Christian; now, professed atheist/agnostic.

Pagan ("Heathen")—One without faith; originally, a "non-convert", not acknowledging the God of Judeo-Christian revelation; today, an irreligious person.

Schismatic (Gk: *Skizein,* to cut, split; a division)—Full believers in the Church while refusing submission to the authority of its vicarious, earthly head, the pope.

Theist—Believes in a supreme being, who created and sustains all things, but does not necessarily accept the doctrine of the Trinity (the Incarnation) or divine revelation.

Heresy
Intellectual (from the mind)—opposed to religious belief

Schism
Volitional (from the will)—offends the union of Christian charity

Julian the Apostate

Julian was an emperor of Rome (361–3) and a great-nephew of Constantine. Even though his famous relative had legalized Christianity, and even though he had been raised a Catholic, Julian renounced his faith and set about reinstating paganism in the Roman Empire. In combating the Church he made an unsuccessful attempt at rebuilding the Jewish temple in Jerusalem. All his anti-Christian efforts and policies failed. He supposedly spoke from his deathbed, ''O Galilean, thou hast conquered,'' finally acknowledging Christ's victory in the world.

Formal Heresy—"prerequisites"

1. Previous valid baptism
2. Persistence of external profession of Christianity
   (lacking this, ''apostasy'')
3. Denial of a truth proposed by the Church as divinely revealed
   (lacking this, ''orthodoxy'')
4. Moral culpability: knowingly refusing a doctrinal imperative
   (lacking this, ''material heresy'')

Vincentian Canon

The widely known three-fold test of orthodoxy, articulated by St. Vincent of Lerins (400–450): ''Care must especially be had that that be held which was believed everywhere *(unique)*, always *(semper)*, and by all *(ab omnibus)*.'' The principles of diffusion, endurance, and universality in this triple norm distinguish a Christian's religious truth (orthodoxy) from error.

Virtues

Grace Builds on Nature

According to Aristotle, for something to build on, grace gets "sanguine," "melancholic," "choleric" or "lethargic" nature. At least that's what Aristotle said were the four human temperaments or dispositions of nature. *We'd* probably say: cheerful, gloomy, temperamental, and apathetic, and then start naming names.

Gradation of Virtues (Hierarchy of Dignity)
- I. Supernatural
  - A. Theological (1. Charity; 2. Hope; 3. Faith)
  - B. Moral (1. Prudence; 2. Justice; 3. Temperance; 4. Fortitude)
- II. Natural

The Theological Virtues

Faith	Hope	Charity

Three Elements of Faith

Knowledge	Assent	Confidence

Qualities of Christian Faith

Universal	Firm	Constant	Living

The Cardinal (Moral) Virtues
Lt: *cardo* (hinge): that on which another thing depends

Prudence	Justice	Temperance	Fortitude

Prudence is the queen, since it controls all others, guiding conduct specifically and practically.

Gifts

The Gifts of the Holy Spirit

According to Isaiah 11.2–3	*According to Paul* 1 Cor 12.8–10
1. Wisdom *(Sapientia)*	Preaching with wisdom
2. Understanding *(Intellectus)*	Faith
3. Counsel *(Consilium)*	Healing
4. Fortitude *(Fortitudo)*	Miracles
5. Knowledge *(Scientia)*	Prophecy
6. Piety *(Pietas)*	Recognizing spirits
7. Fear of the Lord *(Timor Domini)**	Tongues
	Interpretation of Tongues
Traditional	*Translation from The Jerusalem Bible*

*"Reverence for God;" the Hebrew term for religion.

Fear and Love

1. Fear of the Lord–Object: Divine Justice
"The Fear of the Lord is the beginning of Wisdom." **Ps 111.10**
  - a. Filial fear (selfless): fear of offending
  - b. Servile fear (selfish): fear of being punished

2. Love of the Lord—Object: Divine goodness
"Perfect love casts out all fear." **1 Jn 4.18**

Charisms (Gk: *Charismata,* gifts of grace)

Described by St. Paul as extraordinary, supernatural, and transitory gifts given directly for the common good, which is the spiritual welfare of the Christian community. The longest single enumeration is in 1 Cor 12.1–14,40. By category:

Charisms of Administration *(Gifts for shepherding God's people)*
  1. Pastor **Eph 4.11; Acts 20.28**
  2. Administrator **Rom 12.8; 1 Thes 5.12; 1 Tim 5.17**
  3. Minister **1 Cor 16.15; Rom 12.7**

Nihil-obstat Quominus Imprimatur

"Nothing hinders it from being printed". Usually seen in two parts: the *nihil obstat,* or the judgment of the censor that there is nothing contrary to faith or morals, nothing "stands in the way"; and the *imprimatur,* the official permission to print, especially from Church authorities or a censor. Pertaining to other printed "Catholic material"; that is, not by the teaching Church (e.g. council, synod, bishop), but by a member of the Church: represents the approval by a bishop for the publication of a religious work; petitioner can seek it from bishop where he resides, or where work is to be published.

Charisms of Knowledge *(Gifts for the mind, to instruct others in faith)*
  1. Prophet **1 Cor 12.28 see Acts 11.27f; 21.10f; 15.32; 1 Cor 14.3; 14.24–25; 11.5; Acts 21.9**
  2. Evangelist **Acts 21.8; 2 Tim 4.5**
  3. Teacher **Rom 12.7; Eph 4.11; 1 Tim 4.13,16**
  4. Exhorter **Rom 12.8; 1 Tim 4.13; Acts 4.36**
  5. Proclaimer of Wisdom **1 Cor 12.8**
  6. Proclaimer of Knowledge **1 Cor 12.8**

Charisms of Prayer
Gifts of communing with God **See 1 Cor 14.**

Charisms of Service
  1. Almsgiving **Rom 12.8**
  2. Manifestation of Mercy **Rom 12.8**
  3. Helpfulness **1 Cor 12.28**
  4. Leadership **1 Cor 12.28**

Fruits

The Fruits of the Holy Spirit (Gal. 5.22–23)

Traditional	*The Jerusalem Bible*
1. Charity	Love
2. Joy	Joy
3. Peace	Peace
4. Patience	Patience
5. Kindness	Kindness
6. Goodness	Goodness
7. Long-suffering	Trustfulness
8. Humility	Gentleness
9. Fidelity	Self-control
10. Modesty	
11. Continence	
12. Chastity	

Words of Supererogation (Lt: *super,* above; *erogare,* to pay out)
A theological term for "good works" done but not enjoined; actually, the outward expressions of the fruits of the spirit.

The Ten Commandments Ex 20.1–21; Dt 5.1–22

1. I, the Lord, am your God . . . You shall not have other gods besides me.
2. You shall not take the name of the Lord, your God, in vain.
3. Remember to keep holy the sabbath day.
4. Honor your father and your mother.
5. You shall not kill.
6. You shall not commit adultery.
7. You shall not steal.
8. You shall not bear false witness against your neighbor.
9. You shall not covet your neighbor's wife.
10. You shall not covet your neighbor's house . . . nor anything else that belongs to him.

The Two Great Commandments Mt. 22.37, 39

1. You shall love the Lord your God with your whole heart, with your whole soul, and with all your mind.
2. You shall love your neighbor as yourself.

Precepts of the Church
Some duties of Catholic Christians, these were originally approved by the Third Plenary Council of Baltimore, 1884. (De jure means sanctioned by law and designates that which exists legally—because it was legislated— as opposed to de facto, "in reality," which reflects merely custom or practice rather than the law of the land or the Church.)

1. To keep holy the day of the Lord's Resurrection: to worship God by participating in Mass every Sunday and Holy Day of Obligation; to avoid those activities that would hinder renewal of soul and body; for example, needless work and business activities, unnecessary shopping, and so forth.
2. To lead a sacramental life: to receive Holy Communion frequently and the Sacrament of Reconciliation regularly—minimally, to receive the Sacrament of Reconciliation at least once a year (obligatory annually only if serious sin is involved.)—minimally, to receive Holy Communion at least once a year, between the first Sunday of Lent and Trinity Sunday.*
3. To study Catholic teaching in preparation for confirmation, to be confirmed, and then to continue to study and advance the cause of Christ.
4. To observe the marriage laws of the Church: to give religious training (by example and word) to one's children; to use parish schools and religious education programs.
5. To strengthen and support the Church: one's own parish community and parish priests; the worldwide Church and the Holy Father.
6. To do penance, including abstaining from meat and fasting from food on the appointed days.
7. To join in the missionary spirit and apostolate of the Church.

The Man in the Moon and the Sabbath Breaker

Some used to say that it is a man leaning on a fork on which is a bundle of sticks gathered on the Sabbath. This is rooted in the Old Testament episode (Nm 15.32–36) of a man caught gathering wood on the Sabbath. He was put to death.

Some versions of this fable include a dog, as in the prologue of *A Midsummer Night's Dream*. Still others call the man in the moon Cain, with the thorn bush representing the thorns and briars of the fall.

*Commonly referred to as "Easter Duty" in the days when frequent communion was not the norm.

The eight points of the Maltese Cross represent the eight Beautitudes

The Beatitudes Mt 5.3–10; see Lk 6.20–25
("Blessed" or "Blest" or "Happy", depending on the translation)

1. Blessed are the poor in spirit, for theirs is the kingdom of heaven.
2. Blessed are the meek, for they shall possess the earth.
3. Blessed are they who mourn, for they shall be comforted.
4. Blessed are they who hunger and thirst for justice, for they shall be satisfied.
5. Blessed are the merciful, for they shall obtain mercy.
6. Blessed are the clean of heart, for they shall see God.
7. Blessed are the peacemakers, for they shall be called children of God.
8. Blessed are they who suffer persecution for justice sake, for theirs is the kingdom of heaven.

The Seven Beatitudes of the Book of Revelation (NAB translation)

1. Happy are those who read this, or hear it, and heed. **1.3**
2. Happy are the dead who die in the Lord. **14.13**
3. Happy are the vigilant, and the faithful. **16.15**
4. Happy are those invited to the Lamb's wedding feast. **19.9**
5. Happy are those who share in the (first) resurrection. **20.6**
6. Happy those who heed this prophetic message. **22.7**
7. Happy are those who wash their robes, and so enter the City. **22.14**

Evangelical Counsels
Poverty   Chastity   Obedience

See Benedictine's Vow of Stability

The monetary allowance to a vowed religious from the order was called the "peculium".

St. Francis and Lady Poverty

Francis is well known for his "love affair" with Lady Poverty. Francis loved to have nothing. One day he decided to give control of his life entirely to God. He went to his bishop and told him his determination. Francis laid everything he possessed at the feet of his bishop, including the clothes on his back. With that he was able to dance away naked down the street, completely free and dispossessed.

Three Notable Duties ("Eminent Good Works")

Prayer   Fasting   Almsgiving

A "pardoner" was one licensed to preach and collect alms. In the Middle Ages, the name was used for preachers of indulgences who solicited alms for church building and crusade sponsoring.

Prayer

The Hebrew, the Jew, and the Christian have been freed for worship (See Ex 7.16) which shapes us for service.

Jesus Prays

Here are some references to Jesus praying, with an asterisk indicating occasions where the prayer itself is recorded.

> After he was baptized Lk 3.21
> At the beginning of his ministry Mk 1.12
> In a lonely desert place Mk 1.35
> Before choosing the Twelve, all night Lk 6.12–13
> In a deserted place with the Twelve Mk 6.32
> After preaching and healing with the Twelve Mk 6.30–33
> Often in lonely places Lk 5.15
> Before his invitation "Come to me. . . ." Mt 11.25–27*
> Before feeding the five thousand Jn 6.11
> Before feeding the five thousand Mt 14.23
> In seclusion, before eliciting Peter's act of faith L 9.18
> At the transfiguration Lk 9.28–29
> For little children Mt 19.13
> Before the raising of Lazarus Jn 11.41–42*
> In the temple on Palm Sunday Jn 12.28*
> For the disciples (the "high priestly prayer of Jesus") Jn 17*
> For Peter and his faith Lk 22.32
> After the last supper Mt 26.30
> In Gethsemane Mt 26.39, 42, 44*
> On the cross Lk 23.34, 46*

Jesus Teaches about Prayer

> Pray in these words. . . .
>   Lk 11.1f; Mt 6.8f
> Pray in secret Mt 6.6
> Ask and you shall receive Mt 7.7
> Pray in readiness for end times Lk 21.36
> Pray for persecutors Lk 6.28
> The power of united prayer Mt 18.19–20
> Persist Lk 11.5–13

PIETAS

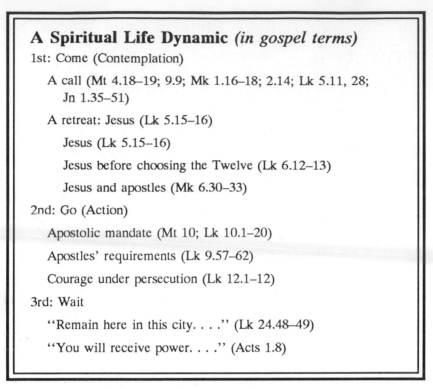

A Spiritual Life Dynamic *(in gospel terms)*

1st: Come (Contemplation)

    A call (Mt 4.18–19; 9.9; Mk 1.16–18; 2.14; Lk 5.11, 28; Jn 1.35–51)

    A retreat: Jesus (Lk 5.15–16)

        Jesus (Lk 5.15–16)

        Jesus before choosing the Twelve (Lk 6.12–13)

        Jesus and apostles (Mk 6.30–33)

2nd: Go (Action)

    Apostolic mandate (Mt 10; Lk 10.1–20)

    Apostles' requirements (Lk 9.57–62)

    Courage under persecution (Lk 12.1–12)

3rd: Wait

    "Remain here in this city. . . ." (Lk 24.48–49)

    "You will receive power. . . ." (Acts 1.8)

CHRISTIANS PRAY

Kinds of Prayer, I

1. **Liturgical** (see chapters 5 and 6)
   Mass, sacraments, and the Liturgy of the Hours—The "source and summit" of Church activity and power (Vatican II, *Constitution on the Sacred Liturgy,* n. 10)
2. **Para-liturgical**
   Lacking full liturgical form as determined by the Church
3. **Devotional/communal** (see chapter 7)
   A. Group (Penance services, Lenten devotions, Rosary, Stations, prayer services, and so forth)
   B. Shared (individual prayer shared—see **Jn 17**)
4. **Personal/private**—prayer "in secret," **Mt 6.6**

Kinds of Prayer, II

1. **Direct Address** (Conversing)
   a. Petition—"Please"
   b. Thanksgiving—"Thank you"
   c. Reparation—"I'm sorry"
   d. Adoration—"I love you"

St. Anthony and the Child Jesus

Once as a guest in someone's home, Anthony was seen through an open window, deep in mediation and communion. He was holding Christ so single-mindedly in his heart that the Christ Child was seen in his arms. Images of Anthony with the child Jesus, the only person other than Mary, Joseph, and Simeon so privileged, are common in church windows and statuary.

2. **Meditation** (Seeking)
    "Considerations and reasonings on a religious truth"
    (divine knowledge; self understanding; life direction/meaning)
    Also known as Discursive Prayer ("reflective"), characterized by reflections of the mind (thoughts).
3. **Contemplation** (Discovering/enjoying)
    "Awareness of God with love and admiration"
    Also known as Intuitive Prayer ("immediately perceptive"), characterized by affective sentiments of the will (feelings).

The Doubting Monk and the Singing Bird

A certain monk of old Hildesheim in Hanover, so the fable goes, doubted how it could be that with God 1000 years are as a day. As he pondered, he listened to the singing of a bird in the woods for three minutes . . . or so he thought, for 300 years had slipped by.

Kinds of Prayer, III

— Access Prayers

Formerly, prayers of a priest before Mass.

— Aspiration ("ejaculation")

Prayerful phrase uttered in one breath.

— Benediction

Generally, a blessing; specifically, the common term for Eucharist Devotion.

— Blessing

Praise; Scripturally: the desire that good fortune attend a person/thing; dedication of a person/thing to God's service. Liturgically, a cleric's sanctification of persons/things to divine service, and/or invocation of divine favor upon.

— Consecration (Ordinary)

A prayer of commitment of self-giving to God through Christ (like St. Ignatius Loyola's). Since it only makes more conscious what happened at baptism/confirmation, it obliges one to no more than "ordinary" discipleship does. Such prayer should always be related to baptism and associated with Eucharist (offertory). The classic form is the renewal of baptismal vows. In recent centuries, particular acts proliferated, often offered involving the inspiration of some saint because of their unique relationship to Christ.

— Consecration (Total)

More all-embracing, beyond normal gospel demands, patterning the spiritual life on Mary, totally dedicated to Christ.

1. Originated by Odilo of Cluny (d. 1049)
2. Perfected by St. Grignon de Montfort (d. 1716)

— Eulogia (Gk: good speaking)

Blessing (a benediction, in apostolic days), or sometimes a blessed object (especially bread).

— Exorcism

The formal exorcism rite is for driving out evil spirits in cases of demoniacal possession and consists of a series of prayers, blessings, and commands spoken by a priest/bishop ("exorcist"); rare today, and only with bishop's permission. Lesser forms, not implying the state of possession, are used in baptism, in the blessings of certain objects and even by some in private prayer.

— Gregorian Chant

The form of musical worship revised and introduced into the liturgy by Pope Gregory the Great (600). Probably derived from Jewish sources, and the oldest chant in current use, it is a form of "plain song," with no definite rhythm.

— Invocation

The prayerful, and humble appeal to God for mercy, love, and/or generally divine assistance. It could also be to angels or saints, for supernatural help.

— Itinerarium

A prayer for a safe journey.

— Novena

A prayer with a specific intention offered nine days in a row, originating in the nine (*novem*) days of prayer by the disciples and Mary between Ascension and Pentecost. Many novenas have been highly indulgenced by the Holy See over the centuries. A "Novena of Grace" was traditionally in March. A "Christmas Novena" begins December 16 and honors the mystery of Christmas. Today the recommended (and only Scriptural) novena is the one before Pentecost.

— Trisagion (try-SAHG-ee-on), Gk: three, holy

A common Eastern Catholic liturgical hymn characterized by a threefold invocation like:

Holy God,

holy and mighty

holy and immortal, have mercy on us. **Modeled on Is 6.3**

Albrecht Durer and the Praying Hands

The hands that have inspired many were originally inspired by a young man named Hans. He and his friend, a youth named Albrecht Durer, were struggling young artists. Around 1490 they were still students, but hindered in their progress by the work that their poverty demanded. The older of the two, Hans, agreed to sacrifice his schooling for a while and work full-time so Albrecht could give full attention to his study. This freed young Durer to pursue the career that produced the treasures for which he is so well known. Hans paid part of the price for this genius with the years of hard manual labor which gnarled his hands and stiffened his fingers. When his friend's success would have enabled him to follow his own dreams of being an artist, he no longer had hands for the sure, delicate brush-strokes of painting. Albrecht Durer, today regarded as the leader of the German Renaissance school of painting, memorialized his friend's sacrifice. He painted his hands, painted them as he had seen them so often: raised in prayer for his success. It is said that The Praying Hands were painted by Albrecht Durer and presented to Hans, whose last name we do not even know.

"Praise God"

A Process of Prayer
1. Listen—"Speak, Lord, your servant is listening."
2. Reflect—"This is the Lord speaking."
3. Wait—"Your will be done." Mt 6.10; Ps 46; 130
4. Receive/respond

The Motive for Prayer
1. To Give (as an end in itself)— Praise and Thanks
2. To Receive (as a means)— Faith, courage, insight, mercy, and so forth.

The Rules of Prayer
Times for Prayer—at specified times and many/any time

Places for Prayer—in specified places and many/any place
Ways of Prayer—with specified words and any/no words

The Object of Prayer
God the Father:
As Jesus did—"MY Father. . . ."
As Jesus taught—"OUR Father. . . ."

Fast and Abstinence

Definitions
Fasting—Limitations on food and drink. In the modern church until 1966, the regulations for days of fast prescribed taking only one full daily meal, plus breakfast and a "collation" (light meal).

Abstaining—In this context, refraining from certain kinds of food or drink, typically meat. From the first century, the day of the crucifixion has been traditionally observed as a day of abstaining from flesh meat ("black fast") to honor Christ who sacrificed his flesh on a Friday.

Obligations
Formerly—Fast days: all Lenten days except Sunday. Fast and abstinence days: Ash Wednesday, Lenten Fridays and Saturdays, Ember Days, certain feast's vigils.

Currently—In Pope Paul VI's constitution *Paenitemini*, 1966:

— the meaning of fasting was explained;

— the obligation was restated;

— the extent of the obligation was changed;

— Ash Wednesday and Good Friday are universal days of fast and abstinence;

The Serpent's Fast

Everyone knows about the serpent in the Garden, and its universal symbolism of temptation and evil. But it seems even the serpent has another, more inspiring side. Surprisingly, it has symbolized repentance, reconciliation, and readiness for Eucharist because of the old fable of its forty-day fast before shedding its skin. There is also an old legend that the serpent quenches its thirst only after leaving its venom in its den lest it kill itself.

— every Friday calls for some act of penance when abstinence from meat is not observed (norm II, 2);

— specific regulations left to bishops in their episcopal conferences.

Eucharistic Fast

A practice from ancient times. Prescribed by Councils of Carthage (254) and Antioch (268). Universal practice by fifth century.

Originally
Fast from midnight, including water and medicine (viaticum being an exception).

— 1953, 1957 (Pope Pius XII): Fast reduced to three hours from solid food and alcoholic drink (from before Mass for the priest and from before communion for the laity); non-alcoholic drink, one hour; water no longer included in fast.

— 1964 (Pope Paul VI): Fast reduced to one hour, including all food and drink, allowing water and medicine anytime.

— 1973 (Pope Paul VI): Fast for the elderly and sick reduced to fifteen minutes, including those attending them if one hour would be too difficult.

When in Rome

"Quando hic sum, non jejuno Sabbato, quando Romae sum, jejuno Sabbato" is the way it comes out in Latin, at least one version, and it's always attributed to St. Ambrose: "When I am here (Milan), I do not fast on Saturday; when I'm in Rome, I fast on Saturday." Or, as we say, "When in Rome do as the Romans do." It's what Bishop Ambrose said when advising Augustine's mother, Monica, who had followed her son to Milan: "When I am here, I do not fast on Saturday; when I am in Rome, I fast on Saturday." Simply put, follow the local customs.

The Penitential Observance of Lent

Historical Background

Even by the time of Christ, fasting and abstaining were venerable traditions of piety among the Jews. The practices were not foreign to Christ (Mt 6.16; Mk 2.20; 9.29) or the apostles (Acts 13.2; 14.23; 2 Cor. 2.27). In the early Church, a two-three day Lenten fast was common. It was not until the fourth century and the Council of Nicea (A.D.) 325 that a forty-day period was mentioned. In the Middle Ages, the rule relaxed somewhat, with a light second meal and fish allowed. From time to time and place to place, there has been variation in practice, but consistency of spirit: the life of a Christian is a life of penance.

Current Practice

See the Code of Canon Law (1983), canon #1249f. They are here outlined:

1. The Seasons of Lent preserves its penitential character.
2. The Days of Penance to be observed are Ash Wednesday and all Fridays in Lent.
3. The manner of fulfilling the precept of penance:
   a. Ash Wednesday and Good Friday are days of fast and abstinence.
   b. All Fridays in Lent are days of abstinence only.
4. Church Law binds as follows:
   a. The Law of Abstinence (not eating meat) obliges those who have completed their 14th year.
   b. The law of fast (only one full meal each day, nothing between meals) obliges those who have completed their 18th year until the beginning of their 60th year.
   c. Proportionately grave inconvenience excuses from the laws of fast and abstinence.
5. The substantial observance of these laws is a grave obligation.
   a. Anyone who neglects all forms of penance violates Divine Law and is guilty of grave sin.
   b. Anyone who occasionally violates the law of fast, and/or abstinence is not guilty of sin.

Almsgiving

Stewardship

The practice of considering and treating all things, the earth and one's own life (time, talent, and treasure) as belonging to God, and oneself as the manager, or "steward," See Lk 12.42; 16.1–8; 1 Cor 4.1–2; 1 Pt 4.10.

In Giving We Receive

"Stone Soup"

Once upon a time, a beggar asked alms at the mansion of a lord. Rebuffed by the servants who claimed they had nothing to give, the beggar replied, "Sorry for it, but will you let me boil a little water to make some soup of this stone?" With their curiosity aroused at such an unusual proposal, the servants readily provided saucepan, water, and spoon. The pauper promptly popped in a stone, savored it, and suggested it needed the flavor of a little salt and pepper. The servants, caught up in the proceedings, shared some of theirs. With a flourish, the beggar stirred, and tasted, and observed that it would certainly be improved with any fragment of vegetable and meat there might be around. His unwitting assistants supplied them. Similarly, with a final fanfare, the beggar accepted a bit of sauce. Then all tasted and enjoyed, with the servants agreeing that stone soup is excellent.

This favorite sixteenth/seventeenth-century story, sometimes called "St. Bernard's Soup" has variations using a horseshoe, or a nail, or a ramshorn, for example, but always the same theme.

"Elijah's Melons"

The story is told of the prophet being denied hospitality: Elijah encountered a peasant bearing melons. When he requested one, he was told they were stones, so Elijah obligingly transformed the melons to stones (and the peasant's falsehood to truth). To this day, certain stones on Mt. Carmel still bear this name.

Tithing
Giving away a portion of one's income, commonly a tenth. In the Old Testament, paying a tenth part of one's property as a tax to one's superior (Gn 14), and also giving a tenth of the fruit of the land and increase of the flocks and herds to God. **See especially Mal 3.10, and also Gn 29.22; Lv 27.30–32; Nm 18.21–32; Dt 12.5, 6, 11, 17, 18; 14.23, 28, 29; 26.12**

Sacrificial Giving
A voluntary, proportionate, systematic, sacrificial, and liturgical giving of money (part of the larger self-giving: time, talent, treasure)

1. Voluntary
   Neither an assessment nor a tax (which the "tithe" became)
2. Proportionate
   Like the widow Jesus praised, though she gave little **Lk 21.2**
   a. The Old Testament "tithe" was literally ten percent (of gross income): that may be too much for some, too little for others
   b. Includes paychecks, dividends, social security payments, allowances, windfalls, etc.
3. Systematic (planned)
   a. Part of the budget
   b. As income is received (not "when somebody needs it")
4. Sacrificial
   a. "Making holy" (the literal meaning of "sacrifice") the earnings and efforts of the week.
   b. If it doesn't hurt (require a sacrifice), it's only a donation, or a contribution, not sacrificial giving, which is a measure of one's trust in God
5. Liturgical
   In Catholic liturgy, the bringing forth of the gifts and the collection of money are both part of the same ritual act (non-givers do not participate in this part of Catholic Eucharistic worship)
   a. Collections at other times and donations in other ways lack this Eucharistic context and don't "consecrate" hours worked and income received
   b. Using envelopes gives witness to commitment
6. Giving (usually divided)
   a. Half is given weekly by way of the local parish collection*
   b. Half is set aside for independent giving (mission appeals, diocesan collections, personal favorite charities, and so forth)

"Church support" is not the same as sacrificial giving, but a by-product of it.

Corporal Works of Mercy

"What you do to the least, you do to me." Mt 25.35-46

1. Feed the hungry.
2. Give drink to the thirsty.
3. Clothe the naked.
4. Shelter the homeless.
5. Visit the sick.
6. Visit the imprisoned.
7. Bury the dead.

Spiritual Works of Mercy

Based on Christ's teachings and Christian practice since the apostles.

1. Counsel the doubtful.
2. Instruct the ignorant.
3. Admonish the sinner.
4. Comfort the sorrowful.
5. Forgive injuries.
6. Bear wrongs patiently.
7. Pay for the living and the dead.

St. Martin and the Shirt Off His Back

As a mere ten year old, Martin became a catechumen on his own initiative. As the son of a military man, however, he was forced into the army against his will when he was fifteen. While stationed at Amiens there was an incident and a vision, well known in tradition and art, which changed his life: On a bitterly cold day, Martin met a poor man, hardly clothed, trembling in the cold and begging from passersby at the city gate. The young soldier had nothing but his weapons and his clothes. He drew is sword, cut his cloak in two, gave one half to the beggar and wrapped himself in the other half. Some of the onlookers mocked him for the figure he cut; others were ashamed for having ignored the man's misery. In his sleep that night, Martin saw Christ dressed in the half of the garment he had given away, and heard Him say, "Martin, still a catechumen, has covered me with this garment." As a result, the story goes, Martin straightaway "flew to be baptized." (Countless times, people ever since have unwittingly referred to this incident and the renowned cloak every time a certain common word is used. See "chapel.")

Hospitality in the Scriptures: Stranger and Guest

Abraham and three visitors (the Lord and two
  messengers) **Gn 18.3–8**
Lot and the two visitors (angels of the Lord)
  Gn 19.1–11
Moses and seven girls (Reuel's daughters; and
  a future wife) **Ex 2.15**
An exception: Jael hosts Sisera and kills him
  Jgs 4.17–22
Gideon and a man (an angel of God) **Jgs 6.19f**
Solomon hosts the Queen of Sheba **1 Kgs 10.1f**
Elijah hosts the 450 prophets of Baal
  1 Kgs 18.19f

Et aperti sunt oculi eorum

The Shunammite woman hosts Elisha **2 Kgs 4.8**
Jacob and a wrestler (an angel) **Gn 32.25f**

"And their eyes were opened," from the Emmaus

Rahab the harlot and Joshua's two spies **Jos 2.1f**
An exception: Holofernes hosts Judith, and is killed **Jdt 12.10f**
Two disciples going to Emmaus and a stranger (Christ) **Lk 24.13–35**
Samaritan woman at Jacob's well and a thirsty stranger (Jesus) **Jn 4.4–42**
Matthew hosts Jesus, tax collectors, and sinners **Mt 9.10–13**
Zacchaeus hosts Jesus **Lk 19.1–10**
Samaritans refusing hospitality to Jesus **Lk 9.51–53**
"He who welcomes you welcomes me" teaching **see Jn 13.20**
  Mt 10.40–42
"Whatsoever you do to the least of my brothers" teaching **Mt 25.31–46**
"Here I stand, knocking at the door." **Rv 3.20**

Divine Ambassadors

The Greeks believed that people in need are the ambassadors of
the gods. Stories of dignitaries and deities in disguise are abundant and universal in folklore—indeed, in the Scriptures
(Abraham's guests, Gn 18, for example, and Raphael in Tobit
5.4f). In the early centuries of Christendom, houses of
hospitality, or hospices, were provided as shelter for the various
"divine ambassadors:" the sick, the poor, the orphan, the old,
the traveler, and the needy of every kind. Bishops originally supervised these houses of hospitality, delegating certain priests
with the administration of their material and spiritual affairs.
Bishops, in fact, were enjoined to have such houses in connection with their churches.

". . . Many Dwelling Places"

Jesus' own experience of homelessness, beginning in infancy, has given his disciples a sensitivity, as well as many stories and traditions.

"A Refuge for the Holy Family"

It's a tradition in south central Italy each Christmas Eve to leave the door of the house open, have the fire lit and the table laid. This posture of hospitality was assumed in case the Holy Family, pursued by Herod's minions, should need a hiding place, or food.

"Gypsies"

"Egyptians" is where the word comes from, at least according to a medieval notion. Among many legends about gypsies, this one says that they are people condemned to wander the earth without rest. Since they refused hospitality to Joseph, Mary, and Jesus during their Egyptian flight, these "gypsies" suffered the same rootless fate.

"St. Joseph Table"

March 19 is the occasion for a traditional show of hospitality, fittingly on the feast of St. Joseph, patron of charity to the poor, a happy home, and peace. The tradition was brought to our country by Sicilian immigrants, and includes inviting to the table all who come to the door. Traditionally, the family table is extended full length and, as the alter used to be, moved against the wall with a statue of St. Joseph surrounded by flowers and candles, as the centerpiece of a shrine. Having enjoyed the hospitality, the fruits and vegetables, the breads and pastries, and the artistry of the hosts, guests move on, making room for more. Beforehand, the priest has blessed the bounty and, afterward, any offering made by guests is given for the poor.

SIN

1. Original (the sin in which we are born)
2. Actual (the sins which we commit, both omissions and commissions)

Original Sin

The Three Great Preternatural Gifts
To which human beings have no title; possessed by Adam and Eve before the Fall.

1. Infused knowledge
2. Absence of concupiscence
3. Bodily immortality

The Effects Of Original Sin
1. Human natural corrupted
2. Understanding darkened
3. Will weakened
4. Strong inclination to do evil

The Four Horseman of the Apocalypse Rv 6.1–8; see Zec 1.8f; 6.1–8
War (white)　　Violence (red)　　Famine (black)　　Death (green)

Flowers in the Garden of Eden

Flowers must have grown in paradise. Legends certainly have. One of them says that there was only one plant salvaged from the Garden of Eden, the *lign aloe*. Adam took with him one of these Paradise Shoots, from which all *lign aloes* have descended. There are many other flowery stories about Eden, like the following:

"The Rose of Paradise"
Before it became a flower of earth, the rose grew thornless in paradise. Only after Adam sinned did it take on thorns to remind mankind of the sin committed, and the fall from grace. The fragrance and beauty remain, however, as a reminder of the splendor of paradise. It continues to be a classic symbol of Mary, the new Eve, the rose without thorns.

"Eve's Tears"
Lilies of the Valley sprung up, it is said, where Eve's repentant tears fell as she was banished from Eden. In England and France, these same flowers are named after the new Eve: "Our Lady's Tears." For centuries, this symbol of humility and purity has been dedicated to Mary.

Actual Sin

St. Paul's "Sin Lists"
1 Cor 5.3–5; 1 Cor 6. 9–10; Gal 5.19–20; Eph 5.5; 1 Tim 1.19–21

Actual Sin
1. Venial (Lt: *venia*, grace, pardon) does not forfeit grace See Mt 12:31
2. Mortal (Lt: *mors, morte*, death) See 1 Jn 5.16–17

Cooperation in the Sin of Another
Causing

1. Advice or Counsel
2. Command
3. Provocation
4. Consent

Approving

5. Praise
6. Concealment or Silence
7. Participation
8. Enjoyment of Results
9. Defense

Greater and Lesser Evils

It was the fifteenth-century theologian Thomas a' Kempis who advised making the best of a bad situation when he said, "Of two evils, the lesser is always to be chosen." *(De duobus malis, minus est semper eligendum)*. If that's not the way he said it, it's the way we repeat it.

The Effects of Venial Sin
1. Lessening of the love of God in the heart
2. Weakening of the power to resist

Three Elements of a Mortal Sin
1. Grievous matter
2. Sufficient reflection
3. Full consent of the will

The Seven Capital Sins
1. Pride
2. Covetousness
3. Lust
4. Anger
5. Gluttony
6. Envy
7. Sloth

The Seven Christian Virtues
1. Humility
2. Liberality
3. Chastity
4. Gentleness
5. Temperance
6. Brotherly love
7. Diligence

The Six Sins against the Holy Spirit (See Mt 12:31–32; I Jn 5.16–17)
All involving a stubborn resistance to inspiration and a contempt for the gifts, therefore "unforgivable" because of the lack of desire for repentance.

1. Despair of one's salvation (of God's mercy)
2. Presumption of saving oneself without merit
3. Resisting the known truth
4. Envy of the graces received by others
5. Obstinacy in one's sins
6. Final impenitence

The Four Sins that Cry to Heaven for Vengeance
1. The voluntary murder Gn 4.10
2. The sin of impurity against nature (sodomy) Gn 18.20
3. Taking advantage of the poor Ex 2.23
4. Defrauding the workingman of his wages Jms 5.4

Speech Abuse
The Divine Praises originated as a reparation for blasphemy and profanity; the Holy Name Society was founded in the thirteenth century to promote reverence for Jesus' name.

1. Disrespecting God
   Generally, "sacrilegious, sacrilege" (Lt: *sacrilegium,* stealing sacred things) is intentional violation of sacred things; a sin against the virtue of religion; normally referring to an action ("desecration"), but also "sacrilegious" talk.
   A. Profanity (Lt: *profanus,* outside the temple): Taking the name of God (Lord, Jesus, Christ) in vain (without due regard for its sacred character).
   B. Blasphemy (Gk: *blasphemein,* to speak ill of): Trivializing, degrading, affronting God.
   C. Cursing: Blasphemy by calling down evil (damnation).
   D. Swearing: Taking an oath; calling God to witness.

"O Blessed Tongue . . ."

Thirty years after his death in 1231, St. Anthony's tomb was opened. Although his body had returned to dust, there was found his tongue miraculously preserved. St. Bonaventure, then Minister General of the Franciscans (of which Anthony was a celebrated member), in veneration of this symbol of sacred eloquence, said, "O blessed tongue that always praised the Lord, and caused others to bless Him, now it is manifest how great your merits were before God." (See "Incorruptibility.")

---

2. Disrespecting Others

"Libel" is a legal term with moral implications: something defamatory written/printed that implicates the publication as unlawful.

A. Gossip: Idle talk.
B. Slander (Lt: *scandalum*, stumbling block, just as "scandal"): verbal defamation of character; character assassination.
C. Detraction: Slander by revealing what is true, but harmful.
D. Calumny (Lt: *calumnia, calvi;* to deceive): Slander by lying (so doubly sinful).
E. Obscenity (Lt: *obscaenitas*, offensiveness, filthiness): Sinfully calculated to arouse sexual pleasure.

Smooth Talkers

They unwittingly quote the Psalmist, who have even spoken a version of the Latin phrase, "*Oleo tranquillior*". It means literally "smoother than oil", and is from the psalms. The whole quote, which has many versions, is "His mouth was as smooth as butter, but his heart was war; his words were smoother than oil, yet they were drawn swords."

3. Disrespecting Truth

"Bearing false witness", in the original context of the Decalogue (Ex 20.16), referring to speaking ("bearing") falsely before a tribunal ("witnessing"). Even well before Christ, it came to mean all telling of untruth.

A. Lying: Speaking a falsehood.
B. Perjury (Lt: *periurium*, false oath): Swearing to a falsehood (lying under oath).

A Friend As Far As to the Altars

Pericles of Athens is said to have responded with this when refusing to swear falsely for a friend. "A friend as far as the altars" ("*Amicus usqua ad aras*" when quoted in Latin) could be a friend to death. It could also be more—where friendship conflicts with religious beliefs or ethics, the good friends draws the line. This is not an admission of friendship's limit; it is a proof of its depth.

THE BIBLE ON THE END AND ETERNITY

The Second Coming (Parousia)/ End of the World

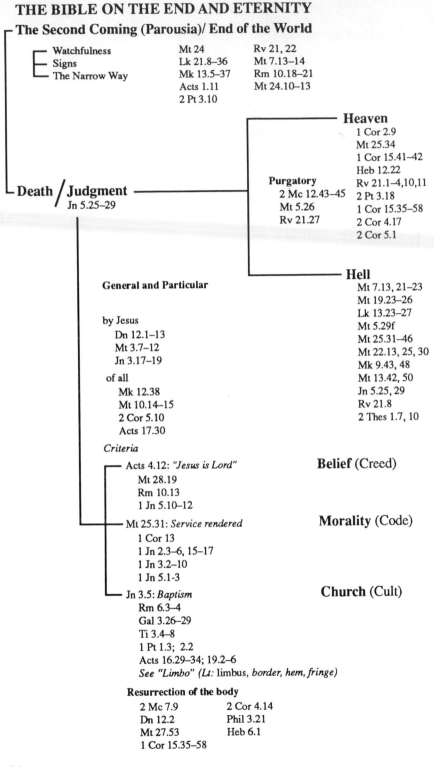

Watchfulness
Signs
The Narrow Way

Mt 24
Lk 21.8–36
Mk 13.5–37
Acts 1.11
2 Pt 3.10

Rv 21, 22
Mt 7.13–14
Rm 10.18–21
Mt 24.10–13

Heaven

1 Cor 2.9
Mt 25.34
1 Cor 15.41–42
Heb 12.22
Rv 21.1–4,10,11
2 Pt 3.18
1 Cor 15.35–58
2 Cor 4.17
2 Cor 5.1

Death / Judgment
Jn 5.25–29

Purgatory
2 Mc 12.43–45
Mt 5.26
Rv 21.27

Hell

Mt 7.13, 21–23
Mt 19.23–26
Lk 13.23–27
Mt 5.29f
Mt 25.31–46
Mt 22.13, 25, 30
Mk 9.43, 48
Mt 13.42, 50
Jn 5.25, 29
Rv 21.8
2 Thes 1.7, 10

General and Particular

by Jesus
Dn 12.1–13
Mt 3.7–12
Jn 3.17–19
of all
Mk 12.38
Mt 10.14–15
2 Cor 5.10
Acts 17.30

Criteria

Acts 4.12: *"Jesus is Lord"*   **Belief** (Creed)
Mt 28.19
Rm 10.13
1 Jn 5.10–12

Mt 25.31: *Service rendered*   **Morality** (Code)
1 Cor 13
1 Jn 2.3–6, 15–17
1 Jn 3.2–10
1 Jn 5.1-3

Jn 3.5: *Baptism*   **Church** (Cult)
Rm 6.3–4
Gal 3.26–29
Ti 3.4–8
1 Pt 1.3; 2.2
Acts 16.29–34; 19.2–6
See "Limbo" (Lt: limbus, border, hem, fringe)

Resurrection of the body

2 Mc 7.9   2 Cor 4.14
Dn 12.2   Phil 3.21
Mt 27.53   Heb 6.1
1 Cor 15.35–58

THE FOUR LAST THINGS

Death   Judgment   Heaven   Hell

Death Talk

Ars Moriendi (Lt: The Art of Dying)
Acquired, it is said, by the practice of right living.

Ante Mortem
Before Death. The period of imminent death. An "antemortem" or deathbed statement (*novissima verba,* "final words"), even legally, is well considered, since a person who is dying is presumed to have no reason to tell anything but the truth.

The Great Promise
The twelfth of the twelve promises from the Sacred Heart of Jesus to Margaret Mary Alacoque (1647–1690). It promises the grace of final perseverance and a safe refuge in the last moment for the dying (on the condition of the nine First Fridays).

The Last Blessing
After "extreme unction," an apostolic blessing with a plenary indulgence: "By the power the Apostolic See has given me, I grant you a plenary indulgence and pardon for all your sins, in the name of the Father . . ."

Litany of the Dying ("Commendation of a Soul Departing")
Part of the liturgy of anointing for those in danger of death, being invocations to the saints to pray for God's mercy.

In articulo mortis ("in the grasp of death")
At the moment of death/before death, especially referring to dying words, a last conscious significant statement (also "in extremis," at the point of death).

Passing Bell
The bell rung when a person was critically ill; to hold at bay any evil that is said to lurk about a dying person that would cling to a soul passing from its body. In addition, this bell announced the passing of a soul from this world to the next, and invited the escorting prayer of the faithful for its safe passage. See the soul bell at the funeral.

Soul Bell
In some locales the parish church bells would be tolled as a parishioner died, and would toll the age of the person at the funeral.

Funeral Rites

Vatican II called for a revision to express the paschal character of Christian death, and also a special Mass for the funeral of a child. Catholic churches in the United States have been using the 1969 Rite of Funerals. Our current Order of Christian Funerals (mandatory since November 1, 1989) contains the 1969 text plus some additions.

1. **Vigil** (and related rites and prayers)
   a. Prayers after death
   b. Gathering in the presence of the body
   c. Transfer of the body to the church/place of committal

   A "wake," now synonymous with the one or two days before a funeral, was historically simply any watch, or vigil, as before a major holiday. Only later did it become, for some, the watch over a body before burial.

2. **Funeral Liturgy**
   "Mass of the Resurrection" is an incorrect title for a funeral and is reserved only for the Easter liturgy itself. It was once called the "Requiem Mass" because of the first Latin word of the Introit, "Eternal rest grant unto them, O Lord. . . ."

3. **Rite of Committal**
   All who die in the Church have a right to a Church burial in consecrated ground. A Catholic cemetery is blessed by a bishop. A Catholic may choose to be buried in a non-Catholic cemetery, in which case their grave could be individually blessed. (A *"Campo Santo"* is a consecrated cemetery, especially one whose surface soil is said to have been brought from Jerusalem, the burial place of Christ.)

Funeral Rites Allowed

For baptized members of another Church/ecclesial community:
1. If this would not be contrary to the wished of the deceased
2. If the minister of the Church in which the deceased was a regular member/communicant is unavailable.

Funeral Rites Denied

Only in the following cases (assuming no sign of repentance before death):
1. *Notorious* apostates, heretics, and schismatics;
2. Those who, for *anti-Christian motives,* were cremated;
3. Manifest sinners for whom a Catholic funeral would scandalize the faithful.

Redemptive Dolphin

A symbol of the redemption, the dolphin is found on some of the oldest tombs. It is thought by some to be the most sophisticated and majestic of all marine life. It was said that it carried the souls of the saved "across the sea" to the land of the blessed.

Tradition and Terminology

Clothing the Dead for Burial

There has been a traditional description:
— Bishops and priests—in their liturgical vestments
— Religious—in their habits
— Lay—appropriately clothed, preferably holding crucifix or rosary

Chapelle Ardente

Chapel for a body to lie in state.

Dies Irae (Lt.: Day of Wrath)

Medieval hymn of Judgment Day, formerly used as a sequence at funerals, and the Mass for the Dead and All Souls' Day. Based on Joel 2.31. Probably written by Thomas of Celano (d. 1255).

Casket Orientation

Caskets at funerals are positioned with the feet of the deceased to the east (oriented); formerly: if a priest, with the head to the east signifying his relative position at liturgy. A person is buried with the feet to the east.

Pall/Pallbearers (Lt: *pallium,* cloak)

A sacred covering; at a funeral, the cloth over a casket, recalling the white garment of the newly baptized; also, at least formerly, a veil placed over a nun at certain orders' profession ceremonies, being an association with both baptism and death.

Latin Inscriptions

R. I. P.—*Requiescat in pace* (may he/she "rest in peace"), a common funeral prayer and grave inscription.

Beatae Memoriae
"Of happy, or blessed, memory," this phrase was not uncommon on tombstones and memorial plaques.

Obiit (OH-be-it)
A common inscription in church records or in cemeteries, "He/she died," followed by the date.

Aetatus suae
There was a day when a tombstone or an old family Bible might read *"Died aetatis suae* 52," or A.S. 52, in the 52nd year "of his/her age." The full phrase is *anno aetatis suae,* "in the year of his/her age."

Hic iacet (or *jacet*)
"Here lies" (tombstone inscription)

Month's Mind
The special Mass offered for a deceased on/near the thirtieth day of their death or burial. (Use of the catafalque has been abolished.)

In Memoriam (Fidelium Defunctorum)
"In memory of the faithful departed." Applied to the means of human assistance to departed in purgatory; now more commonly referring to the cherished memory of the earthly virtues, achievements of the deceased.

Pro-Defunctis
Memorial of the dead.

The Resurrection of the Body

Properties of the Glorified Body

("Sown in weakness, raised in strength" 1 Cor 15.42.)

Body totally submissive to the Spirit

1. Lucidity
2. Agility–movement through space with speed of thought
3. Immortality
4. Impassability
5. Spiritually

Otherwise stated: each will rise

- in his own body (Identity)
- in his entire body (Entirety)
- in his immortal body (Immortality)

The Peacock on the Tomb

As a symbol of resurrection and immortality, the peacock was not uncommon on ancient tombs. Those who die in Christ will be raised to a new and glorious life, because Jesus' flesh did not experience corruption. This glory is represented in the glorious fan tail of the peacock.

The peacock, symbol of the splendor of resurrection

The Phoenix of the Resurrection

According to one legend, this eagle-like bird lives to an age of 500 years whereupon it flies to Heliopolis, Egypt, and incinerates itself upon the temple's high altar. The temple priest finds among the ashes a small worm of sweet savor. From this worm evolves a bird, which attains full growth as the phoenix on the fourth day, departing with its youth renewed. According to another legend the phoenix, having reached 500 years of age, builds a nest of fragrant twigs and spices. These are set ablaze by the heat of the sun (or by the fanning of the bird's wings) and the phoenix is consumed by the fire. Resurrect and young, it rises from the ashes destined to live another 500 years.

Heaven

Abraham's Bosom

Luke's description (16.22) of the abode of the dead for just persons who died before Christ, before they were admitted to the beatific vision; also, heaven.

Beatific Vision

The "blessed" sight of God, especially as a gift at the moment of death.
See Is 6.1–4; Acts 7.55–56.

Paradise (Gk: *paradeisos,* park, Garden of Eden, paradise)

Used three times in Scripture as a synonym for heaven:
1. by Jesus speaking to the good thief Lk 23.43;
2. by Paul about a Christian "caught up into paradise" 2 Cor 12.4;
3. in Rv a reference to "the tree of life in God's paradise" Rv 2.7.

Kingdom of God

New Jerusalem

Seven Heavens

A popular notion, never defined by the Church, that heaven has a seven-tiered hierarchy of beatitude, the highest being seventh heaven.

Limbo

The *limbus* (edge, fringe) of heaven. A Scriptural notion, though the word is not in the Bible; a theological attempt to reconcile the necessity of baptism (Jn 3.2) with God's eternal mercy.

St. Dorothea's Roses

St. Dorothea was a victim of the Diocletian persecution of the early fourth century. According to legend she was scoffed at by Theophilus, the judge's secretary, as she was being led to execution. "Send me some roses and fruit when you get to paradise, Dorothea." Within moments of her execution, an angel appeared to him, bearing a basket of apples and roses inscribed, "From Dorothea, in paradise."

S. Clara abb· S Dorothea v

Gabriel's Hounds

Actually, wild geese in flight ("gabble ratchet"). The common sound of these magnificent birds is not unlike the sound of a pack of hounds in full cry. An old fable had it that this sound was the wail of the unbaptized, wandering the air until Judgment Day.

Angels

Heavenly beings, sexless, of a fixed population, who neither marry or are given in marriage (Mk 12.25); distinct from saints (which human beings may become); mentioned nearly 300 times in the Bible. Following are the nine choirs (classes) of angels, listed in ascending order, named according to their traditionally assigned duties (see Col. 1:16; Rm. 8.37).

Angels
Various symbols: musical instruments, thuribles, shields, scrolls, passion emblems.

Archangels (see below)
Chief angels, mentioned twice in the New Testament (Jude 5.9; 1 Thes 4.16) as distinct from guardian angels; they are messengers from God in significant matters.

Principalities
Carrying scepters with which they direct God's commands. With archangels and angels they are the heavenly multitude that is in God's ordinary and immediate service in what pertains to the visible world. It was said that countries would be assigned to certain principalities.

Powers
Shown with swords, so-called because of their special power in restraining the assault of the evil spirit.

Virtues
Charged with dispensing celestial miracles and accomplishing stupendous works.

Dominations
In royal robes and crowned, for their authority; movers of stars and planets.

Thrones
In a kneeling posture of adoration; in Ps 9.4, "You have upheld the justice of my cause from the Thrones where I sit as righteous judge."

Cherubim (plural of cherub)
Angels of wisdom, guardians and protectors, stationed at Eden (Gn 3.24), erected in gold on the Ark of the Covenant (Ex 25.18), bore Yahweh to the rescue of David (2 Sam 22.11). Picture four-eyed, blue-winged, and presenting a book, representative of their great knowledge.

Seraphim (plural of seraph, "to burn")
Shown with six red wings and eyes; highest, named for the seraphim of Is 6.2. Distinguished by their burning zeal and love for the Trinity.

The Good-Friday Born

There is an ancient superstition that those born on Good Friday— or Christmas Day—have the power to see and command spirits.

The Three Triads of Celestial Hierarchy

Counselors (Angels of the Presence)
    Seraphim (Is 6.2), Cherubim (Ex 10), Thrones
Governors (angels over forces of nature)
    Dominations, Virtues, Powers
Messengers (angels ministering directly to man)
    Principalities, Archangels, Angels

The Seven Archangels

Three of the names are Biblical (the "saints" below); other names and material evolved out of tradition and are gleaned from Jewish apocryphal books (e.g. Enoch). The "Seven" of Tobit (12.15) refers not necessarily to that specific number, but symbolically to all those ministers who are entitled to stand before God, ready to do his bidding. (Meaning of names in parentheses.)

St. Michael *(Who is like God)*
Angel of God's power; leader of the heavenly host (Dn 10.13,21; 12.1; Jude 9; Rv 12.7ff); cast Lucifer and fallen angels from heaven (Rv 12.7–9; see Ez 28.17); disputed with Satan over Moses' body; Israel's protector; leader of the archangels; considered to be the angel who executes the decision on each person's eternal destiny on Judgment Day (hence his scales insignia).

St. Gabriel *(God is My Strength)*
Angel of God's dignity, "Hero of God"; Angel of the Annunciation (Lk 1.19, 26); the "one in rapid flight" (Dn 8.16; 9.21); Angel of the Day of Judgment, blowing his horn for the assembling of the nations.

St. Raphael *(God is My Health)*
Represents Jesus' priesthood; instructor of Tobit and guardian of Tobias; the angel who moved the waters of the pool when Christ worked a miracle in Jn 5.1–4; chief of guardian angels.

Uriel *(God is My Light)*
Interpreter of prophecy; guarded Jesus' tomb (see Mt 28.3); appeared to Ezra in a dream.

St. Michael, the Archangel

Jophiel *(The Beauty of God)*
Represents God's splendor; drove Adam and Eve out of Eden (see Gn 3.24).

Chamael
Angel of God's wrath; wrestled with Jacob; appeared to Jesus in Gethsemane.

Zadkiel *(The Righteousness of God)*
Angel of God's justice; stopped Abraham from sacrificing Isaac.

Jophkiel *(The Purity of God)*
Guided the Jews in the wilderness.

When Blackberries Turn Tasteless

It is on September 29, after which they are left for the birds. This is Michaelmas Day, honoring the archangel who drove Lucifer out of heaven. In honor of the occasion, the devil spits on the blackberries, leaving them tasteless.

Purgatory

The suffering of the faithful which causes a "purging" (of temporal punishment due to sin). Implied in Scripture (Rv 6.9–11; 1 Pt 3.18,19), taught by the early Fathers, and defined by the Church (especially the Council of Florence, 1439).

St. Patrick's Purgatory

There is a cave with this name in Ireland, on an islet in Lough Derg, Country Donegal. In the Middle Ages there was a church and a man-made cavern constructed on the island, and it became a great place of pilgrimage. Behind this island's notoriety was an English Cistercian monk, Henry of Saltrey, who wrote of the adventures and punishments of one Owen, or Sir Owain, a knight of King Stephan's court, who descended into "purgatory" on an Irish island. This popularized the thousand-year-old legend of St. Patrick's Purgatory. The story goes that an earthly purgatory was set up by Patrick, or that God granted him to see—and show—the punishment of sinners, whereby he bolster his teachings with a little demonstration. Patrick would take sinners to this purgatory-on-earth to see the pain and suffering of the souls in purgatory, and thus warn of the evils of sin and the dangers of procrastinating repentance and reparation. This was a three-day retreat, complete with fasting, sleeping on the ground, and sacramental reconciliation.

Indulgences

Remission of temporal punishment due to sin, either partial or plenary (full)

Some Means of Gaining a Partial Indulgence
1. Praying the Magnificat or Hail Holy Queen
2. Praying the Acts of Faith, Hope, and Love and the Creed
3. Making the Sign of the Cross
4. Visit to the Blessed Sacrament
5. Visit to a cemetery

Conditions for Gaining Plenary Indulgence
1. Sacrament of Reconciliation
2. Reception of communion
3. Prayer for the Holy Father

Some Means of Gaining Plenary Indulgence
1. Adoration of the Blessed Sacrament for at least one-half hour
2. Scripture reading for at least one-half hour
3. Way of the Cross
4. Rosary prayed in a church or family group or religious community, etc.

The *Raccolta*

Formerly a book of the prayers and exercises to which indulgences were attached by the Holy See. It included conditions for gaining the indulgence and their application to the souls in purgatory. Now, in another form, "the Enchiridion of Indulgences."

Trick or Treat

On All Souls' Day, the poor begged for food and, in return, would pray for the dead. "Soul cakes" was the name given to the doughnuts they received. The circle made by the hole cut out of the center represents eternity, with no beginning or end.

Hell

The following three words are **not** synonymous, but have at times been loosely translated into English as "hell."

Sheol

(Hebrew; sixty-five occurrences in Old Testament.)

Gloomy abode of the dead beneath the earth, destination of righteous as well as evil: nether world, deeps, grave, pit, personification of death (Mt 16.8). **See Nm 16.33; 1 Sm 2.6–8; 2 Sm 22.6; Jb 11.8; 33.24, 28; Prov 9.18; Ps 9.15; 28.1; 30.3,9; 55.15; 63.9; 88.4; Am 9.2; Is 14.9; 44.23; Ez 31.16–17; 32.21.**

Hades

(Greek version of the underworld; eleven occurrences in New Testament.)

Left as is in some translations, rendered "grave" or "hell" in others. According to Greek myth, Hades was ruled by Pluto and Persephone; a place to which the dead (with coin in mouth) were ferried across the River Styx by the avaricious Charon. Judgment followed, with righteous going to a meadow on the edge of western world (Elysian Fields) and the wicked doomed to eternal suffering in Hades' depths (Tartarus).

Gehenna

(Gk: Valley of Hinnom, deep ravine on southwest side of Jerusalem.)

Long a dumping ground for human waste, corpses, and rotting matter— hence, "incessant fire." Once even the site of human sacrifice. In Jesus' time, a popular symbol for what Christians call "hell." **See Mk 9.43–48; Lk 12.5; Mt 5.29; 18.8; 23.33.**

"He descended into hell."

"He Descended Into Hell"

In the Creed when we say Christ "descended into hell," we mean "hades," or "shoel" (the place of the dead), not "gehenna" (the place of the damned—the hell of punishment). Jesus Christ experienced death completely, going into the "underworld" and "bursting the bonds of hell (limbo)," thereby showing power and authority over all creation, including death, and releasing the souls of the just who were awaiting salvation through his death and resurrection.

The Otter and the Crocodile

Pliny, Plutarch, and other early pagan writers have retold this ancient myth. It was believed that the otter, having coated itself with mud that dried to form a protective coat, was able to slay the crocodile by rushing down its throat and attacking it from within. Christianity has long used this fable, symbol, and analogy to explain the facts of life in Christ, and is no less imaginative than paganism. Finding a Christian significance in this fable, believers have retold it as a sign of how Jesus established his Lordship over sin and death by his descent among the dead.

The Devil: Titles, Cognomans and Euphemisms
The Babylon/Lucifer association and "the five 'I Wills' ": Is 14.12–15. Michael and the battle between good and bad angels: Rv 12.7–9.

Anti-Christ, The
The unnamed personification of resistance to Christ ("evil," "the devil"). Many interpretations, legends, and bigotries have been spawned by the two classic texts, 2 Thes. 2.1–12 and Rv 13. See "666" (Rv 13.18) in symbols chapter particularly. Mentioned specifically in 1 Jn 2.18; 2.22; 4.3; and 2 Jn 7 (identified with unbelievers who deny the Incarnation). Variously associated with historical figures (for example, Caligula and Nero, as well as more bigoted suggestions) and also heresies (as a personification).

Beelzebub
Correctly "Beelzebul" from Baalzebal, Baal (possessor, as in lord of a place), a word used for local divinities, common in Canaan, and later the paganism denounced by Jewish prophets. A demonic deity or influence. Jesus denied that he performed miracles through Beelzebub (Mt 12.24; Lk 11.19–20). Also the contemptuous "Lord of the Flies."

Good Manners and Self-Defense

In the Middle Ages there were those who taught that the devil entered a person through the mouth, at the time of a yawn. So naturally, when you yawn, you cover your mouth, or make the sign of the cross over it.

Belial
Lawless one, worthless. Used as a personification by Paul (2 Cor 6.15);
see 1 Sam 2.12.

Lucifer (Lt: "light bearer")
In patristic literature, identified with Satan, leader of the fallen angels,
and referring to his status before his fall; See Is 14.12–16.

Old Bendy
Because he can bend to anyone's inclinations.

The Devil and the Horseshoe

Legend has it that the devil approached Dunstan, known for his
horseshoeing skills, and asked him to shoe his "single hoof."
The saint perceived his true identity, so secured him fast and did
the job, but inflicted so much pain in the process that the devil
roared for mercy. He was released only on condition that he
would never enter a place where a horseshoe was displayed. (Or
could it have been that ever since when the devil sees the horseshoe he is reminded of the episode, and flees in fear?)

Old Harry
From the personal name, like "Old Nick?" An allusion to "harry" (to
harass, lay waste)?

Old Nick
Maybe related to German nickel, "goblin"; common in the seventeenth
century.

Old Scratch
From *skratta*, an old Scandinavian term for a monster or goblin.

Satan (Hb: "adversary; to plot against another")
Often (usually?) applied Biblically to a human opposer. The three Old
Testament uses for an evil spirit: Zeck 3; Job 1.2: 1 Chr 21.1. Tempted Jesus
Mt 4.11–11, warned about by Paul 1 Cor 7.6.

Serpent
From the story of the Fall (Gn 3). Legend has it that a serpent, remembering his role in the Fall, would flee in terror from a person who quickly
disrobes (representing the devil's repulsion at those who have divested
themselves of sin).

Ancient Folklore and Christian Analogy

Many symbols and comparisons have found their way into Christian folklore by way of the enthusiastic and imaginative teaching of believers. Not surprisingly, temptation and the devil are often the subject. For example:

How the Devil is like the Wolf

The ancients believed that the wolf hunts his victims by night, that he frightens his prey by magnifying his voice, that he approaches his prey against the wind, and that he mutes his footsteps with spittle. This image was readily applied to Satan, deceiving and surprising the unsuspecting.

How the Devil is like the Whale

Whales of such enormous size were believed to exist that sailors landed on them, taking them for desert islands, and built fires. Their fate was sealed when the whale, aroused by the heat, plunged downward and drowned the sailors. Also it was believed that fish would unwittingly swim into the whale's mouth, perceived as a safe harbor. This legend easily lent itself to illustrations of the treachery of Satan, whose designs are not always detected.

St. George and the Dragon

Dragon slaying is a favorite allegory for the victory of Christ's grace over evil. Versions of St. George's conquest are classic. One story goes that he was summoned to subdue a dragon that inhabited a lake in Silene, Libya, and fed on folks in the neighborhood. When he arrived, St. George snatched away the princess Saba who was already in the dragon's clutches as his latest victim. Then he dispatched the monster with his sword. The historical St. George was martyred near Lydda in the early centuries of the Church. Stories of his victory over sin and evil in terms of dragon slaying are rooted in images from the Book of Revelation, and can be compared to similar stories in the lives of Ss. Michael, Martha, Sylvester, and Margaret. Also recall God's original curse of the snake and promise of a victorious redeemer (Gn 3.15) and the New Testament fulfillment depicted in scenes of Jesus and Mary treading on a snake.

End Times Glossary

Abyss Rv 9.1; 20.1
The place of Satan and the fallen angels for the time being (the millennium).

Armageddon *("Hill of Megiddo")* Rv 16.15–16; 20.7–10
Symbol of the final decisive victory over the forces of evil at the end of time (since historically Megiddo was the site of many decisive battles).

Book of the Living Rv 21.27; 3.5; 13.8; 17.8; 20.12–15; Phil 4.3; Dn 12.1
The "record" of the names of the redeemed.

Day of the Lord Rv 6.12f; see Mt 24.29; Am 8.8f; Is 34.3; Jl 2.10; 3.3f
The occasion of the parousia.

Eschatology
A study of the end times, the eschaton.

Fiery Pool of Sulphur Rv 19.20; 20.10; 4.10, 14–15
Symbol of hell (distinct from the "abyss").

First Resurrection Rv 20.4–5
The risen-life experience of those who have died "in Christ" (redeemed) while the messianic age on earth continues.

Gog and Magog Rv 20.8; Ez 38.1–39.20
Symbols of all pagan nations.

Millennialism *(unorthodox, not a Catholic truth)*
Belief in an extended period of prosperity and peace between present
temptation/trial and parousia. A millennialist would call the Catholic position "amillennialist" **see 1 Cor 10.11.**

Millennium *(the "thousand years")* Rv 20.1–6
The long period between Christ's resurrection-victory and the end of the
world. See Rom 6.1–8; Eph 2.1; and John's "realized eschatology": Jn
5.24f; 16.33; 1 Jn 3.14.

Parousia *(Christ's Second Coming)* Rv 1.3, 7; 3.11; 2.7, 10, 12, 20
Christ's return in glory at the end of time.

Rapture 1 Thes 4.17
The union of Christ with the redeemed who are alive at the time of the
parousia.

Satan Chained Rv 20.1–10, 12
As he is now, in the millennium.

Satan Unchained for a Short Time *(the "Little Season")* Rv 20.3, 7
Unclear; possibly a Scriptural statement against millennialism's theory of
pre-parousia prosperity.

Second Death Rv 2.11; 20.6, 14–15; 21.8
The time of the bodily resurrection when sinners receive their final
punishment; i.e. when the dead who did not die in Christ go to hell (said
"not to live" between their death and this "second death," Rv 20.5).

Tribulation Mk 13.1–37; Mt 24.1–44; Lk 21.5–36; see 1 Thes 4.13–18
The word given to the circumstances of the end times, with vocabulary
and images from the apocalyptic (literary style) "Eschatological
Discourse" of Jesus to the disciples. It reflects the prevailing early
Church opinion on the imminent second coming. Its literal/historical ap-
plication is popular with fundamentalists and millennialists.

Tribulation-Rapture Literalist Theories

Pre-Tribulation Rapture
Rapture preceding "tribulation" period (which occurs after Church
period) which ends with parousia.

Mid-Tribulation Rapture
Rapture mid-way through "tribulation" which begins during Church
period and ends with parousia.

Post-Tribulation Rapture
Rapture and parousia part of same intervention which ends "tribulation"
and Church period.

Millennialism Diagrams

Church Period
Millennium
Tribulation
With "Little Season"

Amillennialism

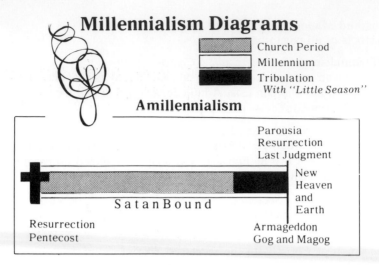

Parousia
Resurrection
Last Judgment

New
Heaven
and
Earth

Satan Bound

Resurrection
Pentecost

Armageddon
Gog and Magog

Postmillennialism

Parousia
Resurrection
Last Judgment

New
Heaven
and
Earth

Satan Bound

Resurrection
Pentecost

Armageddon
God and Magog

Premillennialism

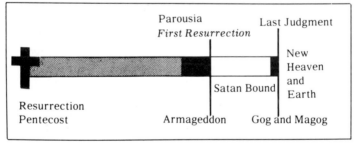

Parousia
First Resurrection

Last Judgment

New
Heaven
and
Earth

Satan Bound

Resurrection
Pentecost

Armageddon

Gog and Magog

108

Scriptural

Definitions of Revelation

1. **Revelation** *(public)*
   Disclosure by God of Himself and His will to humanity; revelation that was objectively complete by the death of the last apostle.
   a. Natural see **Wis 13.1; Rm 1.20**
      When intermediary is world of space and time.
   b. Supernatural see **Heb 1.1–2**
      Far exceeding natural; scripturally, "divine speech."
      (1) Indirectly—through the prophets
          Including the Old Testament, God's inspired Word
      (2) Directly—through His son (the "incarnation")
          Including the New Testament, God's inspired Word
2. **Revelations** *(private)*
   Supernatural manifestation since apostolic times bringing understanding of revelation to a particular person. Compare the claims of cults, like the Mormons' spurious "Maroni revelations."
   a. Sometimes sensory (see Principle Marian Apparitions)
   b. Sometimes merely intellectual (see Dreams)
   c. Sometimes approved by the Church.
      For example, St. Bernadette Soubirous, 1844–79 (Lourdes), and St. Margaret Mary, 1647–90 (the Sacred Heart).
   d. Never adding to the deposit of faith, or requiring assent.
3. **Visions and Apparitions**
   Supernatural experiences wherein objects are seen but not necessarily understood. Either corporeal or sensible; called "theophanies" if of God. See Gn 16.7, 13; Ex 3.2; 14.19, 24; Nn 22.22–35; Jgs 6.11–18.

Dreams in the Scriptures

Abimelech, of God: "Return Sarah to Abraham" **Gn 20.3f**
Jacob at Bethel, of God, a ladder, and a promise **Gn 28.10f**
Jacob, of God: "Go back to Canaan" **Gn 31.11f**
Joseph, of sheaves bowing down **Gn 37.5f**
Joseph, of the sun, moon and eleven stars **Gn 37.9f**
Cupbearer and baker of the Pharoah, interpreted by Joseph **Gn 40.9f**
Pharoah, of seven fat cows and seven skinny cows
Gideon, of a loaf of barley bread, a tent, and a victory **Jgs 7.13f**
Solomon, of God, and a request for wisdom **1 Kgs 3.5f**
Nebuchadnezzar, of a gold, silver, bronze, iron, and clay statue told and interpreted by Daniel **Dn 2.1f**
Nebuchadnezzar, of a tree, interpreted by Daniel **Dn 4.1f**
Daniel, of four beasts, and more **Dn 7.1f**
Joseph, of an angel: "Marry Mary" **Mt 1.20–21**
Astrologers, of a message: "Do not return to Herod" **Mt 2.12**
Joseph, of an angel: "Flee to Egypt" **Mt 2.13**
Joseph, in Egypt, of an angel: "Return to Isreal" **Mt 2.19**
Pilot's wife, of Jesus . . . and upsetting **Mt 27.19**

MAJOR WORLD RELIGIONS

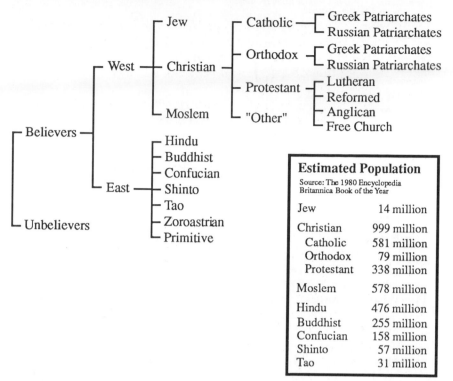

Estimated Population

Source: The 1980 Encyclopedia Britannica Book of the Year

Jew	14 million
Christian	999 million
Catholic	581 million
Orthodox	79 million
Protestant	338 million
Moslem	578 million
Hindu	476 million
Buddhist	255 million
Confucian	158 million
Shinto	57 million
Tao	31 million

RELIGION IN THE WESTERN WORLD

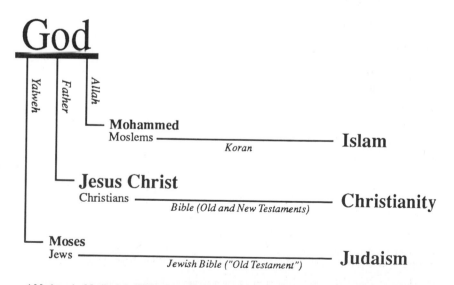

* Moslems (or Muslims) do NOT believe that Jesus is the son of God, but that he is in the line of prophets that ended with Mohammed, the "seal of the Prophets", whose revelations are compiled in the Koran, or Holy Book. There are notable beliefs that Moslems Do share with Christians, namely 1) there is one God; 2) God created the universe; 3) Abraham, Moses and Jesus are in the line of prophets; 4) the day of judgement; 5) heaven and hell; and 6) the resurrection of the body.

THE BOOKS OF THE OLD TESTAMENT

(Parenthesized words are former titles/spellings)

Pentateuch

	Abbrev.	Chap.	
Genesis	Gn	50	
Exodus	Ex	40	
Leviticus	Lv	27	The Torah (Law)
Numbers	Nm	36	
Deuteronomy	Dt	34	

The Historical Books

Joshua *(Josue)*	Jos	24	
Judges	Jgs	21	
Ruth	Ru	4	
1 Samuel *(1 Kings)*	1 Sm	31	Primary Group
2 Samuel *(2 Kings)*	2 Sm	24	(Former Prophets)
1 Kings *(3 Kings)*	1 Kgs	22	Excluding Ruth
2 Kings *(4 Kings)*	1 Kgs	25	
1 Chronicles *(1 Paralipomenon)*	1 Chr	29	
2 Chronicles *(2 Paralipomenon)*	2 Chr	36	Secondary Group
Ezra *(1 Esdras)*	Ezr	10	
Nehemiah *(2 Esdras)*	Neh	13	
*Tobit *(Tobias)*	Tb	14	
*Judith	Jdt	16	Stories with a historical base
Esther	Est	10	Including Ruth
* Maccabees	1 Mc	16	
* Maccabees	2 Mc	15	Later History

The Wisdom Books

Job	Jb	42	
Psalms	Ps (s)	150	
Proverbs	Prv	31	
Ecclesiastes *(Qoheleth)*	Ecc	12	**The Writings**
Song of Songs *(... of Solomon)*	Sg	8	Including Daniel, Ezra, Nehemiah,
(Canticle of Canticles)	Wis	19	Chronicles, Ruth, Lamentations and Esther
*Wisdom	Sir	51	
*Sirach *(Ecclesiasticus)*			

The Prophetic Books   Latter Prophets

Isaiah *(Isaia)*	Is	66	
Jeremiah *(Jeremia)*	Jer	52	
Lamentations	Lam	5	Major Prophets
*Baruch	Bar	6	Excluding Lamentations and Baruch
Ezekiel *(Ezechiel)*	Ez	48	
Daniel	Dn	14	
Hosea *(Osee)*	Hos	14	
Joel	Jl	4	
Amos	Am	9	
Obadiah *(Abdiah)*	Ob	1	
Jonah *(Jona)*	Jon	4	
Micha *(Michea)*	Mi	7	Minor Prophets
Nahum	Na	3	Daniel and Jonah being special cases
Habakkuk *(Habacue)*	Hb	3	
Zephaniah *(Sophonia)*	Zep	3	
Haggai *(Aggai)*	Hg	2	
Zechariah *(Zacharia)*	Zec	14	
Malachi *(Malachia)*	Mal	3	

*Deuterocanonical ("second canon")

These are books of the Bible whose place among the inspired works was debated in the early Church. Their language is Greek (and nor Hebrew like the rest of the Jewish bible). This indicates their late authorship, after the scriptural canon was considered closed by the Jews. These books are found in the Septuagint (ancient Greek translation of the Old Testament) and the Vulgate (Jerome's Latin translation of the Bible). The reformers in the Middle Ages followed the Jewish tradition during the proliferation of published Bibles after the advent of printing. Often these books are included in a section following the Old Testament, sometimes entitled "deutero-Canonicals".

THE BOOKS OF THE NEW TESTAMENT

Gospels

	Abbrev.	Chapters	
Matthew	Mt	28	
Mark	Mk	16	Synoptics
Luke	Lk	24	
John	Jn	21	

History of the Early Christian Church

Acts of the Apostles	Acts	28

Letters ("Epistles")

	Abbrev.	Chapters	
Romans	Rom	16	
Corinthians (2)	(1,2) Cor	16,13	
Galatians	Gal	6	
Ephesians	Eph	6	
Philippians	Phil	4	
Colossians	Col	4	By Paul
Thessalonians (2)	(1,2) Thes	5,3	
Timothy (2)	(1,2) Tim	6,4	
Titus	Ti	3	
Philemon	Phlm	1	
James	Jas	5	
Peter (2)	(1,2) Pt	5,3	
John (3)	(1,2,3) Jn	5,1,1	By Others
Jude	Jude	1	
Hebrews	Heb	13	Anonymous

Apocalyptic

Revelation or, Apocalypse	Rv	22

Deuterocanonicals (Gk: second canon)
These are books of the Bible whose place among the inspired works was debated in the early Church (see footnote on previous page). In the New Testament they are Hebrews, James, 2 Peter, 2 and 3 John, Revelation and Mark 16.9–20. Both Old and New Testament deuterocanonicals are recognized by the Catholic Church as part of the biblical canon. Protestants reject as apocryphal the Old Testament deuterocanonicals as well as the last twelve verses of Mark in the New Testament.

Apocrypha (Gk: hidden)
Originally, works claiming a sacred origin but supposedly hidden for generations. Later, a specific body of literature with scriptural or quasi-scriptural pretensions though not canonical or genuine, composed during the two centuries before Christ and the early Christian centuries. Protestants have often improperly made the term synonymous with deuterocanonical.

St. Jerome and the Lion

The lion is a common feature of story and legend, especially to illustrate the effect of kindness, and the transforming power of gratitude. The following is a Christian version of *Androcles and the Lion*.

The story goes that a lion entered a schoolroom in which Jerome was teaching, and lifted one of its paws. Although the disciples all fled, Jerome noticed that the paw was wounded, and proceeded to extract a thorn from it an dressed the wound. The grateful lion "showed a wish to stay with its benefactor." That is why the saint is commonly depicted accompanied by a lion.

It is not surprising that this story's setting is a schoolroom. Jerome spent much time there. No less than St. Augustine said of him, "If Jerome doesn't know, nobody does, or ever did." A prodigious scholar, Jerome's ultimate work was translating the entire Bible into Latin (the "Vulgate"), like Old Testament from Hebrew and the New from Greek. The Council of Trent, having called for its revision, declared it the authentic text for the Church. Jerome mastered not only languages, notably Latin, Greek, Hebrew and Chaldaic, but also a life of piety. Finally, before the massive undertaking of translating the Bible, he toured the holy land, experiencing the very places hallowed by Christ. This pilgrimage culminated in a five year retreat in the desert of Chalcis for penance, prayer and more study. Settling in Bethlehem, he lived in a cave that was believed to be the birthplace of Christ.

Fearful Thomas

"*Timeo hominea unius libri*" (I fear the man of one book) is a sentiment attributed to Thomas Aquinas. The traditional interpretation was that a person steeped in a single source made a formidable opponent in debate. More recently another interpretation is suggested: there are those for whom a single source is sufficient, with its knowledge, purpose and expressions. They cannot then entertain any truth but that contained in the statements of their one book.

Abbreviation of Books of the Bible

Acts	Acts of the Apostles	2 Kgs	2 Kings
Am	Amos	Lam	Lamentations
Bar	Baruch	Lv	Leviticus
1 Chr	1 Chronicles	Lk	Luke
2 Chr	2 Chronicles	1 Mc	1 Maccabees
Col	Colossians	2 Mc	2 Maccabees
1 Cor	1 Corinthians	Mal	Malachi
2 Cor	2 Corinthians	Mk	Mark
Dn	Daniel	Mt	Matthew
Dt	Deuteronomy	Mi	Micah
Eccl	Ecclesiastes	Na	Nahum
Eph	Ephesians	Neh	Nehemiah
Est	Esther	Nm	Numbers
Ex	Exodus	Ob	Obadiah
Ezr	Ezra	1 Pt	1 Peter
Ez	Ezekiel	2 Pt	2 Peter
Gal	Galatians	Phlm	Philemon
Gn	Genesis	Phil	Philippians
Hb	Habakkuk	Prv	Proverbs
Hg	Haggai	Ps(s)	Psalms
Heb	Hebrews	Rv	Revelation
Hos	Hosea	Rom	Romans
Is	Isaiah	Ru	Ruth
Jas	James	1 Sm	1 Samuel
Jer	Jeremiah	2 Sm	2 Samuel
Jb	Job	Sir	Sirach
Jl	Joel	Sg	Songs of Songs
Jn	John	1 Thes	1 Thessalonians
1 Jn	1 John	2 Thes	2 Thessalonians
2 Jn	2 John	1 Tim	1 Timothy
3 Jn	3 John	2 Tim	2 Timothy
Jon	Jonah	Ti	Titus
Jos	Joshua	Tb	Tobit
Jude	Jude	Wis	Wisdom
Jgs	Judges	Zec	Zechariah
Jdt	Judith	Zep	Zephaniah
1 Kgs	1 Kings		

Languages

According to the American Bible Society, as of 1987, the complete Bible has been translated into 303 of the world's 5000 languages, the New Testament into 670, and at least one book into 911. The examples below are all translations of Jn 3.16: "For God so loved the world. . . ."

Hebrew

כִּי־אַהֲבָה רַבָּה אָהַב הָאֱלֹהִים אֶת־הָעוֹלָם עַד־אֲשֶׁר נָתַן אֶת־בְּנוֹ

Old Testament. (Exception: a few books of late composition were written in Greek; some parts were written in Aramaic, which became the everyday language of the Jews after the Exile, Hebrew being reserved as the language of the Law.)

Greek

Διότι τόσον πολύ ἀγάπησε ὁ Θεὸς τὸν κόσμον, ὥστε ἔδωκε τὸν Υἱόν του

Original language of the New Testament. Also the language of the third century B.C. translation of the Old Testament, the "septuagint", so-called because it was said to have been done by 72 scholars in 72 days (*sept* meaning seven).

Aramaic

Probably spoken language of Jesus. Still the liturgical language of the Chaldean, Malabar, Malankar, Maronite, Nestorian and Syrian Rites.

Latin (same alphabet as English)

The *editio vulgata* ("common edition" or Vulgate), was translated by Jerome about 385–405, but did not appear in print until a thousand years later (1456).

Arabic

أحب الله العالم حتى بذل ابنه الوحيد لكي لآ يهلك كل من يومن

Language of sacred writings of Islam, the Koran.

116

Hebrew   # Greek   # Arabic

Letter	Name	Transliteration	Letter	Name	Transliteration	Letter	Name	Transliteration
א	aleph	- or '	A α	alpha	a	١	alif	-[1]
ב	beth	b,v	B β	beta	b	ب	ba	b
ג	gimel	g	Γ γ	gamma	g	ت	ta	t
						ث	sa	th
ד	daleth	d	Δ δ	delta	d	ج	jim	j
ה	he	h	E ε	epsilon	e	ح	ha	h
ו	vav	v, w	Z ζ	zeta	z	خ	kha	kh
ז	zayin	z	H η	eta	e (or ē)	د	dal	d
ח	cheth	ḥ	Θ θ	theta	th	ذ	zal	th
ט	teth	ṭ	I ι	iota	i	ر	ra	r
			K κ	kappa	k	ز	za	z
י	yod	y, j, i	Λ λ	lambda	l	س	sin	s
כ ך[1]	kaph	k, kh	M μ	mu	m	ش	shin	sh
ל	lamed	l	N ν	nu	n	ص	sad	s
מ ם[1]	mem	m	Ξ ξ	xi	x	ض	dad	d
נ ן[1]	nun	n	O o	omicron	o	ط	ta	t
ס	samekh	s	Π π	pi	p	ظ	za	z
ע	ayin	'	P ρ	rho	r	ع	ain	-[2]
פ ף[1]	pe	p, f	Σ σ,ς[1]	sigma	s	غ	ghain	gh[3]
צ ץ[1]	sadi	ṣ	T τ	tau	t	ف	fa	f
ק	koph	ḳ	Υ υ	upsilon	y	ق	qaf	k[4]
ר	resh	r	Φ φ	phi	ph	ك	kaf	k[5]
שׁ	shin	sh, š	X χ	chi	ch, kh	ل	lam	l
שׂ	śin	ś	Ψ ψ	psi	ps	م	mim	m
ת	tav	t	Ω ω	omega	o (or ō)	ن	nun	n
						ه	ha	h
						و	waw	w
						ي	ya	y

[1]Functions as the bearer of *hamza* (the glottal stop), or as a lengthener of short *a*. [2]A voiced pharyngeal fricative. [3]A voiced velar fricative. [4]A uvular stop. [5]A voiceless velar stop.

[1]At end of word.   [1]At end of word.

117

The Bible in English: A Partial List

1450–1456: the first printed book, the Gutenberg Bible

1380, Wyclif's Bible

Wyclif's Bible refers to two translations of the Vulgate, the first in 1380 and the second later. Neither was actually by Wyclif himself; the second was by one of his followers. The 1380 translation was the first complete English version. It remained unprinted, however, until 1850.

1525, Tyndale's Bible

Tyndale's Bible was the first printed English New Testament (1525, Cologne), to which were later added the Pentateuch (1530) and various Old Testament parts. Tyndale was the translator.

1535, Coverdale's Bible

Coverdale's Bible was the first complete English Bible printed. This was in 1535. Miles Coverdale was the publisher.

1537, Matthew's Bible

"Thomas Matthew" a pseudonym for a Tyndale assistant, collated the previous efforts, beginning the evolution that culminated in the Authorized Version (AV) in 1611.

1539, The Great Bible

The Great Bible was Coverdale's revision of his own 1535 Bible. It was also called "Cromwell's Bible," as it was commissioned by Lord Cromwell.

1539, Taverner's Bible

Taverner's Bible was a translation by the Greek scholar Richard Taverner. It was an independent work; that is, it stood apart from the tradition culminating in the Authorized Version.

1560, The Geneva Bible

The Geneva Bible was a translation by English exiles in Geneva. It was done under Protestant auspices and has a strong Calvinist tone. It was very popular, some 200 editions are known. The first Bible was printed in roman type instead of black letter, with the verses designated, and with explanatory words and phrases set in italics.

1568, The Bishops' Bible

The Bishops' Bible was contributed to by most Anglican bishops. A revision of the Great Bible, it was the foundation of the Authorized Version.

1609, Douai-Rheims

The Douai-Rheims was a translation of the Vulgate with careful comparisons to original Hebrew and Greek by English Catholic scholars mainly Gregory Martin (d. 1582) in France. The New Testament was done at Rheims (1582); the Old Testament at Douai (1609)—the two towns because of the move of English College where the work was done. It was an effort for accuracy more than literary style.

1611, Authorized Version ("King James")
The Authorized Version is thus called because it was authorized by King James I. Hence, it is commonly known as the "King James." It became the standard, though it has been through much revision over the years.

Eighteenth Century, Challoner's Bible
This was a revised version of the English translation of the Douai-Rheims, by a Bishop Challoner (1691–1781). It was virtually "the Catholic Bible" (for English speakers) until the mid-twentieth century.

1885, Revised Version ("English Revised Version")
(New Testament, 1881) This was a British and American revision of the Authorized ("King James") Version by twenty-five English scholars.

1901, "American Standard Edition of the Revised Version" (ASV)
The ASV was a U.S.-published, revised rendition of the King James Bible. It is commonly called the American Revised Version.

1924, Moffat
This was a new translation of the Bible in Modern English by James Moffat. The New Testament was done in 1913.

1944, Knox
The Knox translation was done by Fr. Ronald Knox, from the Vulgate.

1952, Revised Standard Version (RSV)
The RSV is a modern American rendering of the English Bible in The King James tradition.

1958, New Testament in Modern English (Phillips)

1959, Berkeley Version

1965, Amplified Bible

1966, The Jerusalem Bible

1969, Barclay's New Testament

1970, The New English Bible
(New Testament 1961)

1970, The New American Bible

1971, The Living Bible: The Way
(New Testament "Reach Out", 1967)

1971, New American Standard Bible

1973, The Common Bible

1976, The Good News Bible: Today's English Version
(New Testament "Good News for Modern Man," 1966)

The evangelization cross: four tau crosses meeting at the center, with four Greek crosses representing the four corners of the world

Comparing Scripture Translations Lk 11.2-4

Lindisfarne Gospels, c. 950
fader gehalgad sie noma oin tocymaeo ic oin hlaf userne daeghuaemlice sel us eghuelc daege   fgef us synna usra gif faestlice aec pe fgefaes eghuelc scyldge us fgef ne usic onlaed ou in costunge

In Old English (or "Anglo-Saxon"), this is an "inter-linear" translation of the Gospels by the monks of Lindisfarne. They took a copy of the Gospels and printed Anglo-Saxon equivalents above the lines (like a "crib"). This work, now in the British Museum, is the nearest surviving "Bible" handwritten in Anglo-Saxon. It probably borrowed heavily from a now non-existent work of the Venerable Bede from around A.D. 700 (Old English is the original pre-Norman, Germanic stock of English, fifth century—or eighth, according to some—to twelfth century. It is the language of the epic poem, Beowulf of early eighth century.)

Wycliffite Bible, c. 1384
Fadir, halewid be thi name. Thi kyngdom come to. zyue to vs to day oure eche dayes breed. And forzyue to vs oure synnes, as and we forzyuen to each owynge to vs. And leed not vs in to temptacioun.

This Bible is in Middle English, the English language of the period approximately from 1150 to 1475. (Cf. Geoffrey Chaucher, 1340–1400).

Tyndale New Testament, 1526

Oure father which arte in heve, halowed be thy name. Lett thy kyngdo come. Thy will, be fulfillet, even in erth as it is in heven. Oure dayly breed geve us this daye. And forgeve vs oure synnes: for even we forgeve every man that traspaseth vs, and ledde vs not into temptacio, Butt delliver vs from evyll Amen.

The Tyndale New Testament is in early Modern English, post–1475. (Cf. Shakespeare, 1564–1616.)

Coverdale Bible, 1536

O oure father which art in heauen, halowed by thy name. Thy kyngdome come. Thy wil be fulfilled vpon earth, as it is in heauen. Geue vs this daye oure daylie bred. And forgeue vs oure synnes, for we also forgeue all them that are detters vnto vs. And lede vs not in to temptacion, but delyuer vs from euell.

Matthew's Bible, 1537

O oure father which arte in heauen, halowed be thy name. Thy kyngdome come. Thy will be fulfylled, euen in erth as it is in heauen. Oure dayly breed geue vs euermore. And forgeue vs our synnes: For euen we forgeue euery man yt treaspaseth vs. And leade vs not into temptacion. But delyuer vs from euyll.

The Great Bible, 1539

O oure father which are i heauen, halowed be thy name. Thy kyngdome come. They will be fulfylled, eue in erth also as it is in heaue. Oure dayly breed geue vs thys daye. And forgeue vs our synnes; For eue we forgeue euery man that treaspaseth vs. And Leade vs not ito temptacyon. But delyuer vs from euyll.

Geneva Bible, 1560

Our Father, we art in heaue, halowed by thy Name: Thy kingdome come:
    Let thy wil be done eue in earth, as it is in heauuen:
Our daily bread giue vs for the day:
And forgiue vs our sinnes: for euen we forgiue euerie man that is in-
    detted to vs:
    And lead vs not into temptation: but deliuer vs from euil.

Bishop's Bible, 1568

O our father which art in heauen, halowed be thy name, thy Kyngdome come, thy wyll be fulfylled, euen in earth also, as it is in heaven. Our dayly breade geue vs this day. And forgeue vs our synnes: Foe euen we forgeue euery man that trespasseth vs. And leade vs not into temptation, but delyuer vs from euyll.

Rheims New Testament, 1582
Father, sanctified be they name. Thy kingdom come, Our daily bread giue vs this day, and forgiue vs our sinnes, for because our selues also doe forgiue euery one that is in debt to vs. And lead vs not into temptation.

King James Bible, 1611
Our Father which art in heauen, Halowed be they Name, Thy kingdom come, Thy will be done as in heauen, so in earth. Give vs day by day our dayly bread. And forgiue vs our sinnes; for we also forgiue euery one that is indebted to vs. And lead vs not into temptation, but deliuer vs from euill.

English Revised New Testament, 1881
Father, Hallowed by they name. Thy kingdom come. Give us day by day our daily bread. And forgive us our sins; for we ourselves also forgive every one that is indebted to us. And bring us not into temptation.

American Standard Edition of the English Revised Version, 1901
Father, Hallowed be thy name. The kingdom come. Give us day by day our daily bread. And forgive us our sins; for we ourselves also forgive every one that is indebted to us. And bring us not into temptation.

Revised Standard Version, 1946
Father, hallowed be they name. Thy kingdom come. Give us each day our daily bread; and forgive us our sins, for we ourselves forgive every one who is indebted to us; and lead us not into temptation.

The New English Bible New Testament, 1961
Father, thy name be hallowed; Thy kingdom come. Give us each day our daily bread. And forgive us our sins, for we too forgive all who have done us wrong. And do not bring us to the test.

The Jerusalem Bible, 1966
Father, may your name be held holy, your kingdom come; give us each day our daily bread, and forgive us our sins, for we ourselves forgive each one who is in debt to us. And do not put us to the test.

Today's English Version, 1966
Father, may your name be kept holy, May your Kingdom come. Give us day by day the food we need. Forgive us our sins, for we forgive everyone who has done us wrong. And do not bring us to hard testing.

The New American Bible, 1970
Father, hallowed be your name, your kingdom come. Give us each day our daily bread. Forgive us our sins for we too forgive all who do us wrong; and subject us not to the trial.

Christian Roots and Grafts

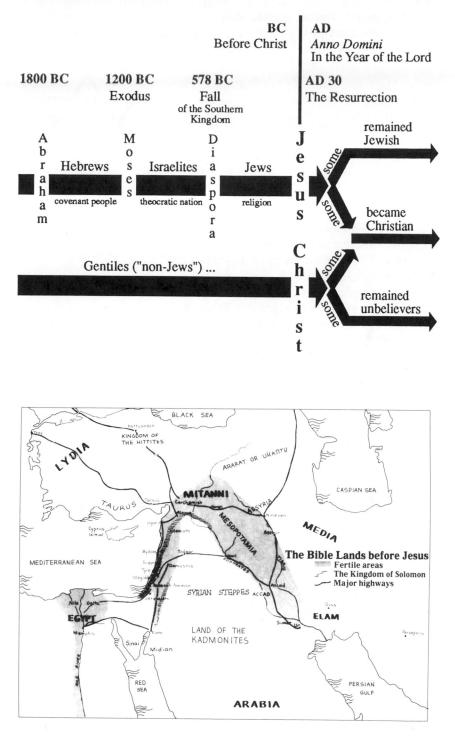

The Bible Lands before Jesus
- Fertile areas
- The Kingdom of Solomon
- Major highways

OLD TESTAMENT HISTORICAL OUTLINE

I. **Origins of Cosmos, Earth, Man**
   - A. Creation
   - B. Paradise — Pre-history
   - C. Original Sin

The Star of David, also known as the "Magen David" ("magen" meaning shield) or "Solomon's Seal," is a symbol of Israel, and the Jewish religion. It is formed by superimposing two triangles.

II. **Hebrew Origins**
   - A. The Patriarchs c. 1850–1600
   - B. The Hebrews in Egypt c. 1600–1250

III. **The State of Israel**
   - A. Origins: Exodus, Desert, Conquest c. 1250–1200
   - B. Period of the Judges c. 1200–1000
   - C. Monarchy: Saul (1000), David (1000–965), Solomon (965–922)
   - D. Divided Monarchy; Rise of Prophecy 922–587
     1. To the fall of the Northern Kingdom (Israel) in 721 (Assyria)
     2. To the fall of the Southern Kingdom (Judah) in 587 (Babylon)
   - E. Babylonian Exile (Captivity) 587–538
   - F. Early Post-Exile Period and End of Prophecy
     1. Restoration: Ezra and Nehemiah
     2. Persian Domination
   - G. Greek Period 333–63
     1. From Alexander to the Seleucids 333–175
     2. The Maccabean Revolt against Syria 175–135
     3. The Hasmonean Era: Jewish independence 135–63
   - H. Roman Period (From Pompey through New Testament times) 63
     Pompey takes Jerusalem and Israel becomes part of Roman Province of Syria.

How Great Thou Art
Wonders Created by the Hand of God
(According to St. Gregory of Tours, about A.D. 550)

The tides of the ocean	The rebirth of the phoenix
The growth of plants from seeds	The cycle of the sun
The volcano Mount Etna	The cycle of the moon

Note: The rebirth of the phoenix is mythological but was accepted as fact in the Middle Ages. There is a pertinent Latin phrase from Psalm 19: *"Caeli enarrant gloriam Dei,"* which means "The heavens declare the glory of God." A simple *"Caeli enarrant"* (CHAY-lee eh-NAH-rahnt) would allude to the planets and stars as brilliant evidence of God's power and wisdom.

The Wonders of the World

The "wonders" of the world of which humans can boast are many, but can perhaps be represented by the celebrated Seven. Interestingly, all are religious monuments, works of piety, except for the Lighthouse and the Gardens:

1. **The Mausoleum at Halicarnassus (Asia Minor)**
   The tomb erected near the present-day Turkish port of Budrum by Artemis (about 350 B.C.?), widow of the prince of Caria, Mausolus (hence the word "mausoleum").

2. **The Temple of Artemis (Diana) at Ephesus**
   A ancient city in west Asia Minor; also site of an early Christian community.

3. **The Hanging Gardens of Babylon**
   Planted on the terraces of the ziggurats (pyramidal temples).

4. **The Statue of Zeus at Olympia**
   Olympia is a plain in ancient Elis, Greece (where the Games were held); by Phidias.

5. **The Colossus of Rhodes**
   A bronze statue of Apollo that stood at the entrance of the harbor of Rhodes, a Greek island in southeast Aegean Sea, between the southwest coast of Turkey and Crete.

6. **The Pharos, the Lighthouse at Alexandria**
   Alexandria is in Egypt; by Ptolemy.

7. **The Pyramids of Egypt (The only extant "Ancient Wonder")**
   Near El Gize, which is near Cairo; especially the one built by Cheops ("Khufu"), king of Egypt about 2650–2630 B.C.

The more "modern" world may not match the mystique of those ancient wonders, but may rival their grandeur with a list of its own:

1. The Coliseum of Rome	5. The Leaning Tower of Pisa
2. The Catacombs of Alexandria	6. The Porcelain Tower of
3. The Great Wall of China	Nankin
4. Stonehenge	7. The Mosque of St. Sophia
	at Constantinople

OLD TESTAMENT "TABLE OF CONTENTS"

I. **Human Origins** Gn 1–11
   A. Creation
      1. 1.1–2.4
      2. 2.4–25
   B. Paradise

   C. Original Sin   **Genesis 1–11**
      1. The Fall 3
      2. Cain and Abel 4.1–16
      3. Adam-Noah generations 4.17–6.4
      4. The Flood 6.5–8.22
      5. God's Covenant with Noah 9.1–17
      6. Tower of Babel 11.1–9
   D. Restoration: the 4th theme of Gn 1–11
      (Alluded to in the divine promises after the Fall; a unifying
      theme of the rest of the Bible and the objective of revelation.)

Choosing People, Chosen People, Chosen One

In the Garden, after the Fall, the God who had created all things
promised to restore all things, "I will put enmity between you and
the woman, and between your offspring and hers; He will strike at
your head, while you strike at his heel." (Gn 3.15). At the heart of
this saving will is divine vocation (call, or election), typically:

1. from before birth (Isaac, Samson, Samuel)
2. of sterile or aged (or virginal) parentage (Isaac, Jesus)
3. from unpromising stock/circumstances (Gideon, Mary)
4. initially causing question/disbelief/self-doubt (Jeremiah)
5. with promise of divine assistance (Moses, Gideon)
6. necessitating an exodus/conversion (Abraham, Paul)

Abraham, Gn 12.1–5	Jeremiah, Jer 1
Isaac, Gn 18.9–15; 21.1–8	Ezekiel, Ez 1–3
Moses, Ex 3.1–12	Zechariah, Zec 1.7–6.8
Gideon, Jgs 6.11f	John the Baptist, Lk 1.5–25
Samson, Jgs 13.2–24	Mary, Lk 1.26–38
Samuel, 1 Sm 1;3.1–14	Joseph, Mt 1.18–24
David, 1 Sm 16.1–13	Jesus, Lk 1.26–38
Elisha, 1 Kgs 19.19f	The Twelve, Mt 4.18–19;
Suffering Servant, Is 49.1	9.9; Mk 1.16–18; 2.14; Lk
Amos, Am 7–9	5.11, 28; Jn 1.35–51
Isaiah, Is 6;40.6–8	Paul, Acts 9.1–16; Gal 1.5

II. **Hebrew Origins** Gn 12–50
    A. Patriarchal Period Gn 12f
        Migration 11.27–12.9
        Melchizedek 14.18–20 (see Is 11.4–9;
          Zec 6.9–15 Ps 110.4; Heb 7)
        Covenant 15.1–18
        Sodom and Gomorrah 18.16–19.29
        Sacrifice of Isaac 22.1–19
        Betrothal of Rebekah 24
        Jacob-Esau conflict 25.19–28.9
        Jacob's dream at Bethel 28.10–22
        The Winning of Rachel 29.1–30
        Jacob-Esau reconciliation 32–33
        Rape of Dinah 34
    B. Joseph Stories Gn 37–50
        The Brothers 37.2–36
        Potiphar's Wife 39.1–23
        Dreams 40–41
        Reunion 42–44
        Disclosure 45.1–28
        Central Theme 45.7–8
        Judah's Speech ("Paragon of Hebrew
        eloquence") 44.18–38
        Jacob in Egypt 46–47
        Deaths 49.28–50.26
        Patriarchal Burials: Gn 23.1–20; 25.9;
          49.31; 50.13
        (Sarah, Abraham, Isaac, Rebekah, Leah,
        Jacob: all at Cave of Machpelah in
        Hebron)
III. **The State of Israel** Ex 1f
    A. National Origins
        Bondage in Egypt Ex 1–5
        The plagues Ex 7.8–12.39
        Escape Ex 13.17–16.36

Genesis 12–50

Melchizedek, offering bread and wine.

Shield of the State of Israel

Exodus Ex 14.21–31 (prose); 15.1–12 (poetry)   **Exodus**
Miriam, prophetess Ex 2.4–8; 15.20–21; Nm 12.1–16; 20.1
Journey from Red Sea to Sinai Ex 15.22–19.2
The quail and manna Ex 16; Nm 11.1–15, 31–34
Water from the rock Ex 17.1–7; Nm 20.2–13
Sinai Covenant Ex 19.1–21.36
The Decalogue Ex 20.1–17 (Cf Dt 5.6–21)
The sanctuary and its furnishings Ex 25–30
The Golden Calf Ex 32

A Horned Moses

Michelangelo's statue of Moses, following earlier paintings, includes horns because of a mistranslation of the Hebrew word for "radiant" in Ex 34.29: "When Moses descended Mt. Siani, he did not know that the skin of his face had become radiant" (formerly "horned"). The same word appears in Hab 3.4, referring to the Lord, with the same translation change made.

Israelite sacrificial and other ritual legislation Lv 1–27
Social laws Lv 19; 25
The reward of obedience Lv 26   **Leviticus**
The first census Nm 1–3
Further legal observances Nm 3–10.10; 28–30
Aaron's Blessing Nm 6.22–27
Journey from Sinai to Moab (thirty-eight years) Nm 10.11–22.1
Jealousy of Aaron and Miriam Nm 12
Reconnoitering Canaan Nm 13–14
Korah's sedition Nm 16
The sin of Moses and Aaron Nm 20.2–13   **Numbers**
Aaron's death Nm 20.22–29
The bronze serpent Nm 21.4–9
Baalam, religious compromiser Nm 22.1f; 31.16 (see Pt 2.15; Jude 11; Rv 2.14f)
The second census Nm 26
The succession of Joshua Nm 27.12–23
Moses' testament: Deuteronomy   **Deuteronomy**
Historical review Dt 1.1–4.43
Exhortation to covenant fidelity Dt 5–11
Keynote of Mosaic law (Cf Jewish "Shema") Dt 6.4–5
Recapitulation/completion of Ex 20–23 (Second Law) Dt 12–26
Synopsis of sacred story Dt 26.5–9

The widow Abigail 1 Sm 25; 30.1–18; 2 Sm 2.2; 3.3;
1 Chr 3.1
Saul pursues David 1 Sm 26
Saul, Samuel, and the Witch of Endor 1 Sm 28.3–25
Saul's death 1 Sm 31

4. King David
Mourning for Saul and Jonathan 2 Sm 1
The Oracle of Nathan ("Magna Charta of Royal
Messianism") 2 Sm 7.8–16 see 2 Chr 17; Ps 89.20–38;
132.11f; Acts 2.30; Heb 1.5
David's prayers 1 Chr 17; 29
Bathsheba 2 Sm 11
Nathan 2 Sm 12 **2 Samuel**
"Court History" 2 Sm 9–20; 1 Kgs 1–2
Absalom 2 Sm 13–18
Rizpah and the longest wake 2 Sm 21.1–10

5. King Solomon
Reign 1 Kgs 1–5; 9–11
Wisdom 1 Kgs 3.16–28; 4.29–34; 10.1–13; 2 Chr 1
Temple dedication 1 Kgs 8; 2 Chr 6–7
The visit of the Queen of Sheba **1 Kings**
1 Kgs 10.1–13

Solomon's Cedar

The cross of the crucifixion has always excited and mystified the imagination. There is a legend that Solomon cut down a cedar tree and buried it. Years later, the pool of Bethesda was built on the very site of this cedar's grave. Still later, when Jesus entered Jerusalem on the Sunday before his death, the ancient cedar rose to the surface of the pool from where it was retrieved. The upright beam of Christ's cross was made from that cedar tree.

D. The Divided Monarchy and the Rise of Prophecy
1. From death of Solomon (922) to fall of the North (721)
Division of the Kingdom 1 Kgs 11–14
The Elijah Cycle 1 Kgs 17–19, 21–2 Kgs 1
The widow of Zarapheth 1 Kgs 17.7–24
The Baal prophets 1 Kgs 18
Jezebel's wrath 1 Kgs 19.1–18
Ahaziah and the captains' fate 2 Kgs 1
Elijah's Ascension 2 Kgs 2.9–14 (see Mt 17.9–13)

2 Kings

Isaiah

The Old Testament prophesying the New: the prophets Isaiah and Daniel foreseeing the Incarnation.

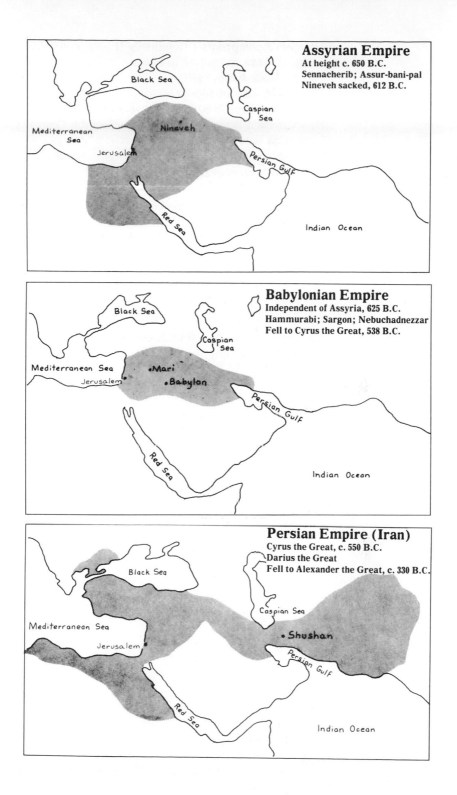

Assyrian Empire
At height c. 650 B.C.
Sennacherib; Assur-bani-pal
Nineveh sacked, 612 B.C.

Black Sea

Caspian Sea

Mediterranean Sea

Nineveh

Jerusalem

Persian Gulf

Red Sea

Indian Ocean

Babylonian Empire
Independent of Assyria, 625 B.C.
Hammurabi; Sargon; Nebuchadnezzar
Fell to Cyrus the Great, 538 B.C.

Black Sea

Caspian Sea

Mediterranean Sea

Mari

Babylon

Jerusalem

Persian Gulf

Red Sea

Indian Ocean

Persian Empire (Iran)
Cyrus the Great, c. 550 B.C.
Darius the Great
Fell to Alexander the Great, c. 330 B.C.

Black Sea

Caspian Sea

Mediterranean Sea

Shushan

Jerusalem

Persian Gulf

Red Sea

Indian Ocean

133

Jeremiah's complaints ("jeremiads")
15.10–21; 18.18–23; 20.7–18 (see Jb 3)
Potter's flask symbol 19
The two baskets of figs 24
Promises of Israel's Restoration 30–32
New Covenant Prophecy ("gospel before the Gospel")
31.31–34
Jeremiah's place in Jerusalem's last days 36.1–40.6
Zephaniah's prophecies, Josiah's
reign 640–609 **Zephaniah**
The Day of the Lord 1 (classic description, see *Dies Irae*)
The remnant 3 (Remnant's hymn 3.14–20)
Nahum prophecies, around 615 (against Nineveh)
The fall of Jerusalem 2 Kgs 24–25 **Nahum**

E. The Babylonian Exile
Lamentations **Lamentations**
Baruch
Habakkuk prophecies **Baruch**
A man questions God (First Jewish example?) 1
Habakkuk's prayer, a religious lyric 3 **Habakkuk**
Ezekiel prophecies
Call 1–4
Revelation of his mission 1–3; 5; 10
First vision 1.4–3.15 **Ezekiel**
Vision of temple abominations 8.1–16
Glory of God departs 8–10
Individual accountability 14; 18; 33.10–20 (see Jer 31.29–30)
Marriage-adultery image 16; 20; 23
The prophet as watchman 33.1–9
The prophet's false popularity 33.30–33
Parable of the shepherds 34
Visions of restored community 36.16–37.14
Dry Bones 37.1–14
Vision of temple restoration 40–43

F. Early Post-Exilic Period
1. Liberation and return **"Second Isaiah"**
Second Isaiah prophecies Is 40–55
Suffering Servant oracle 42.1–4; 49.1–7; 50.4–11;52.13–53.12
Message of deliverance 40
Gift of the restoration 44
Effectiveness of God's Word 55.10–11
Third Isaiah prophecies Is 56–66
True fasting 58
Confessions 59 **"Third Isaiah"**
Glory of the New Jerusalem 60

The Good News **61**
Supplication **62–64**

2. Restoration
Ezra, religious and cultic reformer
The decree of Cyrus (538–529 B.C.) **1**
Samaritan interference **4.1–5, 24**　　　**Ezra**
Temple rebuilding **5–6**
The "Ezra Memoirs" **7–10 (and Neh 8–9)**
Nehemiah, builder and administrator
Prayer **1**
Return to Jerusalem **2**　　　**Nehemiah**
Temple rebuilding **4–6**
Ezra reads the Law **8.1–12**
Confession prayer **9–10**
Haggai prophecies, 520f　　　**Haggai**
Exhortation to rebuild the temple
Zechariah prophecies, 520f　　　**Zechariah**
Promoting temple rebuilding **6.9–15**
Entry of the messiah (see Palm Sunday) **9.9f**
The Day of the Lord (apocalyptic) **14**
Malachi prophecies, around 450　　　**Malachi**
The messenger of the covenant (see Jn the Baptist) **3.1–3**
Obadiah prophecies, fifth century
(see Jer 49.7–22)　　　**Obadiah**
Joel prophecies, around 400
The Day of the Lord **2–3**
Call to repentance **2.12–17**　　　**Joel**
Spirit poured out **3.1**
Last judgment **4.2–21**

G. Post-Exilic Jewish Literature
"Short story" style: How should Jews relate to their Gentile neighbors? (Nationalistic)
1. Esther, late fourth-century Jewess become queen of Persia
Queen Vashti, rebellious beauty **1**
Esther intercedes with Assuerus **5; 7**
Prayers of Mordecai and Esther **13–14**　　　**Esther**
2. Tobit, early second century
Tobit's prayers **3.2–6 8.5–7; 15–17; 13**
Raphael reveals his identity **12.11–22**　　　**Tobit**
3. Daniel, around 165 (Antiochus IV Epiphanes' reign)
Six folk tales about Daniel **1–6**
a. Daniel and his friends in king's palace **1**
b. Daniel's interpretation of an unrevealed dream **3**
c. Shadrach, Meshack, Abednego in the furnace **3**

7. Wisdom (About 100 B.C.)
   On suffering ("The souls of the just are in the hand of God") 3.1–8
   Solomon's prayer 9

Ms. Wisdom

It is not uncommon to hear tell of wisdom as a person. In the Hebrew Bible, "she" is portrayed not as abstract virtue, but a concrete person, divine even (see Prov 1; 8; Sir 1; 24; Wis 6; 9. It would not be an unfamiliar device for Israel's pagan neighbors either, but it is well in line with monotheism as well. The name "Sophia" is derived from the Greek word for wisdom. Legend tells of a Roman widow named Sophia who had three daughters named Faith, Hope and Charity. The whole family was martyred, as the story goes—the three daughters first and then "Wisdom" herself, slain as she prayed for her daughters. Her feast day was Sept 30. Christians see Wisdom personified in Jesus.

I. Rebellion and Jewish Independence
  1. I Maccabees (About 100 B.C.)
     Portrait of Judas Maccabeus 3
     Four laments 1.25–28; 1.36–40; 2.8–13; 3.45
     Three hymns of praise 2.51–65 ("our fathers"); 3.3–9 (Judas); 14.4–15 (Simon)
     The death of Antiochus Epiphanes and the battle of Bethzacharam 6
     Roman alliance 8
     Death of Judas Maccabeus 9.1–22   **Maccabees**
     Simon's rule and death 14
  2. II Maccabees (About 100 B.C.)
     Preface 2
     Heliodorus 3
     The martyrdom of Eleazar and the Seven brothers 6–7

Divine Names/Titles

Below are "The Seven Names of God", traditionally. Over these, the scribes exercised special care, especially mindful of the decalogue mandate (Ex 20.7). Hence, in the Middle Ages, God would be referred to as The Seven.

1. **El**
   Hebrew: common stem word used for deity in semitic languages: earliest Hebrews used it in forming words about God. Etymologically uncertain: power? wholly other? highest? See el root in Michael

(who is like god), Samuel (the name of God), Gabriel (man of God), Israel (one who has striven with God).

2. **Elohim**

Common, appearing several thousand times in the Old Testament; Hebrew plural of El (singular understood); used (or meant) in the plural for pagan gods (Gn 35.2; Ex 18.11; Jesus' cry from the cross, "Eli, Eli. . . ." (Mt 27.46) is a form of this.

3. **Adonai**

Hebrew; Greek: *Kyrios;* Latin: *Dominus;* English: Lord; for late pre-Christian Jews the Hebrew substitute for the unspeakable YHWH.

4. **Yahweh** (or mistakenly Jehovah)

English rendering of the enigmatic sacred tetrogrammaton YHWH with vowels from "Adonai" (Sometimes in late pre-Christian era Jews stopped pronouncing it out of exaggerated reverence and substituted Adonai). God's self-revelation to Moses (Ex 3.14); maybe "I am who am" or "I will be with you" (absolute being). Occurs over 6700 times in Old Testament, more often than all other designations combined. Frequent component for personal names: cf. prefixes Je/Jehu/Jeho and suffixes iah/jah.

5. **Ehyeh-asher-Ehyeh**

6. **(El) Shaddai**

Rendered into Greek "pantocrator" (almighty); according to Gn 17.1; 35.11; Ex 6.3, God used this in speaking to Abraham and Jacob; appears in the celebrated YHWH text; also English "Lord of the Mountain."

7. **Zebaot**

Yahweh Sebaoth
Yahweh (God) of Hosts; not found in the first seven books of the Bible; "Hosts" uncertain: of heaven? armies of Israel?

Malek
"King"; used frequently for Yahweh.

Ancient of Days
Dn 7, 9, 13, 22; emphasizing His eternity compared to the frailty of earthy empires.

Father
Jesus' revelation of God; see **Jn 14.6ff; 16.12–15**

Trinity
God revealed in three Persons: the Father (who is God, but is not the Son or the Holy Spirit), the Son (i.e. Jesus, who is God, but is not the Father or the Holy Spirit), and the Holy Spirit (who is God, but is not the Father or the Son). see **Mt 28.18–20; Jn 14.6ff**

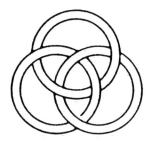

The three interwoven circles of the Trinity.

138

God

English; Latin: *Deus;* Greek: *Theos.*

Jehovah

A non-word; a linguistic mistake. Appeared for the first time in 1530. Since written Hebrew did not use vowels until quite late, the ancient manuscripts read simply YHWH (as it would be in English) for "God". Through the centuries, the name of God came to be considered so sacred that it was not to be pronounced. So wherever YHWH appeared in the ancient text, the scribes added vowel marks signaling the reader to say *"Adonai"* instead of *"Yahweh."* These marks, "vowel pointings," were not separate letters, but smaller symbols usually below a consonant to indicate its vowel sound. When one adds the vowels for *Yahweh*—YHWH—the result, if you're not aware that it is intended that *adonai* is to be read, comes out sounding like "Yahowah" (Jehovah).

Principal Deities of Old Testament Neighbors

Mesopotamia—A triad of Anu, Bel and Ea

Canaan—A pantheon headed by El, son Baal and goddesses (of sex and war) Anath, Astarte, and Asherah (Ashtaroth)

Egypt—A triad of Isis, wife of Osiris and mother of Horus. Also Aton Re.

Philistia—Dagon ("little fish"); also Ashtaroth

Moab—Chemosh

Ammonites—Molech (or Milcom)

Phoenicia—Astarte, Melkart (Baal)

Amorties—Annurru, Asherah

Babylon—Ishtar, Marduk (with which Bel would identify)

The Covenant in the Old Testament

Jer 31.31–34 is the one passage in the Old Testament where the idea of a New Testament is expressly mentioned

1. **Yahweh and Noah** (God and earth) Gn 6.18; 9.8–17
2. **Yahweh and Abraham** (God and individual)
    Repeated to Isaac Gn 26.24, Jacob Gn 28.13–15 and Moses Ex 6.2–4
    a. Promise of numerous descendants Gn 12.2–3
    b. Promise of descendants, land; name change Gn 15.18–21; 17.2–8, 15–16
    c. Sign: circumcision Gn 11.10–11
3. **Yahweh and Moses** (God and community)
    a. Agreements and negotiations Ex 19
    b. Reception of the Law Ex 20–23
    c. Ratification of the covenant Ex 24

The Seven Patriarchs

Adam   Noah   Shem   Abraham   Isaac   Jacob   Joseph

Names for the Chosen People

Hebrew
Abraham (Hebrew)
Semitic language (of the Hebrews), called "the language of the Canaanites" in the Bible.

Israel
Jacob (after the angel renamed him; see Gn 35.10).
The nation of the twelve Hebrew tribes following liberation (exodus) from Egypt under Moses ("Father of his Country").
The Northern Kingdom after the division (922 B.C., end of Solomon's reign).

Judah
Fourth son of Jacob (Israel).
The tribe (descendents) of Judah.
The Southern Kingdom after the division.
All Hebrews left in the Promised Land after the fall of Israel (i.e. Northern Kingdom), 721 B.C.

Jew
From "Judah"; linguistically Latin and Greek.
All Hebrews after the Babylonian captivity (587–538 B.C.).

Names for the Land Promised

The Promised Land
Chosen by God (Gn 15.18) for chosen people led by Moses from Egypt.

Land of Milk and Honey
God's utopian description (Ex) of the Promised Land.

Canaan
Land in the middle of the fertile crescent, between the Jordan River and the Mediterranean Sea occupied by Canaanites whom Israel gradually displaced/absorbed.

Israel
The kingdom established by Moses/Joshua in Canaan, with intermittent independent political rule until 587 B.C., and never since; also "Northern Kingdom" after Israel's split following Solomon's reign.

Palestine
From "Philistine," the name of the area's southern inhabitants.

Judah
The Southern Kingdom after the split following Solomon's reign.

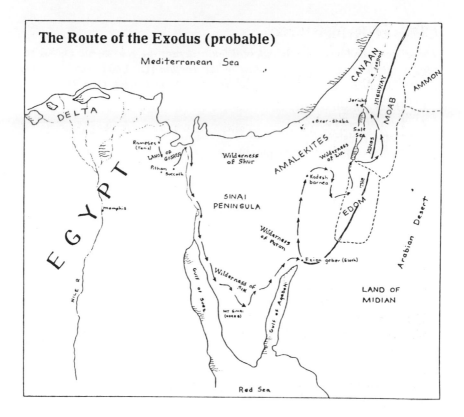

The Route of the Exodus (probable)

Mediterranean Sea

DELTA

EGYPT

CANAAN

AMMON

MOAB

Jericho

Beer-Sheba

Salt Sea

Rameses (Tanis)

LAND OF GOSHEN

Pithom   Succoth

Wilderness of Shur

Wilderness of Zin

AMALEKITES

Kadesh barnea

memphis

SINAI PENINSULA

EDOM

THE

Arabian Desert

Wilderness of Paran

NILE R

Gulf of Suez

Wilderness of Sin

Ezion geber (Elath)

LAND OF MIDIAN

MT SINAI (HOREB)

Gulf of Aqaba

Red Sea

The Holy Land

For Jews, Christians, and Moslems.

Zion

Jebusite city that became Jerusalem. When it was captured by David it was named the Citadel of David (2 Sam 5.7) and assumed a sacred character when he brought to it the Ark of the Covenant. After the temple was built on the northeastern hill ("Mt. Moriah")*, the term Zion or ("Sion") was applied to the hill too. Gradually the name came to be applied to all of Jerusalem (2 Kgs 19, 21; Ps 125; 126), ultimately even to the Holy Land generally, indeed to the Jewish faith itself. (Hence, the modern movement to make Palestine the Jewish homeland is called "Zionism".)

The Jerusalem coat of arms, with lion rampant

---

*Mt. Moriah is the site, according to legend, of King David's tomb and Jesus' last supper. It is also where Abraham intended to sacrifice Isaac, the locale of Jesus' trial, the Dome of the Rock mosque, the Western Wall, the site revered by Moslems as the place from which Mohammed rode a steed to heaven.

Cities of Refuge

These were asylums for "accidental" murderers See Nm 35; Dt 19; Jos 20. *Moses set the first three apart east of the Jordan* (Dt 4.43); *the Israelites under Joshua set the other three apart west of the Jordan* (Jos 21).

1. Bezer (Moab desert)
2. Ramoth—Gilead
3. Golan (Bashan)
4. Kedesh (Galilee, by Naphtali)
5. Shechem (mountain region of Ephraim)
6. Hebron (mountain region of south Judah)

In medieval Europe, churches provided such sanctuary for hunted persons, the altar guaranteeing immunity from arrest. Later, the meanings of these names were "Christianized," that is, applied as characteristics of Jesus, the "refuge of the repentant."

1. "Fortress"—Jesus' strength
2. "High"—Jesus' dignity
3. "Joy"—Jesus' gift
4. "Holy"—Jesus' sanctity
5. "Shoulder"—Jesus' responsibility
6. "Brotherhood"—Jesus' following

Old Testament Places and Things of Worship

Patriarchal Sanctuaries
1. Shechem (Gn 12.6–7; 33.18–20), Abraham's first stop in Canaan
2. Bethel (Gn 12.8; 28.10–22), Site of Jacob's ladder/stairway vision
3. Mamre (Gn 13.18), point of reference for patriarch's graves
4. Beer-Sheba (Gn 26.23–25) Isaac (repetition of Abrahamic) promises

The Tent *("Tabernacle")* **of the Exodus** *(to house the Ark)*
Description Ex 26; 36.8–38

Divine presence Ex 40.34–38; Nm 9.15–23; Ex 33.7, 11; Nm 12.8

The Ark of the Covenant *(housing tablets of the Decalogue)*
Descriptions Ex 25.10–22; 37.1–9; Ex 26.33; 40.21

Religious Significance
> A place of divine presence see 1 Sm 4.7, 22; Nm 10.35; 1 Sm 5; 6.19; 2 Sm 6.7
>
> An archive for the Law see Dt 10.1–5; Ex 25.16; 40.20

Sanctuaries in Israel before the Temple

1. Gilgal Jos 4.19; 7.6; 5.2–9
2. Shiloh Jos 18.1; 21–2; 22.9, 12; 1 Sm 3; Jgs 21.19–21
3. Mizpah Jgs 20.1, 3; 31.1, 5, 8
4. Ophrah Jgs 6.11–24
5. Dan Jgs 17–18
6. Jerusalem

Ark brought by David 2 Sm 6

Altar built on site of future temple 2 Sm 24.16–25

Temple of Jerusalem

1. Built by Solomon on Mt. Moriah around 1000 B.C.
   Destroyed in 587 B.C. in the siege of Jerusalem by Nebuchadnezzar,
   1 Kgs 5–8; 2 Chr 3,5; Ex 40–41.
2. The temple of Zerubbabel (Post-exilic)
   Completed around 515 on the same site. Ezra 3–5.
3. Third
   Begun in 20 B.C. by Herod the Great and destroyed in A.D. 70 in the
   siege of Jerusalem by Vespacian and Titus. This was the conquest
   commemorated in the Roman Arch of Titus, which includes relief
   depictions of the spoils taken from the temple.

Religious Significance

Divine presence 1 Kgs 8.10f; 2 Kgs 19.14; 2 Chr 5.14; Ez 10.4; 43.5;
Ps 27.4; 84 Am 1.2; Is 2.2–3; 6.1–4; Jer 14.21
Warnings about divine gratuity Jer 7.1-15; 6.1–15; (See Ex 8–10)
Sign of divine choice 2 Sm 24.16; 2 Chr 3.1; Ps 68.17; 78.68

Shekinah

Shekinah ("sheh-KEE-nah") is a Hebrew word for the presence
of God on earth, or a manifestation or symbol of His presence, or
His dwelling place. Although not found in the Bible, it was used
by Jews in the late Old Testament period in reference to the
visible majesty of the Divine Presence (see Ex 19.16–19; 40.34–
38; 2 Chr 5.13–14 for allusions). Corresponds to the "glory" of
God (Is 60.2; Rms 9.4) and the cloud of the Israelites journey
(Ex 14.19). The ultimate shekinah is the incarnation of the Son
of God, Jesus Christ.

Altars
Patriarchal altars **e.g. Gn 22.9**
Tabernacle altars (Holocaust; incense) **Ex 27.1–8; 30.1–5; 37.25–28; 38.1–7**
Temple altars
　Solomon's **1 Kgs 6–7**
　Ahaz' ("Damascus Style"; "Ezekiel's") **2 Kgs 16.10–16 Ex 43.13–17**
Religious significance
　Divine hearth **Lv 6.5–6**
　Divine presence **Gn 12.7; 26.24–25**

Menorah
Seven-branched candelabrum
See Ex 25.31–36; 1 Kgs 7.49

Shofar
Ram's horn trumpet
See Nm 19.10; Ex 19.13

Ephod
Article of priestly clothing
See 1 Sm 2.18; 2 Sm 6.14; Ex 29.5; Lv 8.7

Urim and Thummin
Lots used in determining divine will . . . sticks, stones, dice?
See 1 Sm 14.41–42; Ex 28.6–30

The Twelve Tribes of Israel

Founded by the twelve sons of Jacob ("Israel"); mothers' names in parentheses. **(See Gn 35.23–26)**.

1. Reuben (Leah)
2. Simeon (Leah)
3. Levi (Leah)
4. Judah (Leah)
5. Issachar (Leah)
6. Zebulun (Leah)
7. Joseph (Rachel)
8. Benjamin (Rachel)
9. Dan (Bilhah[1])
10. Naphtali (Bilhah)
11. Gad (Zilpah[2])
12. Asher (Zilpah)

The twelve-pointed star of the twelve tribes of Israel.

1. Rachel's maid

2. Leah's maid

Often Levi is not included because they were priestly and not given land but dispersed among other tribes and supported by them. In this case, two of Jacob's grandsons (children of Joseph adopted by Jacob), Ephraim and Manasseh, are considered one tribe, thus keeping the number twelve. When Levi is counted, these two tribes are included with Joseph.

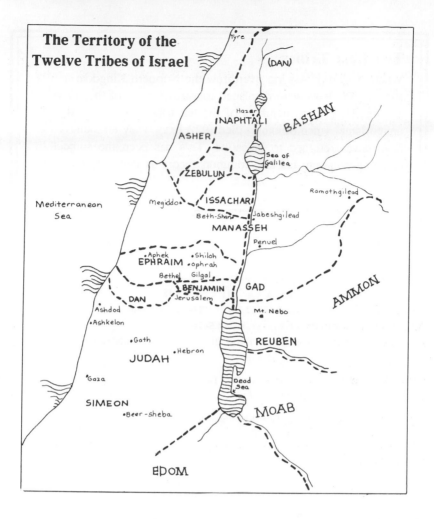

The Territory of the Twelve Tribes of Israel

Tyre

(DAN)

Hazor

NAPHTALI

BASHAN

ASHER

Sea of Galilea

ZEBULUN

Megiddo

ISSACHAR

Ramothgilead

Mediterranean Sea

Beth-Shan

Jabeshgilead

MANASSEH

Penuel

Aphek

Shiloh

EPHRAIM

ophrah

Bethel

Gilgal

BENJAMIN

GAD

AMMON

DAN

Jerusalem

Ashdod

Mt. Nebo

Ashkelon

REUBEN

Gath

Hebron

JUDAH

Gaza

Dead Sea

SIMEON

MOAB

Beer-sheba

EDOM

The Divided Kingdom

The monarchy endured under three kings—Saul, David, and Solomon. After the death of Solomon in 922 B.C., it was divided:

Northern Kingdom ("Israel")
Formed by ten of the twelve tribes in 922 B.C

Included nine dynasties (royal family lines)

Conquered by Assyria in 721 B.C.

Southern Kingdom ("Judah")
Formed by the tribes of Judah and Benjamin in 922 B.C.

Ruled by one dynasty—the royal line of David

Conquered by Babylon in 587 B.C.

145

The Prophets

Prophet and King: A Thorn in the Flesh
Some classic examples:
Samuel and Saul—**1 Sm 9.1f (28.3–25: post-mortem?)**
Gad and David—**1 Sm 22.5; 1 Chr 21; 2 Sm 24.18**
Nathan and David—**2 Sm 7.1f (12.1–12: "The man should die!")**
Ahijah and Jeroboam—**1 Kgs 11.31; 14.5–16**
Elijah and Ahab—**1 Kgs 17–19 (1 Kgs 21: Jezebel; Naboth's vineyard)**
Micaiah and Ahab—**1 Kgs 22.8–28**

Daniel's Vision of the Four Beasts **Dn 7; see Dn 2; 8**
Same significance as Nebuchadnezzar's statue dream, Dn 2.

The four succeeding world kingdoms opposed to Messianic Kingdom:
    Babylonian—Winged lion (gold part of statue)
    Median—Bear (silver part of statue)
    Persian—Winged leopard (bronze part of statue)
        Greek—Horned beast (iron part of statue)

Isaiah, with lips cleansed: "A child is born to us, A son is given to us."

See Rv and this image applied to Roman Empire/Church persecution

Oral Prophets
The oral prophets are distinct from the "literary" prophets whose books are contained in the Bible. There are five major oral prophets
Samuel (enthroned David)
Nathan (advisor to David)
Ahijah (advisor to Jeroboam)
Elijah (led resistance against Baal cult)
Elisha (led resistance against Baal cult)

Literary ("Latter Prophets")
Early, around 721, the fall of the North
    Amos, Hosea (Israel addressed)
    Isaiah, Micah (Judah addressed)
    Jonah (Nineveh addressed)

Pre-Exilic (587) Judah
   Jeremiah, Habakkuk, Zephaniah
   Nahum (Nineveh addressed)
Babylonian Captivity (from 587)
   Ezekiel, Daniel
Post-Exilic Jewish Community
   Haggai, Zechariah, Malachi
   Obadiah (against Edom)
   Joel (the Day of the Lord)

The Seven Women Prophets

(Traditionally recognized in the Old Testament)

Sarah	Miriam	Deborah
Hannah	Abigail	Hulda	Esther

Anna is the only New Testament prophetess named **Lk 2.36–38.**

OLD TESTAMENT/NEW TESTAMENT RELATIONSHIP

Jesus of Nazareth said that he came to fulfill the Law, not destroy it. His life/death/resurrection is a study in fulfillment according to divine plan and difficult to appreciate apart from its Old Testament background and circumstances.

Note Well
1. Jesus' many Old Testament quotations and references;
2. Jesus', the evangelists', and other New Testament authors' Old Testament allusions;
3. Old Testament foreshadowings;
4. Prophecy fulfillment.

Prophecy Fulfillment in Jesus Christ

Jesus would . . .

be God's son (Mk 1.1, 11/Ps 2.7)
be God's glory filling the temple of Mary/Church (Lk 1.35/Hg 2.7)
be born of a woman (Lk 2.12/Is 9.5)
*be born Emmanuel, of a virgin (Mt 1.23; Lk 1.35/Is 7.14)
descend from Abraham (Mt 1.2, 16, 18–25/Gn 12.2; 15.5; 17.2)
descend from David in the tribe of Judah (Mt 1.6, 16, 18–25; Mk 11.9–10;
         Lk 1.32/2 Sm 7.8–16; Ps 89.20–38; 132; Jer 23.5–6; Gn 49.10; Is 9.6; Mi 4.7.)
*be born in Bethlehem (Mt 2.1, 5–6/Mi 5.1; 2 Sm 5.2)
be announced by a star (doubtful) (Mt 2.2/Nm 24.17)
be given homage by Gentiles (Mt 2.11/Ps 72.10f; Is 60.5f; Nm 24.17; Is 49.23)
*come out of Egypt (Mt 2.15/Hos 11.1)

---

*indicates evangelists' explicit reference to prophecy fulfillment. This is not an exhaustive listing. Not surprisingly, Matthew with his Jewish audience provides most. Many of these are unique to him; where there are parallels in the other evangelists reference is usually not made.

Jesus would . . .

*be called a Nazorean (hence: messianic mission to Gentiles?) Mt. 2.23/?;
 see Is 66.18

*be a Galilean, making Capernaum the center of his ministry
 (Mt 4.12f; see Jn 7.40–42/Is 9.1f)

*be announced by a herald's voice in the desert (Mt 3.3/Is 40.3)

*be prepared for by a messenger (Mt 11.10/Mal 3.1)

*be prepared for by the second coming of Elijah (Mt 11.14; 17.10–13;
 Mk 9.11–13/Mal 3.23f)

experience the spirit of the Lord come to rest on him (Mt 3.16–17/Is 11.2)

inaugurate the judgment of the reign of God (Mt 3.12; 13.42, 50/Is 1.25;
 Zec 13.9; Mal 3.2; Is 24.8: 41.16; Jer 7.20; 15.7)

universalize the covenant (Mt 2.1f etc/Is 60.1–6,9,11; see Epiphany)

*bear our infirmities as the Suffering Servant (Mt 8.17; Mk 9.12/Is 53.4)

*be resisted in certain key cities in Galilee (Mt 11.23/Is 14.13f)

*be meek (Mt 12.17f/Is 42.1–4)

*teach a message that would be rejected (Mt 13.14–15; Mk 4.11–12;
 Jn 12.37–41/Is 6.9f; 53.1)

*teach by means of parables (Mt 13.25/Ps 78.2)

*contend with hypocrisy in his hearers (Mt 15.7–9; Mk 7.6–7/Ps 78.36f;
 Is 19.13)

administer the key of the house of David (Mt 16.19/Is 22.22)

be a good shepherd (Mt 18.12–14; Jn 10.1f/Ez 34.1f; Mi 2.12; Zec 11.17)

reconcile parents and children, rebellious and wise (Lk 1.17/Sir 48.10)

bring grace ("living water") (Jn 4.10–14/Is 55.1f)

*teach all for God (Jn 6.45/Is 54.13)

free people with the truth (Jn 8.32/Is 42.7)

open the eyes of the blind (Jn 9.1f/Is 42.7)

*enter Jerusalem meek, astride an ass (Mt 21.5/Is 62.11; Zec 9.9)

*preach the Kingdom of God as a vineyard taken away from Israel
 (Mt 21.33–46; Jn 15.1f/Is 5.1–7

*be rejected as a stone by builders (Mt 21.42/Dn 2.45; Ps 118.22; Is 28.16)

---

*indicates evangelists' explicit reference to prophecy fulfillment. This is not an exhaustive listing. Not surprisingly, Matthew with his Jewish audience provides most. Many of these are unique to him; where there are parallels in the other evangelists reference is usually not made.

Jesus would . . .

*be betrayed by a companion (Jn 13.18/Ps 41.10)

*be betrayed for thirty pieces of silver (Mt 26.14; 27.9–10/Zec 11.12–13)

*be a shepherd struck down while sheep scatter (Mt 26.31/Zec 13.7)

be silent before his accusers (26.63/Is 53.7)

*occasion divine judgment to be worked on his betrayer (Mt 27.3–10/
Jer 18.2f; 19.1f; 32.6–15)

be beaten and spat upon as the Suffering servant (Mt 27.30/Is 50.6)

be stripped of his garments, which would be divided (Mt 27.5/Ps 22.19)

endure public humiliation (Jn 19.5/Is 52.14)

be insulted (Mt 27.39/Ps 22.8)

be taunted for his reliance on God (Mt 27.43/Ps 22.9)

feel forsaken (Mt 27.46/Ps 22.9)

be abandoned (Mt 27.49/Ps 69.21)

thirst on the cross (Jn 19.28f/Ps 69.22; 22.16)

*be pierced by a sword (Jn 19.28f/Ps 69.22; 22.16)

*be killed without his bones being broken (Jn 19.36/Nm 9.12; Ex 12.46;
Ps 34.21)

be buried in someone else's tomb (Mt 27.59–60/Is 53.9)

bear much fruit by dying ("grain of wheat") (Jn 12.24/Is 53.10–12)

Types of Jesus Christ

A "type" is an historical personage/event (strictly speaking) from the past which foreshadows or prefigures a future person/event, which is thereby explained in its richness and significance by the type. It is distinct from a symbol which merely represents ("symbolizes"), and is usually an animal, bird, or inanimate object.

The Annunciation
God announcing to Moses from burning bush the delivery of Israel
announcement of birth of Isaac, of Samson, of Samuel

Incarnation
The fleece of Gideon; Jacob's ladder;
Divine presence in the Dwelling (Ex 40.34/Lk 1.35), in the Temple
(1 Kgs 8.10)

Nativity
Flowering of Aaron's rod; birth of Eve; Moses in the bulrushes

---

*indicates evangelists' explicit reference to prophecy fulfillment. This is not an exhaustive listing. Not surprisingly, Matthew with his Jewish audience provides most. Many of these are unique to him; where there are parallels in the other evangelists reference is usually not made.

Reproaches of Good Friday

The Graded (or Calvary) Cross

"Improperia" (Complaints), recited during veneration of the cross

O my people, what have I done to you?
Wherein have I afflicted you? Answer me.

V. Because I led you out of the land of Egypt.
you have prepared a cross for your Savior.
O holy God! O holy, strong One! O holy, Immortal One, have mercy on us!

V. Because I led you through the desert for forty years, and fed you with manna, and brought you into a land exceedingly good, you have prepared a cross for your Savior! O holy God . . .

V. What more ought I have done for you than I have done;
I planted you, indeed, as my most beautiful vineyard
and you have become excessively bitter to me.
For in my thirst you gave me vinegar to drink.
and with a lance you have pierced the side of your Savior.
O holy God! . . .

The following Reproaches are sung alternately by the cantors.

V. For your sake I scourged Egypt through its first-born;
and you have scourged me and betrayed me.

R. O my people, what have I done to you? wherein have I offended you? Answer me.

V. I led you out of Egypt and drowned Pharoah in the Red Sea;
R. O my people . . .

V. I opened the sea before you;
and you have opened my side with a spear.
R. O my people . . .

V. I went before you in pillar of a cloud;
and you have led me before the judgment-seat of Pilate.
R. O my people . . .

V. I fed you with manna in the desert;
and you heaped blows and scourges upon me.
R. O my people . . .

V. I gave you the water of salvation from the rock to drink;
and you have given me gall and vinegar.
R. O my people . . .

V. For your sake I struck the kings of the Canaanites;
and you have struck my head with a reed.
R. O my people . . .

V. I gave you a royal scepter;
and you have put on my head a crown of thorns.

Presentation
presentation in temple of Israelite firstborn/of Samuel
joy of Jacob at the sight of his long lost son (Simeon and Messiah)

Epiphany
Queen of Sheba visiting Solomon
Abner's visit to David at Hebron
Joseph's brothers bowing before him
Three strong men bringing David water

The star of
the Epiphany

Flight into Egypt
Flight of Jacob to Laban
Moses concealed from Pharaoh's soldiers
David's flight through the window
Two spies' flight from Rahab's house
Jacob's flight into Egypt to escape famine

Holy Innocents
Pharaoh's slaughter of Israelite children; Saul's slaughter of the priests
Rachel bewailing Israel's exile (Mt 2.18/Jer 31.15f)
Athaliah's slaughter of the King's sons

Holy Family in Egypt
The Egyptian migration of Jacob's family

Return from Egypt
Jacob's return to Israel; David's return to Hebron
Moses' return to Egypt

John the Baptist
Isaac/Samuel (faith, parentage, consecration)
Elijah (attire, locale, message, way of life)

Temptation
Esau (birthright); Adam and Eve; Joseph (Potiphar's wife)
Moses overcoming Egyptians and Shepherds; Samson (the lion)
David (the lion; Goliath); Moses on the mountain forty days and nights

Sermon on the Mount
Moses on Mt. Sinai

Raising of Lazarus
Elijah's raising of the son of the widow of Sarepta
Elisha's raising of the Shunammite's son

Transfiguration
Moses' transfiguration
Angel's appearing to Abraham (see Moses and Elijah)
Nebuchadnezzar seeing the three youths in furnace

Messianic Entry into Jerusalem
Elisha met at Bethel by prophets' sons
David's entry in triumph with Goliath's head

Jesus Weeping over Jerusalem
Jeremiah weeping over Jerusalem

Cleaning Out the Temple
Judas Maccabeus purging the profaned temple
King Darius' mandating Ezra to cleanse the temple

Last Supper
Melchizedek's bread offering to Abraham; desert manna
Moses' and Joshua's farewell conversation (Jesus and his disciples)

Prediction of the Passion
Predicted death of Ahab (by Micaiah), of king's servant (by Elisha), and
of Belshazzar (by Daniel)

Agony in the Garden
Abraham escorting Isaac up the mountain
Angel wrestling with Jacob/comforting Elijah

Betrayal
Joseph sold to Ishmaelites/to Potiphar; Joab murdering Abner
Absolom plotting against David; Tryphon betraying Jonathan
Saul jeopardizing David.

Jesus before Pilate
Daniel/Babylonians; Elijah/Jezebel; Job/the devil
Susanna/corrupt judges; Joseph/Potiphar's wife

Crowning with Thorns
Mutilation of David's messengers by King of Ammon
Elisha mocked at Bethel

Jesus Mocked by Soldiers
Elisha/children; Elisha/priests of Baal
Her/Jews; Noah/Ham; Samson/Philistines

Scourging at the Pillar
Lamech tortured by wives; Job by the devil
Achor tied to a tree

A passion
cross: with
thorny crown

Way of the Cross
Isaac with the wood for his own sacrifice
Sarepta women with two cruciform bundles of wood

Crucifixion
Abel's murder; Isaac on Mt. Moriah
Sacrifice of Moabite King's son
Moses' lifting brazen serpent in desert
Joseph's imprisonment with two thieves
Martyrdom of Isaiah/of Jeremiah (traditionally)

The Russian
Orthodox
cross, upper
crossmember:
INRI; lower:
footrest

Seamless Garment
Joseph's coat

Pierced Side
Eve from Adam's side; Moses evoking water from the rock

The New Covenant in Christ's Blood
The Old Testament covenant sealed with the blood of the lamb

Mary's Sorrow
Adam and Eve/Abel; Naomi/sons; Jacob/Joseph (coat)

Descent from the Cross
Rizpah and her sons who were hanged

Burial
Joseph/pit; Jonah/sea; burial of Jacob/of Abner/of Moses

Descent into Hell
Moses/Egypt; Samson/lion; Elijah/priests of Baal
David/Goliath; Joshua/walls of Jericho

Resurrection
Samson carrying off the gates of Gaza
Jonah/whale; Daniel/lion's den; three youths/furnace

The Easter cross, white, with lilies

Women at the Tomb
Reuben looking for Joseph
Daughter of Sion (Song of Songs) searching for her missing spouse

Appearance to Mary
"Resurrection" appearances of Daniel/of Jonah/of three youths

Appearance to the Disciples
Joseph revealing himself to his brothers
Prodigal Son, forgiven by his father (as disciples were for their cowardice)

Thomas
Angel's appearance to Gideon/to Jacob

A seven-pointed star representing the seven-fold gift of the Spirit

Ascension
Elijah's fiery chariot; the translation of Enoch

Pentecost
Stone tablets given to Moses
Descent of fire upon Elijah's altar

Damnation
Expulsion of Hagar and her son
Judgment, destruction of Korah, Dathan, and Abiram/of Sodom/of Jericho
The writing on the wall at Belshazzar's feast

Salvation
Daniel/lion's den; three youths/furnace; Israel/Red Sea
Blood on doorposts

Joseph's brothers/famine; feast of Job's sons
Jacob's ladder

Church
Eight people in Noah's ark
Solomon building his temple (Christ building his Church)
Laying the cornerstone of the temple (Christ)
Isaac meeting Rebecca (Church, the bride of Christ)
Bridegroom meeting bride in *Song of Songs*

Baptism
The flood; red Sea; washing of Naaman the Syrian; water in the desert

Eucharist
Melchizedek bringing bread and wine to Abraham
Elijah fed by angels; manna

Christological Titles *(Principal)*

With representative Scripture references for some; a glossary follows.

Jesus
Given name *Yeshuah*: "Yahweh is salvation." Common enough Jewish name (Mt 1.21). Identifying his mission. (Mt 1.21; Acts 4.12; 10.43; Col 3.17)

Ihs form, with the h decorated as a cross; being the first three letters of "Jesus" in Greek.

Jesus the Nazorean
A "last name," which developed later in history to distinguish among those with the same name. (Surnames usually originated with either occupation, parentage, appearance, or place of origin, as in this case.)

Christ *(over one hundred uses)*
Greek *Christos,* translating Hebrew Masi ah ("anointed one.") The Messiah, the fulfillment of Jewish hope. (See Jn 1.41; 4.25; 10.22–38)

Jesus Christ
From Jesus the Christ, evolving into a kind of proper name.

Rabbi
Teacher (Lk 10.25)

Savior
English expressions from Latin word used for Jesus' given name. (Gn 3.16–17)

Lord
Common expressions used in Middle East, with connotations it still has today. Used as an act of faith in Jesus as Son of God (our Lord and later

as God Himself (the Lord). Reserved for Yahweh in Old Testament. (Jn 20.28; Phil 2.20–11)

Judge
Old Testament forger and leader of the people. Later refers to Jesus' role in the judgment. (Jn 5.22–23)

Priest, Prophet, King
Related terms referring to the fullness of Jesus' role as the Christ.

Lamb of God
Jesus' sacrificial role as the authentic and final passover lamb of Old Testament. (Jn 1.29, 30; Rv 5.6f; 14.1–5; 1 Pt 1.18f; Acts 8.32; See Ex 12; Is 53.7)

Son of David
Jesus as legal claimant to the "throne" of David and the one establishing the kingdom of God, which David established in a political sense. (Jn 18.36)

Son of Man
A favorite of Jesus and used of or by him some eighty-two times making it the most frequently used title in the New Testament (all except one—Acts 7.56—in the Gospel). It is messianic (Dn 7.2–14), and a key to Jesus self-understanding (see Hebrew *bar nas:* the man) as the first of a new race who possesses the life of God. Emphasizes:

1. Jesus' humanity Mt 8.20; 11.19; 12.32
2. Jesus' role Mt 9.6; 12.8; 13.37; 16.13; 20.28; Lk 6.22; 19.10
3. Jesus' destiny Dn 7.13; Mt 24.37

The Word
Jesus as God's definite self-communication Jn 1.1, 14

Alpha and Omega
Jesus as the beginning and the end of human history; from first and last letters of Greek alphabet Rv 1.8; 22.12

Suffering Servant
Applying Old Testament prophecy Is 42.1–4; 49.107; 50.4–11; 52.13–53.12

Son of God
Post-resurrection term, used especially by those with Jewish background. *The* not *a* Son of God, explaining Jesus' nature and role in God's plan for the world (Jn 17.5; Rom 9.5).

Ichthys means fish; its letters were made to stand for "Jesus Christ, Son of God, savior" by the early Christians

Used in All Four Gospel Accounts:
Matthew 3.17; 4.3, 6; 8.29; 14.33; 16.16; 17.5; 26.63; 27.54
Mark 1.1, 11; 3.11; 5.7; 9.7; 14.61,62
Luke 1.32, 35; 3.22; 4.41; 35; 22.70
John 1.34, 49; 3.16, 18; 5.25; 9.35; 10.36; 19.7; 20.31

Jesus Calls Himself Son of God:
Mk 14.61–62; Jn 9.35–37; Jn 10.36

The Father Called Jesus His Beloved Son:
Mt 3.17; 17.5; Mk 1.11; 9.7 Lk 3.22; 9.35

Others Called Jesus Son of God:
John the Baptist Jn 1.34;
Nathanael Jn 1.49;
Martha Jn 11.27;
Roman guard Mt 27.54;
Peter Mt 16.16;
Disciples Mt 14.33;
Gabriel Lk 1.32; 35
evil spirits Mt 8.29; Mk 3.22; 5,7; Lk 4.41

Christological Titles (Glossary)

Advocate, 1 Jn 2.1
Alpha and Omega, Rv 1.8; 22.13
Amen, Rv 3.14
Apostle and High Priest of our religion, Heb 3.1
Author and Finisher of our Faith, Heb. 12.2
Beloved, Mt 12.18
Bread of God, Jn 6.33; 50
  Bread of Life, Jn 6.35
  Bread, living, Jn 6.51
Bridegroom, Jn 3.29
Brother, Mt 12.50
Captain of our Salvation, Heb 2.10
Carpenter, Mk 6.3
  Carpenter's son, Mt 13.55
Chief shepherd, 1 Pt 5.4
Chosen One, Lk 23.35
Christ, Mt 16.20
  Christ Jesus, 1 Tim 1.15, Col 1.1
  Christ of God, Lk 9.20
  Christ the Lord, Lk 2.12
  Christ who is above all, Rom 9.5
Cornerstone, chief Eph 2.21, 1 Pt 2.6
Dayspring, Lk 1.78
Eldest of many brothers, Rom 8.29
Faithful witness, Rv 1.5; 3.14
Favorite, Mt 12.18

First and the Last, Rv 1.17; 2.8
Firstborn from the dead, Rv 1.5
  Firstborn of all creation, Col 1.15
First fruits, 1 Cor 15.20
Friend, Lk 1.24
Friend of tax collectors and sinners, Mt 11.19
Gate of the sheepfold, Jn 10.7
Glory, Jn 12.41; Lk 2.32
Good Shepherd, Jn 10.11, 14
  One Shepherd, Jn 10.16
  Great Shepherd of the Sheep, Heb 13.20
Governor, Mt 2.6
Greater Covenant, Heb. 7.22
Head, Eph 4.16; 1 Cor 11.3; Cor 2.10
  Head of the Church, Col 1.18; Eph 1.22
Hidden manna, Rv 2.17
High priest, Heb 3.1; 4.14; 7.26
Holy One, Acts 2.27
  Holy One of God, Mk 1.25
  Holy servant Jesus, Acts 4.27
Hope, 1 Tim 1.2
Horn of Salvation, Lk 1.69
I am, Jn 8.58
Image of God, 2 Cor 4.5; Col 1.15
Immanuel, Mt 1.23

Inexpressible gift, 2 Cor 9.15

Innocent, 1 Pt 3.18

Intercessor, 1 Jn 2.1

Israel's comforting, Lk 2.25

Jesus, Mt 1.21
  Jesus the Nazarene, Jn 18.5

Just One, Acts 7.52

King, Mt 21.5
  King of Israel, Jn 1.50
  King of Kings, Rv 17.14; 19.16; 1 Tim 6.15
  King of nations, Rv 15.3
  King of righteousness, Heb 7.2
  King of the Jews, Mt 2.2

Lamb of God, 1 Pt 1.20; Jn 1.29, 37; Rv 5.12

Last Adam, 1 Cor 15.45

Leader, Mt 2.6; Heb 2.10

Leader and Savior, Acts 5.31

Liberator, Rom 11.26

Life, Jn 14.6; Col 3.4

Light, Jn 12.35, 1.9
  Light of men, Lk 2.32; Jn 1.4
  Light of the world, Jn 8.12

Lion of the tribe of Judah, Rv 5.5
  (See Gn 49.9)

Lord, Lk 1.25
  Lord, one, Eph 4.5
  Lord and my God, Jn 20.28

Lord both of the dead and of the living, Rom 14.9

Lord God Almighty, Rv 15.3

Lord Jesus (Jesus is Lord), Acts 7.59; 1 Cor 12.3

Lord Jesus Christ, Acts 15.11

Lord of all men, Acts 10.36

Lord of Glory, 1 Cor 2.9

Lord of lords, 1 Tim 6.15

Lord of peace, 2 Thes 3.16

Man, The, Jn 19.6

Master, Mt 17.24

Mediator, 1 Tim 2.5

Messiah, Jn 1.41; 4.25

Mighty God, Is 9.6

Morning Star, 2 Pt 1.20; Rv 2.29; 22.16

Nazarene, Mt 2.23

Passover, 1 Cor 5.8

Power and the wisdom of God, 1 Cor 1.25
  Power for salvation, Lk 1.69

Priest for ever, Heb 5.6

Prince (of life), Acts 3.15; 5.31
  Prince of Peace, Is 9.6
  Prophet of the Most High, Lk 1.76

Radiant light of God's glory, Heb 1.3

Ransom, 1 Tim 2.6

"Behold the Lamb of God." The victorious lamb on the book with seven seals, and the rising sun

THE FOUR EVANGELISTS

Their traditional symbols, the "four living creatures", are taken from (anticipated in?) the prophecy of Ezekiel (1.5–21; 10.20). Of these same living creatures, borrowed by the Book of Revelation (4.6–8), St. Irenaeus says, "The lion signifies the royalty of Christ, the calf his priestly office, the man his incarnation and the eagle the grace of the Holy Spirit."

Matthew Apostle and Martyr

Matthew is called the "divine man," since he teaches about the human nature of Christ and his version of the gospel begins with Jesus' paternal genealogy.

Mark Martyr

Mark is called the winged lion, since he informs us of the royal dignity of Christ and his version of the gospel begins: "The voice of one crying in the wilderness," suggesting the roar of the lion.

Luke Martyr

Luke is called the winged ox, since he deals with the sacrificial aspects of Christ's life and his version of the gospel begins with a temple scene.

John Apostle

John is called the rising eagle, since his gaze pierces so far into the mysteries of heaven and his version of the gospel begins with a lofty prologue that is a poem of the Word become flesh.

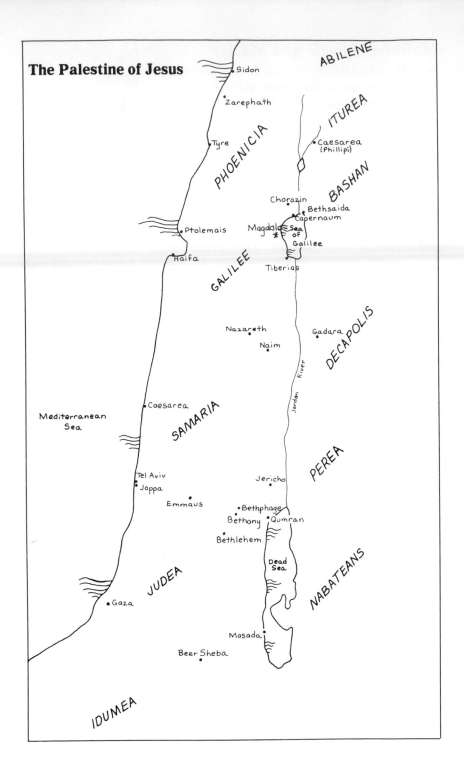

The Palestine of Jesus

ABILENE

Sidon

Zarephath

ITUREA

Tyre

PHOENICIA

Caesarea (Phillipi)

BASHAN

Chorazin

Bethsaida

Capernaum

Ptolemais

Magdala

Sea of Galilee

Haifa

GALILEE

Tiberias

Nazareth

Gadara

DECAPOLIS

Naim

Jordan River

Caesarea

Mediterranean Sea

SAMARIA

PEREA

Tel Aviv

Jericho

Joppa

Emmaus

Bethphage

Bethany

Qumran

Bethlehem

Dead Sea

NABATEANS

JUDEA

Gaza

Masada

Beer Sheba

IDUMEA

Stories of the New Testament

John the Baptist

His ministry Mt 3/Mk 1.1–11/Lk 3.1–20
His execution by Herod, Mt 14.1–12/Mt 6.14–29

The Life of Jesus

Nativity, Mt 1.18–2.15/Lk 1.5–2.40
Early years, Lk 2.41–52
Baptism, Mt 3/Lk 4.21,22/Jn1.29–39
Call of the Apostles, Mt 4.18–22; 9.9, 10.1–5; Mk 3.13–19; Lk 6.12–16;
    Jn 1.35–51
Temptation, Mt 4.1–11; Mk 1.12, 13; Lk 4.1–13
The "Sermon on the Mount", Mt 5–7/Lk6.20–49
The Transfiguration, Mt 17.1–8/Mk 9.1–7/Lk 9.28–36
According to tradition, the Transfiguration took place on Mt. Tabor,
making it the counterpoint to Gethsemane, the place of Jesus agony on
the eve of Good Friday.
Messianic Entry into Jerusalem, Mt 21.1–11/Mk 11.1–11/Lk 19.29–44/
    Jn 12.12–19
The Last Supper, Mt 26.17–35/Mk 14.12–26/Lk 22.1–38
Agony in Gethsemane, Mt 26.36–46/Mk 14.32–42/Lk 22.39–46
Crucifixion, Mt 26.47–27.66/Mk 14.43–15.47/Lk 22.47–23.56/Jn 18; 19
The "Gospel of the Holy Spirit", Acts (cf 13.1–4; 16.6; 19.21; 20.22)

Discourses

Vindication of his authority, Jn 2.18–22
To Nicodemus, Jn 3.1–21
To a Samaritan woman, Jn 4.7–30
Defense of his disciples (not fasting, corn on the Sabbath), Mt 9.14 17;
    12.1–8/Mk 2.18–28/Lk 5.33–39; 6.1–5
Defense of himself (Sabbath healing of withered hand), Mt 12.9–13/
    Lk 3.1–5/Lk 6.6–10
Sermon on the Mount, Mt 5.1 to 7.29/Lk 6.20–49
Testimony concerning John the Baptist, Mt 11.7–19/Lk 7.24–35; 16.16
Instructions for the apostolate, Mt 10.5–42/Mk 6.8–13/Lk 9.3–6; 10.1–12
The bread of life, Jn 6.22–72
Defense of his claim to divinity, Jn 5.19–47
Defense of his disciples (Jewish tradition), Mt 15.1–20/Mk 7.1–23
Promise of primacy to Peter, Mt 16.13–20
Predictions of the Passion and Resurrection, Mt 16.21–23; 17.21–22; 20.17–
    19/Mk 8.31–33; 9.29–31; 10.32–34/Lk 9.22; 9.44–45; 18.31–34
Doctrine of the Cross, Mt 16.24–28/Mk 8.34–39/Lk 9.23–27
Scandal, Mt 18.59/Mk 9.41–49/Lk 17.1–2
Fraternal correction, Mt 18.15–17, 21–22/Lk 17.3–4
Conversation with Martha and Mary, Lk 10.38–42

The adulteress, Jn 8.3–11
The fruitfulness of prayer, Mt 7.7–11/Lk 11.9–13
Defense of his authority Mt 21.23–27/Mk 11.27–33/ Lk 20.1–8
Tribute to Caesar, Mt 22.15–22/Mk 12.13–17/Lk 20.20–26
The Great Commandment, Mt 22.34–40/Mk 12.28–34
Destruction of Jerusalem and the Temple, Mt 24.1–3; 15–22; 32–35/
      Mk 13.1–20; 28–31 The "Little Apocalypse"/Lk 21.5–6; 20–24; 29–33
End of the world and coming of the Son of Man, Mt 24.4–14; 23–31;
      36–51; 25.13/Mk 13.21–27; 32–37/Lk 21.7–19; 25–28; 34–36
Last Judgment, Mt 25.31–46
Discourses at the Last Supper, Mt 26.20–29/Mk 14.17–25/Lk 22.14–38/Jn
      13.2–17.26
Peter the chief shepherd, Jn 21.15–19
Apostolic mandate, Mt 28.16–20/Mk 16.15–18

Parables

The House Built on Rock, Mt 7.24–27/Lk 6.47–49
The Sower, Mt 13.1–23/Mk 4.1–20/Lk 8.1–15
The Seed Grows of Itself, Mk 4.26–29
The Mustard Seed, Mt 13.31–32/Mk 4.30–32/Lk 13.18–19
The Weeds, Mt 13.24–30; 36–43
The Leaven, Mt 13.33/ Lk 13.20–21
The Found Treasure, Mt 13.44
The Precious Pearl, Mt 13.45, 46
The Net, Mt 13.27–50
The Unmerciful Servant, Mt 18.23–25
The Laborers in the Vineyard, Mt 20.1–16
The Two Sons, Mt 21.28–32
The Vineyard, Mt 21.33–46/Mk 12.1–11/Lk 20.9–19
The Marriage Feast, Mt 22.1–14/Lk 14.15–24
The Wedding Garment, Mt 22.11–14
The Ten Virgins, Mt 25.1–13
The Talents, Mt 25.14–30
The Sheep and the Goats, Mt 25.31–46
The Two Debtors, Lk 7.36–50
The Good Samaritan, Lk 10.25–37
The Importunate Friend, Lk 11.5–8
The Rich Fool, Lk 12.16–21
The Servants Who Waited, Lk 12.35–48
The Barren Fig Tree, Lk 13.6–9
The Last Seat, Lk 14.7–11
The Great Supper, Lk 14.15–24
The Lost Sheep, Lk 15.3–7   } Luke's Three Parables of Mercy
The Lost Coin, Lk 15.8–10   } "The gospel within the Gospel"
The Prodigal Son, Lk 15.11–32   }
The Dishonest Steward Lk 16.1–13

The Rich Man and Lazarus, Lk 16.19–31
The Unjust Judge, Lk 18.1–8
The Pharisee and the Publican, Lk 18.9–14
The Gold Pieces Lk 19.11–27

Similitudes and Allegories

"Physician, cure yourself", Lk 4.23
The flavor of salt, Mt 5.13/ Mk 9.49/ Lk 14.34–35
The lamp under a basket, Mt 5.14–15/Mk 4.21/Lk 8.16–18; 11.33–36
The city on a mountain, Mt 5.14
The opponent, Mt 5.25–26/Lk 12.58–59
The lamp of the body, Mt 6.22–23/ Lk 11.33–36
The two masters, Mk 6.24/Lk 16.13
A son's request, Mt 7.9–11/Lk 11.11–13
The tree and its fruit, Mt 7.15–20; 12.33–37/Lk 6.43–45
The physician and the sick, Mt 9.12–13/Mk 2.17/Lk 5.31–32
The bridegroom and the wedding guests, Mt 9.14–15/Mk2.18–20/Lk 5.33–35
A patch of new cloth and an old garment, Mt 9.16/Mk 2.21/Lk 5.36
New wine in old wine-skins, Mt 9.17/Mk 2.22/Lk 5.37–38
Secrets to be revealed, Mt 10.26–27/Mk 4.22/Lk 8.17; 12.2–3
The servant not above the master, Mt 10.24–25/Lk 6.40
The wayward children, Mt 11.16–19/Lk 7.31–35
The divided kingdom, Mt 12.25–26/Mk 3.23–26/Lk 11.17–18
The unclean spirit, Mt 12.43–45/Lk 11.24–26
The wise scribe, Mt 13.52
The defilement of man, Mt 15.10–20/Mk 7.22–23
Blind guides of blind men, Lk 6.39/Mt 15–14
The children's bread, Mt 15.26–27/Mk 7.27–28
Building a tower, Lk 14.28–30
Preparation for war, Lk 14.31–33
The watchful servants, Lk 12.35–38/Mk 13.34
Faithful and unfaithful servants, Mt 24.45–51/Lk 12.42–48
The servant doing his duty, Lk 17.7–10
The body and the eagles, Mt 24.28/Lk 17.37
The thief, Mt 24.43–44/Lk 12.39–40
The fig tree and the branches, Mt 24.32–33/Mk 13.28–29/Lk 21.29–31
The good Shepherd, Jn 10.1–18
The vine and the branches, Jn 15.1–17

The Seven Signs from St. John's "Book of Signs"

1. Changing water to wine at Cana, Jn 2.1–11
2. Cure of royal official's son, Jn 4.43–54
3. Cure on a Sabbath feast, Jn 5.1–15
4. Multiplication of loaves at Passover, Jn 6.1–15
5. Walking on the sea, Jn 6.16–21
6. Cure of man blind from birth, Jn 9.1–34
7. Raising of Lazarus, Jn 11.1–44

Miracles

1. **Nature Miracles**
   Changing water into wine at Cana, Jn 2.1–11
   First miraculous draught of fishes, Lk 5.1–11
   Calming of the tempest, Mt 8.23–27/Mk 4.36–40/Lk 8.22–25
   Multiplication of loaves, Mt 14.13–21/Mk 6.31–44/Lk 9.12–17/Jn 6.1–15
   Jesus' walking on water, Mt 14.22–23/Mk 6.45–52/Jn 6.16–21
   Second multiplication of loaves, Mt 15.32–38/Mk 8.1–9
   Coin in the fish's mouth, Mt 17.24–27
   Cursing the fig tree, Mt 21.18–19/Mk 11.12–14/Lk 13.6–9
   Second miraculous draught of fishes, Jn 21.1–14

2. **Healings**
   Very numerous in Jesus' ministry, and often only referred to scripturally. (Mt 4; Lk 4; Mk 6). Twenty are mentioned specifically:
   Healing of the nobleman's son, Jn 4.46–54
   Cure of the mother-in-law of Peter, Mt 8.14–15/Mk 1.29–31/Lk 4.38–39
   Cleansing a leper, Mt 8.14/Mk 1.40–45/Lk 5.12–14
   Healing a paralytic, Mt 9.1–8/Mk 2.1–12/Lk 5.18–26
   Healing a sick man at Bethesda, Jn 5.1–9
   Restoring a man with the withered hand, Mt 12.9–13/Mk 3.15/Lk 6.6–10
   Healing a centurion's servant, Mt 8.5–13/Lk 7.1–10
   Healing of one blind and dumb, Mt 12.22–27
   Healing a woman with an issue of blood, Mt 9.20–22/Mk 5.25–34/
   Lk 8.43–48
   Opening the eyes of two blind men, Mt 9.27–31
   Cure of the dumb man, Mt 9.32–34
   Healing a deaf and dumb man, Mk 7.31–37
   Opening the eyes of one blind at Bethesda, Mk 8.22–26
   Healing two lunatic children, Mt 17.14–20/Mk 9.13–28/Lk 9.37–43
   Opening the eyes of one born blind, Jn 9.1–41
   Restoring an infirm woman, Lk 13.10–17
   Healing of man with the dropsy, Lk 14.1–6
   Cleansing the lepers, Lk 17.12–19
   Opening the eyes of the blind man near Jerico, Mt 20.29–34/Mk
   10.46–52/Lk 18.35–43
   Healing Malchus's ear, Mt 26.51–52/Mk 14.47/Lk 22.49–51/Jn 18.10–11

3. **Deliverances**
   Evidently very numerous in his ministry, given the scriptural formulas (see Mk 1) that recur. Seven are mentioned specifically:
   Demoniac at Capernaum, Mk 1.23–28/Lk 4.33–37
   Deaf and dumb demoniac, Mt 12.22–29/Mk 3.22–27/Lk 11.14–26
   Gerasene demoniacs, Mt 8.28–34/Mk 5.1–15/Lk 8.26–35
   Dumb demoniac, Mt 9.32–34
   Daughter of Syro-Phoenician woman, Mt 15.21–28/Mk 7.24–30
   Lunatic child, Mt 17.14–21/Mk 9.14–29/Lk 9.37–43
   Infirm woman, Lk 13.10–17

4. Victories over Hostile Wills

It is difficult to distinguish in many instances between a miraculous action of Christ and a merely natural and effective act or influence. (See e.g., Jn 7.30, 44; 8.20, 59, where Jesus disallows his enemies from arresting him.) Most agree that two situations involved the miraculous:

The casting out of the vendors, **Mt 21.12f/Mk 11.15f/Lk 19.45f/Jn 2.13f**

The episode of the escape from the hostile crowd at Nazareth, **Lk 4.28–30**

5. Resusitations

Not truly "resurrections," like Jesus' own. That is, these people were brought back to life; they still had to die eventually.

Raising the daughter of Jairus, **Mt 9.18–19; 23–26/Mk 5.20–24; 35–43/ Lk 8.41–42; 49–56**

Raising the son of the widow of Naim, **Lk 7.11–17**

Raising of Lazarus, **Jn 11.1–44**

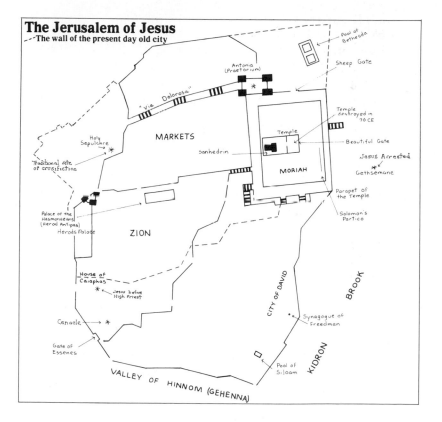

The Jerusalem of Jesus
- - The wall of the present day old city

Pool of Bethesda
Sheep Gate
Antonia (Praetorium)
"Via Dolorosa"
Temple destroyed in 70 CE
Holy Sepulchre
MARKETS
Temple
Sanhedrin
Beautiful Gate
Traditional site of crusifiction
Jesus Arrested
MORIAH
Gethsemane
Parapet of the Temple
Palace of the Hasmonaeans (Herod Antipas)
Herods Palace
ZION
Solomon's Portico
House of Caiaphas
Jesus before High Priest
CITY OF DAVID
BROOK
Cenacle
Synagogue of Freedmen
Gate of Essenes
KIDRON
Pool of Siloam
VALLEY OF HINNOM (GEHENNA)

"They Reclined at Table. . . ."

That's what the Bible says (Mk 14.18), but that's not what most of us see. In our mind's eye, and also in so many Last Supper pictures, we see a more formal seated gathering. As a matter of fact, diners in Christ's time were more likely to recline on floor cushions during meals, since chairs are part of later history. Leonardo da Vinci's Last Supper—with its anachronistic chairs—is a long-time favorite. It was originally (about 1495) painted on the dining room wall of a Milan convent. Although the building was virtually destroyed during World War II, the wall with the unharmed painting remained. The spilled salt? Spilling salt was an evil omen for the Romans. Leonardo alludes to this with his distinctive detail of the overturned salt "cellar." Salt, symbolic of purity and sanctifying effect, was used in Greek and Roman sacrifices, placed on the head of the victim. Superstitions arose regarding spilling this salt.

Luke's Banqueting Scenes

1. Levi's reception for Jesus, 5.29–32
   "eating and drinking with sinners"
2. Simon the pharisee's dinner, 7.36–50
   a woman bathes Jesus' feet
3. At Martha and Mary's house 10.38–42
   Mary chooses the better part
4. A pharisee's dinner 11.37–54
   "Woe to you, pharisees"
5. A leading pharisee's sabbath meal 14.1–24
   "It is lawful to cure on the sabbath?"
6. Parable told at a pharise's meal: the Marriage Feast 14.7–14
   highest place and lowest place
7. Parable told at a pharisee's meal: the Great Supper 14.15–24
   "Bring in the poor and the crippled"
8. Parable of the Prodigal Son 15.11–32
   celebration: "Kill the fatted calf"
9. At Zacchaeus' house 19.1–10
   "I want to stay at your house today"
10. The Last Supper 22.14–38
11. The Emmaus meal 24.13–35
    "with that their eyes were opened"

The Cenacle of St. Mark's Mother

The "upper room" in Jerusalem that was the site of the Last Supper (Mk 14.14; Lk 22.12) is called the "cenacle" (Lt: *coenaculum*, dinning room). Christian piety has also identified it as the place of the Holy Spirit's descent on Pentecost. The Scriptures only say the Eleven repaired to an upper room where they were lodging, gathering regularly in prayer with Mary the mother of Jesus, with some of his relatives and with a group of women disciples.

Passion Foretold

Following the confession by Peter that Jesus is the Messiah, at the high point of Mark's Gospel (8.29), there are three teachings on the passion:

8.31–38

9.30–32

10.32–34

There are, in all, five occasions recorded when Jesus spoke of his death and resurrection:

After Peter's confession,

> **Mt 16.21/Mk 8.31/Lk 9.22**

After the Transfiguration,

> **Mt 17.9, 12/Mk 9.9, 12**

After healing the epileptic,

> **Lk 9.44**

While passing through Galilee,

> **Mt 17.22–23/Mk 9.31**

Near Jerusalem,

> **Mt 20.17–19/Mk 10.32–34/Lk 18.31–34**

Adam's Grave

The Holy Land includes many holy places, but none so venerable, some say, as the Basilica of the Holy Sepulchre in Jerusalem. This favorite place of pilgrimage has many chapels, favorites being St. Helena, and the True Cross . . . and the "Chapel of Adam". The place of the Lord's crucifixion was called Golgotha in Greek—Calvary in Latin, translations of the Hebrew word for "skull". It was so called in tradition, relates Jerome and others, because of the ancient legend that Christ was crucified on the very spot in which Adam was buried, so that the blood of Jesus would have poured down its redemptive stream upon mankind's first guilty head. The skull and cross bones that appear occasionally at the foot of a crucifix are a remnant of this legend. Whatever there is to this, "Golgotha" is a fitting name for this holy hill, possibly resembling a skull in fact or fancy, on which the second Adam's obedience culminated.

INRI

The inscription in "the Three Tongues:"

Iesus Nazarenus Rex Iudaeorum

Jesus of Nazareth, King of the Jews

In the Middle Ages, a thorough knowledge of Hebrew, Greek, Latin was the prerequisite for theological training, and a mark of such an education.

"They Have Pierced My Hands and My Feet"

Although crucifixion was a common form of execution in Jesus' day, later generations were left with only scant scriptural evidence, and their own imagination, to determine details of how, for example, his feet were affixed. Michelangelo's Crucifixion, showing the feet of the crucified Jesus separated, with a nail through each, has influenced more images than recent contemporary archeological and literary evidence.

No Rest for the Wicked

Isaiah has been quoted in Latin, *"Nemo malus felix"* ("No bad person is happy"), and we have said, "No rest for the wicked." If this is true, there is abundant illustration from stories of Pilate's life after Good Friday. They are suitably dramatic. One tradition relates that his life became so unfortunate that he committed suicide in Rome, in the days of Caligula. Thereupon his body was disposed into the Tiber, whose waters became so troubled by evil spirits that his corpse was retrieved and transported to Vienna. A similar disposal was attempted, this time into the Rhone, which washed Pilate's remains into the recesses of a lake on Mount Pilatus, between the cantons of Lucerne and Unterwalden. This is too coincidental to ignore: it is more likely that it was the name that brought the story, not the river that brought the body; "Pilatus" earned its name from the westerly winds that cover it with a white cloud "cap" (Lt: *pileatus; pileus,* felt cap).

The mount named Pilatus has spawned another legend: after Pilate was banished by Tiberius to Gaul he wandered to Mount Pilatus and threw himself into a black lake on its summit. Ever since, the ghost of Pilate reappears on the mountain annually; anyone cursed with a glimpse of the ghost is destined to die before another year is over. (A sixteenth century law did not allow the throwing of stones in the lake, for the fear of bringing a tempest on the country.)

The Seven Last Words

1. Father, forgive them; for they know not what they do. **Lk 23.34**
2. "Woman behold they son! . . . Behold thy mother!" **Jn 19.26–27**
3. I thirst. **Jn 19.28**
4. This day thou shalt be with me in Paradise. **Lk 23.43**
5. My God, my God, why hast Thou forsaken me? **Mt 27.46; Mk 15.34**
6. It is consummated. **Jn 19.30**
7. Father, into Thy hands I commend my Spirit. **Lk 23.46**

Flowers on Calvary

It is not uncommon for a plant to have a Christian fable associated with it, as with the aspen and the passion flower. The red *anemone,* the purple *orchis* (orchid), the *arum,* and the spotted persicaria were all stained red, it is said, by blood falling from the crucified Christ. There is more elaborate symbolism to some: the "Calvary Flower" (common trefoil, *Medicago Echinus*) is said to have sprung up in the footsteps taken by Pilate when he walked to the crucifixion "to see his title affixed" (INRI). There are resemblances in the flower to crucifixion symbols: in the center of each of its three leaves is a carmine spot, which takes on a cross form in the daylight hours. Moreover, the plant sports a little yellow flower that resembles a crown of thorns.

    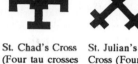

St. Peter's Cross St. Andrew's Cross St. Anthony's Cross (Egyptian, or tau; his origin and monastic locale) St. Chad's Cross (Four tau crosses joined in quadrate) St. Julian's Cross (Four Latin crosses joined saltirewise)

Birds at the Crucifixion

The story of the robin is a favorite, but there are others. Like the Scandinavian legend that explains the origin of the swallow's name: hovering over the crucified Christ, the bird cooed its consolation, "*Svala, svala*" ("Console, console"). Ever since, it has been referred to as the Bird of Consolation, the "Swallow." There is also a Legend of the Crossbill. Longfellow is one who has told this medieval fable of a bird at the cross of Christ. The Savior memorialized its efforts to pull the nails from the cross with its beak. To this day the bird is decorated with distinctive red plumage and obliquely crossed bill, thus meriting a name that always recalls its mercy.

Jesus' Appearances after the Resurrection

According to Matthew
Mary Magdalene and the other Mary visit tomb.
Jesus appears to the women.
Chief priests bribe guards.
Jesus appears to the eleven in Galilee.

According to Mark
Mary Magdalene, Mary mother of James, and Salome visit tomb.
Jesus appears to Mary Magdalene.
Jesus appears to three disciples going to the country.
Jesus appears to the eleven at table.

According to Luke
Mary Magdalene, Mary mother of James and Joanna visit tomb.
Peter runs to tomb.
Jesus appears to two on way to Emmaus, and to Peter.
Jesus appears to the eleven in Jerusalem.
The Ascension.

According to John
Mary Magdalene visits tomb.
Peter and John run to tomb.
Jesus appears to Mary Magdalene.
Jesus appears to the eleven, minus Thomas, Sunday evening.
Jesus appears to the eleven including Thomas, one week later.
Jesus appears to two apostles by Sea of Galilee later.

According to Paul (1 Cor 15.5–8)
". . . he was seen by Cephas, then by the twelve. After that he was seen by five hundred brothers at once. . . Next he was seen by James; then by all the apostles. Last of all he was seen by me, as one born out of the normal course."

According to Luke (Acts 1.3 and 13.31)
"In the time after his suffering he showed them in many convincing ways that he was alive, appearing to them over the course of forty days and speaking to them about the reign of God . . . God raised him from the dead, and for many days thereafter Jesus appeared to those who had come up with him from Galilee to Jerusalem."

Ascension window

173

Church

Revelation/Religion
Divine Initiative/Human Response

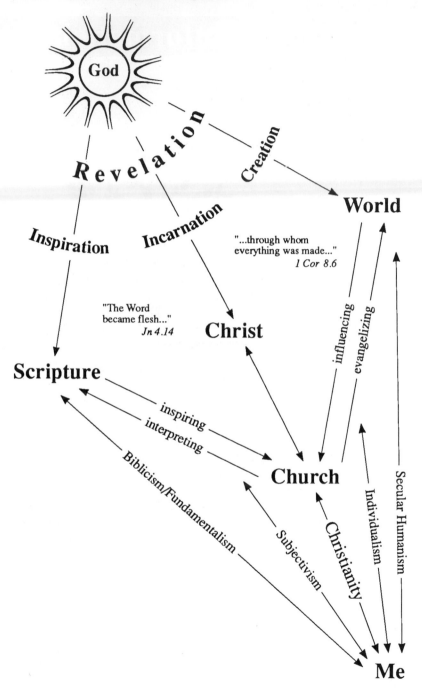

CHURCH

A. **Meanings**
1. Universal
   The Body of Christ
2. Diocesan
   The "littlest Church of all".
   The assembly of many assemblies.

B. **Models** (cf. Avery Dulles, *Models of the Church*)
1. Community
2. Herald
3. Institution
4. Sacrament
5. Servant

C. **A Description**
According to the three determining elements of any group.
1. A shared way of viewing life articulated in a creed ("Philosophy") faith in Christ; Jesus is Lord
2. A shared way of experiencing life articulated in a code ("morality") the corporal and spiritual works of mercy
3. A way of celebrating identity acted out in cult ("ritual") liturgy

D. **Characteristics** (according to Acts 2.42–47)
1. The Teaching of the Apostles (*Didache*)
2. The Communal Life (*Koinonia*)
3. The Breaking of the Bread
4. The Prayers

E. **Mission**
1. Message (*Kerygma*)
   The proclamation of the Good News, the core of which is that Jesus who died is risen and now lives among us (see Rom 16.25). Distinct from the teaching (*Didache*).
2. Fellowship (*Koinonia*)
   The responsibility of Jesus' followers for a visible demonstration of what they are proclaiming in the message. The building of christian community in the bond of faith, hope, and love (see Acts 2.42–47).
3. Service (*Diakonia*)
   The act of healing and reconciling, of binding up wounds and restoring health, as Jesus showed us how.

F. **The Four Marks**
1. One
2. Holy
3. Catholic
4. Apostolic

The pomegranate, filled with seeds, a symbol of the Church

G. **The Three Dimensions of the Church's Communion**
   1. The Church Militant on earth
   2. The Church Suffering in purgatory
   3. The Church Triumphant in heaven

The Fifteen Marks

An expansion of the Four Marks of the Church; according to St. Robert Bellarmine, who lived in the wake of the principal Protestant reformers (1542–1621): a cardinal, Archbishop of Capua and Doctor of the Church.

1. **Name:** Catholic, worldwide and not confined to a particular nation;
2. **Antiquity,** in tracing ancestry directly to Christ;
3. **Duration,** lasting substantially unchanged for centuries;
4. **Extensiveness,** in the number of members;
5. **Episcopal succession,** from the twelve apostles to the current hierarchy;
6. **Doctrinal agreement** between current teaching and apostolic Church;
7. **Union** among members, and between members and visible head (pope);
8. **Holiness of doctrine,** reflecting the holiness of God;
9. **Efficacy of doctrine,** reflecting the holiness of God;
10. **Holiness of life** of representative writers and defenders;
11. **Miracles** worked in the Church and under its auspices;
12. **Prophecy** gift among its saints and spokespersons;
13. **Opposition** aroused on same ground as Christ was opposed;
14. **Unhappy end** of her enemies;
15. **Temporal peace and earthly happiness** of those who are faithful to her teaching and who defend her interests.

Catholic
(Gk: *katholikos;* Lt: *catholicus*)

A. **Literally**
   Universal, general.

B. **Originally** (In reference to the Church)
   By St. Ignatius of Antioch (A.D. 35–107) in
   his letter to the Smyrneans (8,2).

C. **Specifically**
   (four common meanings of "catholic")

1. The Catholic Church as distinct
   from Christian church bodies
   that do not recognize papal primacy.
2. The Catholic faith as the belief of
   the universal body of the faithful
   ("everywhere, always and by all").
3. Orthodoxy as distinguished from
   heresy and schism.
4. The undivided Church before the
   Eastern Schism (A.D. 1054), after
   which the Eastern Church called
   itself "Orthodox" distinguishing
   itself from Christian bodies which
   rejected the definitions of
   Ephesus and Chalcedon on the
   divinity of Christ.

Christ entrusting the keys of
the Kingdom to Peter, building his Church on rock.

D. **Commonly**
   Those Christians who live a continued tradition of faith and worship, and who hold to the apostolic succession of bishops and
   priests since Christ. "Catholic" since:
   it is intended for *all humankind;*
   it is intended for *all time;*
   it is appropriate in *every circumstance* of human life.

"The Spirit of the Lord will fill the whole world. Send forth your spirit and they will
be recreated and you shall renew the face of the earth"

The Apostolic Church

Ascension—Acts 1.1–12
Pentecost—Acts 2
The Ministry of Deacons—Acts 6.1–7
Stephen, the First Martyr—Acts 6.5–15; 7.54–60
Philip and the Ethiopian—Acts 8.26–39
Saul of Tarsus—Acts 9.1–32
Peter and Cornelius—Acts 10
Peter in Prison—Acts 12.1–19
The First Council—Acts 15.1–35
Paul in Prison—Acts 16.16–40
The Riot of the Ephesus Silversmiths—Acts 19.23–41
Paul's Voyage to Rome—Acts 27; 28

The Eight Kerygmatic Sermons in Acts

In 1 Cor 15.1–11 Paul writes of Christ's resurrection as the core of the message ("that which has been handed on"), the foundation of Christian faith, and calls it "the preaching", "the proclamation" (Heb: Kerygma).

Six to Jews (Five by Peter, the sixth by Paul):

2.14–36   3.12–26   4.8–12   5.29–32   10.34–43   13.16–41

Two to Gentiles (by Paul):

14.15–17   17.22–31

An Outline Chronology of the Early Church

These are all first-century dates and approximate in most cases. At least three dates from secular history, however, are established ones and helpful in determining dates in early Church history, namely Herod Agrippa's reign in Judea (44–44; see Acts 12), Festus' appointment as governor at Caesaria (60; see Acts 24.27), and Nero's reign as Roman emperor (63–67).

By putting 19 ahead of each year and "contemporizing" the events, one gets a better sense of the lapse of time between these events and their relationship to each other. By considering first-century events like twentieth-century ones chronologically, one can better see the written Word (the Bible) as the Church's inspired reflection on the interpretation of its experience of the Incarnate Word (Jesus Christ).

180

Numbers in parentheses are Acts of the Apostles references. Bold face indicates New Testament book.

"Saul, Saul, why do you persecute me?"

1930	Formation of the Church in Jerusalem (2)
1931/2	Stoning of Stephan, first martyr (7,8)
1931/2	Saul's conversion (9)
1934/5	Paul's first visit to Jerusalem (as a Christian)
1944	Paul's second visit to Jerusalem (11.27–30)
1945–48	Paul's first missionary journey: Galatia (13–14)
1950	The Council in Jerusalem
1950–53	Paul's second missionary journey: Greece (16–18)
1951	**1 Thessalonians** (from Corinth)
1952	**2 Thessalonians** (from Corinth)
1954–57	Paul's third missionary journey: Ephesus (19, 20)
1955/6	**1 Corinthians** (from Ephesus)(16.8)
1956/7	**2 Corinthians** (from Philippi)
1956/7	**Galatians** (from Philippi)
1957	Paul in Jerusalem (20.16)
1958–60	Paul in Caesaria
1960–61	Paul's journey to Rome (27, 28)
1961–63	Paul's first Roman captivity (28.16)
c. 1962	**Philemon**
c. 1962	**Colossians**
c. 1962	**Ephesians** (to churches in Asia Minor)
c. 1963	**1 Timothy** (between first and second captivities)
c. 1963	**Titus** (between first and second captivities)
c. 1963–65	Paul's second captivity
c. 1965	**2 Timothy**
c. 1965	**Hebrews** (in Italy, by Apollos?, towards end of Paul's life?)
c. 1965	Paul executed (during Nero's reign, 63–67)
c. 1970	**The Gospel according to Mark** ("John Mark," Peter's interpreter, in Rome? to Gentile Christians)
c. 1975	The Gospel according to Luke; Acts (the physician, friend of Paul)
c. 1985	The Gospel according to Matthew (in Jewish milieu)
1990s	The Gospel according to John (the "beloved disciple")— 19.35; 21.24—himself? in Ephesus?)
1990s	**The Book of Revelation**

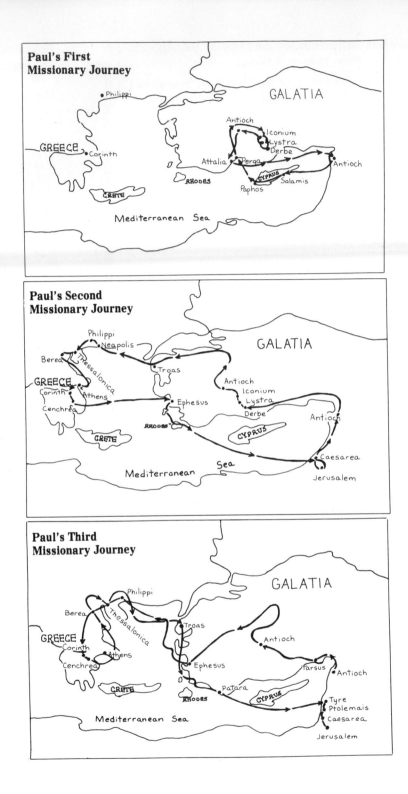

Paul's First Missionary Journey

GALATIA

Philippi

GREECE
Corinth

Antioch
Iconium
Lystra
Derbe
Attalia Perga
Antioch
RHODES CYPRUS
Paphos Salamis
CRETE
Mediterranean Sea

Paul's Second Missionary Journey

GALATIA

Philippi
Neapolis
Berea
Thessalonica
Troas
GREECE
Corinth
Athens
Antioch
Iconium
Lystra
Ephesus
Derbe
Cenchrea
Antioch
RHODES
CYPRUS
CRETE
Caesarea
Mediterranean Sea
Jerusalem

Paul's Third Missionary Journey

GALATIA

Philippi
Berea
Thessalonica
Troas
GREECE
Corinth
Antioch
Athens
Cenchrea
Ephesus
Tarsus
Patara
Antioch
CRETE
RHODES
CYPRUS
Tyre
Ptolemais
Caesarea
Mediterranean Sea
Jerusalem

182

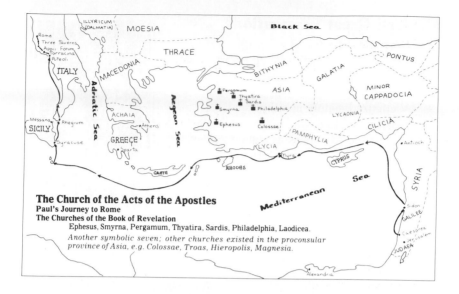

The Church of the Acts of the Apostles
Paul's Journey to Rome
The Churches of the Book of Revelation
 Ephesus, Smyrna, Pergamum, Thyatira, Sardis, Philadelphia, Laodicea.
 Another symbolic seven; other churches existed in the proconsular
 province of Asia, e.g. Colossae, Troas, Hieropolis, Magnesia.

God's Irresistible Call

In the apocryphal *Acts of St. Thomas* there is a story that Thomas was missioned to India, and when he resisted, Christ appeared and sold him as a slave to an Indian prince who was visiting Jerusalem. Thus is was that he went to India. As time went on, he baptized the prince as well as many others, and there was martyred finally at Meliapore.

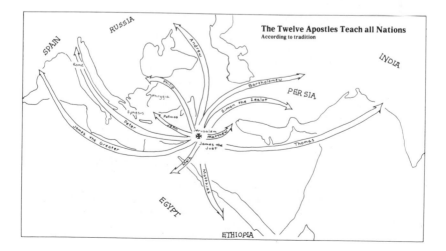

The Twelve Apostles Teach all Nations
According to tradition

The Ten Great Persecutions

S·Stephanus · S·Laurentius

1. **Nero** (54–68)
   Accused Christians of being enemies of mankind.
2. **Domitian** (81–96)
   Victimized mainly nobility.
3. **Trajan** (98–117)
   Considered Christians as state enemies.
4. **Marcus Aurelius** (161–180)
   Confiscated Christian's property and tortured his victims.
5. **Septimus Severus** (193–211)
   Outlawed conversion to Christianity.
6. **Maximius Thrax** (235–238)
   Persecuted clergy.
7. **Decius** (249–251)
   Ordered the death of any citizen refusing to sacrifice to the state gods.
8. **Valerian** (253–260)
   Outlawed Christian assembly, persecuting mainly clergy and nobility.

The Tears of St. Lawrence

On August 10, A.D. 258, the deacon Lawrence was strapped to a gridiron and burned. As has been repeated so often, he asked to be turned when "one side was done." It so happens that on the three nights following this anniversary each year, the early morning sky is streaked with one of the most spectacular meteorite showers of the year. Such celestial events were never meaningless to the medieval mind: these "falling stars", falling at the rate of more than one every minute, were called the "tears of St. Lawrence," spangling the dark sky like drops of glimmering gold, shed from heaven for the cruelty of humanity.

---

9. **Aurelian** (270–275)
   Allowed the anti-Christian laws, although without seriously enforcing them.
10. **Diocletian** (284–305)
   Reversing Aurelian's policy, engineered the bloodiest Roman persecution.

The Edict of Milan (313) gave Christianity legal status, ending the age of persecution.

THE EPISCOPACY

Bishop
The "ordinary" of a diocese with personal jurisdiction as a successor of the apostles over people within his diocese or "see."

Pope
The bishop of Rome, successor of St. Peter, first among equals (bishops) and visible head of the Catholic Church

The Universal Hierarchy
Entered through episcopal (bishop) ordination, the fullness of Holy Orders.

The Holy See
The papacy: the office in terms of its jurisdiction and court.

Miter and crosier symbols of episcopal office

No Pope Peter

The tradition of popes changing names upon election traditionally dates from Sergius IV (1009–1012). The story retold is that his name was Peter di Porca, and he changed it, deferring to St. Peter, considering it unseemly to style himself Peter II. Actually, prior to this, some popes had changed their names to drop a name of pagan origin. The tradition allows pontiffs to show esteem for a predecessor, signal a goal or style they want to have, and demonstrate a total commitment to the office.

Species of Bishops

Patriarch

There are seven bishops, including the pope, who are called patriarchs. Historically, the patriarchates (jurisdictions) were Rome, Antioch, and Alexandria, plus Constantinople in 381 and Jerusalem in 451. The Eastern Rite Catholic patriarchs have jurisdiction over the faithful in their Churches throughout the world and are subject only to the Pope. Currently, there is an Eastern Patriarch in Alexandria for the Coptic Catholics; three in Antioch for the Syrian Catholics, the Greek Melkite Catholics, and the Maronite Catholics; in Babylon for the Chaldean Catholics and in Cilicia for the Armenian Catholics. Finally, there is a Latin Rite Patriarch in Jerusalem. All of the faithful in these jurisdictions are fully Catholic, sharing the doctrines and sacraments of the universal Church, although their liturgical rites are very different.

Archbishop

The leader of the principal see within a particular province (region, jurisdictional unit). Other sees (dioceses of the same region) are said to be suffragan to the archbishop, and so their bishops are suffragan to the archbishop. His immediate jurisdiction, however, pertains only to his own diocese. He is often called a metropolitan if he is an ordinary (and not merely titular or auxiliary) because of the importance of his see city.

Cardinal

An (arch) bishop of a higher rank, given special recognition/responsibility in the universal Church (with no increase in regional jurisdiction); a papal elector (their eligibility ceasing at age eighty). From Lt: *cardo* (hinge): that on which another thing depends, so "principal"; their red hat became customary after Innocent IV (1245), as they were ". . . ready to lay down their life for the Gospel." A "prince of the Church," because of his ecclesiastical equivalency to a prince in a monarchy. Cardinals in the privileged confidence of the pope are called *a latere* (ah LAH-tehr-eh) cardinals. It means "from the side." The designation of a cardinal *in pectore* ("in the breast") means it is still secret, and not yet publicly announced.

The Sacred College (College of Cardinals)

It has existed since the early church, though its exact origins are unclear. By the eleventh century, this was a body with great influence, the pope's principal advisors on both governance and doctrine. It included bishops, priests, and some deacons of Rome and surrounding dioceses. In the time of Pope Nicholas II (1509), cardinals became papal electors. Today the College still functions in an advisory capacity to the pope, and can have not more than 120 cardinals under age eighty, and thus eligible to elect a pope. (The "Consistory" is a Church court, commonly referring to the assemblage of cardinals presided over by the pope for deliberation; either secret, if only cardinals are present; semi-public, if bishops participate; or public, if other prelates are invited.)

Metropolitan (see *archbishop*)
An archbishop with suffragan bishops under him, the "metropolis" being the mother church of an area that includes other see churches. In the Greek Church, the hierarchy is patriarch, then metropolitan, then archbishop.

Primate
Formerly, a bishop with authority (though never according to canon law) over a national territory, and not merely over his own diocese/province; has authority for convoking and presiding over national councils, and hearing appeals. Today, only an honorific title.

Suffragan Bishop
A bishop not a metropolitan or archbishop, but relative to one. So called because they can be convened to give their "suffrage" (vote, consent, approval). Also a generic designation for a bishop without his own see specifically auxiliary, coadjutor, and titular bishops.

Titular Bishop
Has no regional jurisdiction. Such a bishop may be entitled *"in partibus infidelium,"* ("in the lands of the infidels") or simply *"in partibus,"* literally, designating a bishop with the title but not the jurisdiction of a particular area.

Vicar Apostolic
A bishop appointed to act as representative of the pope in an area not yet designated a diocese. (Originally a bishop to whom the pope delegated some of his jurisdiction.)

Auxiliary Bishop
Aid to a bishop; without personal jurisdiction (that is, not an ordinary).

Coadjutor Bishop (Lt: *ad, juvare,* to help)
An auxiliary with right to succession.

The Five Patriarchates

Christianity was first established in the eastern (Greek) part of the Roman Empire. (Note the Greek language of the Christian Scriptures and early Christian writing.)

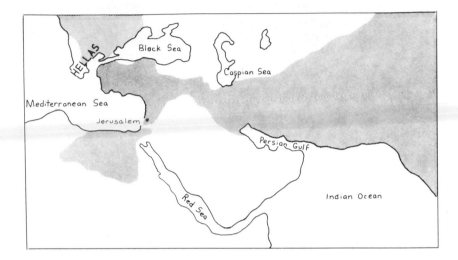

Peter and Paul took Christianity to Rome. In A.D. 330 Constantine made Constantinople the capital of the Roman Empire, raising its position as a see city.

By the end of the fourth century, Christendom was dominated by these five great centers and their bishops (patriarchs):

Alexandria
Antioch
Constantinople
Jerusalem
Rome

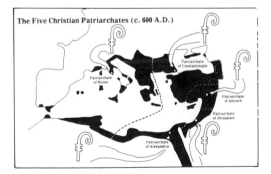

The Five Christian Patriarchates (c. 600 A.D.)

In A.D. 395 the Empire was divided into East (with the ecclesiastical seat in Constantinople) and West (with the seat in Rome).

Thereafter, the patriarchates of Antioch, Jerusalem, and Alexandria gradually came to acknowledge the leadership of Constantinople. Their loss of universal Christian prominence was complete when absorbed by Islam (A.D. 632–638).

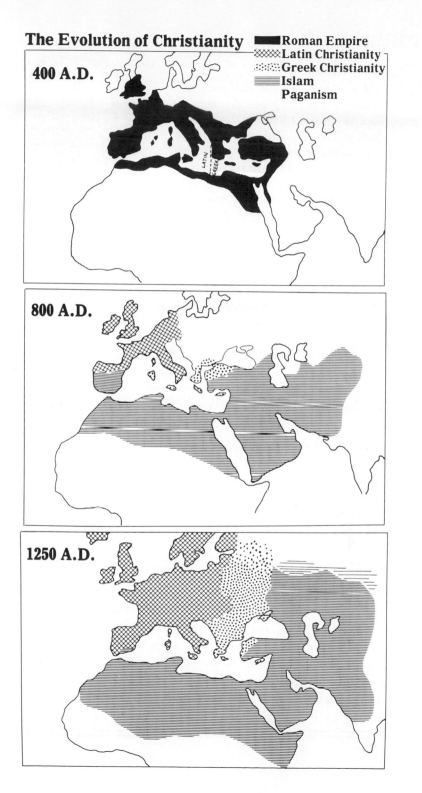

The Evolution of Christianity

Roman Empire
Latin Christianity
Greek Christianity
Islam
Paganism

400 A.D.

LATIN
GREEK

800 A.D.

1250 A.D.

THE PAPACY

Papal Election

A **conclave,** since 1274, is the enclosure of cardinals to elect a pope. Changes by Pope Paul VI included limiting the number of electors to 120 and, if no one is elected in three days, requiring a day of prayer, allowing for conversation among electors. There was a tradition that cardinals in conclave were reduced to bread and water rations if a pope was not elected in five days. In 1271, the deadlocked cardinal electors were finally locked in with no supplies.

Tiara and crossed keys—symbols of papal office

The **chamberlain** becomes head of the college and directs the conclave, *januis clausis* (behind closed doors), at the death of a pope.

A **papabile** is one likely to be pope.

The **Sistine Chapel** is the locale of the conclave.

When all the **canopies** except the one of the newly elected are lowered over their chairs, a cardinal knows he is elected pope.

Black smoke emerging from the Vatican indicates no decision; white smoke, *"Habemus papam"* ("We have a pope").

The **pontificate,** or patriarchate, of a pope begins when he accepts election.

Resignation of a pope would be to the college of cardinals.

An **interregnum** (*"sede vacante"*) is the period between the death of a pope and the election of a successor.

"Sic transit gloria mundi"

Thomas a Kempis spoke thus, in commenting on the vanity (fleeting nature) of human life, "thus passes the glories of world." It has been preserved in its Latin condition in the papal coronation: a rope bundle is burned and, as the flame dies, the words are spoken, *"Pater Sancte"* (Holy Father), *sic transit gloria mundi."*

Popes of the First Century

1. St. Peter (Simon Bar-Jona); Bethsaida, Galilee; d. about A.D. 67
2. St. Linus; Tuscia; 67–76
3. St. Anacletus (Cletus); Rome; 76–88
4. St. Clement; Rome; 88–97
5. St. Evaristus; Greece; 97–105

Apostolic Succession

The continuity of shepherding responsibility given by Christ to the Church leadership (Jn 20.23, Mt 28.19); hence, the unbroken line of authority passing from the apostle Peter to each of his legitimate successors. This empowers ("legitimizes") the sacramental ministry of a parish priest since he is ordained by a bishop who is consecrated by a successor of St. Peter.

Popes of the Twentieth Century

256. Leo XIII (Gioacchino Pecci); Carpineto, Anagni, Italy; 1878–1903
257. St. Pius X (Giuseppe Sarto); Riese, Treviso, Italy; 1903–1914
258. Benedict XV (Giacomo della Chiesa); Genoa, Italy; 1914–1922
259. Pius XI (Achille Ratti); Desio, Milan, Italy; 1922–1939
260. Pius XII (Eugenio Pacelli); Rome, Italy; 1939–1958
261. John XXIII (Angelo Giuseppe Roncalli); Sotto il Monte Bergamo, Italy; 1958–1963
262. Paul VI (Giovanni Battista Montini); Concessio, Brescia, Italy; 1963–1978
263. John Paul I (Albino Luciani); Forno di Canale, Italy; 1978
264. John Paul II (Karol Wojtyla); Wadowice, Poland; 1978–

A Distinctive Pope

Our 264th pope is the youngest pope chosen since 1846 (fifty-eight years of age in 1978), the only pope elected from a Communist country, the only Polish pope, the first pope since Pius II in the fifteenth century to be a man of letters and the first non-Italian pope since the Dutch Adrian VI who died in 1523 (fifty-eight of the 264 popes have been non-Italian, including fifteen Greeks, fifteen Frenchmen, six Germans, and an Englishman).

A Resigning Pope

In 1294, Pope St. Celestine V (Peter di Morone), without precedent, voluntarily resigned after five months in office. He was an eighty-four-year-old hermit when elected pope to follow Nicholas IV. Very soon he realized that he lacked the competence and experience for such a leadership task, and was unable to cope with the pressure from secular rulers. He therefore issued a constitution declaring a pope's right to resign, which was accepted by the cardinals. Two years later he died and, in 1313, was canonized.

First, Last and Only Popes

John II, 533—first pope to change his name (His given name having been Mercury, the name of a pagan deity)

Adrian IV 1154–59—only English pope ("Nicholas Breakspear")

Gregory XII, 1415—last pope to resign

Felix V, 1440—last anti-pope

Adrian VI, 1522–23—last non-Italian pope (from Utrecht, Holland)

Marcellus II, 1555—last pope to keep his own name (Marcello Cervini)

Pius X, 1903–14—last pope to be canonized (beatified in 1951)

John XXIII, 1958–63—was an army chaplain and a World War II corpsman

Paul VI, 1963—first pope to address a United Nations General Assembly

Paul VI, 1963–75—canonized most saints (to date)

John Paul II—only Polish pope and first non-Italian in 450 years

Papal Titles

Pope (A.S. "papa"; Gk *pappas,* childlike "father")
Not uncommon designation in the early Church, Leo the Great (440–61) first using it officially, Gregory VII (1073–85) first reserving it to the bishop of Rome; paternal authority, after the example of Christ.

Bishop of Rome
"First among equals" (*primus inter pares*), paradoxically; the pope is a bishop, the fullest office of Holy Orders. Vatican I defined that the successors of Peter in primacy are the bishops of Rome.

Vicar of Christ
As representative of Christ, the Head of the Church; adopted by Innocent III (1198).

Successor of St. Peter, Prince of the Apostles

Supreme Pontiff of the Universal Church

Pontiff: Lt, *pons, pontis* (bridge); *facio, fecit* (to do, make); so *pontifex* (pontiff): bridgebuilder. Originally any bishop, "one in charge of the bridges" (high priest), later reserved for the supreme or sovereign (first) pontiff (the bishop of Rome). With antecedents in the Roman religious office of *pontifex maximus,* bridge builders between gods and men.

Patriarch of the West (see "Patriarch")

Primate of Italy (see "Primate")

Archbishop and Metropolitan of the Roman Province

Servus servorum Dei (Lt: "servant of the servants of God')'
First used by Pope St. Gregory the Great (590–604), after Mk 10.44; in common use after Pope Gregory VII (1073–1085).

Sovereign of Vatican City

Dear Pope

Pope John Paul II gets more letters than any of his predecessors, from a whole range of correspondents: some, like heads of state, send communication by way of diplomatic pouch. Others deliver themselves, by way of the Swiss guards at the bronze door, the main entrance to the Apostolic Palace where the pope lives. Most, however, simply mail their letters to the pope like any other letter. It is the Vatican Secretariat of State who first receives them. Here they are sorted, divided mainly into eight language categories: Italian, English, French, Spanish, Portuguese, German, Polish, and Latin. Letters in other languages go to translators. Ultimately, almost all letters addressed to the pope go to him. The Secretariat staff, prior to delivering the pope's mail, sorts the letters into envelopes according to subject matter, and summarizes the contents on a paper attached to the envelope. (It takes nine priests working full time to read, summarize, and often respond to just the English-language letters. Only the Italian-language correspondence, with its greater volume, requires a larger staff.) Even letters destined for a specific office, like the Doctrine of the Faith, go to the pope if they are addressed to him. In most cases, letters are answered by the Secretariat of State, or by the Congregation which handles the topic of the letter. Personal responses from the pope are rare, usually to heads of state.

Papal Statements

Non Possumus

Spoken by the pope in response to a suggested innovation in doctrine—"We cannot." These words are from the Acts of the Apostles, when Peter and John were asked to stop preaching.

Anathema
Solemn condemnation, Scriptural in origin (see St. Paul: "If anyone preaches to you a gospel besides what you have received, let him be anathema," Gal. 1.9). Declares that some teaching or position contradicts Catholic faith and doctrine. The form *anathema sit* (let him be anathema, excommunicated) probably first used in fourth century.

Apostolic Brief
Less formal than a Bull, regarding less serious matters; sealed with a representation of St. Peter landing his fishermen's net.

Apostolic Bull
Solemn, formal document regarding serious matters, it opens with the current pope's name, *"Servus servorum Dei"* (Servant of the Servants of God) and *"ad perpetuam rei memoriam"* (Lt: for the perpetual remembrance of the thing). It closes with its place of origin, date of issue and the year of the current pontificate. So-called because of the leaden seal *(bulla,* Lt) on the document.

Encyclical
Letter (usually doctrinal) to universal college of bishops or certain nation's bishops.

Great Social Encyclicals

Rerum Novarum (Leo XIII, 1891)	Condition of the Working Class
Quadragesimo Anno (Pius XI, 1931)	Renewal of the Social Order
Mater et Magistra (John XXIII, 1961)	Christianity and Social Progress
Pacem in Terris (John XXIII, 1963)	Peace on Earth
Populorum Progressio (Paul VI, 1967)	Development of Peoples

Ex Cathedra (Lt: "from the chair")

The Church's visible seat of authority is the chair of St. Peter; this visible symbol is occupied day by day by his successor, the Bishop of Rome, exercising universal authority with his brother bishops.

Indult

The Holy See's temporary favor allowing a bishop to do something not otherwise allowed.

In petto (Italian; Lt: *in pectore,* in the breast)

Something done privately, or held in reserve; used for cardinals chosen but not yet announced.

Motu proprio (Lt: by one's own accord)

A letter which the pope himself writes, signs, and issues on his own initiative.

Pontifical Letter

Letter of explanation (of a certain doctrinal point), instruction, congratulation, and so forth.

Urbi et Orbi (Lt: *to the city*—Rome—and *to the world*)

The solemn papal blessing given from St. Peter's balcony on special occasions.

"Defender of the Faith"

This title, *"Fidei Defensor"* (abbreviated F.D.), is not one the pope takes; it's one the pope gives. Or gave. It is one of the many titles of the English Kings, first applied in 1521 by Pope Leo X to Henry VIII for his treatise *Assertio Septem Sacramentorum.* That was then. Come 1534, after continued conflict with papal power, he obtained the "Act of Supremacy" from Parliament creating a national church, "Anglican," apart from the Catholic Church, and appointed the king protector and sole supreme head of church and clergy of England. Thomas More, his chancellor, was executed for refusing to acknowledge this. His suppression of monasteries, confiscation of their properties, and beheading of two wives are other stories of the first Defender of the Faith.

Papal Places

Vatican City

The geo-political area, recognized by the Treaty of the Lateran (1929), including the buildings of the Holy See (109 acres, slightly less than a square mile). Napoleon had annexed the Papal States and made Pope Pius VII his prisoner, who excommunicated him. Its parish church is St. Ann's.

The Order of St. Gregory the Great

An order originally established by Pope Gregory XVI in 1831 to honor citizens of the Papal States. In modern times the Holy Father confers this order on those who are distinguished for personal character and reputation or for some significant accomplishment. It has civil and military divisions, and three classes of knights.

Vatican City coat of arms; similar to the pope's

Vatican (Lt: *Vaticanus,* a hill in Rome)
The papal palace and the popes' residence since the Avignon Papacy in the fourteenth century, before which the residency was at the Lateran. It has 10,000 rooms and hallways, and 997 stairways, including thirty hidden ones.

Lateran Palace

An edifice in Rome, used as the papal residence from the fourth century (when it was given to Pope Miltiades by Constantine) until the fourteenth century (when Pope Gregory XI returned from Avignon and took up residence at the Vatican). The Church of St. John Lateran adjoins it.

Vaticanus and *Quirinal* are two of the seven hills on which ancient Rome was built. "The Vatican" refers to papal authority and government whereas "the Quirinal" refers to Italian civil authority and government. There is also the Esquiline (of the miraculous fall of snow) and the Capitoline (one which the ancient Temple of Jupiter was built).

The *Scala Sancta*

The twenty-eight marble steps (now covered with wood) in the Lateran that lead to the papal chapel. Believed to be the steps of Pilate's praetorium, sanctified by Jesus' use during the passion. Brought to Rome by St. Helena, they are often climbed by pilgrims on their knees.

Swiss Guards and Designer Clothes

Since the fourteenth century, they are the official Vatican police officers and the pope's body guards. Their red, yellow, and blue uniforms were designed by Michelangelo. They number 110, plus six officers, their main responsibility being guarding the apostolic palaces. These soldiers are veterans of the Swiss military, and also diplomatic enough to handle the occasional charlatans who arrive in clerical clothing, insisting they are expected for dinner with the pope.

The Sistine Chapel *(from Pope Sixtus IV under who it was designed)*

Main chapel of Vatican palace and private chapel of the pope, whose altar (of mother of pearl) only he uses. Locale for papal election conclaves. Designed by Giovanni de Dolci; painted by Michelangelo, 1475–83; dedicated to Our Lady of the Assumption.

Peter's Pence

This is the annual universal collection among Catholics for the pope to help defray the costs of the pope's travels to the poorer Third World countries, and of the administration of the Holy See. The collection began in the ninth century when King Alfred the Great of England assessed a penny tax from each landowner in his realm. He rendered the proceeds to the pope as a form of financial aid. This tradition, discontinued at the Reformation, was reinstated by Pope Pius IX in the 1860s.

Castel Gandolfo

The papal summer residence named after the town in which it is located some fourteen miles southeast of Rome. Begun by Pope Urban VIII in the seventeenth century.

Papal Things

Flag
White and gold, with the Vatican seal on the white half.

Radio Station
HVJ (designed and supervised originally by Guglielmo Marconi).

Printing Press
"Vatican Polyglot Press."

Newspaper
A daily, *L'Osservatore Romano;* the first copy of the original edition was received by the Holy Father.

Harbor
The Civita Vecchia, northwest of Rome.

Phone
6982

Address
Palazzo Apostolico Vaticano, Vatican City, Europe 00121

Appearances
The Holy Father addresses visitors in St. Peter's Square on Sunday, at noon, with a general audience on Wednesdays.

Theologian ("Master of the Sacred Palace")
Always a Dominican.

Representatives
Apostolic Delegate (papal liaison to the Church in a given country) or nuncio (papal ambassador, diplomatic representative to a civil government).

Papal Coffin
According to the Vatican protocol, when a pope dies, the body, along with medals struck during his pontificate, are placed in a cypress coffin. This coffin is then placed in one of lead which bears the pope's coat of arms and death certificate. This is all housed in an oak casket. This is not to symbolize anything, but simply to conserve and preserve, and (ceremoniously) provide identification.

The Ecumenical (General) Councils

An Ecumenical Council is a gathering of the bishops of the world called together by the pope to share the responsibility of teaching and guiding the Church. There have been twenty-one such world wide councils.

198

1. Nicaea I, 325
2. Constantinople, 381
3. Ephesus, 431
4. Chalcedon, 451
5. Constantinople II, 553
6. Constantinople III, 680–681
7. Nicaea II, 787

These first seven, "The Seven Great Councils of the Early Church," are the only ones on which the Eastern and Western Churches agree; they are the only test of orthodoxy among the Eastern Churches separated from Rome.

8. Constantinople IV, 869–870
9. Lateran I, 1123
10. Lateran II, 1139
11. Lateran III, 1179
12. Lateran IV, 1215
13. Lyons I, 1245
14. Lyons II, 1274
15. Vienne, 1311–12
16. Constance, 1414–18
17. Basel-Ferrara-Florence, 1431–45
18. Lateran V, 1512–17
19. Trent, 1545–63
20. Vatican I, 1869–70
21. Vatican II, 1962–65

Documents of Vatican II

The Council was called by Pope John XXIII, who died before it was over; presided over by Pope Paul VI, who called its documents "the greatest catechism of our times"; lasted from 1962–1965 with about 2500 bishops attending. Also present were leading Catholic theologians and teachers (periti; peritus, singular), religious, and lay people to contribute to the discussions. Non-Catholic observers and delegates were also present and given the opportunity to speak.

Constitutions
The Church *(Lumen Gentium)*
Divine Revelation *(Dei Verbum)*
Liturgy *(Sacrosanctum Concilium)*
The Church in the Modern World *(Gaudium et Spes)*

Decrees
Communications, Ecumenism, Eastern Churches, Bishops, Priestly Formation, Religious Formation, Laity, Priests, Missions

Declarations
Education, Non-Christians, Religious Freedom

Coats of Arms

Emblems of nobility, the "achievements" are of military origin and a by-product of medieval feudalism. Consisting of certain tinctures (metals and colors) and figures, they were later adopted by ecclesiastical dignitaries and religious communities to symbolize special characteristics of the person or community. The arms of the (arch)diocese occupy the left side of the shield; personal arms, the right.

Papal

(Illustration at left): Tiara ("triple crown," "triregnum"); crossed keys, one gold, one silver, in saltire (crossed); no motto; first used officially in the thirteenth century.

Cardinal

(Second illustration at left): Red pontifical hat and fifteen red tassels in five rows on each side.

Archbishop

(Third illustration at left): Green hat and ten green tassels in four rows on each side; gold cross with double crossbeam, sometimes flanked by miter and crosier (curved outward).

Bishop

(Fourth illustration at left): Green hat and six green tassels in three rows on each side, gold cross with single crossbeam, sometimes flanked by miter and crosier (curved outward).

Bishop, Auxiliary or Coadjutor

Same as bishop/archbishop but no diocesan arms (personal arms displayed on whole shield).

Bishop (Archbishop), Eastern Rite

(Third illustration): Same except tassels are purple, and miter and crosier are in the eastern style.

Abbot

Same as bishop, (minus cross) except tassels are black (Benedictine) or white (Cistercian or Premonstratensian) and crosier is curved inward (with veil attached to knob).

Archdiocese, Diocese or Abbey
(Illustration at right): These arms appear as part of the individual's coat of arms (see above), or alone: miter surmounting shield, with no personal arms attached.

The "M" of the Archbishop

As a young Polish priest, he had consecrated himself to the Blessed Mother—as he would one day teach the world: "spiritually taking her into his home," as the apostle John had done. So it was not surprising, when he became an archbishop, that he would choose to recognize her with a large "M" on his coat of arms. But when Archbishop Karol Wojtyla was elected pope, the designers of the papal coat of arms objected. They insisted that a star or a crown would be more appropriate. In the argument that ensued, Pope John Paul II remained adamant. His coat of arms would still have the "M" of the houseguest of his soul.

Mottoes

Integral part of Catholic history, motivating the faithful (Some are cited first in their more common Latin original.)

Always go forward and never go back—Fr. Junipero Serro

Deo Favente (with God's favor)—Invoking or citing God's cooperation

Deo Gratias—We end the liturgy, as we could many undertakings, "thanks be to God"

Deo Iuvante, or *Juvante* (with God's Help)

Deo Volente, D.V. (God willing)

For the Greater Glory of God (*Ad Majorem Dei Gloriam*)—A.M.D.G.—St. Ignatius; the Jesuits

"God Wills It"

The faithful who gathered to hear Pope Urban II in 1095 at the Council of Clermont responded *"Deus Vult,"* which became the battle cry of the First Crusade, at the end of the eleventh century, which resulted in the recovery of the Holy Land from the Muslims.

Heraldic Cross Patee, fitched at the bottom, representing the crusaders, and the cross they would implant in the ground.

It is Better to Light One Candle than to Curse the Darkness—The Christophers

Lift up your Hearts (*Sursum Corda*)—from Christian heraldry; a phrase used in the liturgy (preface)

Praise Always to God (*Laus Deo Semper*)—Common for saints, especially monastics

Pray and Labor (*Ora et Labora*)—St. Benedict

There is Nothing without God (*Nihil sine Deo*)

To God Who is the Best and the Greatest (*Deo Optimo Maximo*— D.O.M.)—the Benedictines

To Restore all Things in Christ—Pope St. Pius X

Totally Yours (*Totus Tuus*)—Pope John Paul II

Non-Catholic Mottoes

Annuit Coeptis—"He (God) has favored our undertaking"— From Virgil's *Aeneid,* this saying appears on the reserve side of the United States' Great Seal, which appears on the one dollar bill. With such an application of the phrase, this country joins many others in believing that God takes special interest in particular societies.

Dominus Illuminatio Mea ("The Lord is My Light")—motto of Oxford University

Veritas Vos liberabit ("The Truth shall make you free")—Johns Hopkins University

Insignia (The Traditional Ceremonial)

Episcopal

Buskins—decorative stockings

Cappa Magna—cape with trim and silk or fur-lined hood

Crosier (late Lt: *crocia,* crook)—pastoral staff; turned outward when carried within his diocese, inward when without; (since the eleventh century the pope has not carried one)

Dalmatic—squarish, chasuble-like garment worn over the alb; proper to a deacon

Gloves

Gremial veil—lap cloth (used during ordinations)

Mantelletta—knee-length, sleeveless vestment of silk or wool

Miter (Gk: headband, turban)—ceremonial headgear (for abbots too): folding, two-piece stiffened hat of silk or linen, joined with soft material allowing it to be open or folded flat; usually with two fringed lappets (*"infulae"*) hanging on the back; removed for prayer; according to occasion/liturgical season, either: (1) Golden, (2) Precious or (3) Simple (white, formerly for use on Good Friday/funerals)

Morse—ornamental clasp for a cope

Mozzetta—short, front-buttoning cape

Pectoral Cross—necklace cross (in common use since seventeenth century)

Ring—gold, third finger right hand; formerly kissed respectfully by one on bended knee; formerly with an amethyst stone

Bishop in violet mozzetta over rochet and violet cassock; zuchetto on head.

Bishop in violet mantelletta (faced in red) over rochet and violet cassock; violet biretta on head.

Archbishop in full pontificals with miter on head and crosier in hand. Pallium is over chasuble, under it is dalmatic and tunic.

Rochet—surplice-like vestment of linen (or lawn)
Sandals
Skullcap—"zuchetto"; purple (red for cardinals, white for popes)
Staff—"crosier" (late Lt: crocia, crook)
Tunicle—chasuble-like vestment, formerly proper to a sub-deacon

Archepiscopal (same as episcopal, plus:)
Cross—having an additional, and shorter, crossmember
Pallium

Papal
Epigonation—Eucharistic vestment, representing the spiritual sword of
  justice: embroidered, stiff garment hanging diamond-shaped from
  the waist to below the right knee; (actually Greek and Armenian
  rite, but worn also and only by the pope in the West)
Falda—white silk vestment from the waist to ground, over cassock
Fanon—scarf-like vestment
Ring (of the Fisherman)—bestowed at election, inscribed with St. Peter
  fishing; used for sealing documents; ceremoniously broken at his
  death
Sedia Gestatoria—portable throne
Subcinctorium—broad, embroidered silk maniple
Tiara—beehive-shaped triple crown of richly ornamented gold cloth,
  topped by a gold globe and cross

The Papal Crown

The tiara is a development of the medieval papacy, above and beyond the miter of other bishops (and popes of the first five centuries); symbolic interpretations of its significance abound, but primarily it represents his triple authority as pontiff: serving the Church militant, suffering and triumphant; according to another interpretation, the first circlet symbolizes the pope's universal episcopate, the second, his primacy of jurisdiction, the third, his temporal influence. Formerly the crowning marked the beginning of a pontificate, a tradition changed by Pope John Paul I (1978) and continued by Pope John Paul II (1978–) when they were invested with the pallium instead. The tiara does remain part of the papal coat of arms and Vatican flag.

Religious Life

Religious Order

Generally: a community of men or women (usually under solemn vows as priests, brothers, or nuns) living a stable manner of life in which they observe the evangelical counsels by means of the vows of poverty, chastity, and obedience. (Technically, one bound only by simple vows is called a sister.) Not attached to a diocese (as a so-called secular or "diocesan" priest is), they usually live a communal life with a specific apostolate and a particular spirituality. Traditionally they have been either active or contemplative, and wore the distinctive "habit."

"Exclaustration" is permission for religious to live outside the community for a specified time (with vows still binding).

A religious order is technically distinct from a religious institute, though basically equivalent, distinguished only by certain points of canon law.

Second Order

Feminine counterpart of a religious order whose founder first established an order of men (notably Franciscans and Dominicans).

Third Order

Association established by a religious order; originated by Franciscans and Dominicans in the thirteenth century. Today there are many, and either:

1. Regular (T.O.R).—religious (in community, under vows)
2. Secular ("Tertiaries")—lay

Brother/Nun

Member of a religious order/community who has taken solemn vows. (Technically, one bound only by simple vows is called a sister.)

Religious Rule

The plan of life and discipline by which religious strive to Christian perfection and accomplish the mission proper to their order.

Vows

Solemn vows include those taken by members of religious orders after a period of temporary, simple vows. They are absolute, irrevocable vows under which ownership of property is prohibited and marriage is invalid. Simple vows, whether temporary or perpetual, allow ownership of personal property. Nuns tend to live cloistered lives, while sisters usually pursue ministries outside the convent.

Canons

Certain orders of religious men distinct from monks because of certain duties, often attached to a particular church (often a cathedral), shrine, or ecclesiastical function. They are either:

1. "Regular"—Priests under public religious vows, living in a religious order community. (Any cathedral to which they were attached was "monastic.")

2. "Secular"—Priests in community, but not under public vows or of a religious order. (Any cathedral to which they were attached was "diocesan.")

Scapular

Primarily and originally a garment, the frock-like working habit of the Benedictines; a long, shoulder-width piece of material, put on over the head, that would cover a person's front and back, like a durable apron. With the rise of the third orders in the thirteenth century, it evolved into a more symbolic garment ("the yoke of Christ"), a monastic overtone in many religious habits. It was modified, becoming part of the habit, then worn under clothing (two small double squares of cloth suspended on strings). Finally, a "lay" scapular evolved, a devotional article worn by anyone, but especially as a sign of membership in a confraternity; two small rectangles of cloth worn front and back, connected by ribbons and worn under clothing.

The Five Scapulars

Special devotion to five of the eighteen most familiar that are Church approved:

1. The Brown Scapular of Our Lady of Mt. Carmel
2. The Red Scapular of Christ's Passion
3. The Black Scapular of the Seven Sorrows of Mary
4. The Blue Scapular of the Immaculate Conception
5. The White Scapular of the Holy Trinity

The Brown Scapular (the most celebrated; "the scapular")
Worn by members of the Confraternity of Our Lady of Mt. Carmel. Associated with the Sabbatine (Saturday) Privilege which promises that the qualified wearer will be delivered from purgatory on the Saturday after death. This pious belief originated in a vision of Pope John XXII in 1322 (the documentation of which has been now judged to be spurious).

Our Lady of Mount Carmel

This is the patronal feast of the Carmelite order. Pious legend tells how in the thirteenth century (the "Age of Faith") the Carmelite, St. Simon Stock, asked Mary to grant a special privilege to his order. And so it happened that on a certain day the Blessed Virgin appeared to him, with a brown scapular in her hand, saying, "Here is the privilege I grant to you and to all children of Carmel. Whoever dies clothed in this habit shall be saved." This is the traditional prayer of Our Lady of Mount Carmel:

"O beautiful Flower of Carmel, most fruitful vine and splendor of heaven, O holy and singular one who brought forth the only Son of God while remaining still a pure virgin, watch over us this night. O Star of the Sea, O Mother of Christ, show us you are our mother, too."

The feast of Our Lady of Mt. Carmel is July 16, and it commemorates eighteen various scapular devotions, including the Brown scapular.

The Green Scapular
Not a scapular in strict sense, but more a "cloth medal." Immaculate Heart on one side, prayer on the other; special efficacy bringing the lapsed back to practice of the faith.

Scapular Medal
In 1910 authorized by Holy See as a substitute for scapular (that is, with same privileges attached). Sacred Heart on one side, Mary on the other.

The Ascetic St. Giles

The story goes that Giles, a hermit, was accidentally wounded in the knee by Childeric, the King of France, who was out hunting. Giles remained crippled for life because he refused treatment for the injury "that he might better mortify the flesh."

He is pictured with a hind, alluding to the form which providence took for him in his asceticism: to his cave by the mouth of the Rhone a "heaven sent hind" would come daily to give him milk.

Historically, churches dedicated to him were often ones on a city's outskirts, even outside its walls, thus the only churches accessible for cripples and beggars who were not allowed in the city.

A. Anchorites (Contemplatives)

Gk: *recluse;* hence one who retires from world activity to contemplation. The original "monks" (Gk: *monachos,* living alone, solitary).

1. **Hermits**
   Withdrawing to desert places, living in essential simplicity, subsisting on manual labor; for example, the Augustinian Recollects (Discalced hermits); see St. Anthony, first famous hermit.
2. **Anchorites**
   Most radical, solitary, with only the essentials of food and cover.

Stylites or Pillar Ascetics

Ascetical zealots of the early and medieval Church (chiefly in Syria) who confined themselves to the top of pillars. Especially Simeon Stylites of Syria, (390–459) who reputedly spent forty years on pillars, each higher and narrower, the last being sixty-six feet high. Also Daniel the Stylite of Constantinople (d. 494) who lived thirty-three years on a pillar, often nearly blown off by the storms of Thrace.

B. Cenobites (Monastics)

Lt: *Coenbium,* monastery; Gk: *Koinos* common; *bios,* life.

A monk or nun living in a religious community. Most are called monks, even though historically (and etymologically) this meant a solitary religious; now monks lived in common in monasteries, taking the three vows according to a specific rule. St. Pachomius (290–346), an Egyptian, is the founder of cenobitic life in the East, having drawn up the first systematic rule of life for a religious community; St. Basil (329–379) modified it; St. Benedict, whose Rule developed it, fitted it to the West.

Generally, cenobites are members of these three orders (and four smaller ones):

1. **Benedictine Monks** (Black Monks)
    St. Benedict, c. 530, founder at Subiaco and Monte Cassino; sanctifying the Church's day (Liturgy of the Hours); studying, teaching, and laboring.

Vow of Stability

An oath taken under the Rule of St. Benedict to stay attached to the monastery of one's profession (thus fostering, in the spirit of St. Benedict, unity around one abbot and continuity of each monastery as a family).

---

2. **Carthusian Monks**
    Founded by St. Bruno of Cologne, about 1086, when he retired with six companions to the solitude of LaGrande Chartreuse, northeast of Grenoble.
3. **Cistercian Monks** (a reform of the Benedictines)
    Founded in Burgundy in 1098 by Robert, Benedictine abbot of Moleme, at Citeaux ("Cistercian") as a reform of the Benedictines. Sometimes called "Bernardines" after their patron St. Bernard of Clairvaux (about 1200).
4. **Trappists**
    A reformed branch of the Cistercians originated in France in 1098 under the leadership of St. Robert Moleme and St. Stephen Harding. After 1664 the name "Trappist" became common, with the reforms instituted by Armand Jean le Bouthillier de Rance (1626–1700) at the order's monastery of La Trappe in Normandy. Rance, imposing a strict rule of fasting, prayer, meditation, and manual labor, believed monasticism should be basically penitential.

5. **Basilian Monks**

   A general name for various religious institutes who have inherited the spirit of St. Basil (329–379), though with no uniform rule. There are five distinct Basilian orders of men and four congregations of women. It has been said that it is "an order from which have come fourteen popes, 1800 bishops, 3000 abbots and 11,000 martyrs."

6. **Premonstratensians** (Norbertine Fathers)

   A cloistered order of Augustinian canons founded by St. Norbert (1120) in the diocese of Laon, France. So-called because in a vision "a place (meadow) was pointed out" *(pre 'montre'; pratum monstratum)*. Inspired by and imitating the Cistercian ideal, by taking the more flexible Augustinian Rule instead of the Benedictine. As "canons" they were clergy living in community, and not monks.

7. **Augustinian Canons**

   An order of men founded by Ivo, Chartres bishop in the eleventh century, following the traditional Rule of Augustine.

C. Mendicants (Friars; Lt: *frater,* brother)

(Lt: *mendicus,* beggar; an infirm, wretched person)

An order that does not own property in common, but is required to work or beg for their living; also not bound to one monastery by a vow of stability.

The California Missions

There were many parish centers established along the west coast among the American Indians by Catholic missionaries from Spain. Between 1769 and 1845, it was followers of Francis who founded the missions in Upper California along the *El Camino Real* ("The Royal Road"). Although generally later than those the Jesuits and Dominicans in "Lower California" (Mexico), these twenty-one of the Franciscans are best known; namely, from south to north and about a day's journey apart:

San Diego	Santa Inez	Santa Cruz
San Luis Rey	Purisima Concepcion	San Juan Bautista
San Juan Capistrano	San Luis Obispo	Santa Clara
San Gabriel	San Miguel	San Jose
San Fernando	San Antonio de Padua	San Francisco
San Buenaventura	Soledad	San Rafael
Santa Barbara	San Carlos or Carmelo	San Francisco Solano

Originally the name only applied to Franciscans and Dominicans. In time, the name and privileges were extended to Carmelites (1245), Hermits of St. Augustine (1256) and Servites (1424). Later, other orders were also accorded the title.

1. **Franciscans** (OFM—Order of Friars Minor) Founded by Francis of Assisi in 1209; "Gray Friars" because of the indeterminate color of habit (which is now brown).
    a. Friars Minor (OFM) Keeping the radical rule of St. Francis including poverty, abstinence, and preaching.
    b. Friars Minor Conventual (OFM Conv.) Modified rule; relaxed rule about holding property; habit: black tunic, white cord.
    c. Friars Minor Capuchin (OFM Cap.) (Lt: *capuc*e, pointed cowl) Most radical, established in 1525; relying on begging of lay brothers. Franciscan Nuns

    Instituted by St. Francis in 1212; named after the first abbess, Clare of Assisi, (hence Poor Clares, or Clares); through reforms: Colettines, Gray Sisters, Capuchi Nuns, Sisters of the Annunciation, Conceptionists, Urbanists.

St. Clare receiving the blessing of St. Francis on the Poor Clares

2 **Dominicans**—(OP—Order of Preachers) "Friars Major"; founded by St. Dominic in 1215; "Black Friars," from their black cloaks; one of the Church's intellectual pillars; personified in the renowned Dominican Thomas Aquinas. "Hounds of the Lord" (*dominican*s).

3. **Carmelites** Organized as mendicant friars by St. Simon Stock (d. 1265); "White Friars," because of the color of their habit.
    a. "The Order of Our Lady of Mt. Carmel" Founded by St. Berthold about 1154 in Palestine; rule set down in 1209; claiming continuity with a rule given by John, patriarch of Jerusalem (about 400), and the record of Elijah's life on Mt. Carmel. Their ancestors include hermits on Mt. Carmel from ancient times.

St. Dominic

b. Discalced Carmelites (Lt: *calceos,* shoe; hence "barefooted") Carmelite nuns following the reforms in the order by Teresa of Avila (1515–82); and men following John of the Cross (1542–91). There was an independent Calced branch also.

St. Francis Xavier, great pioneer missionary to the East Indies and Japan; one of the first seven Jesuits who dedicated themselves to God at Montmartre in 1534.

4. **Augustinians**
   This is a generic name for many institutes (orders) whose religious life is based on the Rule of St. Augustine (d. 430). There are fourteen distinct Augustinian communities, including hermits (or friars), which included Martin Luther.

5. **Servites** ("Order of the Servants of the Blessed Virgin Mary")
   Founded in Florence in 1233 by seven city councilors (canonized as "The Seven Holy Founders").

6. **Jesuits** (Lt: *Jesus* plus *-ite* suffix meaning "associated with")
   The Society of Jesus (S.J.), founded by St. Ignatius Loyola in 1513 ("We are a little battalion of Jesus"). First purposes were defending the faith in the wake of the break-up of the Church and evangelization among the unchurched. Their general has been referred to as "the black pope."

The Little Flower

Thérèse Martin entered a Carmelite convent at age fifteen. As Sister Therese of the Child of Jesus, she lived a hidden life. She was just twenty-four when she died. The world came to know her through her autobiography, *The Story of a Soul.* She described her life as "a little way of spiritual childhood." She lived each day with unshakable confidence in God's love. What matters in life is "not great deeds, but great love." "My mission—to make God loved–will begin after my death," she said. "I will spend my heaven doing good on earth. I will let fall a shower of roses." This is the reason St. Thérèse's emblem is a crucifix covered with a profusion of roses.

RITES OF THE CATHOLIC CHURCH

Not in the **liturgical** sense of rituals, but in the **ecclesial** sense of

— a special tradition
— a style or way of living Christianity
— a cultural mentality toward practicing the Gospel
— a community of faith with a distinct ancient tradition

There is a **Latin** Rite ("Roman", "Western") as well as various **Eastern** Rites.

These two basic "Churches," Latin and Eastern, are the same

— in one profession of faith,
— in one celebration of the seven sacraments ("mysteries"),
— in one hierarchical unity;

but are uniquely different

— in distinct approaches to theology, spirituality, liturgy, Church law;
— in particular cultural and linguistic influences;
— because of autonomy and independence.

Evolving throughout Church history, and based on the culture of a particular time, place and group of the faithful, these are all Catholic (in union with Rome). The distinction "Eastern" or "Western" depends on their area of origin within the Roman Empire. The Latin ("Roman") rite prevails in the Western Church (hence "Roman Catholic").

Western (Latin)

1. **Roman**
2. **Other minor**
   a. Of locales:
      Mozarabic (Toledo, Spain)
      Ambrosian (Milan, Italy)
   b. Of religious orders:
      Dominican, Carmelite, Carthusian

Eastern (There are more than 600,000 in the United States)

All have non-Catholic counterparts except Maronites. All are practiced in the United States except Alexandrian.

1. **Byzantine** (6,000,000) Used by fourteen major groups:

Albanian	Georgian	Italo-Albanian	Russian	Ukrainian
Bulgarian	Greek	Melkite	Ruthenian	Yugoslav
Byelorussian		Hungarian	Rumanian	Slovak

2. **Chaldean** (2,500,000)
   Chaldean in the Middle East, Europe, Africa, and the Americas; Syro-Malabarese in India
3. **Alexandrian** (2,000,000)
   Coptic in Egypt; Abyssinian in Ethiopia
4. **Antiochene** (1,900,000)
   Malankarese in India; Maronite worldwide (mainly Lebanon) Lebanese Syrian, Syria, Iran, Egypt, Turkey
5. **Armenian** (375,000)
   The Near East, Europe, Africa, the Americas, Australia

Catholics may fulfill worship obligations in any rite, with no restrictions.

European Co-Patrons

Pope John Paul II named SS. Cyril and Methodius "co-patrons" of Europe, along with beloved Benedict. Today, all the nations where these two evangelists and pastors brought the gospel and ministered are behind the Iron Curtain. They are the apostles of the southern Slavs, fathers of the Slavonic liturgy and patrons of Christian unity. From the capitals of the Greek alphabet, they invented the Cyrillic-glagolithic alphabet as a conveyor of the Byzantine liturgy and the Bible to the Serbs, Bulgarians, Ukrainians, and Russians.

Genealogy of Christian Churches/Nationalities/Liturgies

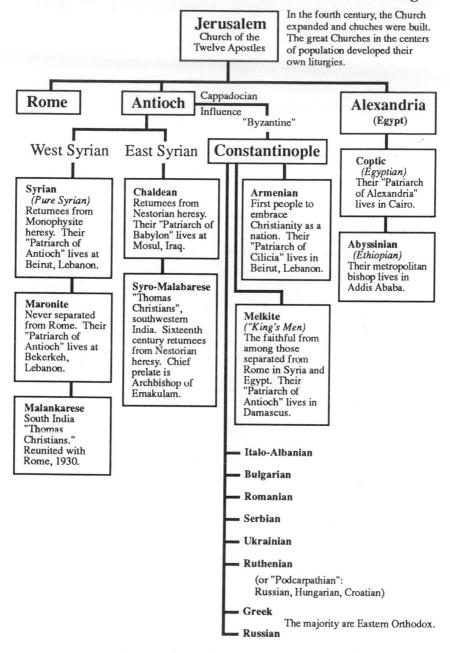

Jerusalem
Church of the
Twelve Apostles

In the fourth century, the Church expanded and chuches were built. The great Churches in the centers of population developed their own liturgies.

Rome

Antioch Cappadocian Influence "Byzantine"

Alexandria
(Egypt)

West Syrian   East Syrian   **Constantinople**

Syrian
(Pure Syrian)
Returnees from
Monophysite
heresy. Their
"Patriarch of
Antioch" lives at
Beirut, Lebanon.

Chaldean
Returnees from
Nestorian heresy.
Their "Patriarch of
Babylon" lives at
Mosul, Iraq.

Armenian
First people to
embrace
Christianity as a
nation. Their
"Patriarch of
Cilicia" lives in
Beirut, Lebanon.

Coptic
(Egyptian)
Their "Patriarch
of Alexandria"
lives in Cairo.

Abyssinian
(Ethiopian)
Their metropolitan
bishop lives in
Addis Ababa.

Maronite
Never separated
from Rome. Their
"Patriarch of
Antioch" lives at
Bekerkeh,
Lebanon.

Syro-Malabarese
"Thomas
Christians",
southwestern
India. Sixteenth
century returnees
from Nestorian
heresy. Chief
prelate is
Archbishop of
Ernakulam.

Melkite
("King's Men)
The faithful from
among those
separated from
Rome in Syria and
Egypt. Their
"Patriarch of
Antioch" lives in
Damascus.

Malankarese
South India
"Thomas
Christians."
Reunited with
Rome, 1930.

— **Italo-Albanian**

— **Bulgarian**

— **Romanian**

— **Serbian**

— **Ukrainian**

— **Ruthenian**

    (or "Podcarpathian":
Russian, Hungarian, Croatian)

— **Greek**

    The majority are Eastern Orthodox.

— **Russian**

Bishops of these chief centers are called **"patriarchs"**
Their territories are called **"patriarchates"**
Those in union with Rome: **Eastern Rite or Greek Rite Catholics**
Those not in union with Rome: **Eastern Orthodox**

Patriarch ("Prince of the Fathers")

Without jurisdiction except in virtue of some particular law. In the order of precedence:

Patriarch   **Primate**   **Metropolitan**   **Bishop**

In order of dignity, the patriarch of Rome precedes those of:

Armenian   **Maronite**   **Melkite**   **Chaldean**

Minor patriarchs:

Venice   **Lisbon**   **West Indies**   **East Indies**

Since the Eastern Schism their importance, except for that of the pope, has diminished. Rights:

1. Ordain all bishops of their patriarchate
2. Consecrate the holy chrism
3. Summon synods
4. Send the *omophorion* (pallium) to their metropolitans
5. Hear appeals from lower courts

They are the highest rulers in their churches, with only the pope having authority over them.

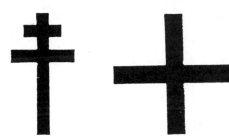

The Patriarchal Cross, the shorter crossmember representing the inscription INRI

Greek Cross

Russian Orthodox; lower crossmember representing footrest

Orthodox (or "Eastern Orthodox")

Eastern Rite Churches that are not Catholic. *So-called after the Great Schism (division, "cutting") of 1054, though a natural division of a sort existed long before the political. A milestone was the division of the Roman Empire into East and West by Theodosius in 395. Principally:*

1. **Greek Patriarchates** (Jurisdictions)
   Constantinople, Alexandria, Antioch, Jerusalem
2. **Russian Patriarchates** (Jurisdiction)
   Moscow

PROTESTANTISM

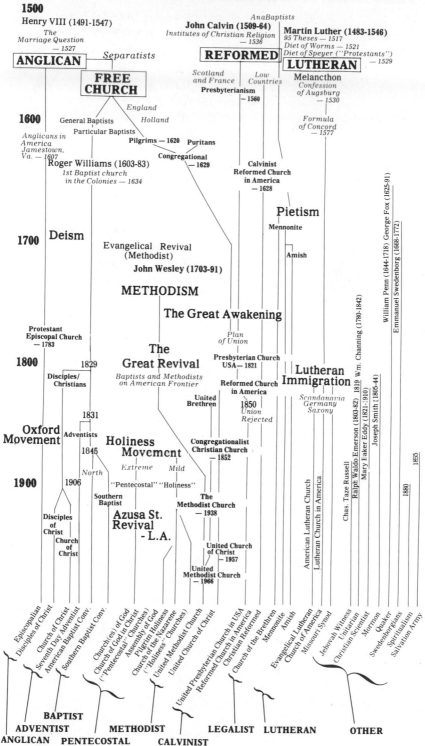

1500

Henry VIII (1491-1547)
The Marriage Question — 1527

ANGLICAN

Separatists

AnaBaptists
John Calvin (1509-64)
Institutes of Christian Religion — 1536

Martin Luther (1483-1546)
95 Theses — 1517
Diet of Worms — 1521
Diet of Speyer ("Protestants") — 1529

REFORMED

LUTHERAN

FREE CHURCH

Scotland and France
Presbyterianism — 1560

Low Countries

Melancthon
Confession of Augsburg — 1530

1600

England
General Baptists
Holland
Particular Baptists

Pilgrims — 1620   Puritans

Congregational — 1629

Formula of Concord — 1577

Anglicans in America Jamestown, Va. — 1607

Roger Williams (1603-83)
1st Baptist church in the Colonies — 1634

Calvinist Reformed Church in America — 1628

Pietism

Mennonite

1700   Deism

Evangelical Revival (Methodist)
John Wesley (1703-91)

Amish

METHODISM

The Great Awakening

Plan of Union

Protestant Episcopal Church — 1783

1800   1829
Disciples/ Christians

The Great Revival
Baptists and Methodists on American Frontier

Presbyterian Church USA — 1821

Reformed Church in America

Lutheran Immigration

Scandanavia Germany Saxony

United Brethren

1850
Union Rejected

1831

Oxford Movement   Adventists
1845

Holiness Movement
Extreme   Mild

Congregationalist Christian Church — 1852

1900   1906

"Pentecostal" "Holiness"

Southern Baptist

The Methodist Church — 1938

Disciples of Christ

Azusa St. Revival - L.A.

Church of Christ

United Church of Christ — 1957

United Methodist Church — 1966

William Penn (1644-1718)   George Fox (1625-91)

Emmanuel Swedenborg (1688-1772)

Wm. Channing (1780-1842)

1819

Ralph Waldo Emerson (1803-82)

Chas. Taze Russell

Mary Baker Eddy (1821-1910)

Joseph Smith (1805-44)

1855

1880

Episcopalian
Disciples of Christ
Church of Christ
Seventh Day Adventist
American Baptist Conv.
Southern Baptist Conv.
Church(es) of God
Church of God in Christ
("Pentecostal" Churches)
Assembly of God
Pilgrim Holiness
Church of the Nazarene
("Holiness" Churches)
United Methodist Church
United Church of Christ
United Presbyterian Church in USA
Reformed Church in America
Christian Reformed
Church of the Brethren
Mennonite
Amish
Evangelical Lutheran
Church of America
Missouri Synod
American Lutheran Church
Lutheran Church in America
Jehovah Witness
Unitarian
Christian Scientist
Mormon
Quaker
Swedenborgians
Spiritualism
Salvation Army

ANGLICAN   BAPTIST   ADVENTIST   PENTECOSTAL   METHODIST   CALVINIST   LEGALIST   LUTHERAN   OTHER

217

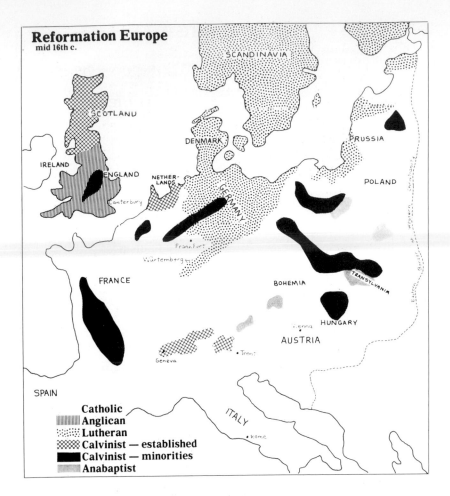

Reformation Europe
mid 16th c.

Catholic
Anglican
Lutheran
Calvinist — established
Calvinist — minorities
Anabaptist

Cuis regio eius religio—Literally, "Whose the region, his the religion," this means that, religiously, a territory would be what the leader was.

Protestant Confessions of Faith *(Principal)*

Lutheran Augsburg Confession (1530)

Calvinist Catechism of Geneva (1542–45)

Reformed Heidelberg Catechism (1563)

Reformed Belgic Confession (1561)

Anglican Thirty-nine Articles (1563)

Presbyterian Westminster Confession (1648)

Canterbury Cross

Catholicism in Mary's Land

In 1607, Lord Baltimore sent ships, the Ark and the Dove, to "the New World," Maryland to establish an English Catholic Plantation. In 1620, there were no Catholics leaving Southampton on the Mayflower. In 1776, one signer of the Declaration of Independence, and only one, was Catholic: Charles Carroll of Maryland. (In spite of the prejudice against Catholics at the time, "nativism," he served a career as a public servant. Called by some "the most distinguished Catholic layman in American history, Carroll was a dedicated patriot.) In the Revolutionary War, a Catholic, Casimir Pulaski, was an American general. It was not until 1831, during the presidency of Andrew Jackson, that a Catholic served in the United States cabinet: Attorney General Roger B. Taney. It was not until 1928 that a Catholic, Al Smith, ran for president, and 1960 before one, John Kennedy, won. In 1963, Pope John XXIII was posthumously awarded the U.S. Presidential Medal of Freedom. In the 101st Congress (1989) there were 138 Catholics: nineteen in the Senate and 119 in the House. Today, there are thirteen Catholics; including Junipero Serra, honored in statuary hall.

SACRED PLACES

Cathedral

The church of the diocesan Church; bishop's "chair" *("cathedra")*. It is traditionally located in the "see city" from which the diocese takes its name. The pastor of the cathedral is the ordinary (bishop or archbishop), hence, the priest who actually conducts the cathedral parish and its affairs has the title rector, not pastor or parish priest.

Pro-Cathedral

A church a bishop uses as a cathedral (for his *cathedra*) until a permanent, suitable church is built; with the same rights and privileges as a cathedral.

Church (A.S.: *circe;* Germ: *kiricha;* Gk: *kuriakon,* adjective being *kuriakos:* "of the Lord")
Gathering place for the local community's worship.

Basilica

A. One of the seven main churches of Rome ("major basilicas" and ancient pilgrimage churches.

    1. St. Peter (Basilica for the Patriarch of Constantinople)

    The largest church building in Christendom (covering about four acres), it was completed in 1626 and is maintained by the *sampietrini,* a permanent group of skilled workers and artisans representing every trade. It is fronted by "St. Peter's Square" which is encircled by the Bernini Colonnade (after its designer). Its bell, weighing around ten tons, is rung on special occasions.

    2. St. John Lateran—the "Mother Church;" archbasilica for the patriarch of the West (the pope)

    3. St. Mary Major Basilica—for the patriarch of Antioch

    4. Holy Cross in Jerusalem (within Rome proper)

    5. St. Paul's Outside the Walls—for the patriarch of Alexandria

    6. St. Lawrence Outside the Walls—for the patriarch of Jerusalem

    7. St. Sebastian Outside the Walls

B. Other churches

"Minor basilicas," given basilica status and ceremonial rights according to certain criteria. (In the fourth century it became customary to position a basilica so that its altar would be over the grave of a martyr.)

Basilica Honors and Accoutrements

The "pavilion" and bell are the two public indications of basilica status in a church's sanctuary. The pavilion, or umbrella, originates in the oriental courtesy and honor accorded a visiting potentate when appearing in public ceremony, shielding him from the sun. In deference to the pope on his occasional visits, Rome eventually adopted the device and practice for its basilicas; later, it spread to minor basilicas as well. The bell also probably has origins in the papal visit, for announcing his presence at the church door. It represents the building's belfry, being in effect a portable and elaborately mounted version, and is carried, along with the pavilion, in all processions. By virtue of its rank, a basilica also has the distinction of its own Coat of Arms ("Armorial Shield").

Chapel

Place of liturgical worship for a community other than a parish (school, hospital, convent, seminary, and so forth); a room within a building, or a separate building; Lt: *cappella,* originally a shrine for preserving the cloak (*cappa*) of St. Martin of Tours.

The Little Cloak

The word "chapel," interestingly, comes from the famous story of St. Martin and the beggar. "Cloak" in Latin is *cappa,* and *cappella* is the diminutive. In Old French the same word is *chapele,* and that was the name given to the oratory in which the alleged *chapele* of St. Martin was preserved. And so it is that a "chaplain," originally, was a "keeper of St. Martin's cloak."

Oratory

Place of prayer other than a parish church, designated by ecclesiastical authority for Mass and devotions; public, semi-public or private (which is a private family chapel).

Shrine

Designated devotional place, usually for reasons of historical event or specific association; for example, Lourdes (France), Fatima (Portugal), Montserrat (Spain), Guadalupe (Mexico). Focuses of pilgrimages and, commonly, approved miraculous phenomena.

Consecration of a Church

Only certain churches have the distinction of being a consecrated church, provided they (1) are debt free, and (2) have an altar based on a solid foundation resting on the ground. Twelve eye-level candle sconces and crosses, representing the teaching of the twelve apostles, encircling its inside walls, signal this particular dignity. Ceremonies of consecration include blessing the cornerstone, washing the altar (using wine) and using holy water (including salt, wine, and ashes). "Brands" on a church that has been consecrated are small crosses in circles. A church is *desecrated* by a notorious crime within its walls; for example, willful murder or use of holy things for unholy purposes. It must then be reconsecrated before it may be used for divine services.

Temple
The Jewish holy place; destroyed (as a specific place) in A.D. 66.

Synagogue
Gathering place of Jews for worship.

Mosque
Gathering place of Moslems for worship.

Pilgrimage

A journey to a holy place,

1. as a form of religious devotion,
2. as an act of penance (even barefooted) or
3. to seek the intercession of a saint.

A classic pilgrimage is the Moslem journey from Mecca to Medina to commemorate Muhammad's hegira or "flight."

Chief Western Pilgrimage Shrines

England	France	Germany	Italy	Spain
Canterbury	Fourviere	Oetting	Rome	Compostella
Walsingham	Puy	Zell	Loretto	Guadalupe
	St. Denis	Cologne	Assisi	Montserrat
		Trier		
		Einsiedeln		

The Three Primary Middle Ages' Pilgrimage Routes
Sign of a pilgrim Church, in search of a future and permanent city: popular in eleventh and twelfth centuries, slackened during Renaissance and Reformation, declined by eighteenth century.

1. To Jerusalem
    The Holy Land
2. To Rome
    Seat of the Western Church, rich in history of the martyrs
3. To Santiago de Compostella (Spain)
    Tomb of the apostle James, first of the apostles martyred

---

The Santiago Trail

This historically most popular pilgrimage, "pathway to conversion and extraordinary witness to faith" (Pope John Paul II), is a network of pilgrimage roads, five major routes with spacious and spectacular churches (like Vezelay, Poitiers, Aulnay, Le Puy, St. Sernin at Toulouse) and hospices all along its way.

The Pilgrimage of the Way of the Cross

A Christian's faith never required pilgrimage to Jerusalem as a Moslem's did to Mecca (commemorating Muhammad's hegira, or "flight"). However, the Holy Places have been transported to church walls throughout the Catholic world in the form of the Stations of the Cross. Although the *Stabat Mater* and Good Friday's "We adore thee, O Christ . . ." have become traditional, the devotion itself only requires the movement from one station to the next. The stations themselves, despite the elaborate depictions that have evolved, are mere wooden crosses.

Tradition says Mary daily retraced the *via dolorosa;* however, it was only in the Middle Ages that devotion to Christ's passion flourished. The early Christians' focus was on the risen Christ. The medieval mind, however, captivated by Christ's suffering humanity, sought to tread his very steps. Those with time and money could; others had the Holy Land brought to them, in the form of "stations," reproductions of the Holy Places in their own place.

The Franciscans, receiving custody of the Holy Places in 1343, stirred an interest in the passion among the faithful. The Franciscan St. Leonard of Port Maurice, the "preacher of the Way of the Cross," spread the devotion in the eighteenth century, making it possible even for non-Franciscan churches to have the stations (previously not allowed). From the beginning, there have been more and less than fourteen. In 1975, Pope Paul VI approved a new set of stations which includes a fifteenth, the resurrection.

Foderunt:manus:meas:et:pedes:meos.

Main Periods of Church Architecture

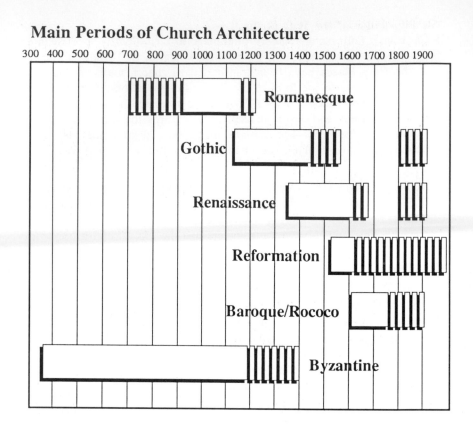

300 400 500 600 700 800 900 1000 1100 1200 1300 1400 1500 1600 1700 1800 1900

Romanesque

Gothic

Renaissance

Reformation

Baroque/Rococo

Byzantine

"Solomon, I Have Surpassed You"

Constantinople on the Bosporus was the capital of the Eastern Empire. It was there—modern day Istanbul, Turkey—that the emperor Justinian built, at a staggering cost, the Church of St. Sophia in the early sixth century. The most ambitious building ever undertaken, it was to be the greatest church of the Byzantine empire. Justinian himself apparently thought it was, reputedly proclaiming at its consecration, "Solomon, I have surpassed you." In 1453, this celebrated Christian church became an Islamic mosque as Constantinople fell to the Turks (which explains the Arabic texts of Islam and whitewashed mosaics).

Romanesque and Gothic

In these periods, the evolution of the window provides a way to date and name an architectural style.

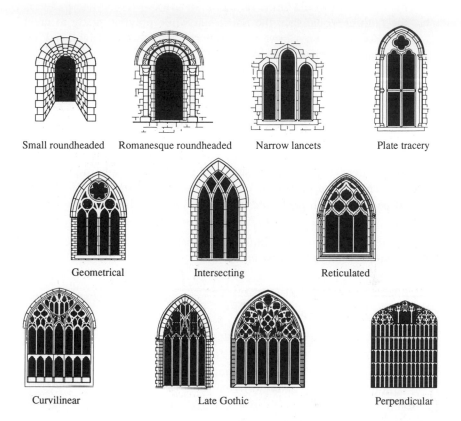

Small roundheaded   Romanesque roundheaded   Narrow lancets   Plate tracery

Geometrical   Intersecting   Reticulated

Curvilinear   Late Gothic   Perpendicular

Roman and Byzantine

The Latin Cross and the Steeple
In the west, church buildings followed a Roman style and the basilica plan, typically in the shape of a Latin cross (hence no natural center), with its nave, transept, and apse.

The Greek Cross and the Dome
In the east, the Greek cross allowed for a central-plan building, which was typically topped with a massive dome. This gilded dome's radiance lent an aura of mysticism, so typical of eastern Christianity, whose very architecture suggested heaven on earth. Its next most distinguishing characteristic is the use of mosaics.

Church Building *(Exterior)*

Orientation

The great churches of Europe were commonly positioned with the axis of their nave pointing due east (Lt: *orient*), thus "oriented" so that:

   a.   the rising sun would shine on the altar;

   b.   the faithful would face the rising sun while praying, ready to greet the glorious risen Christ who will put darkness to flight and inaugurate a new day;

   c.   it would face Jerusalem, so honoring the city of David which many medieval maps showed as the center of the world, with east rather than north appearing at the top.

This was mandated since the tenth century, and a custom observed long before, except by Emperor Constantine, so St. John Lateran, St. Peter's and San Lorenzo's are exceptions. In modern times this practice has become impractical, depending on shape of property; still the altar end is "the east end." Liturgically, a custom arose of facing east during the creed to *enact* the faith *professed* in the Dayspring and Sun of Righteousness.

(The east end was where the building's construction normally began, so often its style predates the west end.)

St. Thomas the Builder

Legends of Thomas in India abound. In one, the King of the Indies, Gondoforus, gave a small fortune to Thomas to build a palace. Thomas turned around and spent it on the poor, thus "building a superb palace in heaven." Hence he is called by some patron of architects and masons, and his symbol is the builder's square. In another, Thomas saw the king trying in vain to haul ashore a huge beam of timber. Even with men and elephants he failed. So Thomas asked to have the beam, intending to use it in building a church. His request being granted, he hauled the beam ashore with a string.

Belfry
Tower on a church, with or without bells.

Buttress
External reinforcement, strengthening walls and supporting roof of a Gothic church.

Campanile
Bell tower (separate from a church building).

Carillon
Set of bells (about twenty-two, technically—a lesser number would be "chimes") developed in the seventeenth century for playing songs mechanically. (In England, the "change ringing"—of six or more bells in intricately varying sequences is more popular.)

Devil's Door
A small door of some old churches' north wall, or baptistery wall, to "let out the devil" during a baptism or communion service; it was common for the superstitious to consider the north side of a church "Satan's side," where the devils lurked to prey on the unwary.

Door
Symbolic of gates of heaven (often red for the blood of Christ).

Gargoyle
Water spouts/decorations in the form of often unsightly human/beast heads on Gothic churches; symbolic of evil exorcised by the gospel.

Leper Window
Medieval; a low window in a church's chancel wall, often shuttered or iron barred, enabling lepers to attend mass while remaining outside.

Spire
Point of a steeple or tower, symbol of humanity's aspiration to be united with the Creator.

Squint
A small opening in the sanctuary wall giving visual access to ceremonies within; this enabled the ancient anchorites to assist at mass.

Steeple (tower)
Functioned to support a spire, a symbol of local pride, making the building more visible; also to support bells. Medieval cathedrals have as many as nine, but most commonly either a single tower at west end; or twin towers, one at either side of the west front, with a third large tower at the crossing (of cruciform style building).

West Front
Most deliberated feature of the classic cathedrals and larger churches. This large facade, incorporating the entrance to the building, was thought to represent the gates of heaven. Large windows are typical on its upper face, with twin towers becoming the norm in the eleventh century.

227

Church Building *(Interior)*

This list includes more permanent, stationary features of a church, some liturgical, some architectural. For liturgical vessels, and other more portable objects used in liturgy, see the chapter on liturgy.

Directions

East: God's side, with His throne; **west:** man's side; **south:** saints' and angels' side (where the sun shines most); **north:** devil's side. This north side was once called the Bachelor's Porch where there were benches down the aisle. This was the place for servants and the poor (male; female, similarly, on the south side). Further, there was a superstition about only evildoers being buried on the north side of a graveyard, symbolized by the want of sun.

Altar

The table of solid or suitable material for the meal of sacrifice, the Eucharist; a symbol of Christ. Traditionally made of stone or at least containing a consecrated stone and containing in a "sepulcher" relics of the martyrs (and sometimes incense grains), enclosed in it by the bishop at its consecration; recalling masses offered in catacombs, and Christ's union with the faithful in Eucharist. Rests on the sanctuary level called the predella. Represents, according to early Fathers, the mediating power, between heaven and earth, of the Word of the Gospels and the grace of the sacraments.

Altar Cloth

A (usually) white linen to cover the altar; formerly three required.

Altar, Privileged (formerly)

One with certain indulgences attached when used in liturgies for the deceased.

Altar Rail *("concelli")*

Low, gated demarcation between sanctuary and church body over which communion was formerly distributed.

"I will go in to the altar of God, to God who gives joy to my youth" (From Psalm 42, used as a "prayer at the foot of the altar"

Altar Stone ("portable altar")
The stone in the altar, technically identified as the altar itself, usually being only large enough to hold the chalice and paten and seated in a receptacle that leaves its top flush with the altar. Its upper surface bears five crosses, for Christ's wounds, where anointings were made in its consecration; near its edge is a sepulcher or cavity in which are sealed relics of two martyr saints. Formerly required; since Vatican II "commended," with an emphasis on the importance of verifying authenticity.

Ambry (Lt: *armaria,* cupboard)
The receptacle, often in/on sanctuary wall labeled O.S. (*olea sancta,* holy oils), for the stocks of consecrated oils. Formerly used more generically for a storage area for liturgical items.

The ambry with crown stoppers on the oils; victorious, regal, and sorrowful.

Antependium
Banner-like cloth "hung before" altar, pulpit, etc., usually a single piece.

Apse
Semicircular, often domed, projection; altar (east) area.

Baldacchino (Italian for Baghdad, whence came precious building materials)
Canopy or dome over altar or bishop's chair. The most famous is in St. Peter's in Rome, designed by Bernini.

Baptistery
Baptismal font and area.

The Womb of the Baptistry

The baptistry is the womb of Mary, Mother of the Church, and also the womb of Holy Mother Church whose pattern and promise is Mary. She is expectant in a kingdom yet-to-be, and fruitful in a kingdom here-and-now. At the womb of the baptistery, we encounter her, pregnant with Christ.

Bier
Structure on which coffin is placed.

Brass
A church brass is a latten funeral effigy affixed to a tombstone on the floor of a church, popular in the fourteenth, fifteenth centuries. (Latten is an alloy made of brass, or to resemble it, hammered thin and used in church vessels.)

Cathedra
Bishop's chair in a cathedral church.

Ceiling with open dome
According to the early Fathers, a symbol of the firmament, often including a figure of Christ the Pantocrator ("Ruler of All"), who is the omnipresence and is over the assembly.

Cerecloth
Moisture resistant altar cloth under the fair linen.

Chair
Seat for celebrant, the presiding minister of the assembly.

Chancel (Lt: *cancellus,* screen)
Area around the altar for clergy choir, from the Roman custom of separating lawyers from the public in court by a lattice screen. See the more liturgical "sanctuary."

Credence Table (It: *credenza,* shelf, buffet)
Side table for articles used at mass, especially bread and wine.

Crucifix
Cross bearing figure of crucified Christ (*corpus*). (The more the sacrificial aspect of the Eucharist—"the unbloody sacrifice of Calvary"—is emphasized, the more prominent is the crucifix above the altar; see "reredos.")

The Nine Crosses

Ancient architects would refer to "the nine crosses," nine being the trinity of trinities, the perfect plural (thrice three, which is the perfect unity), this helped make mystique built in.

Altar cross

Processional cross

Rood cross (on loft)

Reliquary cross

Consecration cross

Pectoral cross

Spire cross

Marking cross

Cross pendant over altar

Crypt
Vault under a church.

Dossal
Large ornamented wall tapestries; formerly often hung behind an altar in the absence of a reredos.

Fair Linen
Fine linen cloth covering the altar, traditionally with a cross in each corner and one in the center representing the five wounds of Christ.

Fald Stool
A portable, folding chair for the bishop's use at formal liturgical ceremonies.

Floor
Symbolic of the world, and the way of the pilgrim people, according to early Fathers.

Font
Baptismal/holy water dispensary.

Frontal (Full altar frontal)
A hanging, covering the entire front of an altar from top to floor.

Frontlet
Usually two strips, narrower than an antependium, over an altar and hanging down the front.

Icon (Gk: image, representation)
A religious image, primarily of Christ but also of Mary and the saints, which is painted according to a conventional model or symbolism and which is part of a place and act of worship. Iconography grew out of Eastern (Byzantine) Christianity and reached its highest point, some would say, in the Russian Orthodox Church. In the Eastern Church iconographic art has sacramental overtones and developed with the divine liturgy of which it is an organic part. As a visual expression of revelation, it corresponds to the Word of God, which is a written expression.

Lectern
Place for song leading and all non-scriptural speaking.

Mensa
Top of consecrated altar.

Narthex
Pre-nave entrance/lobby/portico area.

Nave (Lt: *Navis,* ship)
The central and primary structural feature, from entry to sanctuary, so called because of its resemblance to the ship of the era. Symbol of the sensory world, and humanity, according to early Fathers.

Ombrellino
Canopy for the Blessed Sacrament in procession.

Parament (Lt: ornament)
A decoration, usually of cloth, especially in a tapestry form, but including even chasubles and chalice veils; often appliqued. See antependium, frontal, dossal.

Predella
Benches in a place of worship.

Prie-dieu ("pre-dew")
Kneeler (French: pray to God).

Pulpit (ambo)
Place for Scripture proclaiming and preaching; common only in the later Middle Ages; prior to this a bishop preached from the *cathedra.*

Reconciliation Room (confessional)
Place for celebrating Sacrament of Reconciliation, either a booth with screens between priest/celebrant/confessor and penitent, or a room with option to pray with priest face to face.

Reliquary
A place in which a relic is sealed and kept; of varying size, from portable objects to actual caskets.

Repository
A shrine ("side altar") or secondary chapel where the Blessed Sacrament that was consecrated on Holy Thursday is reposed until the Easter Vigil.

Reredos *(retable, altar-piece)*
Richly carved or painted or decorated structure forming back of altar, usually of wood or stone, sometimes including overhanging shelf, frame, and so forth.

Rood Screen
Ornamented altar screen, usually surmounted with a crucifix, separating sanctuary from nave. Properly "rood" (rod) is the crucifixion cross (crucifix) which was originally enshrined on the stone or wooden screen. This came to be ornamented with saintly statuary and symbols.

Rose Window
A circular window embellished with tracery that is symmetrical around the center.

Sacrarium *("piscina", Lt: fish)*
A sacristy sink with a drain

The altar and reredos of St. Adrian's

directly into the earth for the fitting disposal of water used from some sacred purpose.

Sacristy *(vestry)*
Room for sacred vessels and vestments.

Sanctuary
Traditionally, the altar, pulpit, and chair area are usually set apart structurally and symbolic of the spiritual world and humanity's spirituality— according to early Fathers. As the place of holiness and nearness of God, "sanctuary" is now understood more broadly as the whole worship space, created by the gathered faith community, and not limited to the part of the church for the activity of ordered and specific ministries.

Sanctuary Lamp
Light indicating presence of reserved Sacrament, the real presence of Christ (formerly fifty-one percent beeswax, as were altar candles).

Sanctuary Screen *("Iconostasis")*
(A part of Eastern Rite tradition) Symbolic of the unity of the divine world and the human world, the reconciliation achieved between God and His creation, according to early Fathers.

Sedilia
Series of usually three seats for officiating clergy. Historically often positioned on the south side of the sanctuary.

The Simple Harmonic Motion of a Sanctuary Lamp

As a young man in Pisa, Galileo would attend Mass at the Duomo, Pisa's magnificent Cathedral whose bell tower is the famous Leaning Tower of Pisa. The sanctuary lamp of this church is suspended from the ceiling on a long cable. On one particular day he attended Mass, Galileo—being Galileo—observed something as the newly lit sanctuary lamp was swinging back and forth: each complete swing of the lamp took exactly the same amount of time. When its arc was large, the lamp would swing more rapidly; as the swinging slowed, the arc decreased. However, the total amount of time for each swing was always exactly the same. How did he know that? He timed it using his pulse. Galileo's lamp, as it is now called, is still there in the Duomo. Iconoclasts say that according to the church records the lamp wasn't installed until ten years after Galileo died. Believe what you will, but Galileo really did make this discovery about motion that led immediately and directly to the invention of the first accurate clocks: using a pendulum as a timing element. The kind of motion he was studying that day at mass is called "simple harmonic motion."

Steps (to the altar)
Symbolic of spiritual ascent to Christ, according to early Fathers. Their Latin name, *graduales,* gave their name to the antiphon formerly sung between epistle and Gospel at high mass as the proclaimer climbed the steps of the altar. (See "Gradual" psalms of the Old Testament.) Also, by association, the book of the mass music (graduals, introits, kyries, gloria, credo, and so on).

Superfrontal
A covering for the front of the altar proper (the depth of the altar/table top), often attached, or extended only partly over the front edge.

Tabernacle
Safe-like, secure place of reservation for the Blessed Sacrament, the consecrated hosts to be used for distribution to shut-ins, the sick, and the dying. (The watch-shaped container for transporting the host is called a *pyx.*) Sometimes a veil (*canopaeum*) covers it, of white, gold, or the color of the feast or season.

Vestibule
Lobby; small antechamber between two doors of a church.

Residences

Monastery (Gk: *monazein,* to live alone)
Place where religious dwell in seclusion; historically referring to the cloistered, contemplative life where the entire Liturgy of the Hours is celebrated in common. Usually quadrangular in structure.

Cloister
The covered walk of a monastery; hence, belonging to a monastery.

Refectory (Lt: *refectorius,* refreshing)
The dining room of a monastery or convent.

Abbey
An independent monastery with a required minimum of religious, led by an abbot (or abbess). Most are quadrangular, except Carthusian which have cottages for individual monks. Most abbeys are either Benedictine or Carthusian.

Friary
A brotherhood of (or monastery for) friars.

Motherhouse
Originally the autonomous monastic institution with jurisdiction over daughter houses (monasteries) that derive from it.

Priory
A monastery governed by a prior(ess); either autonomous ("conventual") or dependent upon an abbey or motherhouse (obedientiary). A cathedral priory (in England) is a monastery attached to a cathedral church.

Convent (Lt: *convenire,* to convene)
The residence of religious, commonly women, under a superior. Traditionally, six professed women must cohabit before the place qualifies as a religious community house.

Rectory
Residence of a rector (see Rector).

Parsonage
Residence of a parson (see Parson).

Manse (a farm, from Lt: *manere,* to dwell)
The residence (and land) occupied by a minister; formerly, the dwelling of a landlord; a mansion. See "mensa" in the Catholic tradition: the portion of the church property for supporting the clergyman.

Glebe
Property permanently assigned for maintaining a parish. A glebe house is a parsonage or manse.

Liturgical

Liturgical Prayer

1. Trinitarian (Centered on Christ)
2. Ecclesial (Rooted in the Church)
3. Scriptural (Nourished by the Bible)
4. Sacramental (Celebrated by the Eucharist/Sacraments/Hours)
5. Structural (Ordered through the calendar of feasts/seasons)

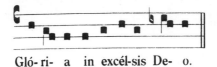

Gló- ri- a   in excél-sis De- o.

"Glory to God in the highest."

Sacrament (Lt: *sacramentum*; Gk: *mysterion*)

In the Old Testament:

1. A touchpoint with divine saving reality . . .
   (a visible, tangible, audible expression of an invisible)
2. for the sake of an oath of allegiance to God
   (love in response to love, and a pledge of fidelity to a faithful God).

For the Ancient Jew
Under the thigh of the patriarch was the **sacrament**
(Yahweh resides in the **seed of life**)

1. The touchpoint,
2. to make an oath.

For the Christians
A. Jesus is the **Sacrament**. . . .
    1. where Life is to be found.
    2. To touch Jesus is to have contact with the Father.
B. The Church is a kind of **sacrament** . . . .
    1. in which Jesus translates his person and saving action.
    2. The "body" of Christ (1 Cor. 12.12f).
C. The seven-fold ministry of initiation, healing, vocation is sacramental
    1. These are touchpoints (points of contact with Jesus) . . .
    2. to draw the people of God to oaths of allegiance . . .
       a. to love Him above all things, and
       b. to love neighbor more than self.

The Sacraments: Signs, Words and Scriptures

Baptism
Pouring of water
	"I baptize you in the name of the Father, and the Son, and the Holy Spirit."	Necessity of rebirth, Jn 3.5;
		Institution by Christ, Mt 28.18–20;
		In the early Christian community:
		    Acts 8.26–39; (the Ethiopian eunuch)
		    Acts 16.16f (the jailer of Paul and Silas)
		    Acts 19.1–7 (the disciples in Ephesus)
		Paul's theology of baptism:
		    Rom 6.3–11; Meaning, effect: Gal 2.19–20; 3.14;
		    3.26–29; Eph 1.3–5; 2.4–10; Col 1.14; 2.9–13;
		    3.1–3; 1 Pt 1.3–5;

Confirmation Anointing with oil	"Receive the seal of the Holy Spirit" (said by the bishop or priest.)	Acts 8.14–17; 9.17–19; 10.5; 19.5 Ti 3.4–8
Eucharist Bread and wine	The Eucharistic prayer within the liturgy with its institution narrative: "This is my body . . . this is my blood . . ."	Roots in Jewish passover, Ex 12.1–28; Melchisedech's offering, Gn 14.18; The priesthood of David, Ps 110 The priesthood of Jesus, Heb 8–10 Multiplication of loaves, Jn 6.1–15 The Bread of Life, Jn 6.25–71 The Last Supper, Mt 26.26–28; Mk 14.22–25; Lk 22.7–20 The Emmaus event, Lk 24.13–53 Apostolic Church, Acts 2.42–47; 20.7 The meaning and effect of Eucharist, 1 Cor 10.16–17.

Reconciliation
 	
Contrition and confession
	"God the Father of mercy, through the death and resurrection of His Son, has reconciled the world to himself, and sent the Holy Spirit among us for the forgiveness of sins; through the ministry of the Church may God grant you pardon and peace, and I absolve you from your sins in the name of the father, and of the Son, and of the Holy Spirit."	Sin lists
		1 Cor 5.3–5; 6.9–10; Gal 5.19–20; Eph 5.5; 1 Tim 1.19–21
		Jesus' mission
		    Mk 2.16–17 ("I have come to call sinners . . . ")
		    Lk 7.47–50 (Mary Magdalen)
		    Lk 19.7–10 (Zaccheus)
		Christ's continued ministry in the Church
		    Jn 16.1–8 (Coming to the Paraclete)
		    Mt 16.13–19 (Keys of the Kingdom)
		    Jn 20.19–23 (Commissioning the Church)
		    Acts 9.1–5 (Saul's conversion)
		Early Church ministry to post-baptismal sin
		    Mt 18.15–18 (Fraternal correction/Church authority)
		    2 Thes. 2.6, 14–15 (Excommunication)
		    1 Tim 1.19–20 (Ostracization)
		Reconciliation before communion
		    Mk 11.25 ("When you pray, forgive . . .")
		    Mk 5.23–24 ("If you bring your gift. . .")
		Scandal, Mt 18.5–7

Anointing of the Sick Anointing with oil and imposition of hands	"Through this holy anointing may the Lord in his love and mercy help you with the grace of the Holy Spirit." ("Amen") "May the Lord who frees you from sin save you and raise you up. ("Amen")	Institution, Jas 5.13–16 The ministry of the community to the sick, Is 52.13–53.12 1 Cor 12.12–22, 24b–27; Mt 25.31–40 Suffering, 2 Cor 12.9–10 Anointing the sick, Is 61.1–3a; Jn 9.1–7 Healing, 1 Kgs 19.1–8; Acts 4.8–12 (3.1–10) Mt 8.1–4 (5–17) Healing and forgiveness, Jb 7.12–21; Mk 2.1–12 Faith, Jb 3.1–3, 11–17, 20–23; Is 35.1–10 Hope and confidence, Jb 19.23–27a (7.1–4, 6–11); Rom 8.18–27 1 Cor 1.18–25; Mt 8.1–4; 25.31–40 The power of prayer, Jb 7.12–21; Jas 5.25–16; Lk 11.5–13
Matrimony Mutual consent to live together as husband and wife	The external expression of this through an interchange with Church witness (priest) as he elicits from them their intention (questions preceding vows) and their consent (wedding vows).	The question of divorce, Mt 19.3–12 (Mk 10.2–12) Christian wives and husbands, Eph 5.25–32 A believing spouse consecrates a partner, 1 Cor 7.12–16
Holy Orders Laying on of hands	The prayer to the Holy Spirit in the preface of the ordination Mass.	Presbyters installed in the early Church, Acts 14.22–23 The priestly role, Heb 5.1–10 Counsel to Timothy, 1 Tim 4.12–16 Exhortation to faithfulness, 2 Tim 1.6–8 Apostolic charge, 2 Tim 4.2, 5.7–8 Qualities of a presbyter, Ti 1.5–9.

THE SEVEN SACRAMENTS

Definitions

1. **Outward signs instituted by Christ to give grace.**
2. **Signs of worship** communicating the grace of Jesus' death, resurrection, and ascension.
3. **Tangible expressions of intangible grace.**
4. **Real symbols** ("They accomplish what they signify.")
   In the way that Jesus is "symbol" or "sacrament" of the Father, really God, yet distinct; tangible, and efficacious. ("To have seen me is to have seen the Father.") ("No one comes to the Father but through me.")

Listed

Three of Initiation—**baptism, confirmation, Eucharist**
Two of Healing—**reconciliation, anointing**
Two of Service to Community—**marriage, holy orders**

Former Terminology

1. **The Last Sacraments**
   Those received before death: reconciliation, Eucharist ("viaticum"), anointing.
2. **Sacraments of the Living**
   Requiring state of grace for fruitful reception, though none would be thereby invalid (except Eucharist; see sacrilege): confirmation, Eucharist, matrimony, holy orders.
3. **Sacraments of the Dead**
   Conferring, or restoring, sanctifying as well as actual grace, can be, and often are, received validly and fruitfully when not in state of grace: baptism, reconciliation, anointing
4. **Sacraments that can be received only once**
   Those which impart a spiritual mark, "character": baptism, confirmation, holy orders.

CHRISTIAN INITIATION

Baptism—Who I am—sharing the **identity** of Jesus
   as a member of the risen body of Christ that is the Church
Confirmation—What I do—sharing the **mission** of Jesus
   as a member of the risen body of Christ that is the Church
Eucharist—Where I am going—sharing the **destiny** of Jesus
   as a member of the risen body of Christ that is the Church

Rite of Christian Initiation of Adults

First Step: Acceptance Into the Order of Catechumens
Introductory Rite

> First Instruction; Opening Dialogues; First Promise; Exorcism and Renunciation of Non-Christian Worship; Signing the Forehead and the Senses; Giving New Name; Additional Rites; Entry into the Church

Liturgy of the Word *As usual until after homily:*

> Presentation of the Gospels
> Prayer for the Catechumens and Dismissal

Liturgy of the Eucharist as usual
Concluding Rite

Second Step: Election or Enrollment of Names
Introductory Rites as usual
Liturgy of the Word *As usual until after the homily:*

> Presentation of Candidates; Admission (Election), Prayer for the Elect and Dismissal

Liturgy of the Eucharist *as usual*
Concluding Rite

Scrutinies and Presentations
Between Election and Initiation (Lent)

> Scrutinies (*Three: on 3rd, 4th and 5th Sundays of Lent*)
>> Homily; Prayer in Silence; Prayer for the Elect; Exorcism; Dismissal followed by Eucharist

> Presentations
> Of the Creed (*during the week after 1st scrutiny*)
>> Readings and homily
>> Handing over of the Profession of Faith
>> Prayer over the Elect
> Of the Lord's Prayer (*during the week after the 3rd scrutiny*)
>> Readings
>> Gospel reading of Lord's Prayer (Mt 6.9–13) and homily
>> Prayer over the Elect

Third Step: Celebration of the Sacraments of Initiation
When during Easter Vigil, following blessing of water, when outside this normal time, following homily.

> Instruction by Celebrant; Litany of the Saints; Blessing of Water; Renunciation; Anointing with oil of catechumens; Profession of faith; Rite of Baptism (including white garment, candle); Confirmation

Eucharist *as usual*

RCIA Terms

Catechumen (Gk: *Katecheein,* to put in the ear)
One being taught "by word of mouth," one preparing for and being catechized for initiation. The term "candidate" is used, and is appropriate because of the white *(candidus)* garment used in baptism; in about 1600 the word came into the English language for one seeking public office (whether candid or not), echoing the candidacy of the catechumen as well as the candidacy of politicians in ancient Rome wearing white togas as a symbol of purity. The Baltimore Catechism was the dominant catechetical tool in the United States for generations, was approved by the Third Plenary Council of American Bishops at Baltimore in 1884.

Sponsor

— Only an active member is able to sponsor an inquirer.

— A baptismal sponsor must be sixteen and confirmed.

— A confirmation sponsor may be of either sex.

Neophyte (Gk: *neophytos,* newly planted)
The baptized, especially those newly initiated; they were also called *Illunimati,* because they were illuminated by the Holy Spirit, as the lighted candle signifies. The alb-like vestment of the newly baptized, the white garment *(chrisom),* signified cleansing and putting on Christ. Formerly, if a baptized child died within a month, the garment was used as a shroud and the infant was called a chrisom child.

The Three Valid Methods of Baptism

Aspersion
In exceptional circumstances: mere sprinkling.

Affusion (Infusion)
By pouring; a practice already in the first century, according to the *Didache.* St. Paul was baptized in a private house (Acts 9.17–18), and St. Peter baptized his jailer's family presumably still in the prison area (Acts 16.33). Many have concluded these baptisms—and others—were done either by sprinkling or pouring, since no river or stream is mentioned, and since pools/tubs were rare among the poor.

Immersion
Dipping, plunging; generally used in the early Church, common in the Eastern Church and certain Protestant traditions; since Vatican II, permissible in the Latin Rite.

Naming

See God's name. A name is regarded as a manifestation of one's being: Scripturally it is not only the title by which a person is called, but the term by which a person is identified.

The Holy Name Society

A confraternity of men originating at the Ecumenical Council of Lyons (1274), promoted by the Dominicans, and dedicated to promoting love, reverence for the name of God, Jesus; and discouraging profanity, blasphemy, perjury, and all improper language.

First Name

Christian name, personal name. In Genesis God gave Adam the responsibility to name that over which he was given authority. Parents choose. Name changes: change of vocation/identity.

Confirmation Name

Individual chooses. Baptismal name personally chosen?

Last Name

Family name, "surname" (Old Fr: *sur-*, from Lt: *super-:* over, above). The name over and above Christian name. Even parents do not choose.

Greek capital letters, first three letters of Jesus' name in Greek (the line at the top indicating abbreviation)

Originated in late tenth century, widely used only much later. Mainly, they define or specify according to:

1. Parentage (patronymic)
2. Trade, occupation
3. Personal, physical characteristics
4. Place of residence

"What Name Do You Give Your Child?"

The Catechism of the Council of Trent (sixteenth century) directed that the baptismal name should be taken from some person whose eminent sanctity has been recognized. Actually, naming after saints was a common practice centuries before this in France and Germany, and by the thirteenth century, throughout Europe. This was a major change in Ireland, where Gaelic Christians had been reluctant to use hallowed names, like Mary. Those named after the Blessed Mother, "Muire" in original Gaelic, were called "Maire," or a similar variation. Today, the revised Code of Canon Law simply says, "Parents, sponsors and the pastor are to see to it that a name alien to a Christian sense is not given".

Names and Name Changes

Relate to creation and recreation (conversion), respectively. In Semitic thought a name conveyed the reality of that person (note that God named John and Jesus, among others). A name change is a scriptural expression for a new state of happiness, a new way of life, new life. "You shall be called by a new name . . ." Is 62.2 (see also Is 65.15, Rv 2.17; 3.12; 19.12).

Abram **Gn 11.27**	Abraham **Gn 17.5**
Sarai **Gn 11.29**	Sarah **Gn 17.15**
Jacob **Gn 25.26**	Israel **Gn 35.10**
Simon **Mt 4.18**	Peter **Mt 16.18**
Saul **Acts 7.58**	Paul **Acts 9.1–30; 13.9**

The Juniper

One of Miguel Serra's favorite books was the *Little Flowers of St. Francis,* and his favorite character was the playful monk, Brother Juniper. Of him Miguel exclaimed, "Would to God that I had a whole forest of such Junipers!" It was the brother's humor that Miguel admired, but more, it was his total selflessness and deep concern for the needs of his companions. On Sept. 15, 1731, Miguel knelt before the provincial and made his vows as a Franciscan. His name? . . . the jolly, holy jester of St. Francis, Juniper (in Spanish, *Junipero*).

Becoming a Catholic

1. From infancy:
     baptism—confirmation—Eucharist
2. From non-Catholic, Christian adulthood:
     (reconciliation)—"reception"—confirmation—Eucharist
3. From non-Christian adulthood:
     baptism—confirmation—Eucharist

Apologia Pro Vita Sua—

After John Henry Newman, the well-known Anglican theologian, became a Catholic in 1845, he wrote a religious autobiography (1864), *A Defense of His Life,* as a defense of the things he did in his life by explaining the basis for his faith. He was made a cardinal in 1879. Although it could refer to anyone's *"apologia,"* that phrase has become synonymous with Newman's masterpiece.

Rite of Reception of Baptized Christians into Full Communion

Reception takes place, ideally, within Mass, after the homily.

1. Profession of faith by assembly and one being received
2. Declaration of reception by the bishop (or priest taking his place)
3. Sacrament of Confirmation
4. General intercessions
5. Sign of peace
6. Liturgy of the Eucharist, in which the person receives communion for the first time with the members of the Catholic community

---

A Covenant of Salt

There was an ancient practice of partaking of the same salt with one with whom a covenant was entered. This signaled its permanence, given the natural properties of the preservative salt. Hence the proverbial "covenant of salt." The tasting of salt by those sharing a table is a venerable symbol of alliance and friendship. The Lord made one with Aaron and his family.

> It is a covenant of salt ("inviolable covenant") forever before the Lord, to thee and to thy sons. (Nm 18.19)

In His instructions to Moses on the ritual of sacrifices God said:

> However, every cereal offering that you present to the Lord shall be seasoned with salt. Do you let the salt of the covenant of your God be lacking from your cereal offering. On every offering you shall offer salt. (Lev 2.13)

King Abijah declared (2 Chr 13.5) that when the Lord God gave the Kingdom of Israel to David, it was by a covenant of salt.

In the same spirit, it was not an uncommon practice among Christians to put salt into a coffin when burying a believer. Because salt is a symbol of immortality—being by nature a preservative—it was part of the baptismal ceremony (until the 1969 revision) to put salt on the child's tongue:

> Receive the salt of wisdom, may it be for you a propitiation into eternal life.

Just as the baptismal candle and white garment have found their way into the funeral liturgy, so in another era did salt. Thus on the occasion of this ultimate birth, the devil was given another taste of grace, for which he has a hatred.

EUCHARIST

Celebrating the Eucharist (definitions)

1. **Thanksgiving**
2. **Word** (of God's love, who is Christ)
   a. of compassion, and
   b. of confrontation
3. **Sacrament** (Lt: *sacramentum;* Gk: *mysterion*)
4. **Sacrifice** (Lt: *sacrum*, holy; *facere*, to make)
   Its significance still in the fire of Old Testament sacrifice:
   a. purifying   c. illuminating
   b. consuming   d. warming
   From holocaust, to sacrifice, to Christian mission:
   To **purify,** one is **consumed** in giving **light** and **warmth**
5. **Presence** ("Real" presence, not merely a sign, or symbolic)
   a. the poor Jesus; b. the obedient Jesus; c. the chaste Jesus
6. **Worship** (old Eng: to declare the worth of another)
   The three dimensions of Eucharistic worship:
   a. past (commemorative)—memorial of Christ's sacrifice
   b. present (affective)—celebration of saving grace
   c. future (prognostic)—sign of hope, pledge of glory
7. **Mystery**
   a. of revelation (God's Word of love to us)
   b. of religion (our word of loving response)

The Real Presence

Although this phrase has come to mean the Body and Blood of Christ present in the Eucharist, it is really only one part of a larger whole, whose other parts include:

1. in the graced human person
   (a "temple of the Holy Spirit"—1 Cor 3.16–17)
2. in the least of the brothers and sisters (Mt 25–40)
3. where two or three gather in his name (Mt 18.20)
4. in the Church
5. in the liturgical celebrations of the Church
6. in the Mass
7. in the person of the priest
8. in the preaching
9. in the Scriptures read
10. in the praying and singing of the Church

Receiving the Eucharist *(synonyms)*

1. **Altar bread**
2. **Blessed Sacrament**
3. **Body of Christ** (also the Church)
4. **Communion** (also the result)
5. *Eulogia* (Gk: "good speaking"). An ancient term, more commonly used for any blessed object
6. **Eucharist** (also the whole liturgy, by metonymy)
7. **Host** The Latin word for a sacrificial lamb is *hostia* (a larger animal is a *victima*)
8. **Sacrament (the** sacrament)
9. *Viaticum* (Lt: *via*, way)
   So-called when receiving by the dying because of the natural meaning: supplies for a journey; traveling provisions
10. **Wafer**

Pope St. Pius X, the Pope of the Eucharist, (1903–1914), encouraged the frequent reception of Holy Communion, especially by children.

Legend of St. Gertrude

She is the patroness of travellers, since in her life she established hospices of pilgrims. This gave rise to the legend that St. Gertrude harbored souls on the first night of their three-day journey to heaven. Historically, she was an abbess, and the aunt of Pepin, who was Charles Martel's father. (d 664)

"Both forms" (or species) means both bread and wine. **"Intinction"** is receiving communion under both forms by dipping the host in the chalice. Utraquists (Lt: *utraque specie,* both species), or "calixtines" (Lt: *calix,* chalice), were an unorthodox group of fifteenth century Bohemians who believed communion could only be received under both kinds.

Christmas Tree, Fruit Tree

Medieval mystery plays employed fir trees, decorated with apples, to symbolize the Garden of Eden with its tree of life and forbidden fruit. Long after the mystery plays, the Germans remembered the tree, modifying its decoration by adding sacramental wafers along with the apples, relating the eating that brought death with the eating that brings life. As the decorations became more elaborate, the symbolism of the fall and redemption faded: apples were joined by oranges and then brightly colored balls, while wafers became cookies cut in the shape of angels, stars, animals, and flowers.

The Mass in A.D. 150

By the apologist Justin, martyr, this passage is from his First Apology, *67, which was rediscovered in the sixteenth century.*

"On the day called Sunday there is a meeting in one place of those who live in cities or the country, and the memoirs of the apostles or the writings of the prophets are read as long as time permits. When the reader has finished, the president in a discourse urges and invites us to the imitation of these noble things. Then we all stand up together and offer prayers. And, as said before, when we have finished the prayer, bread is brought, and wine and water, and the president similarly sends up prayers and thanksgivings to the best of his ability, and the congregation assents, saying the Amen; the distribution, and reception of the consecrated elements by each one, takes place and they are sent to the absent by the deacons. Those who prosper, and who so wish, contribute, each one as much as he chooses to. What is collected is deposited with the president, and he takes care of orphans and widows, and those who are in want on account of sickness or any other cause, and those who are in bonds, and the strangers who are sojourners among us, and, briefly, he is the protector of all those in need."

A Chronology of Changes in the Mass (selected)

1922—Assembly permitted to make responses
1953—Modification of the Eucharistic fast
1953—Permission for afternoon and evening Mass
1956—Revision of the rites of Holy Week
1964—Use of the common spoken language approved
1965—Last Gospel and "Leonine" prayers after Mass eliminated
1967—Purple allowed instead of black in Masses for the dead
1968—Three additional Eucharistic Prayers authorized
1969—"Instruction" on Masses in the home
1970—New Order of Mass (Replacing sixteenth century "Tridentine" Mass and including:)
    —clear structure of Word and Sacrament
    —new lectionary
    —reinstated Prayers of the Faithful
1970—New Lectionary introduced, including:
    —Mark and Luke added to Matthew for Gospel readings
    —three-year Sunday and two-year daily cycles of readings
    —three readings instead of two on Sunday
    —psalm responsories
1970—Sunday Mass on Saturday approved, where necessary
1973—Special guidelines for Masses with children
1974—New Roman missal (Sacramentary); the first in 400 years
1977—Communion in the hand allowed
1978—Permission given for lay Eucharistic ministers

Structure of the Liturgy of the Mass

"The Breaking of the Bread" (Acts 2.42, 46); "High" Mass was the *missa solemnis,* "solemn mass," a phrase translated—and often spoken—before the renewal of the liturgy.

1. **Introduction**
   Greeting   Penitential Rite
   (Gloria)   Opening Prayer
   Concluded by **amen** of opening prayer
2. **Liturgy of the Word**
   First Reading   Response
   (Second Reading)   Gospel
   Homily   Creed
   Intercessions
   Concluded by **amen** after intercessions
3. **Liturgy of the Eucharist**
   a. Preparation ("set the table . . .)
      Concluded by **amen** of prayer
      over the gifts
   b. Eucharistic Prayer (. . . say grace . . .)
      Concluded with its own amen—the "Great Amen"—as it is a presidential prayer in itself
   c. Communion (. . . share the food.")
      Concluded by **amen** of prayer after communion
4. **Dismissal**

"Behold the Lamb of God . . ."

Principal Parts of the Mass

1. Liturgy of the Word
2. Liturgy of the Eucharist

Formerly, the first part, known as the "Mass of the Catechumens," was seen only as preparatory for the "Mass of the Faithful" with its principal parts of offertory, consecration, and communion.

Ordinary Time Readings: Outline

Sundays

	Second Reading				Gospel Reading		
Sun.	Year A	Year B	Year C	Sun.	Year A	Year B	Year C
2	1 Cor 1	1 Cor 6	1 Cor 12	2	John 1	John 1	John 2
3	1 Cor 1	1 Cor 7	1 Cor 12	3	Mt 4	Mk 1	Lk 1 & 4
4	1 Cor 1	1 Cor 7	1 Cor 12–13	4	Mt 5	Mk 1	Lk 4
5	1 Cor 2	1 Cor 9	1 Cor 15	5	Mt 5	Mk 1	Lk 5
6	1 Cor 2	1 Cor 10–11	1 Cor 15	6	Mt 5	Mk 1	Lk 6
7	1 Cor 3	2 Cor 1	1 Cor 15	7	Mt 5	Mk 2	Lk 6
8	1 Cor 4	2 Cor 3	1 Cor 15	8	Mt 5	Mk 2	Lk 6
9	Rom 3	2 Cor 4	Gal 1	9	Mt 7	Mk 2	Lk 7
10	Rom 4	2 Cor 4–5	Gal 1	10	Mt 9	Mk 3	Lk 7
11	Rom 5	2 Cor 5	Gal 2	11	Mt 9–10	Mk 4	Lk 7
12	Rom 5	2 Cor 5	Gal 3	12	Mt 10	Mk 4	Lk 9
13	Rom 6	2 Cor 8	Gal 4–5	13	Mt 10	Mk 5	Lk 9
14	Rom 8	2 Cor 12	Gal 6	14	Mt 11	Mk 6	Lk 10
15	Rom 8	Eph 1	Col 1	15	Mt 13	Mk 6	Lk 10
16	Rom 8	Eph 2	Col 1	16	Mt 13	Mk 6	Lk 10
17	Rom 8	Eph 4	Col 2	17	Mt 13	John 6	Lk 11
18	Rom 8	Eph 4	Col 3	18	Mt 14	John 6	Lk 12
19	Rom 9	Eph 4	Heb 11	19	Mt 14	John 6	Lk 12
20	Rom 11	Eph 5	Heb 12	20	Mt 15	John 6	Lk 12
21	Rom 11	Eph 5	Heb 12	21	Mt 16	John 6	Lk 13
22	Rom 12	Jas 1	Heb 12	22	Mt 16	Mk 7	Lk 14
23	Rom 13	Jas 2	Philemon	23	Mt 18	Mk 7	Lk 14
24	Rom 14	Jas 2	1 Tim 1	24	Mt 18	Mk 8	Lk 15
25	Phil 1	Jas 3	1 Tim 2	25	Mt 20	Mk 9	Lk 16
26	Phil 2	Jas 5	1 Tim 6	26	Mt 21	Mk 9	Lk 16
27	Phil 4	Heb 2	2 Tim 1	27	Mt 21	Mk 10	Lk 17
28	Phil 4	Heb 4	2 Tim 2	28	Mt 22	Mk 10	Lk 17
29	1 Thes 1	Heb 4	2 Tim 3–4	29	Mt 22	Mk 10	Lk 18
30	1 Thes 1	Heb 5	2 Tim 4	30	Mt 22	Mk 10	Lk 18
31	1 Thes 2	Heb 7	2 Thes 1–2	31	Mt 23	Mk 12	Lk 19
32	1 Thes 4	Heb 9	2 Thes 2–3	32	Mt 25	Mk 12	Lk 20
33	1 Thes 5	Heb 10	2 Thes 3	33	Mt 25	Mk 13	Lk 21

Ordinary Time Readings: Outline—*Continued*

Weekdays

First Reading			Gospel	
Week	Year 1	Year 2	Week	
1	Heb	1 Sm	1	
2	Heb	1 Sm	2	
3	Heb	1 Sm	3	
4	Heb	2 Sm; 1 Kgs 1–16	4	
5	Gn 1-11	1 Kgs 1–16	5	Mark
6	Gn 1-11	Jas	6	
7	Sir	Jas	7	
8	Sir	1 Pt; Jude	8	
9	Tb	2 Pt; 2 Tim	9	
10	2 Cor	1 Kgs 17–22	10	
11	2 Cor	1 Kgs 17–22; 2 Kgs	11	
12	Gn 12-50	2 Kgs; Lam	12	
13	Gn 12-50	Am	13	
14	Gn 12-50	Hos; Is	14	
15	Ex	Is; Mi	15	
16	Ex	Mi; Jer	16	Matthew
17	Ex; Lv	Jer	17	
18	Nm; Dt	Jer; Na; Hb	18	
19	Dt; Jos	Ez	19	
20	Jgs; Ru	Ez	20	
21	1 Thes	2 Thes; 1 Cor	21	
22	1 Thes; Col	1 Cor	22	
23	Col; 1 Tim	1 Cor	23	
24	1 Tim	1 Cor	24	
25	Ezr; Hg; Zec	Prv; Eccl	25	
26	Zec; Neh; Bar	Jb	26	Luke
27	Jon; Mal; Jl	Gal	27	
28	Rom	Gal; Eph	28	
29	Rom	Eph	29	
30	Rom	Eph; Phil	30	
31	Rom	Phil	31	
32	Wis	Ti; Phlm; 2, 3 Jn	32	
33	1, 2 Mc	Rv	33	
34	Dn	Rv	34	

Lectionary

"Collection of readings" (Scripture), assigned by the Church in both organic* and thematic* cycles for liturgical proclamation. The present one was introduced March 22, 1970, and is comprised of:

1. three-year cycle of Sunday readings
2. two-year weekday cycle
3. one-year sanctoral cycle
4. variety of other readings for various occasions
5. responsorial psalms and alleluia verses

General Principles of the New Lectionary

Gospel *(both Sundays and weekdays)*
During Ordinary Time: Readings are "organic".* Notice this on the tables; for example, Matthew one year, Mark the next, and so on.

For special feasts and seasons: Readings are "thematic."** (Easter and Christmas readings, for example.)

First Reading *(Sundays)*
Old Testament readings, chosen thematically; there is no table of these readings, since no pattern could be illustrated. The choices show clearly the unity and relationship between the Old and New Testament.

Second Reading *(Sundays)*
The choices are organic, as the tables illustrate, providing a semi-continuous reading of Paul and James. (Peter and John are read during the Easter and Christmas seasons.)

First Reading *(weekdays)*
Organic, again, although more selective than on Sundays, since both Testaments are used: Old Testament, limited; New, extensive. (As with the second reading on Sundays, this reading is usually unrelated to the Gospel (and the first reading), although grace has its way. Sometimes the Thematic Principle works within the Organic: for example, Daniel and Revelation are assigned at the end of the liturgical year because of their eschatological ("end times") themes.

The "Last Gospel" was the one at the end of the Mass (before the reform of the liturgy), usually Jn 1.1–14 except on days in Lent and various other occasions.

---

*Organic ("Semi-) continuous text" reading; reading through a particular book or letter; picking up one week later where last week left off. "Organic" in that the particular book or letter is treated as a whole, and not "as related to something else".

**Thematic as applied to a reading: chosen not for its own sake, but for its relationship to a theme chosen beforehand or suggested by another reading, or by a feast day, for example.

Sequence (Lt: *sequentia,* a following, sequence)

Hymn of joy; of varying length and meter, sung or recited before the Gospel on certain feasts. Three remain in the revised liturgy (Pentecost's is called " The Golden Sequence"):

1. The *Victima Paschali* ("Paschal Victim")—Easter
   By Wipo of Burgundy (d. 1050)
2. The *Veni Sancte Spiritus* ("Come Holy Spirit")—Pentecost
   Probably by Stephen Langton (d. 1228), archbishop of Canterbury
3. The *Lauda Sion* ("Praise O Sion")—Corpus Christi
   By St. Thomas Aquinas in 1274

The *Dies Irae,* formerly common in requiem Masses, is not a liturgical sequence, strictly speaking.

Preaching

I. Generically
   A. **Sermon**
      A talk on a religious topic, usually at a worship service.
   B. **Homily**
      Explaining the Scriptures in light of the here and now situation so as to elicit a response of Eucharist: the interior and liturgical praise of God:

      1. present the mystery of Christ, based on readings and Mass texts;
      2. apply Scriptures to daily Christian Life; and
      3. connect Liturgy of the Word with Liturgy of the Eucharist.

II. Specifically
   A. **Pre-evangelization**—addresses the human situation
      object: readiness
   B. **Evangelization**—proclaims who Jesus is
      object: conversion
   C. **Catechesis**—explains religion, God, Jesus
      object: understanding
   D. **Homily**—demonstrates what the Lord is doing
      object: Eucharist, to bring worshipper to say from the heart:
      "It is right to give Him thanks and praise." (Preface)

Dabitur vobis—An old idea that a preacher does not prepare because "it will be given to you" in the pulpit.

253

General Intercessions

The faithful exercise their priestly function when they intercede for all humankind. Usually the sequence of intentions is:

A. **Introduction** (presidential)
1. for the needs of the Church;
2. for public authorities and the salvation of the world;
3. for those oppressed by need; and
4. for the local community.
B. **Responses to each** (congregational)
C. **Conclusion** (presidential)

"Fruits of the Mass"

The spiritual benefits derived form the liturgy, difficult as spiritual things are to measure. According to traditional Catholic teaching—and a human understanding of what God does in His wisdom and love—the fruits are three-fold:

1. The universal Church is graced, in the mystery of God's love, by every Mass said in the world.
2. The person/intention for whom the Mass is offered is graced, according to the intention of the priest-celebrant.
3. The priest who offers it is graced.

Sacramentary

The celebrant's book; the part of the Roman Missal containing mainly the Mass prayers and rubrics, excluding the readings (lectionary). In use until into thirteenth century. The main three (prime sources of liturgical history) being:

Leonine Sacramentary

The oldest, wrongly attributed to Pope Leo I, in use fourth–seventh centuries. Has no Eucharistic prayer or ordinary, but many propers, "orations" (collections, secrets, post communion prayers) and prefaces, as well as ordination forms. Much from here is still used.

Gelasian Sacramentary

Sixth-eighth centuries (pre-Gregorian), ascribed to Pope Gelasius I (492–96). Earliest known Roman Missal with feasts arranged according to liturgical year. Includes Roman Canon in virtually the same form in current use.

Gregorian Sacramentary (or Sacramentary of Adrian I)

Attributed to Pope St. Gregory I, and includes: (1) ordinary of the Mass; (2) propers of the Mass (excluding Masses after Epiphany and Pentecost; (3) ritual prayers for ordinations.

The Eucharistic Prayer

The "Roman Canon", the first (of the current four) Eucharistic prayers, is from the sixth century and is based on the Gelasian Sacramentary. It was called by some the "*Te Igitur*" after its first Latin words meaning "You, therefore . . .", Latin words still referring to the Eucharistic prayer (and also to the sacramentary). This central proclamation of the Liturgy of the Eucharist is a prayer of thanksgiving and sanctification, and consists of:

1. **Thanksgiving,**
   expressed especially in the preface, for salvation or some specific aspect of it;

2. **Acclamation,**
   in the so-called "Seraphic Hymn," or "Holy, holy . . ." ("Sanctus" in Latin) because it was sung by the seraphim (Is 6.3); all proclaim, united with the angels, the holiness of God; it concludes with Mt 21.9, the Palm Sunday acclamation (which quotes Ps 118.26);

3. **Epiclesis,**
   invoking the Holy Spirit, asking that the gifts be consecrated and become a source for salvation; in the Orthodox Church, considered essential for the validity of the Eucharist; since Vatican II, all Eucharistic prayers include it;

4. **Institution and Consecration Narrative,**
   in the words and actions of Christ at the Last Supper;

5. **Anamnesis,**
   acclaiming, at Christ's command, Christ's presence: passion, resurrection and ascension;

6. **Offering,**
   of the victim in memorial, whom the Church becomes in Eucharist, to the Father in the Spirit;

7. **Intercessions,**
   expressive of the Eucharist as an assembly's celebration with the whole Church of heaven and earth and for the Church and all her members living and dead;

8. **Doxology,**
   expressing praise of God, confirmed and concluded by the acclamation of the people.

Languages of a Catholic Tradition

Hebrew, Aramaic, Greek and Latin are all represented; some are used, in this age of the vernacular, in translation; others remain in beloved use in their original form, exactly as our ancestors spoke them.

Adoramus te, Christe (Latin): "We adore you, Christ"
A translation is still commonly used fourteen times during the Stations of the Cross (. . . because by your holy cross you have redeemed the world").

Alleluia (Hebrew): "Praise the Lord"
Christians "fast" from this acclamation during Lent.

Amen (Hebrew): "It is true," or "So be it"
First and foremost, a word of commitment to what has been spoken; also a title for Christ (Rv 3.14).

Deo gratias (Latin): "Thanks be to God"
A response to Scripture in the liturgy.

Dominus vobiscum (Latin): "The Lord is with you"
A common Christian greeting, used liturgically for Mass

Fiat voluntas tuas (Latin): "Let your will be done"
The familiar phrase from the Lord's prayer. The same "*fiat*" is spoken by Mary in her celebrated response in the Annunciation, "Let it be done (to me according to your word)", Lk 1.38.

Gloria in excelsis Deo (Latin): "Glory to God in the highest"
See "Angelic Hymn", and the "Greater Doxology".

Hosanna (Hebrew): originally an acclamation for safety, salvation
Still used in the "Holy, Holy" of our English liturgy.

Kyrie eleison (Greek): "Lord, have mercy"
A Greek prayer kept even when Latin became the liturgy's vernacular

Marana tha (Aramaic): "Our Lord has come", or "Come, our Lord"
See I Cor 16.22; in Rv 22.20 is the similar "Come, Lord Jesus"

Mea culpa (Latin): "Through my fault"
The prayer of many a *Confiteor* ("I confess . . .").

Sanctus (Latin): "Holy"
A translation of the Hebrew "*Hagios*"; used regularly in the acclamation of the preface of the Eucharist prayer.

Veni, Sancte Spiritus (Latin): "Come, Holy Spirit"
"Golden Sequence."

On the other hand: It was in 1986 that the Vatican approved a translation of most parts of the Mass into Navajo, the first Native American language to be so approved. (It had been given "liturgical language" status in 1983, which enabled the translation to proceed.) Following Navajo, Choctaw became a liturgical language in 1984, with a translation into that language approved in 1987.)

Liturgical Objects and Vessels

A *sacristan* is one in charge of sacred articles/vestments; the *sacristy*, similarly, is the room, usually near the altar, for storage of liturgical things (and for vesting, for some). Both words come from the Latin word for "holy," as does the word *sexton* (church custodian; grave digger).

"Sacred Vessels," properly, are those receptacles and utensils which come into direct contact with the Blessed Sacrament (chalice, paten, ciborium, pyx, capsula, lunette and monstrance). Other "vessels" traditionally included cruets, lavabo dish, thurible, boat, and aspergillum.

Amphora (Gk: *amphi*, both sides; *phero*, to carry)
A wine vessel for Mass; tall, two-handled, often pottery. (Symbolically inscribed ones were found in catacombs.)

Ampullae
Two-handed vessels for holding oils, or burial ointments.

Aspergillum (sprinkler)
An instrument (brush, perforated container) for sprinkling holy water; the pail for holy water: aspersory.

Candles
See sacramentals.

Capsula
The container for reserving the consecrated host for exposition in the monstrance.

Censer
A vessel for burning incense (mixture of aromatic gums) at solemn ceremonies whose rising smoke symbolizes prayer. Also called a "thurible," a "thurifer" being its user. The supply container for the incense is called a boat.

Chalice
A cup that holds the wine (grape, "fruit of the vine"). Formerly of precious metals: if not gold, gold plated inside. Since Vatican II, it must at least be a non-porous material of suitable dignity. Consecrated with holy chrism by a bishop; also "consecrated by use" (contact with Christ's blood). Eight inches was the traditional and common height. Christ's Last Supper chalice is the centerpiece of the medieval Holy Grail legends (see next page).

Chalice Veil *(no longer in common use)*
Covers the chalice and paten from the beginning of Mass until the offertory and after the ablutions (of the same color as the vestments).

Ciborium
Container for hosts distributed in communion; similar either to paten (larger) or chalice (with cover).

The Holy Grail

This is the legendary cup identified with the chalice of the Last Supper. Popular folk etymology explained the word as meaning "real blood" (hence "Sangrail," or "Sangreal"). Actually it is from an old word meaning platter, and is a symbol of Christian purity, or its reward. The quest for the Holy Grail has formed the basis for many a popular story, the most well known (from Arthurian romances) being the legend that Joseph of Arimathea preserved it, receiving into it some of Christ's blood at the crucifixion. This Joseph is the one in whose own tomb Christ was buried (Mt 27.57–60; Mk 15.42), a wealthy man who had appeared earlier in the Gospel as a secret believer. During his subsequent forty-two year imprisonment, legend relates, he was miraculously kept alive by the Holy Grail. Upon his release in 63 A.D. by Vespacian, he bore the relic, along with the spear with which Longinus pierced Christ's side, to England, Glastonbury county, Somerset, where it disappeared. In this famed place, designated as the King Arthur's burial place (Avalon), Joseph rested his staff which took root as the legendary Glastonbury Thorn which leafs out every Christmas eve. (There is a variety of hawthorn still claiming this fabled lineage). It was also in this place that he founded the famed abbey—the first Christian church here—and proceeded with the conversion of the Britons.

There are many other legends involving the Grail, like the one that has it that it was delivered from heaven by angels and entrusted to a body of knights who guard it on a mountaintop. When approached by anyone whose purity is imperfect, it disappears. Its quest became the principal source of adventures of the Knights of the Round Table. Malory's *Morte d'Arthur* and Tennyson's *Idylls of the King* are favorite English versions.

Corporal
A square of linen cloth placed upon the altar and upon which the chalice and paten are placed. (Its container, when not in use, is called the burse.)

Crescelle
The "knocker" formerly used in place of the bell (consecration etc.) during Holy Week.

Cruets
Water and wine containers; an "A" and "V" would indicate *aqua* (water) and *vinum* (wine).

Finger Bowl and Towel
Used for the rite before Eucharistic prayer. The linen for drying was called a *"manuterge."*

Lavabo Dish
Saucer for the celebrant's ceremonial washing of fingers (so-called from the first words of the prayer formerly used by the priest, "I will wash my hands among the innocent." Ps 26.6

Liber Usualis (no longer in use)
Contains most of the Gregorian chants and readings for the Mass and the Divine Office.

Luna (lunette)
See monstrance.

Monstrance ("Osterorium")
Container for the host in exposition of the Blessed Sacrament, commonly surmounted by a cross. The glass-sided, removable receptacle at its center, the luna (or lunette), actually holds the host.

Ordo
Mainly, an annual calendar of directions for each day's Mass and Liturgy of the Hours.

Pall
A stiff square of linen used to cover the chalice.

Paten
A flat saucer of the same material as the chalice for the host (unleavened wheat bread).

Processional cross
Mobile, leads procession and recession of liturgical ministers, placed in the sanctuary to signal the presence of the assembled praying community.

Purificator
A band of linen used to cleanse the chalice.

Pyx
The container for conveying the communion host outside of church and Mass.

Roman Missal (Lt: *missalis,* pertaining to mass)
The liturgical book, combining mainly sacramentary and lectionary, which became advantageous since the ninth century. The liturgical restorations of Vatican II involved separating these two books.

Thurible
See censer.

The Six Points of Ritualism

Sanctioned for the Anglican Church (High Church) in the days of Edward VI, it is said, and never authoritatively suppressed or forbidden:

wafer bread	liturgical vestments	incense
mixed chalice	altar candles	eastward orientation

Liturgical Vesture

Alb
A long, loose-fitting tunic worn under other vestments, common to all ministers in worship. Adaptation of fourth-century Greek and Roman undertunic. Symbolizes the garment in which Pilate clothed Christ; also purity of the soul required for Mass. Also the garment of the newly baptized.

Amice
A white linen square worn over the neck and shoulders under the alb. Formerly used as a cape to cover the priest's head.

Biretta *(no longer in common use)*
Square cap with three ridges or peaks. Worn mainly by principal ministers on the way to and from the altar. In its place, religious cover their heads with amice and hood.

Cassock
Full length, fitted robe for ordinary use; black (priest), purple (bishop), red (cardinal), white (pope).

Chasuble
The external garment, worn by the (main) celebrant of the Eucharistic liturgy, with stole worn over it (or, depending on style, under it). Sometimes designed as a chasualb serving the purpose of both vestments.

Cincture
A cord used to belt the alb.

Cope
Long cloak with a fastening in front, worn on solemn occasions and specified ceremonies (for example, Eucharistic benediction) outside of Mass.

Dalmatic
Sleeved outer garment, fashioned after the chasuble, worn by a deacon in place of a chasuble; patterned on the royal vest of Dalmatia, once worn by kings at solemnities like coronations.

Humeral Veil (Lt: *humerus*, shoulder)
Wide scarf worn over the shoulders for carrying the sacred vessels or the Blessed Sacrament.

Maniple *(no longer in common use)*
An ornamental strip of cloth pinned or tied to the left forearm signifying authority; formerly a handkerchief worn on or carried in the left hand.

Orphrey (Lt: *aurum*, gold; Phrygian)
The painted or embroidered images or symbols on a chasuble, front and back, and around a cope's opening.

Pallium (Lt: covering)
A liturgical vestment symbolizing the fullness of episcopal (bishop's) office; thus worn not only by the pope, but also by metropolitan archbishops (archbishops with suffragan dioceses related to them) and patriarchs; also symbolic of personal loyalty to the pope and, thereby, the sign of unity between a local Church and the universal Church. It is a white, woolen, circular, two-inch band worn loosely around the neck, breast, and shoulders. It has a weighted pendant front and back, each ornamented with six black silken crosses, and extending nearly to the waist. When an archbishop receives a pallium (from a pope) he may exercise metropolitan jurisdiction. Should he transfer to another archdiocese, he is vested in a new pallium. (It is worn for such liturgical ceremonies as priest ordinations, bishop consecrations, and church dedications.)

St. Patrick, with the crosier and pallium of his office.

261

Pallial Mystique

The pallium is made from the wool of two lambs, representing Christ, the Lamb of God and the Good Shepherd. These animals are furnished from the lambs raised by the convent of St. Agnes in Rome and chosen and blessed each year on her feast day (Jan.

21) for their quality and whiteness. The lambs are sent to the Benedictine Sisters of St. Cecilia in Trastevere. There they are cared for and shorn, and the pallia are woven from the wool.

On the eve of Ss. Peter and Paul (June 29) the pallia are laid upon the tomb of St. Peter in the Basilica, to rest above his body for the night, "contracting a share of apostolic authority." Following the vesper service on the feast day itself, they are placed on the high altar to be blessed by the pope and placed on his own shoulders. After the ceremonies, the pallia are placed in a silver urn and enclosed in a cabinet under the Altar of Crucifixion, over the traditional tomb of St. Peter. Here they await delivery by papal embassy to the metropolitans or patriarchs who will wear them. The pallium is buried with the churchman when he dies.

Stole
Sign of priestly office, worn in administration of sacraments. A narrow strip of cloth of a liturgical color worn over the shoulders; on a deacon, worn over right shoulder and crossing to the left side of the body.

Surplice
Vestment of white linen with wide sleeves worn over cassock, often used by ministers other than celebrant; sometimes worn by a priest for administration of the sacraments.

Liturgical Colors

Black: Death, Mourning, Despair
May be used for Masses for the dead (as well as violet and white)

Blue
Not an approved liturgical color; see violet below. Also see Marian Blue.

Green: Hope, Growth, Increase, Life, Immortality, Fidelity
Used on Sundays in Ordinary Time

Red: Sacrifice (Blood—Life Itself), Charity, Zeal, Holy Spirit
Used on commemorations of our Lord's passion (Passion Sunday, Good Friday), the apostles, evangelists, and martyrs for the faith; Pentecost.

Rose: Subdued Joy, Relieved Repentance
May be used on Gaudete Sunday (third of Advent) and Laetare Sunday (fourth of Lent)

Violet: Sorrow, Penitence, Preparation
Used during seasons of Advent and Lent. Often called purple, it has a variety of shades ranging from blue-violet to red-violet. Whereas the traditional ''Roman purple'' is actually a red-purple, a more blue-purple has prevailed in other parts of Europe. Some have taken advantage of this hue variation to differentiate between Lent (redder shades) and Advent (bluer).

White: Innocence, Purity, Virginity, Victory, Joy
Used on all occasions of the joyful and glorious mysteries of our Lord (like Christmas and Easter), of Mary (like the Annunciation), of angels, and of saints who were not martyrs; traditionally worn on celebrations honoring John the Baptist, the Chair of Peter, and the Conversion of St. Paul. May be used for funerals.

Liturgical Gesture and Posture

Sign of the Cross
Externalizing anything done in the name of the Lord; blessing self or marking another in baptism, confirmation, anointing, and so on.

Benediction
Latin Form Thumb and first finger extended, last two fingers closed; representing the Trinity: the strong thumb, the Father; the long middle finger, the Son; and the first finger, the Holy Spirit, proceeding from the Father and the Son.

Greek Form First finger extended, second finger curved, thumb and third finger crossed, fourth finger curved (thus forming Greek letters ICXC, the first and last letters in Greek of Jesus Christ).

Bowing
Profound (from the waist), simple (reverent nod).

Folded Hands
Traditional prayer posture. (Arms folded, palms inward, is a fuller sign of prayerfulness, attentiveness to the divine presence, and humility.)

Pretzels

The word come from "pretoila," Latin for "little reward." That's what the snack was called because of the legend of a seventh-century monk who made them and gave them as little rewards to children for learning their prayers: he took a strip of bread dough that was leftover, twisted it into the shape of arms folded in prayer, and baked it. What a nice little reward! Pretzel.

Genuflection
Bending the right knee to touch the floor as an act of worship. (Since the 1973 Instruction on Worship of Eucharist outside Mass, this "single" genuflection before the Blessed Sacrament, whether reserved or exposed, is called for, and not a "double" (both knees), that formerly was used before the exposed Sacrament.)

Invocation
Arms extended, palms down; blessing, invoking Spirit.

Kneeling
In the strict sense, the posture of repentance and private adoration.

Orans
Open hands, palms up (Ex 17.11–13).

Prostration
To lie face down (not supine). Its two most common uses are Good Friday (by main celebrant) and ordination (by candidates for orders). Kneeling on both knees with head bowed is a form of prostration.

Sitting
Passive posture of reflection and receptivity.

Standing
Active posture of receptivity, respect and readiness for mission.

SACRAMENTS OF HEALING

Reconciliation and Healing

Forli, Italy, was once part of the Papal States and governed by the pope. A man named Peregrine, born around 1265, grew up there, and was active in an anti-papal, opposition party. The Prior General of the Servants of Mary, Philip Benizi (now canonized), was sent to preach reconciliation in Forli. Peregrine obstructed him, heckled him. His political fervor even brought him to strike Philip—an action that became a turning point.

Peregrine changed. His dynamic energies began to be channeled in another direction. Philip's preaching had provoked reaction as well as attraction: Peregrine eventually entered the Servants of Mary himself, at about the age of thirty, pronouncing his vows in the Servite Priory in Siena, Italy. Peregrine's transformed zeal took him back to Forli where he was to live out his life. His fervor that had been so intense politically was no less so spiritually. He became a special advocate of the sick, the poor, and those on the edge of society. He assumed special penances, one of them—standing whenever it was not necessary to sit—led to varicose veins.

His condition worsened, becoming an open, running sore which was diagnosed as cancer. The wound became so extreme, odorous, and painful as to require amputation. This was another turning point for Peregrine. Now he is sixty. The one who had seen ugliness and suffering and served and supported others now faced the ugliness and suffering in himself. The healer was wounded and the servant needed to be served. He went to the faith he had preached to others, and the goodness of God he had ministered so long. The night before the surgery, in the priory chapel room, he prayed before the image of the Crucified. In the prayer-filled sleep that followed, he envisioned his crucified Lord descending the cross and touching his cancerous leg. Upon awakening, he discovered his wound healed.

The reputation of this beloved holy man grew as the years passed. Twenty years later, on May 1, 1345, he died at age eighty. He was canonized in 1726 and is universally invoked as the patron of cancer victims. (The National Shrine of St. Peregrine is in Chicago, St. Dominic Church.)

RECONCILIATION ("Penance"; "Confession")

The Four Traditional Parts of Reconciliation
1. Contrition—internal attitude of sorrow and repentance.
2. Confession—clear telling of sin for which absolution is requested.
3. Absolution—emphasizing healing power of Jesus.
4. Satisfaction—penance, reform of life, amends.

Going to the Table, Not Confession

The "Penitential Rite" is not to be confused with the Sacrament of Reconciliation. Lacking sacramental absolution, it is an understated, preparatory and optional rite, to help the assembly reflect on their spiritual condition and bring a humble attitude to worship. At times, a sprinkling rite may replace it, recalling the waters of baptism as well as the tears of repentance.

The Three Elements of Contrition
1. Hatred of the sin (mind)
2. Grief (heart)
3. Firm purpose of amendment (will)

The Four Qualities of Genuine Contrition
1. Internal
2. Supernatural
3. Universal (extending to all sins)
4. Sovereign (recognition of sin as the greatest evil)

Sacramental Seal
The obligation of secrecy enjoined on the minister of reconciliation.

Under the Rose

"*Sub rosa*," some would say. In any language it means "in strictest confidence." Beginning in the sixteenth century, the rose was occasionally enshrined over a confessional symbolizing the sacramental seal. Its origin is obscure. It may refer to the myth of Cupid bribing Harpocrates (the god of silence) with a rose so that he would not reveal the amorous activities of Venus, the goddess of sensual love (and well known for practicing what she preached). A rose over a dining room table means that anything spoken around the table is to remain in the room.

Outline of the New Rite of Penance

Form 1 Reconciliation of Individual Penitents	Form 2 Reconciliation of Several Penitents with Individual Confession, Absolution	Form 3 Reconciliation of Several Penitents with General Confession, Absolution
Introductory Rite		
1. Sign of the Cross 2. Priest draws penitent to faith and trust in God's healing mercy and welcomes the penitent	1. Hymn/antiphon/psalm 2. Dialogue salutation—priest/congregation 3. Oration by priest: exhortation, statement of purpose, invitation to pray, silent moments, prayer	1. Hymn/antiphon/psalm 2. Dialogue salutation—priest/congregation 3. Oration by priest: exhortation, invitation, silence, prayer
Celebration of the Word		
3. (Recommended) Priest offers text with announcement of God's mercy and call to conversion	4. (Obligatory) One text (Gospel) or several, Response and/or silence 5. Homily 6. Examination of conscience	4. (Obligatory) One text (Gospel) or several, Response and/or silence 5. *"Monitio"* (homily and examen), drawing out confession of sinfulness
Reconciliation Rite		
4. Confession and possible advice from priest; suggested penance 5. Prayer of penitent in which sorrow is expressed 6. Absolution, with gesture of imposed hands	7. General confession of sin using Confiteor, litany, hymn 8. Individual confession 9. Individual absolution	6. General confession (some sign by those desiring to receive, e.g. kneeling or head bowed litany, Confiteor) 7. General absolution*
Concluding Rite		
7. Praise of God in dialogue with priest 8. Dismissal of penitent: prayer of proclamation	10. Proclamation praising God's mercy, (hymn, antiphon, psalm or prayer of priest). 11. Blessing of all 12 Dismissal dialogue priest/congregation	8. Proclamation of God's mercy 9. Blessing of all 10. Dismissal

*General absolution may be given only in restricted circumstances as described in the new Rite of Penance and determined by the national episcopal conference. (1) Danger of death. (2) Number of penitents: insufficient number of confessors to hear individual confessions properly within a suitable period of time, requiring penitents (through no fault of their own) to go without sacramental grace or holy communion for a long time.

The keys represent the Church's power to bind and to loose, to open and to close."

Censures
Each is surrounded by technicality, and can take many forms.

Interdict (On a Place or its Inhabitants)
Withholds certain privileges from the faithful who remain, however, in communion. For example, attendance at liturgical services, Christian burial, some of the sacraments. The bishop of La-Crosse, Wisconsin, imposed an interdict in 1975 because of the false apparitions of Necedah.

Excommunication ("anathema," if formal)
Generally, affects one's ability to receive the sacraments, notably Eucharist; it pertains to one's relationship to the communion of the faithful, and depends on such factors as public obstinancy. Remitted by pope, bishop or in certain cases even by a priest confessor.

Vitandus
Most severe form of excommunication; public excommunication by name by the Holy See; literally, "to be avoided" ("except in the case of husband and wife, parents, children . . .") A remedial measure reflecting St. Paul's mandates to the early Christian community (2 Thes 3.6,14–15).

Abortion and Excommunication
"A person who actually procures an abortion incurs an automatic (*latae sententiae*) excommunication." So says the new code of Canon law, practically repeating the 1917 code. This penalty:

1. Includes accomplices without whom abortion would not have happened.
2. Presumes other requirements of the law are present:
   a. The abortion was intended and successful (that is, not an accidental loss of child or miscarriage).
   b. The woman knew of this penalty attached to the law.
   c. She was at least eighteen at the time of the abortion.
   d. She had full use of reason (not retarded/psychologically disturbed).
   e. She did not act out of serious fear.

This excommunication can be remitted by the local bishop. (Confessors have been delegated by many bishops to absolve from this penalty—at least in the case of a first abortion.)

THE ANOINTING OF THE SICK

According to the Church's "Rite of Anointing and Pastoral Care of the Sick," the following are among those who should be anointed:

1. Those whose health is seriously impaired by sickness or old age
2. Those about to undergo surgery because of a serious illness
3. Elderly weakened by age, even if no serious illness is present
4. Sick children who are sufficiently mature to be comforted by the sacrament

Snakes and Healing

A single snake wound about a staff is the symbol of Asclepius, the ancient Greek god of medicine (the Roman version being Aesculapius). Serpents were sacred to Asclepius, maybe because of the superstition that they are able to renew their youth by a change of their skin. Since 291 B.C. there was a temple dedicated to Asclepius on Tiber Island (in Rome). In the Christian era, there was a church built in honor of St. Bartholomew on the same island to which healing hostelries were annexed, thus illustrating the mutual relationship of the ministry and the profession.

The caduceus, often confused with the medical symbol, is another symbol, similar but definitely distinct. Twin snakes intertwined on a winged staff, it is the symbol of Mercury, messenger of the gods and god of merchants. (He got it from Apollo in exchange for the famous lyre he made out of a shell.)

Others, putting all this serpentine pagan mythology aside, prefer to believe that the snake-on-the-stick symbol derives from the Biblical story in Numbers 21. The Lord directed Moses to make a seraph and mount it on a pole. The repentant Israelites, dying from the attack of the seraph serpents, would be healed with just one look.

Either way, the snake-encircled-staff is one thing, and the caduceus is something else again.

A Wounded Healer

There was once a man of God who was afflicted with pestilence and the plague. Some call him St. Roch (rosh) and some Roque (rock), and he represents every wounded healer, since he "worked miracles on the plague-stricken, while he was himself smitten with the same judgment." He is sometimes pictured seeking healing: garbed as a pilgrim, he is presenting a wound on his thigh to an angel for its healing touch. Legend also relates of God's providence to him in a story of a hound bearing bread to him daily as he perished of pestilence in the forest.

MARRIAGE

Constituative Elements of Matrimony

1. **Readiness**
2. **Capacity** (that is, lack of:)
    A. "Impeding" impediments
       rendering the marriage "illegal" (canonically), but valid (sacramentally)
    B. "Diriment" impediments
       rendering the marriage invalid (e.g. existing bond, Holy Orders, solemn vows, lack of age, consanguinity)
3. **Public Ratification** (with two witnesses, the Church/priest)*
    A. Receives intentions (permanence/fidelity/children)
    B. Elicits vows
4. **Sexual Consummation**

Banns (A.S.: *bannan*, to summon; later: to proclaim)

It is an ancient custom to publicize a marriage in the parishes of the marrying party for the purpose of discovering any impediments to the marriage. Anyone with such knowledge was conscience bound to reveal it to the pastor. Originally it was done after the second reading.

Marriage as Metaphor Rv 19.7 21.1–22.5 Hos 1–3 Sg Jer 2.2

The Covenant—is like a marriage (Hos 2.16–22; Is 54.4f; 62.5; Ez 16.6–14)
Idolatry (sinning)—is like adultery (Hos 2.4–15; Ez 16.15–63; 23.1–21)
Christ—is like a bridegroom (Mt 9.15; 25.1–13; Jn 3.29)
The Church—is like a bride (2 Cor 11.2; Eph 5.22–27)

*The ring is a symbol of fidelity and permanence. (See Ring in Symbols chapter).

Mothers' Day

The fourth Sunday of Lent has always been the joyful one, "Laetare Sunday," after the first words of the Introit, "Rejoice with Jerusalem." At the mid-way point of Lent is offered a respite to the season's rigors. Additionally, there was the ancient practice of handing over the Apostle's Creed to the catechumens that day (or during the week prior), the last and decisive step for those to be initiated and reborn at the Easter Vigil. The "sponsoring community" would have been deeply conscious of its own spiritual birth and life. Not surprising, the ancient and indulgenced custom of visiting one's mother church or cathedral developed on this same day, "Mothering Sunday." Small countryside chapels served as the weekly gathering places for liturgy, but on this Sunday all would go to the mother church of the parish, where they had been baptized, with their offerings. In a natural evolution of this "pilgrimage," children would also return home to spend the day with mother and parents, with "mother cakes" and simnel cakes prepared specially for the occasion. Roses were the traditional flowers for the day, naturally, because rose was the color of the vestments and the decoration on the altar. After Mass, the roses were taken to mothers. One tradition presents Mothering Sunday as an honor to St. Anne, the Blessed Mother's mother, when children would "go a-mothering" and bring flowers, gifts, and sweets to their mother. Long before Anna Jarvis held her service to honor all mothers in 1907, or Woodrow Wilson proclaimed the second Sunday in May "Mothers' Day" in 1914, folks were honoring mothers, spiritual and natural, and mid-Lent Sunday had become a day of family reunion and festivity.

Mothers' Patrons

St. Monica is the celebrated patron of mothers, given her experience with the wayward son-become-saint, Augustine. Anne, mother of the mother of the Savior, is another natural as a mother's patron. There are other saints who are also mothers of saints, though less well known: Blanche, mother of Louis; Bridget, mother of Catherine of Sweden; Elizabeth, mother of John the Baptist; Emelia, mother of Basil the Great; Margaret of Scotland, mother of David; Philippa, mother of Theodore; Sophia, mother of Charity, Faith, and Hope; and Sylvia, mother of Gregory the Great.

The End of a Marriage Bond

1. **Death**
2. **Dissolution**
   a. Pauline Privilege (unbaptized parties; see 1 Cor 7.12–16)
   b. In privilege of the faith (one party unbaptized)
3. **Annulment** ("invalidation")
   a. Lack of freedom
   b. Intention against permanence/fidelity/children
   c. Inadequate mental competence
4. **Lack of form**
   (A marriage outside the Church with no dispensation)

HOLY ORDERS

Major Orders

Bishop ("episcopacy"), the fullness of Holy Orders

Priest ("priesthood"), a participation in the ministerial priesthood*

Deacon ("diaconate"), a participation in the ministerial priesthood

Today, as in the early Church, offered as a permanent office; also transitional step toward fuller exercise of Orders. A candidate for the permanent diaconate must be thirty-five years old, and may be married (however, once ordained he may not remarry should his wife die).

---

*Traditionally, a distinction is made between (1) *Secular Priests*, that is, those living in daily contact with the world, notably **diocesan priests,** sharing/assisting the bishop's pastoring of a diocese, vowing celibacy (single for the Lord) and obedience to the bishop; and (2) *Religious (Order) Priests*, those living in monastic and/or community life.

Minor Orders *(formerly)*

A "subdiaconate" has been suppressed, as have the other minor orders:

Lector (reader)

Exorcist (casting out devils)

Acolyte (light bearer/server)

These were stages of preparation for priestly ministry following upon tonsure (initiation into clerical state). Today largely unused, or integrated and exercised within normal Church life and ministry in the broad sense.

"Tonsura," a Shaving

Originally, a priestly practice dating from the fifth–sixth century of shaving the head, or part of it, symbolic of the crown of thorns. More recently and with secular clergy, only a token clip was retained, with no literal tonsure worn after the ordination. Historically among "regular clergy" (religious), this took as many forms and symbolisms as religious garb took. A classic example would be the former Dominican practice of shaving the whole crown above the top of the ears. In 1972, tonsure was discontinued and instead, entrance into the clerical state has been joined with the diaconate.

Liturgy of Ordination

Calling of the candidate
Presentation of the candidate
Election by the bishop and consent of the people
Instruction
Examination of the candidate
Promise of obedience
Invitation to prayer
Litany of the Saints (candidate prostrates)
Laying on of hands
Prayer of consecration
Investiture with stole and chasuble
Anointing of hands
Presentation of gifts
Kiss of peace

A Clerical Glossary

Celebret (Lt: let him celebrate)
A document stating a person is a priest in good standing and requesting that he be permitted to say Mass; requiring the signature of his bishop (or superior).

Exeat
Official permission for a priest to leave his diocese or a monk his monastery ("let him go forth").

Excardination
Release of a cleric from the jurisdiction of one bishop to another (who would "incardinate" him).

Faculties
Practically, the right granted by an ordinary (bishop) to a priest for administering the Sacrament of Reconciliation; technically, referring to rights granted by the pope to ordinaries, and ordinaries to priests, enabling the exercise of the ministry for the sake of the faithful in their jurisdiction.

Sinecure (Lt: *sine cura;* "without cure/care")
Salary without responsibility. A position (and salary), a benefice, without pastoral responsibility (care for souls).

Garb
Clerical Dress (uniforms)—worn for work
Liturgical Dress (vestments)—worn during liturgy
Religious' Dress (habits)—worn after postulancy (upon novitiate)

The Roman Collar
In the early Church, priests wore contemporary dress, just as the Lord was not distinctive, but common in dress. In 313, the Edict of Milan put the Church and Her priests in a different posture in society. Marks of distinction and signs of respect would not be surprising, although most changes were more liturgical than public.

It was in the Middle Ages, and among religious, not secular clerics, that distinctive dress definitely evolved. Over time, the full-length work apron of the Benedictines, for example, became the black "scapular" that distinguished this religious community. Mendicant orders as well, like the Franciscans and Dominicans, adopted a comparable habit.

Some form of clerical dress among some secular priests probably arose in the eighth century with a directive to them suggesting a distinctly religious mode of dress. Some say that the Roman collar evolved from this. Others say it has a military origin. Still others explain that diocesan clergy, unlike religious, had no uniform habit but only street clothes. It was the common cloak that evolved into a cassock, and the Roman collar from this (or under it): when high, detachable collars on shirts became the fashion for men, secular priests followed suit, except reversing the collar so the opening ended up in back and a white band in front. Under the upturned collar of the cloak-become-cassock, this white band became a Roman collar. For all of this, there is mention of a collar by the Second Council of Nicaea (A.D. 787), explaining its symbolism in terms of poverty, to this, the Council of Trent (1545) added the symbolism of dignity; and, in 1931, the symbolic meaning of protection was added in the decrees of a Sacred Congregation.

Various Titles Used for Those in Holy Orders

For those in the universal hierarchy (pope, cardinal, archbishop, patriarch, primate). The phrase *Dei gratia,* "by the grace of God", sometimes following a title expresses the divine vocation.

Abbot (Aramaic *abba, father), Abbess (feminine)*
A monastic superior, fixed as a title by St. Benedict; elected, usually for life, by the secret ballot of his community; has paternal authority within his monastery, and also quasi-episcopal authority in the Church because of the territorial jurisdiction. Insignia are pectoral cross and ring; as a bishop, has priority over a prior, whose priory is within his jurisdiction (the territory of the abbey).

Bishop (Gk: overseer)
Pastor of a diocese.

Celebrant
Ordained clergyman officiating.

Chaplain (guardian of the *cappella:* the cloak of St. Martin)
A clergyman ministering to a group other than a congregation.

Clergyman (Clergy from Gk: *Kleros,* portion; see Dt. 18.2; Acts 1.17)
"The Lord is their inheritance"; an ordained minister of Word and Sacrament; in 1 Pet 5.3 the Church is called God's portion, or lot; in the Old Testament the tribe of Levi was so-called.

Ad clerum—A statement "to the clergy", instead of *ad populum,* to the people.

Curate
One with the care (cura) of souls, especially a parish priest. Often used for pastor's assistant or associate. See curator, overseer. French: cure (Lt: cura); for example, the Cure or Ars.

Deacon (Gk: servant)
Ordained clergyman of the first rank; either a permanent vocation or a transitional step toward fuller exercise of orders as a priest or bishop.

Dom (Lt: dominus, master, lord)
Used by religious of Benedictine, Carthusian, and Cistercian Orders; originally applied to pope, later to bishops, then to monks.

Father (see: Spanish padre)
A title given to priests that emphasizes family relationships, common among Catholics.

Man of the Cloth
"Cloth" refers to vestments, the distinctive dress expressive of the office; formerly, the distinctive garb of any trade, restricted to the clergy's cloth around the seventeenth century.

Minister (Lt: "mini", little things)
Emphasis on service ("doer of little things") contrasted with magister (Lt: magi) suggesting triumphalism ("doer of great things").

Monsignor
Title of honor, derived from the Italian word for "my lord." It originates in feudal Europe when clergy designated with this courtly title of distinction were considered to be connected in some way with the papal household. It is still a practice in some dioceses for a bishop to recommend and the pope to approve this designation for certain diocesan clergy. (Technically: either prothonotary apostolic, domestic prelate, or papal chamberlain.)

Parson (M.E.: persone, person; persona, mask)
Emphasis on role (alter Christus, other Christ); pre-reformation meaning: "Person of the Church" (Persona Ecclesiae), priest in charge of a parish; now referring mainly to Anglican ministers.

Pastor (Lt: shepherd)
Head of a parish; favorite in the early Church.

Preacher (Lt: praedicare, to speak before)
Emphasis on function of proclaiming God's Word.

Prelate (Lt: praelatus, carried before)
Designating one promoted, ranking above, one in an office with jurisdiction over other clergy, which would include especially cardinals and bishops; by association, other more historically ephemoral positions of honor (monsignore).

Presbyter (Gk: elder)
Presider in the community.

Priest (Eng: corruption of presbyter)
Common with Catholic, Orthodox, and Episcopal.

Prior (Lt: former, first, superior)
A superior in a monastery that, usually, is a dependency of an abbey, hence "prior simplex."

Provincial
The superior of an order's monastic houses in a province.

Rector
Popularly, a pastor: the chief clergyman of a parish, (hence, the residence called a "rectory"); common with the Episcopal. Technically, the head of a religious community of men or of an educational institution. Canonically, the priest in charge of a church that is not (only) parochial (for example, a cathedral).

Reverend (Lt: *reverentia*)
An epithet of respect, having the same root as reverent, revered and reverence (the virtue that honors those with dignity).

The Four Forms of Reverence

(corresponding to the four forms of dignity)
1. Familial reverence—toward parents (or those taking their place)
2. Civil reverence—toward civil authorities
3. Ecclesiastical reverence—toward those in the service of the Church
4. Religious reverence—toward any person/place/thing related to God

---

Right Reverend
This use of the adjective "right" has the archaic meaning of "in great degree," "extremely"; it is sometimes used in reference to bishops, abbots, and monsignors.

Superior
Generic term, often synonymous with abbot or prior; one in authority in a religious order.

Vicar (Lt: in place of)
Clergyman who serves in place of the rector.

The Liturgy of the Hours

The Church's full cycle of daily prayer, daily opened with the *Venite Ex-sultemus* (Ps 95). The fulfillment of the obligation to pray at stated times: in the morning, in the evening and before retiring. Called the Divine Office ("sacred duty"), it was updated by Vatican II and published as The Liturgy of the Hours in 1971. The book used for its celebration was called the Breviary. Called *opus Dei* ("work of God") by the Benedictines.

Obligation

Those in major orders (bishops, priests and deacons), as well as certain religious communities, have been obliged, historically, to celebrate this liturgy. The mandate to pray the Liturgy of the Hours belongs to the whole Church. ("*The Little Office of the Blessed Virgin Mary,*" introduced by St. Peter Damian in the eleventh century, is a version of the Hours traditionally used by many religious communities and members of sodalities.)

Formerly

Traditionally, there were seven canonical hours ("Seven times a day do I praise you," Ps 119.164), chanted in monastic communities. With much variation, the pattern was seven daytime Offices and the night Office:

1. Matins (Fr: morning; for the early hours, after midnight)
2. Lauds (Lt: praise, from Ps 148–150)
3. Prime ("first": 6 am)
4. Terce ("third": 9 am)
   This midmorning prayer's opening hymn commemorated the Spirit's descent upon the Apostles; now, along with Sext and None, part of the Middle Hour.
5. Sext ("sixth": noon)
6. None ("ninth": 3 pm)
7. Vespers ("evening," hence the medieval English term "evensong")
   Compline (from *completorium*, "completing" day's services)

Currently

Morning and Evening Prayer are restored as the most important "hinges" of each day's Office.

- 1st Hour: Office of Readings (corresponding to ancient Matins)
  Not an "hour" (time) in the sense the other hours are, but two readings: one Biblical and one patristic (Fathers) or hagiographical (saints).

- 2nd Hour: Morning Prayer ("Lauds")

- 3rd Hour: Daytime Prayer ("Middle Hour")
  Reducing to one the "Little Hours" of Prime, Terce, Sext and None for those not saying the Office in choir (depending upon the time one has the choice of midmorning, midday, or midafternoon).

- 4th Hour: Evening Prayer ("Vespers")

- 5th Hour: Night Prayer

Elements of the Liturgy of the Hours

Morning Prayer	Daytime Prayer	Evening Prayer	Night Prayer
Introduction (Invitatory) Verse Antiphon Psalm 95	Introduction Verse Doxology Alleluia	Introduction Verse Doxology Alleluia	Introduction Verse Doxology Alleluia
			Examination of Conscience —Penitential Prayer
Hymn	Hymn	Hymn	Hymn
Psalmody Psalm Old Testament Canticle Psalm	Psalmody Psalm Psalm Psalm	Psalmody Psalm Psalm New Testament Canticle	Psalmody
Reading —pause for reflection	Reading —pause for reflection	Reading —pause for reflection	Reading —pause for reflection
Responsory	Responsory	Responsory	Responsory
Gospel Canticle —of Zechariah		Gospel Canticle —of Mary	Gospel Canticle of Simeon
Intercessions		Intercessions	
Lord's Prayer		Lord's Prayer	
Final Prayer —Trinitarian ending	Final Prayer —simple ending	Final Prayer —Trinitarian ending	Final Prayer —simple ending
Conclusion	Conclusion	Conclusion	Conclusion
			Marian Antiphon

PRINCIPAL SACRAMENTALS

Holy Objects (ashes, bells, candles, crucifixes, holy water, images, incense, medals, oils, palms, rosaries, scapulars). (Disposal by burial where there will be no desecration; or burning, or pouring liquids directly into the ground.) Holy Actions (blessings, exorcisms, sign of the cross)

Holy Oils (O.S., *Olea Sancta*)

In 1970 it was declared that, if necessary, holy oils may be from any plant and not only from olives. The blessing of oils has traditionally been done on Holy Thursday by a bishop at a cathedral. The supply distributed to local churches is kept in the ambry, and the unused portion, a year later, burned in the sanctuary lamp.

• Used in the sacraments which impart a sacramental character:

Baptism   Confirmation   Holy Orders

• Used in the sacrament of healing:

Anointing of the sick

• Used in the blessing of various objects.

1. **Chrism** (S.C., *Sacrum Chrisma*)
   Used in baptisms, confirmations, and orders.
   Also for blessing tower bells, baptismal water; and for consecrating churches, altars, chalices, and patons; a mixture of olive oil and balsam (or balm).

2. **Oil of Catechumens/Of the Saints**
   (O.C., *Oleum, Catechumenorum* O.S., *Oleum Sanctorum*)
   Used in baptism, whence the name.
   Also for consecrating churches, blessing altars, ordaining priests.

3. **Oil of the Sick** (O.I., *Oleum Infirmorum*)
   Used in the Sacrament of Healing/Anointing.

Blessed Oils

The Church also recognizes the use of blessed oil by a lay person, as other sacramentals which "extend and radiate the sacraments" (as holy water or candles do, for example.) The purpose would normally be for healing and protection, and the method, a simple signing of the forehead (or appropriate part of the body) with a cross using the oil.

St. Aidan's Cruse of Oil

In his Ecclesiastical History the Venerable Bede relates (735) that St. Aidan entrusted a cruse of oil to a young priest who was to escort a maiden to King Oswin for his wedding. In case of troubled waters the oil was to be used for calm. A storm did arise and Aidan's oil reduced the trauma.

Bells

Blessing of Bells
There is a solemn ceremony done by a bishop; the bells are washed with holy water, anointed with holy oils inside and out, and prayed over: that at the sound of these bells, evil spirits may be put to flight and God's people summoned to prayer. (There is also a simple blessing.)

Bells Silenced
Formerly, from Holy Thursday (the Gloria) until the Easter Vigil (the Gloria), commemorating Christ's passion.

Bells Ringing
A *single swinging bell* traditionally called people to church. Pulled by a bell rope, the pivoted bell would swing, causing the clapper inside to strike it. As the bell swings toward and then away, tone and volume change, creating the familiar "ding, dong."

Pealing bells (two or more swinging), synonymous with celebration, produce a random, beautiful sound, given the difference in speed and sound between lighter and heaver bells (as in the famous and beautiful St. Anne de Beaupre three-bell Angelus).

A *tolling bell* is stationary, struck by a heavy clapper, producing a stately, solemn sound, as for funerals. The *De Profundis*, the methodical, solemn toll of the bourdon bell (the bell of lowest pitch in a carillon) marked the end of the day at 9 P.M., the traditional occasion of the common community night prayer for the faithful departed. See "Soul Bell."

Angelus Bell
Consisting of three strokes, each followed by a pause, then nine strokes while the Angelus prayer is being finished.

Church Bell
Originally an "Ave bell," inviting worshippers to prepare with a Marian prayer, more than a "church-going bell."

Sance/Sacring/Sanctus Bell
The bell rung during the Mass (a practice which began in the sixth century), traditionally: at the *sanctus,* to signal the consecration (*"hanc igitur"*), institution (three times each at "elevation" of host and chalice), three times before the priest's communion (*"domine, non sum dignus"*) and in some places again three times before congregation's communion.

Sick Call
The ring of a bell announces the presence of the Eucharist and the service of a priest.

Tower Bell
Dawn, noon, and evening ringing is traditional, as well as during the elevation, in another era, inviting people through the countryside to join the prayer.

Incense

Symbolic in its burning (zeal, fervor), its fragrance (virtue) and its rising smoke (acceptable prayer, as noted in **Psalm 141.2**).

Veneration is shown by incensing, as in the incensation of the altar, the book of the Gospel, the gifts, the people, and the body of the deceased during a funeral. Five grains of it are deposited in the Paschal candle at the Easter Vigil, representing Christ's five wounds. The old blessing of incense included the prayer, "Be blessed by Him in whose honor you will burn."

Frankincense

This is the main ingredient, *boswellia carterii,* of the incense used in today's liturgies. A resin produced by a family of desert trees that grow in southern Arabia, it is derived from a sap that dries, forming crystalline lumps of an amber/gold color. For Christians, it has a rich prayer and purification symbolism. From earliest Christian days, it has been associated with Christ, beginning with the magi gift (Mt 2.10–11). Even before that, the Jews regarded its rich spicy scent as a pure offering, pleasing to God. Even beyond Judeo-Christian circles, frankincense has been prized for centuries in Palestine, Egypt, Greece, and Rome not only as a way to honor gods, but as a medicine, and as a base for perfume.

The old procedure for incensing the gifts according to the rubrics of the Roman missal: 1–6 in the form of a cross, 7–9 in a circle:

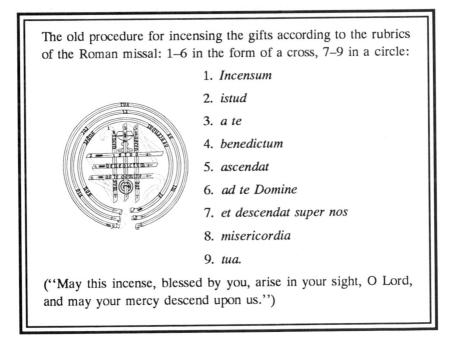

1. *Incensum*

2. *istud*

3. *a te*

4. *benedictum*

5. *ascendat*

6. *ad te Domine*

7. *et descendat super nos*

8. *misericordia*

9. *tua.*

("May this incense, blessed by you, arise in your sight, O Lord, and may your mercy descend upon us.")

Candles

Altar candles (formerly, at least fifty-one percent beeswax) Expressing "devotion or the degree of festivity" according to the *General Instruction of the Roman Missal*, on or around the altar.

Baptismal Candle
Its lighting (from the Christ candle) and presentation are part of Christian initiation.

Christ Candle or Paschal Candle
A prime Christ/Easter symbol; remains lit, from its enthronement during the Easter Vigil, throughout "The Great Feast" (the fifty days of Easter) until it is extinguished and transferred to a less prominent, though visible, place on Pentecost. Thereafter, it is used for its resurrection symbolism at baptisms and funerals.

Sanctuary Candle/lamp/light
Signaling Blessed Sacrament presence.

Triple Candle
At the Easter Vigil it was lit by the deacon chanting *Lumen Christi* (Light of Christ) while the choir answered *Deo Gratias* (Thanks be to God). From this the paschal candle was then lit. Today the paschal candle is lit directly from the new fire.

Unity Candle
A recent innovation for weddings, doing the wedding ring one better: using a single candle flanked by two others representing the couple (and their baptism?).

"I Am the Light of the World"

It is still an optional part of the Easter Vigil to "stress the Christ Candle's dignity and significance" by decorating it with a cross ("Christ yesterday and today/the beginning and the end"), the Greek *alpha* and *omega,* and the numerals of the current year (". . . all time belongs to him/and all the ages/to him be glory and power/through every age for ever. Amen."), and then inserting five grains of incense in the cross ("By his holy/and glorious wounds/may Christ our Lord/guard us/and keep us. Amen.").

Vigil Candles/lights
Representing the prayerful vigilance of expectant faith.

Blessed Candles
Those for home use, blessed on Candlemas.

Candlemas Day

Old Simeon sand, "Lord, now lettest thy servant depart in peace, according to thy word, for mine eyes have seen the glory of thy salvation . . . ."—and if that sounds familiar ("mine eyes have seen the glory of the coming of the Lord"), it's because this is where Julia (Ward Howe) got her idea for "The Battle Hymn of the Republic."

The occasion of Simeon's song, the *"Nunc Dimittis,"* was the presentation of Jesus in the temple, and it's all in Luke 2. In the East, and in the early Middle Ages, it was called the *"Hypapante,"* or "Meeting," (between Jesus, Simeon, and Anna). It's an "epiphany" too, part of the Lord's whole pattern of manifestation: nativity, magi visit, baptism, first miracle at Cana. It was also known as "Feast of Simeon, the Old Man."

When the feast was later adopted in the Western Church ("Roman Catholic"), the increasing devotion to the Blessed Mother made it a day to honor her: "the Purification," which was of course the reason for the presentation. In common with all Jewish mothers, Mary took her child to the temple after forty days, the period during which she was excluded from public worship according to the Law of Moses (Lev 13). To this day, the feast is kept forty days after Christmas, but called "The Presentation of the Lord," a "Dominical" feast, and not a Marian one.

The English name Candlemas, "Candle Mass," was common because the Mass has often been preceded by the blessing and distribution of candles—at least since the seventh century—probably to symbolize Christ's role as Light of the World. What better way to give the Season of Light's victory over darkness one last hurrah? Some suggest that the candle association grew out of the light processions in honor of Mary in Rome on the occasion, which were a Christian substitute for the ancient torch parades.

Though the revised calendar has overshadowed this lightsome feast, we may still like to keep at least a remnant of the Christmas season's greenery and lights til now, in order to keep the old Christmas to Candlemas Season. (But not a day longer! There's an old legend that houses will be haunted by goblins that are still decorated for Christmas after Candlemas eve.)

The Flame of Faith

Christmas Candles

Several centuries ago in Ireland, during the suppression of Catholicism by the English persecution, priests were driven to visiting homes in secret, where Mass could be said at night. At Christmastime, the Catholic families would leave their doors unlocked and put candles in the windows that would guide priests to their homes. Any soldiers noticing the open doors and lit candles were simply told that it was to welcome Mary and Joseph on Christmas Eve. The signal remained, as the soldiers dismissed the story as harmless superstition.

"Candles in a Storm"

Faith in things unseen can be bolstered by things seen—like a burning candle. Especially during a storm (including those within), forgetfulness of the Guardian threatens heart and home. And so popular piety would light a candle—blessed at Candlemas, of course—for protection, if not from the storm, then at least from the thunder and lightning of fear itself.

Holy Water

Used for baptizing, and to recall it; symbolizing exterior and interior purity; blessed in solemn ritual during the Easter Vigil; in "mini fonts" at church doorways and in homes, for use coming and going; sometimes sprinkled on individuals/assemblies/objects as part of a blessing; part of the revised penitential rite.

Asperges

The old Latin name used for the ceremony of holy water sprinkling at Mass; from the first words of the psalm used in the rite, "You will sprinkle me with hyssop . . .". The asperges is replaced in the Easter season by the hymn *Vidi Aquam*, "I beheld Water" (from Ez 47 and Ps 117.1).

Medals

To commemorate, memorialize, inspire; of or about the Lord, the Blessed Mother, the saints. (See "Miraculous Medal.")

Scapulars

Originally, part of the habit of a religious. (See Scapular.)

Palms

Received and used on Palm Sunday as a prayerful reminder of Christ's triumphant entry into Jerusalem and his death and resurrection. After Palm Sunday, it has become tradition to display them, often in some artistic form (braided, woven, crosswise), often along with a crucifix or sacred picture. On the following Ash Wednesday, they may be burned, with the ashes then used for the beginning of Lent.

Ashes

Used principally for Ash Wednesday markings, altar consecrating, church dedicating.

Liturgical Year

TIME

1. Quantity: *chronos* . . . "time" . . . ("What *chronos* is it?")
   (The time when something happens)
2. Quality: *kairos* . . . "opportunity" . . . ("Once upon a *kairos* . . .")
   (The time of something religiously significant)

"Be sure you make the best use of your *kairos*." Col 4.5 also Eph 5.16
"Be on guard, you never know when the *kairos* will come." Mk 13.33

The Calendar

The civil calendar is, as it were, the "nature" on which grace builds the liturgical year. Our current calendar is the Gregorian (or Reformed, or New Style), which is the civil year according to the correction made on the Julian calendar by Pope Gregory XII in 1582.

The Julian (Old Style) Calendar

In 46 B.C., Julius Caesar attempted to adapt the calendar year to the time required by the earth to make one complete revolution around the sun (a "solar year"). He established the current number of days per month, and incidently, gave his name to the fifth, "July." He alloted 365 1/4 days per year, the "common year," with the quarter day included by adding one day every four years, "leap year."

The Gregorian (New Style, or Reformed) Calendar

By 1582 the calendar was reading March 11 at the time of the vernal equinox, (which had occurred on "March 25" in Caesar's day. On a solar calendar, such annual and predictable solar phenomena (seasons) should have been "immovable feasts" falling on the same date every year. This should be as true as the lunar phenomena (full moons) being "immovable feasts" on a lunar calendar (see 14th Nisan and the Jewish lunar calendar). But even with Caesar's system, man's calendar and mother nature were not keeping in step. This was because his allotment of 365 1/4 days per year was eleven minutes and 10 seconds too much. The sun was faster than Julius calculated and, by 1582, was two weeks ahead. Two astronomers, Lilius and Clavius, calculated the astronomical year to be 365.2422, and not 365.25. In this calendar reform, Gregory therefore decreed that an exception to leap year would be made whereby the intercalary day would not be added in centenary years not divisible by 400 (hence, 1600 and 2000 would be leap years, and 1700, 1800 and 1900 would not be, because of this exception). Gregory then selected March 21 as the equinox date, because that is when it was in the year of the Council of Nicea (which fixed the dating of Easter). Then, on October 4, 1582, he suppressed ten days, making 1582 the year that October 15 followed October 4. Immediately. By the simple new formula, the same error was prevented from happening in the future (except for the one day every thirty-five centuries). At first, Protestant countries refused to use the Reformed Calendar; it was adopted in England finally in 1752, and in Russia in 1918.

The Year

This Dominical Year

The current year, a year of our Lord *(anno Domini)*, is a number based on the supposed year Jesus Christ was born, devised by Dionysius Exiguus (d. A.D. 550). The consensus of modern scholarship is that the actual birth was several years earlier, either between seven B.C. and four B.C., based on the death of Herod the Great (Mt 2.19) in four B.C., or in A.D. six, based on the great taxation of Quirinius (Lk 2.1–2).

Numbering Years

Christian A.D.: Lt, *Anno Domini ("In the Year of the Lord");* B.C.: Before Christ

Hebrew A.M.: Lt, *Anno Mundi* ("In the Year of the World"). In the Hebrew tradition, the year of creation corresponds to 3761 B.C.

Moslem A.H.: Lt, *Anno Hegira* ("In the Year of the Hegira"). Muhammad's flight from Mecca to Medina in A.D. 622, beginning the Muslim era

Roman A.U.C.: Lt, *Ab Urbe Condita* ("From the Founding of the City"), speaking of Rome, and 753 B.C.

Generic C.E.: Common Era; B.C.E.: Before the Common Era

There is no religious significance to the *"ides"* of a month (as the *ides of March*, popularized by Shakespeare's play *Julius Caesar,* the day of the Emperor's assassination). The *"ides,"* the *"calends,"* and the *"nones"* are simply the three specific days each month that the Romans used when they divided the year into twelve months to compute the divisions. The *ides* are always either the 13th or the 15th.

Good Luck and Amazing Grace

In more superstitious times, grace may have been amazing enough, but luck was too good not to want. In Highland Scotland, for example, it was believed that June 9 was the luckiest day of the whole year, especially those years when it fell on a Thursday. Why June 9th? That was the day St. Columba died, in 597, and so became his feast day. More edifying than superstition is the amazing grace at work in evangelists. . . . like Columba. He was a priest who determined to convert the Picts to the Lord, relying not on good luck, but on grace. He embarked with twelve disciples around 563 to build a church and a monastery on the island of Iona, near Scotland.

The Seasons

Ember Days

These are nature feasts spiritualized from pagan practices at the changes of the seasons (A.S. *ymbren,* running about, revolution)—three days of prayer, fasting for spiritual renewal and blessings on the seasons, four times a year: the Wednesday, Friday, and Saturday of the weeks which would include: St. Lucia's Day, Dec. 13 (the third Sunday of Advent); the First Sunday in Lent; Pentecost; and Holy Cross Day, Sept. 14. (Ember Days and Ember Weeks were fixed by the Council of Placentia, 1095).

The Months

Names of the Months of the Year

January—Janus, god of doors
With two faces, looks forward to current year as well as back at former

February—Lt: *Februa*
Roman festival of expiation celebrated on the 15th of month (*februare,* to expiate); hence, month of expiation

March—Mars, god of war

April—Lt: *aperier:* **to open**
In the midst of European spring and buds open; or *Aphro* (Gk, shortened Aphrodite, goddess of love), for the time when human fancy turns to love

May—Ancient Italic goddess Maia
"The greater goddess," "the increaser," hence month of growth

June—Roman clan *Junius*

July—Julius Caesar

August—Caesar Augustus
August: *augurs*; so "consecrated by or undertaken under favorable signs"

September—Lt: *septem* **(seven)**
Seventh month in Roman calendar; *ber:* probably "month of". For the Romans, September through December were the "seventh" through the "tenth" months since March was the first month of the year.

October—Lt: *octem* **(eight)**

November—Lt: *novem* **(nine)**

December—Lt: *decem* **(ten)**

Dedication of the Year

January—Holy Childhood	July—Precious Blood
February—Holy Family	August—Blessed Sacrament
March—St. Joseph	September—The Seven Sorrows
April—Holy Spirit*	October—The Holy Rosary
May—Mary	November—Souls in Purgatory
June—Sacred Heart	December—Immaculate Conception

*also Holy Eucharist, which is the risen Christ, whose Paschal Mystery is usually celebrated in April.

290

The Week

Names of Days of the Week

Christians call the first day of the week "The Lord's Day" (Rv 1.10), after Jesus' resurrection. Otherwise, the days of the week take their names from pagan sources, according to the belief in the influence of the planets (which included for the ancients the sun and the moon) on certain days. Planetary names are derived from names of Roman gods which gave their names, or their Germanic equivalent, to our weekdays. Curiously, while the names of months have a Roman origin, days are Anglo-Saxon:

Sunday—Sun's Day
Monday—Moon's Day
Tuesday—Tiu's (Mars) Day (god of war)
Wednesday—Odin's Day (god of storms)
Thursday—Thor's (Jove's/Jupiter's) Day (god of thunder)
Friday—Frigg's (Venus') Day (goddess of marriage)
Saturday—Saturn's Day (god of time)

Dedication of the Week

Sunday—Holy Trinity
Monday—Souls in Purgatory/Holy Spirit
Tuesday—Guardian Angel
Wednesday—St. Joseph
Thursday—Blessed Sacrament
Friday*—Precious Blood
Saturday**—Mary

Why Seven?

A solar year, and a lunar month, and a twenty-four-hour day are naturals, but a seven-day week is a supernatural. Seven is holy. Seven is magic. Seven days make a week. This was determined even by the author of Genesis—or God Himself—who created the world, and rested from it, in seven days, or one "week." So this seven-day cycle from the beginning was religious. The Romans' week was also seven days, naming them as they did after the heavenly bodies of the sun, the moon, and the planets (five of which they knew). Seven . . . one week's worth of days.

*See First Fridays and Sacred Heart devotion.
**Popular Marian veneration on Saturday originated in the ninth century in a weekly memorial of Jesus' passion. The thinking seemed to be that while Jesus was in the tomb Mary in her vigil alone never doubted. See "Five First Saturdays" and "Immaculate Heart of Mary devotion."

The Date of Easter

The date of Easter is based on the resurrection of Jesus, three days after his crucifixion which occurred on Passover, the fourteenth of the month of Nisan, according to the Jewish calendar. Much debate and conflict has been spawned by efforts to determine this date annually. The difficulty comes in translating an "immovable feast" from a lunar to the Christian solar calendar (Julian, and now Gregorian), on which it becomes a movable feast. The Council of Nicaea in 325 placed Easter on the first Sunday following the first full moon after March 20 (which is the vernal equinox, when the sun is directly above the earth's equator). This date allowed pilgrims to have moonlight for traveling to the great Easter festivals of that day. Easter may be as early as March 22 and late as April 25.

The Movable Feasts (dependant upon the date of Easter)
Always fall on the same day of the week, regardless of the date.

1. Sexagesima—60 days before
2. Ash Wednesday—40 days before
3. Palm Sunday—the Sunday before
4. Good Friday—the Friday before
5. Ascension—40 days after
6. Pentecost—seventh Sunday after
7. Trinity—eighth Sunday after

The Immovable Feasts (always fall on the same date each year)

The "Quarter-Days"
1. Annunciation ("Lady Day")—March 25
2. Nativity of John the Baptist—June 24
3. Michaelmas Day—September 29
4. Christmas—December 25

The fleur-de-lys, a stylized lily, is a classic Marian symbol.

Other lesser
1. Circumcision—January 1
2. Epiphany—January 6
3. All Saints—November 1
4. The Apostles' days

Poor Friday

Some say Friday is a good day for bad things. Some say that Adam and Eve fell from grace on a Friday, and that the Flood started on a Friday, and that Solomon's Temple fell on a Friday. Jesus Christ was crucified on a Friday. "Bad Friday"? A Church that can call Adam's fault happy will call Friday's crucifixion good, and Christ's bad day Good Friday. (If the Head has a penchant for paradox, so will the Body.)

By the Dark of the Moon

Planting potatoes on Good Friday is legendary, partly because of a rule by those who plant by the moon: vegetables that produce above ground should be planted by the light of the moon (from the day of the new moon to the day of the full moon), whereas underground vegetables should be planted by the dark of the moon (from the day of the full moon to the day of the new moon). Remember that Easter comes on the first Sunday after Spring's first full moon, and add the mystique of That Day, and there is the tradition of planting potatoes on Good Friday. In some climes.

A Glossary, Just on Time

Tide

Through the ages people have thought of time as a vast, flowing sea, with its ebb and flow, its rising and falling. Just as the tide has its ebb and flow, so an occasion has a build up, and a denoument. So naturally, it became traditional for a feast—a festive moment—to have a season: not just time, but a tide. So Christmas time becomes Yuletide, and so on with Shrovetide, Eastertide, Witsuntide: time flowing through the seasons, even as it does through the day: noontide, eventide, all with their glad or sad tidings.

Octaves

An octave is a feast day plus the seven days following it. They were numerous before Vatican II, with their daily commemoration in the Liturgy of the Mass and the Hours, taking precedence over other feasts. Now there are two: Easter and Christmas.

-mas

There is an ancient pattern of suffixing feast days with these letters meaning "Mass of", for example, Christmas, Candlemas, Michaelmas, Martinmas.

Ferial Day

A day with on special feast.

THE LITURGICAL YEAR

Through the course of a year, the Church experiences and celebrates redemption in Christ. In head and members, the Church is shaped anew through the various festivals and seasons of the liturgical year.

Sundays

Sunday is the day the Church celebrates the Paschal Mystery, the "Lord's Day" (see Rv 1.10) according to the apostolic tradition, the day of Jesus' resurrection from the dead. After the Sundays of Advent, Lent, and the Easter season, this "original feast day" does not admit of the permanent assignment of another celebration, with the following exceptions:

Holy Family—Sunday after Christmas

Epiphany—Sunday after January 1*

Baptism of our Lord—Sunday after January 6

Holy Trinity—Sunday after Pentecost

Corpus Christi—Sunday after Holy Trinity*

Christ the King—last Sunday of the liturgical year

Ordinary Time

"Ordinary Time" is the name given to the thirty-three/thirty-four weeks (depending upon Easter) in the course of the year apart from Advent/Christmas and Lent/Easter which celebrate no particular moment or aspect of the Christian mystery, but rather the fullness of our faith.

Ordinary Time's pre-Lenten phase begins Monday after the Baptism of our Lord and includes what were formerly called the Sundays after Epiphany and the suppressed Sundays of Septua/Sexa/Quinquagesima.

It is interrupted Tuesday before Ash Wednesday for Lenten and Easter seasons and is resumed again Monday after Pentecost and continues until the end of the Church year. This "second phase" includes:

Trinity Sunday—Sunday after Pentecost

Corpus Christi—Sunday after Trinity Sunday

Christ the King—last Sunday of the Church year

*In the U.S. where it is not a holiday.

Advent

Advent is the expectation of the Christ and is penitential in tone. It is four weeks long, or slightly less, the first two focusing on Jesus' final coming as Lord and Judge. The final eight days anticipate his coming in history (Christmas). Since the tenth century, the first Sunday of Advent has marked the beginning of the (Western) Church year.

Gaudete Sunday

Third Sunday of Advent, expressing the joyful note of anticipation in a season that was seen traditionally as penitential.

Date and Time of Christ's Birth (story)

Originally, Jesus' birth was celebrated as part of the Feast of Epiphany. Around the year 330, however, the Church in Rome assigned Christmas to December 25. There were some early Fathers and writers who claimed that Dec. 25 was Christ's actual birthdate, although there was never an official reason given for the ecclesiastical decision. Church scholars contend that the date was chosen to counteract the pagan feast of the "Birthday of the Sun," which also took place on Dec. 25. The tradition of a midnight mass on Christmas originated in the pious belief that Christ was born at that hour. Don't look for historical evidence.

Christmas Season

The Christmas Season is the celebration of Jesus' birth and epiphany (manifestation). It is second in significance only to the Easter season.

Christmas—December 25
Holy Family—Sunday after Christmas
Mary, Mother of God—January 1
Epiphany—Sunday after January 1
Baptism of our Lord, Sunday after Epiphany

When Is a Christmas Carol Not a Christmas Carol?

When it's "Good King Wenceslaus." He "look'd out, on the feast of Stephen, when the snow lay all about, deep and crisp and even," and that date was enough to enshrine this popular English carol of the last century as a Christmas favorite. The story, however, isn't about the Christmas spirit, though set on the day after that great feast, but about the spirit of Wenceslaus, doing the work of Christmas. The words were written by a nineteenth-century hymn writer to fit a thirteenth-century air, using a miracle attributed in medieval legend to St. Wenceslaus.

Its five verses tell of the good king noticing a poor man, gathering fuel. Determining from a page who the man was and whence he came, the king said, "Bring me flesh, and bring me wine, bring me pine logs hither; thou and I will see him dine, when we bear them thither." Forth they went, against the bitter weather, page and king. On the way, the page's heart failed, threatening his life as well as the mission of mercy. "Mark my footsteps, my good page, tread thou in them boldly: thou shalt find the winter's rage freeze thy blood less coldly." Its last verse earns its popular place in people's hearts as a most worthy Christian, if not Christmas, carol: "In his master's steps he trod, where the snow lay dinted; heat was in the very sod which the saint had printed. Therefore, Christian men, be sure, wealth or rank possessing, ye who now will bless the poor, shall yourselves find blessing."

What earns Wenceslaus his favored place as patron and hero is not legend but history: he was an effective ruler in difficult times, faced with factionalism within and the threat of Bavaria without, and with the reconciliation of Christian and non-Christian parts of Bohemia. With the birth of a son, his brother Boleslav lost his hopes of succession, as well as all sense of right and wrong, and murdered Wenceslaus on the way to church.

Getting Ready for Lent

The three Sundays before Lent amounted to a pre-Lented "season," which prepared for Lent, which prepared for Easter, and so were dropped because of their redundancy. Septuagesima, Sexagesima and Quinquagesima could not literally be the 70th, 60th and 50th Sundays before Easter, but the titles were used presumably to correspond with the older term Quadragesima (40th), the first Sunday of Lent.

"Shrovetide," the three days before Ash Wednesday, got its name from "Shrove Tuesday," which got its name from the reconciliation sought before Lent (to shrive—shrove, shriven) is to hear confession, assign penance, and give absolution. One is shriven of guilt through repentance, making these days of glad tidings, sport, and merriment before the rigors of Lent. Hall Sunday, Hall Monday, and Hall Night were names used for the same time and same reason: "hall" is a contraction of hallow, which means holy, festive. Still others would speak of "Merry Monday." This preparation is partly play.

Feasting—food and drink—became the staples of the play, preparing oneself as well as ones house for the fasting. And so the names came: "Carling Sunday," from the custom, especially in northern Europe, of eating parched peas fried in butter (carlings). And the quite unpuritanical "Blue Monday," if the day were spent in dissipation, which, some say, gives a blue tinge to everything, which is why blue has come to mean under the influence. For others, these two days were Callop Monday and Pancake Day, because of the foods specially prepared and served then. The practice originated in the effort to use up eggs, milk, and lard before Lent, with its strict conditions for fasting. And finally Fat Tuesday, "Mardi Gras" in French, the carnival celebration and feasting on rich foods and pastries in anticipation of the rigors of Lent, and in order to use up such foods that were not even kept in the house for the fast.

Springtime New Year's

The Mardi Gras that New Orleans imported from France resembles New Year's Eve, because they're related. In ancient times, the year began in spring and was celebrated in primitive renewal rites, like the modern orgiastic New Year's Eve celebrating. "Carnival" ("farewell to meat" in Latin) originally designated this pre-Lenten season for Christians, lasting sometimes from Epiphany to Ash Wednesday, sometimes only a few days, but always culminating on Fat Tuesday, "Mardi Gras."

Lenten Season
A penitential season of six Sundays and forty weekdays that prepares for the high feast of Easter, beginning on Ash Wednesday and ending with the evening Mass of the Lord's Supper on Holy Thursday (not Holy Saturday noon, as formerly).

Historically the step-by-step preparation period for catechumens (those being initiated into the Church) for the Paschal Mystery. Thus also a renewal of the faithful's baptismal commitment.

"Lent," from the Anglo Saxon lencten (spring); lenctentid (springtide) was the Saxon name for March because it is the month in which days begin to lengthen (also a root of "lent"). The Great Fast took this name, falling as it does largely in the month of March.

Traditions and Terminology

Fourth Sunday of Lent
The fourth Sunday of Lent has had many aliases:

Laetare Sunday—After the first words of the Introit: Laetare Jerusalem (Rejoice with Jerusalem) (Is 66.10). The halfway point and a respite in the penitential season, signaled by the rose vestments instead of violet. There is a joyful note at this point in Lent because of the ancient practice of "handing over" the Apostles' Creed to catechumens, the last and decisive step for those preparing for baptism.

Mothering Sunday

Reflection Sunday—Because the Scripture included the story of Joseph feeding his brothers (first reading) and Jesus feeding the multitude (Gospel), on this day in certain locales it was traditional to serve rich "simnel" cakes. Ornamented with scallops, they commemorated the food spoken of in the readings.

Rose Sunday—Because of the papal blessing of the golden rose.

The Golden Rose
This is a floral spray blessed by the pope on the fourth Sunday of Lent and sent to some notable person or institution to acknowledge and honor special service, loyalty. There is a small container of musk and balsam in the heart of its principal rose. (The golden rose is a symbol of spiritual joy.)

Lenten Veil

Once upon a time it was the tradition to cover all crucifixes, statues, and pictures in purple cloth from two Sundays before Easter until Good Friday. Those were the days when the fifth Sunday of Lent, one week before Palm Sunday, was called "Passion Sunday" (or "Judica Sunday," after the first word of the Introit "Judge me, O Lord . . ." from Psalm 43). The veiling referred to the closing words of the Sunday's Gospel (Jn 8.46–59), "They took up stones, therefore, to cast at him. But Jesus his himself, and went out of the Temple." The Lenten veil also expressed the sorrow of the Church at this time. As a matter of fact, the Roman Missal still says, in a note on Saturday of the fourth week of Lent, that this tradition may be observed, keeping the veiling until the beginning of the Vigil. Also, the unveiling of the cross prior to veneration on Good Friday is still an optional part of the liturgy.

Holy Week

This was the common terminology for Lent's culmination and Easter's advent. With the renewal of "Triduum" language and chronology—Lent is maintained until the Mass of the Lord's Supper; the Great Three Days are celebrated; and the Great Feast (Easter) is sustained for fifty days.

Fig Sunday

Palm Sunday, for the figs eaten that day, memorializing the fig tree cursed by Christ after his entry into Jerusalem (Mk 11).

Spy Wednesday

Alluding to Judas agreeing with the Sanhedrin to betrayal (Mt 26.3–5, 14–16).

The Triduum

Celebrates the heart of Christian faith, to which all leads and from which all flows: Jesus' redemptive death and resurrection; related to the Church year as Sunday is to each week.

Begins with—the evening Mass of the Lord's Supper,

> Continues through—Good Friday and Holy Saturday,

> Culminates in—the Easter Vigil, and

> Concludes with—Evening Prayer of Easter Sunday.

(Easter Sunday is both the final hours of the Triduum and the first hours of The Great Fifty Days.)

Traditions and Terminology

Maundy Thursday
An ancient name for Holy Thursday, from Jesus' words that day (and a former antiphon of the day): *"Mandatum novum da nobis"* (A new commandment I give you), Jn 13.34. The phrase began the ancient foot-washing ceremony. Also called "Shear Thursday," because of an ancient practice of trimming hair and beard, sign of spiritual preparation for Easter.

Tre Ore (It: "Three Hours")
Refers to Christ's three hours on the cross, and to the noon to three Good Friday service. It was traditionally a series of homilies on the seven last words, along with song, silence, and stations. Eucharist was allowed to follow it, "presanctified," because it came from Holy Thursday's consecration. Hence this service came by the title "Mass of the Pre-Sanctified," although it remains the only day of the year without a celebration of the Eucharist ("The Eucharist has died.").

The Great Service of Light
Though not the heart of the Easter Vigil, it is symbolically rich and a favorite "adjective" for the Exultet, readings, and glorious Eucharist that follow it. Celebrated in the Middle Ages, it may even go back to the fourth century. The light of the Paschal Candle represents the light Christ brought to a darkened world. It was all the more powerful as a symbol in the days when fire was struck from flint—of necessity, reminding the believer of the flame of faith which is struck from Christ, the cornerstone of the Church.

Tenebrae (Lt: darkness)
A public singing of matins (a night office) and lauds (morning office), part of the old form of the Liturgy of the Hours. During the evenings of the Triduum, it had a tone of mourning and a ceremony of light, using a triangular stand with fifteen candles. One by one, these were extinguished until, after the last candle, a prayer was offered in darkness, one candle was relit, and the assembly dispersed in silence.

Liturgical Terminology

According to the Roman Missal, Holy Thursday's service is called "The Evening Mass of the Lord's Supper", Good Friday's is called "The Celebration of the Lord's Passion", and Easter Sunday's services are called "The Easter Vigil—Easter Sunday's services during the night" and "Easter Sunday".

Even though the Roman Missal does not call for a "Sunrise Service," as it does a "Mass at Dawn" on Christmas (the so-called Mass of the Shepherds), it has become popular as a relatively recent innovation. Some would credit the Moravians, Czechoslovakian immigrants who introduced the custom in the late eighteenth century.

Easter Season

Easter Season refers to the Great Fifty Days from Easter Sunday to Pentecost Sunday. A celebration of resurrection from the death of sin to life of grace. The last ten days (Ascension Thursday through Pentecost) focus on the promise of the presence and power of the Holy Spirit. The fiftieth Day (*"pente-"*) is seven (the perfect number) squared, plus one (the first day of the New Life). The word probably has roots in the Norse term *"Eostur,"* the season of the rising sun, or the time of the new birth of Spring. Both these meanings lent themselves well as Christian symbolism for the new life of the Risen Christ, the eternal light.

The Egg Roll

In 1873 when President and Mrs. Hayes had an Easter Monday egg roll on the White House lawn, they could not have known that it would start a tradition, and may not have known that it was more than a game long before they made it famous. Long before, the egg roll imitated the rolling away of the stone from Christ's tomb. Rutherford and Lucy were simply pleasing their eight children.

"Low Sunday" *(English)*
The Sunday after Easter, contrasting it with the high feast of Easter. The tradition was to consider the octave day as belonging to the feast, so that Easter would last eight days including two Sundays: Easter itself (the "high" one) and the following Sunday (the "low" one). It was common with the ancients for those who had been baptized during the year to commemorate the event on this Sunday or on *Laetare* ("Annotive Sunday").

Expectation Week
An old term designating Easter's culmination: the days between Ascension Thursday and Pentecost when the apostles prayed with expectant faith for the Paraclete. The "novena" prayer form originated with this advent of the Holy Spirit: the nine (*novem*) days between Christ's ascent and the Spirit's descent.

Christ Candle
Formerly, the Christ candle was extinguished on Ascension Thursday, representing the physical departure of Christ from the earth; now, it remains prominent through Pentecost for the entire Easter season.

Whit Sunday
Pentecost, named after the neophytes' white ("whit"), worn for the fifty-day Easter feast, from their initiation at the Easter Vigil until the commemoration of the gift of the Spirit.

HOLIDAYS AND ANNIVERSARIES

In the course of the year the Church:

1. **Celebrates** the mystery of the risen Christ (see list below),
2. **Honors** Mary (see list below), and
3. **Venerates** saints as examples for the living.

Holy Days of Obligation

Conferences of Bishops are free to set their own, with the Vatican's approval. Current practice is to retain at least two: Christmas and one feast honoring Mary. In the United States, six (besides Sundays) are retained.

1. All Sundays	7. Immaculate Conception
2. Christmas	8. Assumption
3. Epiphany*	9. St. Joseph**
4. Ascension	10. SS. Peter and Paul**
5. Corpus Christi*	11. All Saints
6. Mary, Mother of God	

The Hierarchy of Eucharistic Liturgies

With their abbreviations used in the following pages.

S—Solemnites. Liturgies celebrating events, beliefs, and personages of greatest importance and universal significance in salvation history; their observance begins with Evening Prayer I of the preceding day.

F—Feasts. Liturgies of lesser significance.

M—Memorials *(obligatory or optional).* Liturgies of the least significance; Those significant only to a local country, church, or religious community are called optional memorials and designated herein with a blank space where there would otherwise be a S, F or M.

Masses Celebrating the Mystery of Jesus

S Christmas—December 25
F Holy Family—Sunday after Christmas
S Epiphany—Sunday after Holy Family
F Baptism of our Lord—Sunday after Epiphany
F Presentation—February 2
S Annunciation—March 25
S Resurrection—Easter Sunday
S Ascension—40 days after Easter
S Corpus Christi—Second Sunday after Pentecost
S Sacred Heart—Friday after Corpus Christi
F Transfiguration—August 6
F Triumph of the Cross—September 14
F Dedication of St. John Lateran—November 9
S Christ the King—Last Sunday of Ordinary Time

The Chi Rho, prime symbol of Christ

*transferred to nearest Sunday in the United States

**obligation removed in the U.S. by U.S. bishops

Masses Honoring Mary, the Mother of God

"Lady Day" originally referred to the feast of the Annunciation, March 25, but has later come to mean any Marian feast.

12–8	S	Immaculate Conception
12–12	M	Our Lady of Guadalupe
1–1	S	Mary, Mother of God
2–11		Our Lady of Lourdes
5–31	F	Visitation
		Immaculate Heart (Saturday after Sacred Heart)
7–16		Our Lady of Mt. Carmel
8–5		Dedication of St. Mary Major
8–15	S	Assumption
8–22	M	Queenship
9–8	F	Birth
9–15	M	Our Lady of Sorrows
10–7	M	Our Lady of the Rosary
11–21	M	Presentation

S Petrus Anost S Paulus

Solemnities of the Church Year

12–8	Immaculate Conception
12–25	Christmas (with an octave)
1–1	Mary, Mother of God
	Epiphany—Sunday after Jan. 1
3–19	Joseph, husband of Mary
3–25	Annunciation
	Resurrection—Easter Sunday (with an octave)
	Ascension—forty days after Easter
	Pentecost—fifty days after Easter
	Corpus Christi—second Sunday after Pentecost
	Sacred Heart—Friday after Corpus Christi
6–24	Birth of John the Baptist
6–29	Peter and Paul, apostles
8–15	Assumption
11–1	All Saints
	Christ the King—last Sunday in Ordinary Time

GENERAL ROMAN CALENDAR

(Including, in italics, feasts proper to the calendar of the United States' dioceses.)

S—Solemnity F—Feast M—Memorial blank—Optional Memorial

ab—abbot	*b—bishop*	*e—evangelist*	*po—pope*
r—religious	*ap—apostle*	*d—doctor*	*m—martyr*
pr—priest	*v—virgin*		

January

1. S Octave of Christmas; Solemnity of Mary, Mother of God
2. M Basil the Great and Gregory Nazianzen, *b/d*
4. *M Elizabeth Ann Seton, r*
5. *M John Neumann, b*
6. S Epiphany; Bl. Andre Besette, *r*
7. Raymond of Penyafort, *pr*
13. Hilary, *b/d*
17. M Anthony, *ab*
20. Fabian, *po/m;* Sebastian, *m*
21. M Agnes, *v/m*
24. M Francis de Sales, *b/d*
25. F Conversion of Paul, *ap*
26. M Timothy and Titus, *b*
27. Angela Merici, *v*
28. M Thomas Acquinas, *pr/d*
31. M John Bosco, *pr*

Sunday after January 6, F, Baptism of the Lord

St. Distaff's Day

This "Rock Day" (rock being an archaic name for a distaff) was January 7, the day after the Christmas holidays and of return to work: women to domestic duties and men to the fields. "Celebrated" in some locals with the farm laborers soliciting money door to door for their frolic, all the while dragging their "fool" plough festooned in white ribbons and flowers. The banquet queen was called Bessy.

St. Agnes' Flowers

Snowflakes, that is, according to some ancients.

Candlemas Day

Although now overshadowed on the revised liturgical calendar, February 2nd bore a weather folklore long before the shadowy groundhog. Farmers found the day a good time to make weather predictions, applying the theory that the rest of the winter would be the opposite of that on Candlemas. There is an old English song,

> "If Candlemas be fair and bright,
> Come, Winter, have another flight;
> If Candlemas bring clouds and rain,
> Go, Winter, and come not again."

Which means, if the sun casts a shadow on Candlemas you can expect more winter, but if there is no shadow, the end of winter is close at hand. Does this sound familiar? If it sounds like the old groundhog story, it's because this is where it comes from— except that the one about the groundhog originated only about a hundred years ago. (A groundhog? That's what people in some parts used to call a woodchuck, which is the largest member of the squirrel family.)

February

2. F Presentation of the Lord
3. Blase, *b/m;* Ansgar, *b*
5. M Agatha, *v/m*
6. M Paul Miki and companions, *m*
8. Jerome Emiliani
10. M Scholastica, *v*
11. Our Lady of Lourdes
14. M Cyril, *monk,* and Methodius, *b*
17. Seven Founders of the Servites
21. Peter Damain, *b/d*
22. F Chair of Peter, *ap*
23. M Polycarp, *b/m*

Saint's Day or What?

St. Valentine was a third-century Christian martyr whose feast day is kept on February 14th. Actually he is one of ten St. Valentines, including a ninth-century pope (and these ten are among about 40,000 recognized saints, of whom only a fraction are commemorated on the calendar!). There are various explanations for the connection between his name and the current "Valentine" practices, none of which have anything to do with his life.

Regarding February 14's "original": he was a priest, possibly a bishop, and a physician from the city of Rome. He was beheaded on the 14th. It could be said that it was because of his love for the Lord and His people that his name has become so commonly associated with the devotion of lovers for beloved, children for parents, and friends for friends.

But wait! There's more: People in medieval times believed that birds paired off on February 14th, and that this was the special day, according to natural law, for love to abound and triumph. What a natural time for young men and women to do the same, or at least to send a love token; hence, "love birds," and "valentines."

And finally, not to omit the dependable old Romans: In mid-February, they celebrated a festival called Lupercalia to honor Lupercus, their version of the Greek god Pan. Part of the festivity was for young men to draw names for women dance partners. If enamorment ensued, so would engagement—the next mid-February, romantically enough. If this doesn't sound familiar enough, these betrothals were sealed with a gift exchange.

Christianity has often baptized practices as well as people, Valentine's Day being a classic example, at least according to some theories. Pan's passion rites prompted the Church to promote a purity rite instead, memorializing St. Valentine, especially since his feast day was handy by. Part of the plan was to substitute saints' names for women's names. Such piety was no match for passion and romance; all that stuck was "Valentine's Day." Whatever origin you choose, or connection you make, one thing is sure: Valentines are sent as signs of love, devotion or affection, and they are received as a thoughtful gesture and a nice compliment.

March

4. Casimir
7. M Perpetua and Felicity, *m*
8. John of God, *r*
17. Patrick, *b*
18. Cyril of Jerusalem, *b/d*
19. S Joseph, husband of Mary
23. Turibius de Mongrovejo, *b*
25. S Annunciation

The Return of the Swallows

It is the eaves of Mission San Juan Capistrano (if not the nearby shopping mall) to which the swallows return each March 19 to nest. It's on October 23 that they head south, as punctually as they came six months earlier.

The Catholic Worker

The feast of St. Joseph the Worker is secondary to Joseph's high feast day (March 19). It was established to counter the communist May Day celebration by offering a Christian view of work, and a prime example in the husband of Mary.

April

2. Francis of Paola, *hermit*
4. Isidore, *b/d*
5. Vincent Ferrer, *pr*
7. M John Baptist de la Salle, *pr*
11. Stanislaus, *b/m*
13. Martin I, *po/m*
21. Anselm, *pp/m*
23. George, *m*
24. Fidelis of Sigmaringen, *pp/m*
25. F Mark, *e*
28. Peter Chanel, *pr/m*
29. M Catherine of Siena, *pr/m*
30. Pius V, *po*

April Fools!

Tradition has it that April 1 is April Fools' Day because it was on that day that Noah sent doves from the ark to check for dry land before the flood had abated. (Actually, it was the first of "Nisan," the first month of the Jewish year and roughly equivalent to our April.) This first dispatch of course was a wild goose chase, to use another fowl metaphor. Even though Noah might object to the implication that he was just fooling, the doves' frustrated mission is commemorated in today's April Fools' tricks.

Legend of the Cuckoo

There is an old folk rhyme: "The cuckoo sings from St. Tiburtius' Day to St. John's Day" (April 14–June 24).

May

1. Joseph the Worker
2. M Athanasius, *b/d*
12. Nereus and Achilleus, *m;* Pancras, *m*
14. F Matthias, *ap*
15. *Isidore*
18. John I, *po/m*
20. Bernadine of Siena, *pr*
25. Venerable Bede, *pr/d;* Gregory VII, *po;* Mary Magdalene de Pazzi, *v*
26. M Philip Neri, *pr*
27. Augustine of Canterbury, *b*
31. F Visitation
    First Sunday after Pentecost S: Holy Trinity
    Thursday after Holy Trinity S: Corpus Christi
    Friday after Trinity Sunday S: Sacred Heart
    Saturday after Trinity Sunday: Immaculate Heart of Mary

June

1. M Justin, *m*
2. Marcellinus and Peter, *m*
3. M Charles Lwanga and companions, *m*
5. M Boniface, *b/m*
6. Norbert, *b*
9. Ephrem, *deacon/d*

11. M Barnabas, *ap*
13. M Anthony of Padua, *pr/d*
19. Romuald, *ab*
21. M Aloysius Gonzaga, *r*
22. Paulinus of Nola, *b;* John Fisher, *b/m,* and Thomas More, *m*
24. S Birth of John the Baptist

St. John's Wort

These little sunbursts—*hypericum perforatum*—are full of legend, "enlightened" legend, not surprisingly. They appear around St. John's midsummer feast (June 24). Six months from this night, one of the shortest of the year, is Christmas Eve, one of the longest, and the birthday of the Light of the World, Jesus Christ, six months younger than his forerunner, the Baptizer.

It is said that these little flowers first opened on John's feast, to catch and reflect the glorious sun. Daylight—and the sun at this time of the year—are in triumph over the night, proclaiming, even as John himself did, the advent of Christ, the rising sun. St. John's Wort is one of the world's treasured wildflowers, with plenty of legend to go with its natural beauty.

Legends like how it'll stop a witch in her tracks, according to the English ("Trefoil, vervain, John's Wort, dill,/Hinder witches of their will."); like how it'll give protection, according to the German tradition of tossing a wreath of them upon on the housetop; like how it'll ward off witches and wickedness when hung in the house, according to the Swedes and the Norwegians; like how, dipped in olive oil and preserved, it's a balm for the wounded, according to the Sicilians; like how it neutralizes hydrophobia (water fear) according to the Russians; like how it's predawn dew, rubbed on the eyelids, will preserve the eyes, the body's source of light. Happy feast of St. John the Baptist!

27. Cyril of Alexandria, *b/d*
28. M Irenaeus, *b/m*
29. S Peter and Paul, *ap*
30. First Martyrs of the Church of Rome

July

3. F Thomas, *ap*
4. Elizabeth of Portugal; *Independence Day*
5. Anthony Zaccaria, *pr*
6. Maria Goretti, *v/m*
11. M Benedict, *ab*
13. Henry
14. Camillus de Lellis, *pr;* Bl. Kateri Tekakwitha, *v*
15. M Bonventure, *b/d*
16. Our Lady of Mount Carmel
21. Lawrence of Brindisi, *pr/d*
22. M Mary Magdalene
23. Bridget, *r*
25. F James, *ap*
26. M Joachim and Ann, parents of Mary
29. M Martha
30. Peter Chrysologus, *b/d*
31. M Ignatius of Loyola, *pr*

August

1. M Alphonsus Liguori, *b/d*
2. Eusebius of Vercelli, *b*
4. M John Vianney, *pr*
5. Dedication of St. Mary Major

Grandparents' Day

Ss. Joachim and Anne are beloved in the Church, though little is written down about them in the Bible. Not even their names are recorded. According to ancient tradition, Anne and her husband Joachim were married for decades and still waiting for a child. In answer to their prayers, an angel appeared and told them they would soon receive a child who "shall be spoken of in all the world." They had a little girl, and named her Mary. The Eastern churches have honored this sainted couple for centuries on September 9, the day after their daughter's birthday. On the revised Roman calendar, this "feast of grandparents" is July 26.

6. F Transfiguration
7. Sixtus II, *po/m,* and companions, *m;* Cajetan, *pr*
8. M Dominic, *pr*
10. F Lawrence, *deacon/m*
11. M Clare, *v*
13. Pontian, *po/m,* and Hippolytus, *pr/mn*
14. M Maximilian Mary Kolbe, *pr, m*
15. Assumption

┌───┐
│ **The Gossamer Legend**   │
│   │
│ This delicate, filmy cobweb, prevalent in the air and on the grass │
│ and bushes, especially in autumn, is explained in a fine legend. It │
│ is the delicate thread unravelling from the Blessed Virgin's wind- │
│ ing sheet, falling to earth in her assumption. The word, however, │
│ comes from "goose summer" which was a name for St. Martin's │
│ summer because of the goose legend, which is another story. │
└───┘

16. Stephen of Hungary
19. John Eudes, *pr*
20. M Bernard, *ab/d*
21. M Pius X, *po*
22. M Queenship of Mary
23. Rose of Lima, *v*
24. F Bartholomew, *ap*
25. Louis; Joseph Calasanz, *pr*
27. M Monica
28. M Augustine, *b/d*
29. M Beheading of John the Baptist, *m*

September
3. M Gregory the Great, *po/d*
8. F Birth of Mary
9. M Peter Claver, *pr*
13. M John Chrysostom, *b/d*

14. F Triumph of the Cross
15. M Our Lady of Sorrows
16. M Cornelius, *po/m* and Cypian, *b/d*
17. Robert Bellarmine, *b/d*
19. Januarius, *b/m*
20. M Andrew Kim Taegon, Paul Chong Hasang and companions, *martyrs*
21. F Matthew, *ap/e*
26. Cosmas and Damian, *m*
27. M Vincent de Paul, *pr*
28. Wenceslaus, *m; Lawrence Ruiz and companions, martyrs*
29. F Michael, Gabriel, and Raphael, *archangels*
30. M Jerome, *pr/d*

October

1. M Theresa of the Child Jesus, *v*
2. M Guardian Angels
4. M Francis of Assisi
6. Bruno, *pr;* Bl. Marie-Rose Durocher, *v*
7. M Our Lady of the Rosary
9. Denis, *b/m* and companions, m; John Leonardi, *pr*
14. Callistus I, *po/m*
15. M Teresa of Avila, *v/d*
16. Hedwig, *r; Margaret Mary Alacoque, v*
17. M Ignatius of Antioch, *b/m*
18. F Luke, *e*
19. Isaac Jogues and John de Brebeuf, *pr/m,* and companions, *m*
23. John of Capistrano, *pr*
24. Anthony Claret, *b*
28. F Simon and Jude, *ap*

All Saints' Day

"Memorial Day"—not in May, as it is in America, but on November 1st, and prolonged through the month, the time in the natural cycle for harvest and dying. We used to call it "the month of the poor souls," but many today rather say "the month of all saints," or holy souls or "Memorial Month." Actually the Catholic's "Memorial Day" is plural, including "All Souls' Day," November 2. We distinguish between our loved ones in heaven, "all saints," who pray for us, and our loved ones who have died, for whom we are moved to pray, the poor souls who still may be undergoing the purging process of death-to-self that follows repentance. In this month of harvest and dying, the Church memorializes the dead and recognizes Jesus as Lord of the living and the dead. Memorial Month.

November

1. S All Saints
2. All Souls
3. Martin de Porres, *r*
4. M Charles Borromeo, *b*
9. F Dedication of St. John Lateran
10. M Leo the Great, *po/d*
11. M Martin of Tours, *b*
12. M Josaphat, *b/m*
13. *M Francis Xavier Cabrini, v*
15. Albert the Great, *b/d*
16. Margaret of Scotland; Gertrude, *v*
17. M Elizabeth of Hungary, *r*
18. Dedication of the Churches of Peter and Paul, *ap*
21. M Presentation of Mary
22. M Cecilia, *v/m*
23. Clement I, *po/m,* Columbian, *ab*
30. F Andrew, *ap*

Last Sunday in Ordinary Time
S: Christ the King

December

3. M Francis Xavier, *pr*
4. John Damascene, *pr/d*
6. Nicholas, *b*
7. M Ambrose, *b/d*
8. S Immaculate Conception
11. Damasus I, *po*
12. *M Our Lady of Guadalupe;* Jane Frances de Chantal, *r*
13. M Lucy, *v/m*
14. M John of the Cross, *pr/d*
21. Peter Canisius, *pr/d*
23. John of Kanty, *pr*
25. S Christmas
26. F Stephen, *First Martyr*
27. F John, *ap/e*
28. F Holy Innocents, *m*
29. Sylvester I, *po*

Sunday within the octave of Christmas or Dec. 30 F: Holy Family

The Shrine of the Immaculate Conception

Mary is the patroness of the United States, especially honored in this monument which is the second largest church in the country (seventh largest in the world). Like the medieval cathedrals, it is constructed entirely of masonry, with no steel structure. Begun in 1920 and dedicated in 1959, the Shrine was funded by millions of Catholics and is situated by the campus of the Catholic University in Washington, D.C. Its sixty chapels feature the Church's rich Marian devotion, including Queen of Peace, Our Lady of Czestochowa, and Our Mother of Sorrows.

Santa Nicholas

Our ubiquitas, gift-bearing "Santa Claus" originates in that gift-giving bishop, Nicholas, of Myra, Asia Minor. In the beginning, it was more a matter of justice than generosity that caused him to give the gift that started the tradition. At least according to one of many colorful legends, he supplied three bags of gold, anonymously, to three sisters who were being reduced to prostitution because their poor father was unable to provide their dowries. (His gifts, tossed in the window, landed in the girls' stockings which were hung by the mantle with care. Sound familiar?)

Throughout the centuries, this generous, compassionate bishop has been a favorite in the Eastern Church, and gift giving a favorite memorial on his feast, December 6. In an outpouring of zealous—if superficial—piety, some reformers banished him from calendar and custom, replacing him with a secular but still gift-giving counterpart: "Father Christmas" being the English version, "Pere Noel" the French. But the durable bishop survived the purge and still lives in a kind of reincarnation.

While the basic fact—giving—still remains, and his name—Saint Nikolaas, Sinterklaas, Santa Claus—is still close, his image has changed. Credit (or blame) for this goes to two. First, to Dr. Clement Moore, a theologian, for authoring "A Visit from St. Nicholas" (also known as "The Night before Christmas) in 1822. That's where Bishop Nicholas gets embellished with toy bag, pipe, reindeer, sleight, and a chimney entrance. Moore had ample resources in the Dutch immigrants who brought Sinterklaas to the New World in spite of themselves (their Calvinism, that is).

What imagination lacked, Thomas Nash supplied in his *Harper's Weekly* cartoons of the 1860s and '70s. It was his pen that fleshed out the image—and the frame—of Santa Claus. But underneath it all, there is still the robed gift giver of Myra, Nicholas.

Although St. Nicholas devotion is largely submerged in contemporary Santa Clause extravagance, some, on Santa's original feast (December 6) have a St. Nicholas breakfast. In honor of this Byzantine Bishop's justice and generosity, food and clothing are collected for the needy.

Saints on the General Roman Calendar

Achilleus, May 23
Agatha, Feb. 5
Agnes, Jan. 21
Albert the Great, Nov. 15
Aloysius Gonzaga, June 21
Alphonsus Liguori, Aug. 1
Ambrose, Dec. 7
Andrew, Nov. 30
Angela Merici, Jan. 27
Ann, July 26
Anselm, April 21
Ansgar, Feb. 3
Anthony, abbot, Jan. 17
Anthony Claret, Oct. 24
Anthony of Padua, June 13
Anthony of Zaccaria, July 5
Athanasius, May 2
Augustine, Aug. 28
Augustine of Canterbury,
   May 27

Barnabas, June 11
Bartholomew, Aug. 24
Basil the Great, Jan. 2
Bede, Venerable, May 25
Benedict, July 11
Bernard, Aug. 20
Bernardine of Siena, May 20
Blase, Feb. 3
Bonaventure, July 15
Boniface, June 5
Bridget, July 23
Bruno, Oct. 6

Cajetan, Aug. 7
Callistus I, Oct. 14
Camillus de Lellis, July 14
Casimir, March 4
Catherine of Siena, April 29
Cecilia, Nov. 22
Charles Borromeo, Nov. 4
Charles Lwanga, June 3
Clare, Aug. 11
Clement I, Nov. 23
Columban, Nov. 23
Cornelius, Sept. 16
Cosmas, Sept. 26
Cyprian, Sept. 16
Cyril, Feb. 14
Cyril of Alexandria, June 27
Cyril of Jerusalem, March 18

Damasus, Dec. 11
Damian, Sept. 26
Denis, Oct. 9
Dominic, Aug. 8

Elizabeth Seton, Jan. 4

Elizabeth of Hungary, Nov.
   17
Elizabeth of Portugal, July 4
Ephrem, June 9
Eusebius of Vercelli, Aug. 2

Fabian, Jan. 20
Felicity, March 7
Fidelis of Sigmaringen,
   April 24
Frances of Rome, March 9
Frances Xavier Cabrini,
   Nov. 13
Francis of Assisi, Oct. 4
Francis of Paola, April 2
Francis de Sales, Jan. 24
Francis Xavier, Dec. 3

George, April 23
Gertrude, Nov. 16
Gregory the Great, Sept. 3
Gregory Nazianzen, Jan. 2
Gregory VII, May 25

Hedwig, Oct. 6
Henry, July 13
Hilary, Jan. 13

Ignatius of Antioch, Oct. 17
Ignatius Loyola, July 31
Irenaeus, June 28
Isaac Jogues, Oct. 19
Isidore of Seville, April 4
Isidore the Farmer, May 15

James, apostle, July 25
James, apostle, May 3
Jane Frances de Chantal,
   Dec. 12
Januarius, Sept. 19
Jerome, Sept. 30
Jerome Emiliani, Feb. 8
John I, May 18
John, apostle, Dec. 27
John Baptist, birth, June 24
John Baptist, beheading,
   Aug. 29
John Baptist, de la Salle,
   April 7
John de Brebeuf, Oct. 19
John Bosco, Jan. 31
John of Capistrano, Oct. 23
John Chrysostom, Sept. 13
John of the Cross, Dec. 14
John Damascene, Dec. 4
John Eudes, Aug. 19
John Fisher, June 22
John of God, March 8
John of Kanty, Dec. 23

John Leonardi, Oct. 9
John Neumann, Jan. 5
John Vianney, Aug. 4
Joachim, July 26
Josaphat, Nov. 12
Joseph, March 19
Joseph the Worker, May 1
Joseph Calasanz, Aug. 25
Jude, Oct. 28
Justin, June 1

Lawrence, Aug. 10
Lawrence Brindisi, July 21
Leo the Great, Nov. 10
Louis of France, Aug. 25
Lucy, Dec. 13
Luke, Oct. 18

Marcellinus, June 2
Margaret Mary Alacoque,
   Oct. 16
Margaret of Scotland, Nov.
   16
Maria Goretti, July 6
Mark, April 25
Martha, July 29
Martin I, April 13
Martin de Porres, Nov. 3
Martin of Tours, Nov. 11
Mary Magdalen, July 22
Mary Magdalen de Pazzi,
   May 25
Matthew, Sept. 21
Matthias, May 14
Methodius, Feb. 14
Monica, Aug. 27

Nereus, May 12
Nicholas, Dec. 6
Norbert, June 6

Pancras, May 12
Patrick, March 17
Paul, apostle, June 29
Paul, conversion, Jan. 25
Paul of the Cross, Oct. 19
Paul Miki, Feb. 5
Paulinus of Nola, June 22
Perpetua, March 7
Peter, apostle, June 29
Peter, chair of, Feb. 22
Peter, martyr, June 2
Peter Canisius, Dec. 21
Peter Chanel, April 28
Peter Chrysologus, July 30
Peter Claver, Sept. 9
Peter Damian, Feb. 21
Philip, apostle, May 3
Philip Neri, May 26

Pius V, April 30
Pius X, Aug. 21
Polycarp, Feb. 23
Pontian, Aug. 13

Raymond of Penyafort, Jan. 7
Robert Bellarmine, Sept. 17
Romuald, June 19
Rose of Lima, Aug. 23

Scholastica, Feb. 10
Sebastian, Jan. 20

Seven Founders of Servites,
    Feb. 17
Simon, apostle, Oct. 28
Sixtus II, Aug. 7
Stanislaus, April 11
Stephen, Dec. 26
Stephen of Hungary, Aug. 16
Sylvester I, Dec. 31

Teresa of Avila, Oct. 15
Thérèse of the Child Jesus,
    Oct. 1
Thomas, apostle, July 3

Thomas Aquinas, Jan. 28
Thomas Becket, Dec. 29
Thomas More, June 22
Timothy, Jan. 26
Titus, Jan. 26
Turibius of Mongrovejo,
    March 23

Vincent, Jan. 22
Vincent Ferrer, April 5
Vincent de Paul, Sept. 27

Wenceslaus, Sept. 28

Feasts Eliminated in the Revised Calendar

In most cases, these were not eliminated because they were judged non-existent or lacking in holiness, but because in many cases all that remains certain is their name, or because they lack universal significance.

January
5—Telephorus; 6—Higinus; 19—Marius, Martha, Audifax, Abacus; 28—Agnes (a duplicated feast)

February
6—Dorothy; 15—Faustinus and Jorita

March
4—Lucius; 10—40 Holy Martyrs

April
17—Anicetus; 22—Soter and Cajus; 26—Cletus and Marcellinas

May
12—Domitilla; 14—Boniface of Tausus; 25—Urban I; 26—Eleutherius; 30—Felix I

June
12—Basilidis, Cyrinus, Nabor and Nazarius; 15—Modestus and Crescentia

July
10—Seven Holy Brothers; 11—Pius I; 17—Alexius; 18—Symphorosa and her seven sons; 20—Margaret of Antioch; 28—Victor I; 28—Innocent I.

August
22—Hippolytus (a duplicate feast); 26—Zephyrinus

September
1—Twelve Holy Brothers; 16—Lucy (a duplicated feast); 16—Geminianus; 19—Companions of St. Januarius; 20—Eustace and Companions; 23—Linus; 23—Thecla; 26—Cyprianus and Justina.

October
5—Placid and Companions; 8—Sergius; 21—Ursula and Companions; 26—Evaristus

November
10—Tryphon, Respicius and Nympha; 25—Catherine of Alexandria

December
4—Barbara

Christopher

There is an ancient allegory of a giant named Christopher who was approached by a child who desired to cross a river. The giant obliged but found the burden of the child to increase with every step he took in the crossing. "Chylde," he said, "thou hast put me in grete peryll. I might bere no greater burden." "Marvel thou nothing," the child responded, "for thou hast borne all the world upon thee, and its sins likewise." ("Christopher" means Christ bearer, and the river is the river of death.) In some stories this Christopher was a burly third-century youth named Offero (Bearer) who "served God and man" by carrying people through a treacherous river that had taken the lives of many. (His cultus was not originally part of the liturgical tradition of Rome.)

St. Christopher and the child

Secular and Sacred Celebrations

Some Church traditions, rituals, holydays, and anniversaries are the descendants (or counterparts) of secular versions; others—or the same ones, for that matter—are the ancestors for still other secular versions. In some cases, the Church has borrowed or baptized; in others, the Church has been borrowed from, or secularized. The following story about Thanksgiving is a good study.

There are many other "Catholic counterparts," ancient Church customs with secular reincarnations as well as secular festivals with sacred ones. The relationship is not always as evasive as St. Martin's goose; for example, see:

1. Candlemas Day
2. Valentine's Day
3. Mothering Sunday
4. Rogation Days
5. All Saints'/All Souls' Day
6. St. Nicholas

Though motives and meanings may vary, traditional holidays and rituals are surprisingly catholic. These are merely examples of the grafting, transplanting and inheriting that is part of Catholic, if not human, history.

Turkey or Goose

Even though the centerpiece of contemporary Thanksgiving dinner is a turkey, goose was the required main course at the venerable Martinmas feast, and some say this November 11th tradition is the ancestor of our Thanksgiving. There is no doubt that both have harvest in common. There is plenty of doubt, however, about the rest.

It's Martin's kindness to a beggar on a wintery day is his best-loved story, but the ones about the goose, though less edifying, are certainly no less interesting. Although it was traditional to slaughter an ox—for distribution to the poor—on his feast, it is the roast goose that has become notorious. The legend behind this is that St. Martin, annoyed by a goose, ordered it to be killed and served up for dinner. After dining on the goose, Martin died. Thereafter, on the anniversary of Martin's demise—and the goose's—a goose is sacrificed to St. Martin.

In another story, Martin was hiding out in a barn because he didn't want to be bishop, the honking of a goose gave him away. While that may have been enough to make him want to kill it, we know that eating a goose that day didn't kill him, because he lived on to, in fact, be a bishop, which didn't kill him either.

In a much more pious vein, Dr. Parsch (*The Church's Year of Grace*) ignores all this and suggests that the custom simply served as a kind of Mardi Gras before the beginning of the Advent fast ("St. Martin's Lent"), which prevailed during the Middle Ages, and which began earlier than Advent does now.

In addition to all this is the September 29 feast of Michaelmas, or St. Michael and All Angels, and one of the quarter-days (when rents are due). There is a centuries-old tradition of eating goose on this feast also, a practice which could have arisen simply because geese were in good supply and condition at this time of the year and were often presented by tenants to landlords, we are told, as a propitiation.

For all of this, Martin deserves a goose as one of his common symbols. As for the quest for Thanksgiving's origin, whether in the roast goose feast of Michaelmas or Martinmas, it may all be a wild goose chase.

THE JEWISH CALENDAR

The Day

The natural day was from sunrise to sunset (civil day: sunset to sunset). Hours were counted from 6 A.M. and 6 P.M. Four watches divided the night: the first, 6–9.00 P.M.; the second, 9–midnight; the third midnight–3:00 A.M.; the fourth, 3–6:00 A.M.

The Sacred Year

Month Name	Equivalent	Feasts
1. Nisan (Abib)	March-April	Passover
2. Lyar (Ziv)	April-May	
3. Sivan	May-June	Pentecost
4. Tammuz	June-July	
5. Ab	July-August	
6. Elul	August-September	⎰ Trumpets
7. Tishri (Ethanim)	September-October	⎱ Atonement
8. Marcheshvan (Bul)	October-November	Tabernacles
9. Chislev	November-December	Hanukah
10. Tebeth	December-January	
11. Shebat	January-February	
12. Adar	February-March	Purim

Sabbaths and Jubilees

Every seven days—the sabbath (the seventh day).
After seven weeks—the jubilee day (the fiftieth day).
In the seventh month—*Rosh Hashanah*.
In the seventh year—the sabbatical year*.
After seven times seven years—the jubilee year (the fiftieth year)*.
(the "Sabbath of the Sabbatical Years" or "the Holy Year")

*Commemorating the Exodus:
1. Fields left fallow for this one year (Ex 23.10; Lev 25.2–7; Dt 15.1–11)
2. Land restored to those from whom it had been dispossessed
3. Release of those obliged into hired service (Lv 25.1–34, 39–54; 27. 16–24)

The Seven Set Feasts

The Three Great Festivals
(when males were required to be presented to God)

1. Passover (*Pesach*)
   Or Festival of Unleavened Bread; Lv 23.4–14; begun on the eve of the 14th Nisan; the festival of redemption and deliverance.
2. Pentecost (*Shovuos*)
   Or Festival of Weeks (or Harvest, or First Fruits); Ex 23.16; Lv 23.15–21; sixth *Sivan* (50th day after Pentecost); spring feast of thanks; ended the weeks of the grain harvest; a covenant renewal.
3. Tabernacles (*Sukkos*)
   Or Feast of Ingathering (or Booths); Lv 23.33–43; begun on the eve of 15th *Tishri;* celebrated the autumn harvest.

The Two Festivals of Awe
4. Trumpets (*Rosh Hashanah*)
   Or Day of Awe; Nm 28; Lv 23.23–25; first and second *Tishri;* Jewish New Year, contrition.
5. Atonement (*Yom Kippur*)
   Or Day of Awe; Lv 10.1–2; 16; 23.26–32; tenth *Tishri;* Great Day of the year, fast day, repentance.

The Two Lesser Festivals
6. Hanukkah (*Chanukkoh*)
   Or Lights; Book of Maccabees; 25th *Chislev;* commemorates the revolt and victory of the Hasmoneans; religious liberty and patriotism.
7. Purim
   Or Mordecai Day; Book of Esther; 14th *Adar;* Jewish deliverance.

The seven-branched candlestick

Dreidel (Hanukkah Game)

Jewish game of chance. A dreidel is a four-sided top, each side bearing the initial letters of the words in the saying *Nas gadol hayah shom* ("a great miracle happened here").

Devotions I—
Adoration
of God

DEVOTIONS IN CATHOLIC TRADITION

Historically

Devotions (evolving historically, admitting of great pluralism depending on times, places and people) have dotted the Catholic year:

Benediction	Stations of the Cross
Various novenas	St. Mark's Day Procession
Nine First Fridays	May Devotions
First Saturdays	May Crowning
Candlemas Day	Rogation Days
St. Blaise	Forty Hours
Ember Days	First Communion Ceremonies
St. Joseph Day	Corpus Christi Procession
Lenten Devotions	Sacred Heart Devotions

Plus innumerable personal devotions (to various saints) that embellished private prayer.

Distinctions

In their "reincarnations" from one era to another, and from one culture to another, there are:

1. Changeless, essential elements (basic meanings)
2. Changeable, secondary elements (forms/language/images)
   That is, particulars popular at a certain time/place, often through the efforts of certain individuals.

Currently

Devotions are "warmly commended" by Vatican II, but "should be so drawn up that they harmonize with the liturgical seasons, accord with the sacred liturgy, are in some fashion derived from it, and lead the people to it. . . ." *Constitution on the Sacred Liturgy (n. 13).*

Principles

Although distinct from Liturgical Prayer, Devotional Prayer is governed by the same principles:

1. Mediated by . . . . . **Christ** ("Trinitarian")
   To the Father, in union with the Holy Spirit
2. Aware of . . . . . **the Church** ("Ecclesial")
   Not overly individualistic and subjective
3. Include . . . . . **Bible readings** ("Scriptural")
   See #35, *Constitution on the Sacred Liturgy*
4. Associated with . . . **the sacraments** ("Liturgical" "in accord with")
5. Related to . . . . . . **the liturgical calendar** ("Structural," "harmonizing with")

Devotional Objects

It is not uncommon for devotion to Christ, Mary, and the saints to include material objects, from pictures to scapulars to relics. The "material object" has often given to devotion its title: Sacred Heart, for example.

Object of Devotions

It is, however, the "formal object"—the meaning behind it, we would say—that gives any devotion its true significance and meaning. It may be a specific attribute of the person, or mystery of their life, but the real point of all the devotions is always the same: the *person*, be it Christ, Mary, or one of the saints.

DEVOTION TO THE EUCHARIST

Corpus Christi

Commemorating the Last Supper, Holy Thursday is the "Eucharistic Feast." In its liturgical setting, however, it could not bear the devotional practices that piety required in its love for the Body of Christ, nor could it adequately allow for the joy that wanted expression, given the sorrowful mysteries of Holy Thursday and Good Friday. Hence, there was a movement that began in twelfth-century Belgium for a special feast to honor the Blessed Sacrament. It was Pope Urban IV who first established the feast, and, most notable, commissioned the great Dominican scholar, Thomas Aquinas, to compose liturgical texts for it.

Eucharistic Processions

This was an early element in Corpus Christi devotions, emphasizing Christ's real Eucharistic presence. The Blessed Sacrament was carried through the town after Mass on its feast day (beneath its festive "*ombrellino*," or canopy). These processions came to include a version of the Roman "stations": stops at various points and, with Eucharist exposed on a simple altar, a sung Gospel passage, hymn, harvest blessing, and benediction.

The *Infiorata*

"Carpet of Flowers" is a monastic tradition hundreds of years old, honoring the Blessed Sacrament. There was a custom of strewing flowers in the path of the Eucharistic procession on the feast of Corpus Christi. From this practice evolved the art of designing panels made with flowers depicting religious themes and scenes for use on Corpus Christi.

Forty Hours' Adoration

This devotion of the Blessed Sacrament commemorates the forty hours Jesus was entombed. It originated at Milan in 1534 and was propagated by the Jesuits under St. Ignatius. It spread to many countries by the end of the eighteenth century. St. John Neumann (1811–60) is credited with establishing it in the U.S. Where it is more feasible, the forty hours are interrupted for the night and extended over three days: The first and third days include liturgies of the Blessed Sacrament; the second day, a liturgy for peace; the solemn closing of Forty Hours included the Litany of the Saints with procession and benediction of the Blessed Sacrament.

Visit to the Blessed Sacrament

This has taken various forms, depending upon culture, era, and personal preference. It acknowledges the presence of Christ in the Holy Eucharist ("real presence") outside of Mass ("abiding presence"). The genuflection (or a deep bow, common in the Eastern Church) is a traditional gesture of respect, as is a bow or tip of the hat while passing a church.

Perpetual Adoration

Perpetual Adoration means that the Blessed Sacrament is exposed and adored around the clock.

Eucharistic Devotion

A liturgical renewed "Benediction," as it was formerly called (Italics below indicate options.)

Introductory Rite
Call to Worship
Expression of Worship—appropriate song and/or psalms

Liturgy of the Word
Incensation of the Scriptures
Proclamation of the Word
Response—prayer or song
Homily and/or Silent Meditation

Liturgy of the Eucharist
Exposition of the Blessed Sacrament*
Incensation of the altar of sacrifice
Exposition on the altar of sacrifice (two candles sufficient)
    Incensation of the Blessed Sacrament
    Song of Exposition
    Blessing with the Blessed Sacrament ("Benediction")
Prayer—silent or vocal
Reposition

Concluding Rite
Canticle—of Zachariah, Mary, or Simeon
Prayers of Intercession
Concluding Prayers
Blessing and Dismissal

Hymns in Honor of the Blessed Sacrament

"Panis Angelicus" (Bread of Angels)

Part of seven-stanza *Sacris Solemniis,* one of the jubilant and celebrated Corpus Christi hymns by Thomas Aquinas (a Matins and processional hymn). Its last two stanzas comprise the hymn *"Panis Angelicus."*

Panis angelicus fit panis hominum;	The bread of angels
Dat panis coelicus figuris terminum:	becomes the bread of man;
Ores mirabilis! manducat Dominum	The bread of heaven
Pauper, servus, et humilis.	puts an end to symbols:
	O wonder! The poor, servant, lowly
	man feeds upon his Lord.

Te trina Deitas unaque poscimus;	You, God, three and one,
Sic nos tu visita, sicut te colimus;	visit us as we pray to you:
Per tuas semitas duc nos quo tendimus;	by your footsteps guide us
Ad lucem quam inhabitas.	on our way to the light which you
	inhabit.

"O Salutaris Hostia" (O Saving Victim)

Part of *Verbum Supernum Prodiens,* "The Divine Word coming forth," the Corpus Christi Lauds hymn by Thomas Aquinas. It is based on a more ancient hymn (of the incarnation) that has the same title. Its last stanza before the customary conclusion in honor of the Trinity is the beloved *O Salutaris:*

O Salutaris hostia,	O Saving Victim, opening wide
Quae caeli pandis ostium,	The gate of heav'n to man below!
Bella praemunt hostilia:	Our foes press on from ev'ry side:
Da robur, fer auxilium.	Thine aid supply, Thy strength bestow.

Uni trinoque Domino,	To thy great name be endless praise,
Sit sempiterna gloria,	Immortal God—head, One in Three;
Qui vitam sine termini	Oh, grant us endless length of days
Nobis donet in patria.	When our true native land we see.

Pange Lingua (and Tantum Ergo)

"Praise, O Tongue" is the name of two famous liturgical hymns. This one, whose first line continues *gloriosi corporis mysterium,* ("the mystery of the glorious Body"), is a Corpus Christi Vespers hymn by Thomas Aquinas. Along with many other hymns, it is modeled on the more ancient holy cross hymn *Pange Lingua.* With various translations in all modern languages, it has been used as a Blessed Sacrament hymn for Holy Thursday and Corpus Christi processionals as well as for Forty Hours' Adoration. Its last two versus, "Tantum ergo," form a traditional Benediction hymn. It has long been used to accompany the procession of the Eucharist to its repose after the Holy Thursday service.

Pange lingua gloriosi, Corporis mysterium
Sanguinisque pretiosi, Quem in mundi pretium
Fructus ventris generosi Rex effudit gentium.

Sing my tongue, the Savior's glory, Of His flesh the myst'ry sing;
Of the Blood all price exceeding, Shed by our immortal King,
Destined for the world's redemption, From a noble womb to spring.

Nobis datus, nobis natus Ex intacta Virgine,
Et in mundo conversatus, Sparso verbi semine,
Sui moras incolatus Miro clausit ordine.

Of a pure and spotless Virgin Born for us on earth below,
He, as Man, with man conversing, Stayed, the seeds of truth to sow;
Then He closed in solemn order Wondrously His life of woe.

In supremae nocte coenae, Recombens cum fratribus,
Observata lege plene Cibis in legalibus,
Cibum turbae duodenae Sedat suis manibus.

On the night of that last supper Seated with His chosen band,
He, the Paschal victim eating, First fulfills the Law's command;
Then as food to all His brothern Gives Himself with His own hand.

Verbum caro, panam verum Verbo carnem efficit:
Fitque sanguis Christi merum, Et si sensus deficit,
Ad firmandum cor sincerum Sola fides suficit.

Word made Flesh, the bread of nature By His word to Flesh He turns;
Wine into His Blood He changes, What though sense no change discerns?
Only be the heart in earnest, Faith her lesson quickly learns.

Tantum ergo Sacramentum Veneremur cernui:
Et antiquum documentum Novo cedat ritui;
Praestet fides supplementum Sensuum defectui.

Down in adoration falling, Lo! the sacred Host we hail;
Lo! o'er ancient forms departing, newer rites of grace prevail;
Faith for all defects supplying where the feeble senses fail.

Genitori, Genitoque Laus et jubilatio,
Salus, honor, virtus quoque Sit et benedictio:
Procedenti ab utroque Comparsit laudatio.

To the everlasting Father, and the Son who reigns on high,
With the Spirit Blest proceeding forth from Each eternally,
Be salvation, honor, blessing, might and endless majesty.

Adoro Te

A communion song by St. Thomas Aquinas (thirteenth century), a prayer for before or after receiving Eucharist. These verses of it are a translation by Gerard Manley Hopkins (1844–1889).

Adóro te devóte, latens Déitas,
Quae sub his figúris vere látitas:
Tibi se cor meum totum súbjicit,
quia te contémplans totum déficit.

Godhead here in hiding, whom I do adore
Masked by these bare shadows, shape and nothing more,
See, Lord, at they service low lies here a heart
Lost, all lost in wonder at the God thou art.

Visus, tactus, gustus in the fállitur;
sed audítu solo tuto créditur.
Credo quidquid dixit Dei Fílius:
nil hoc verbo veritátis vérius.

Seeing, touching, tasting are in thee deceived;
How says trusty hearing? that shall be believed:
What God's Son has told me, take for truth I do;
Truth himself speaks truly or there's nothing true.

O memóriále mortis Dómini,
Panis vivus vitam praestans homini,
praesta meae menti de te vívere,
et te illi semper dulce sápere.

O thou our reminder of Christ crucified,
Living Bread the life of us for whom he died,
Lend this life to me then: feed and feast my mind,
There be thou the sweetness we were meant to find.

Iesu, quem velátum nunc aspício,
oro fiat illud quod tam sítio:
ut, te reveláta cernens fácie,
visu sim beátus tuae glóriae.

Jesus whom I look at shrouded here below,
I beseech thee send me what I thirst for so,
Some day to gaze on thee face to face in light
And be blest for ever with thy glory's sight.

The Legend of the Pelican

The pelican is a favorite symbol of the Eucharist and redemption because of the ancient belief that the female pelican would rip  open her breast to feed her young with her own life blood, to avert their starvation in famine. In another legend, the pelican is the enemy of the serpent whose stings bring death to the young. The mother pelican, mourning over her dead brood, incinerates herself, and her warm blood restores their lives.

DEVOTION TO THE SACRED HEART

Devotion to the Sacred Heart is a wor-
shipful relationship to the person of
Christ and his redeeming love, under
the aspect or symbol of his heart.

One of the forms of the Sacred Heart

Scriptural Origins

1. **The love of God** for mankind
   Like a mother for her infant
   (Is 49.14–15)
   Like a husband for his wife
   (Hos 2.9–27)
2. **The human heart** understood as
   central to the person God writing His covenant on human hearts
   (Jer 31.31–34)
3. **The Jesus of John's Gospel:**
   a. At the Feast of Tabernacles (Jn 7.35–41)
       "From within him rivers of living water shall flow."
   b. On the cross (Jn 19.34)
       When blood and water flowed from his pierced side
   c. As risen Lord (Jn 21.25)
       With his wounds still visible

Historical Evolution

1. **Between A.D. 800 and 1000,** Jesus' heart evolved as a symbol for
   the venerable devotion to the humanity and wounds of Christ.
2. **St. John Eudes (1601–1680)** promoted devotion to the Sacred
   Heart and to the Heart of Mary, prompting Pope Pius XI to call him
   the Father of the cultus for the Hearts of Jesus and Mary.
3. **St. Margaret Mary's apparitions of Christ (1673–1675),** telling
   of his concern about the indifference and coldness in the world in
   response to his love. He asked her to promote
   a. devotion to his heart, symbolic of his love for all;
   b. frequent communion in a spirit of reparation, especially on the
       first Fridays of the month;
   c. holy hours and other devotions.
4. Through St. Margaret Mary Alacoque's Jesuit spiritual director,
   Claude de la Colombiere, **promotion by the Jesuits** became part of
   their institute, notably through the Apostleship of Prayer (Sacred
   Heart League), who popularized the Morning Offering and widely
   distributed the Sacred Heart badge.
5. **Pope Pius XII encyclical in 1956 on the Sacred Heart,
   "Haurietis Aquas."**

The Promises Of Our Lord

To Saint Margaret Mary for souls devoted to his Sacred Heart. Implicitly approved by the Church in her canonization (1920).

1. I will give them all the graces necessary in their state of life.
2. I will establish peace in their houses.
3. I will comfort them in all their afflictions.
4. I will be their strength during life and above all during death.
5. I will bestow a large blessing upon all their undertakings.
6. Sinners shall find in My Heart the source and the infinite ocean of mercy.
7. Tepid souls shall grow fervent.
8. Fervent souls shall quickly mount to high perfection.
9. I will bless every place where a picture of My Heart shall be set up and honored.
10. I will give to priests the gift of touching the most hardened hearts.
11. Those who shall promote this devotion shall have their names written in My Heart, never to be blotted out.
12. I promise you in the excessive mercy of My Heart that My all-powerful love will grant to all those who communicate on the First Friday in nine consecutive months the grace of final penitence; they shall not die in My disgrace nor without receiving their Sacraments; My Divine Heart shall be their safe refuge in this last moment.

Enthronement of the Sacred Heart (See Promise nine above.)
This is the formal and communal acknowledgement of the sovereignty of the Heart of Jesus over a Christian family. The "apostle" of this practice was Fr. Mateo Crawley-Boevey (1875–1960), a South American Sacred Heart priest. Approved by Pope St. Pius X, the steps of the ceremony are:

1. Blessing of the home (optional),
2. Blessing of the image/picture,
3. Placing of picture in place of honor,
4. Apostles' Creed,
5. Explanation of enthronement,
6. Act of Consecration and Prayer of Thanksgiving,
7. Blessing of the family, and
8. Signing of a document and "report card".

Traditional Practices of the Sacred Heart Devotion

Act of Consecration

Renewing the gift of ourselves that was made in baptism/confirmation (and marriage/holy orders). Implies a total surrender to Christ in gratitude, promising fidelity.

- **A most ancient form** dates from the fifteenth century, popularized by the Benedictine monks at the Abbey of St. Matthias, Trier, Germany.

- **Proliferated** after St. Margaret Mary and later through the Apostleship of Prayer's Morning Offering as a personal and daily consecration.

- **Formalized** in 1925 by Pope Pius XI who ordered an annual, pubic consecration of the human race on the feast of Christ the King:

Most sweet Jesus, Redeemer of the human race, look down upon us humbly prostrate before Thine altar. We are Thine, and Thine we wish to be; but to be more surely united with Thee, behold, each one of us freely consecrates himself today to Thy most Sacred Heart. Many, indeed, have never known Thee; many, too, despising Thy precepts, have rejected Thee. Have mercy on them all, most merciful Jesus, and draw them to Thy Sacred Heart. Be Thou King, O Lord, not only of the faithful who have never forsaken Thee, but also of the prodigal children who have abandoned Thee; grant that they may quickly return to their Father's house, lest they die of wretchedness and hunger. Be Thou King of those whom heresy holds in error or discord keeps aloof; call them back to the harbor of truth and the unity of faith, so that soon there may be but one fold and one Shepherd. Grant, O Lord, to Thy Church assurance of freedom and immunity from harm; give peace and order to all nations, and make the earth resound from pole to pole with one cry; Praise to the divine Heart that wrought our salvation; to it be glory and honor forever. Amen.

Acts of Reparation

An act of reparation is a conscious turning to God, change of heart and reconciliation with others, leading to and flowing from the Sacrament of Reconciliation.

First Fridays (See Promise twelve above.)

These are memorials of Good Friday, and a response in loving praise and gratitude for the grace flowing from the heart of the Lamb of God, who takes away the sins of the world.

Holy Hour
Commemoration of Jesus' agony in the garden ("Could you not stay with me for one hour?"—Mt 26.40).

Morning Offering
The Morning Offering is inspired by Christ's requests to St. Margaret Mary. It was initiated by Jesuit Fr. Gaulrelet (1844). Popularized since 1860 by the Apostleship of Prayer (League of the Sacred Heart), it associates one's "prayers, works, joys and sufferings" with the offertory of the Church's Eucharist (Dogmatic Constitution on the Church, no. 34; 1 Pt 2.5)

Agony in the Garden

DEVOTION TO THE PASSION

Devotion to Christ's passion, the heart of Christian redemption, is at the heart of Christian spirituality. Just as Eucharistic devotion and Sacred Heart devotion have their feasts, so does devotion to Christ's passion: the Triumph of Holy Cross (September 14). At the Good Friday service, this devotion is expressed most beautifully and solemnly in The Veneration of the Cross.

The Veneration of the Cross
The sacramentary still suggests the ancient songs, traditionally including:

1. **Ps 67.2** ("May God be gracious and bless us . . .") words similar to the priestly blessing of Nm 6.22–27.
2. **The Reproaches** (Quoting Ps 136)
   Although still included in the sacramentary as an option, various official groups have discouraged their use, since they are so capable of inspiring an anti-Jewish spirit. The venerable trisagion ("Holy God; Holy, Mighty One . . .") is the traditional (and usable) refrain for the first part of the Reproaches.

3. *"Pange Lingua"*

Honoring and addressing Christ's cross, this celebrated hymn (once sung at Passiontide Matins) is one of the Church's most beautiful poems and has been used for Good Friday veneration since the ninth century. It has inspired many other hymns, most notable the Eucharistic hymn by Thomas Aquinas with the same title. Written in 602 by Venantius Fortunatus, bishop of Poitiers, it is familiar to many because of its refrain, "Faithful Cross" (*Crux Fidelis*):

Faithful Cross, above all others,
    One and only noble Tree,
None in foliage, none in blossom,
    None in fruit thy peer may be;
Sweetest Wood, and sweetest Iron;
    Sweetest weight is hung on thee.

Sing, my tongue, the glorious battle,
    Sing the last, the dread affray;
O'er the Cross, the Victor's trophy,
    Sound the high triumphal lay,
How, the pains of death enduring,
    Earth's Redeemer won the day.

He, our Maker, deeply grieving
    That the first-made Adam fell,
When he ate the fruit forbidden
    Whose reward was death and hell,
Marked e'en then this Tree the ruin
    Of the first tree to dispel.

Thus the work for our salvation,
    He ordained to be done;
To the traitor's art opposing,
    Art yet deeper than his own;
Thence the remedy procuring
    Whence the fatal wound begun.

Therefore, when at length the fullness
    Of the appointed time was come,
He was sent, the world's Creator,
    From the Father's heavenly home,
And was found in human fashion,
    Offspring of the Virgin's womb.

Lo! he lies, an infant weeping,
    Where the narrow manger stands,
While the Mother-Maid his members,
    Wraps in mean and lowly bands,
And the swaddling clothes is winding
    Round his helpless feet and hands.

Thirty years among us dwelling,
    His appointed time fulfilled,
Born for this, he meets his Passion,
    For that this he freely willed:
On the Cross the Lamb is lifted,
    Where his Life-Blood shall be spilled.

He endured the nails, the spitting,
    Vinegar, and spear, and reed;
From that Holy Body broken
    Blood and Water forth proceed:
Earth and stars, and sky and ocean,
    By that flood from stain are freed.

Bend they boughs, O tree of Glory!
    Thy relaxing sinews bend;
For a while the ancient rigor,
    That thy birth bestowed, suspend;
And the King of heavenly beauty
    On thy bosom gently tend.

Thou alone was counted worthy
    This world's ransom to uphold;
For a shipwrecked race preparing
    Harbor, like the ark of old;
With the Sacred Blood anointed
    From the smitten Lamb that rolled.

Vexilla Regis

By the sixth-century bishop, Venantius Fortunatus (as *Pange Lingua,* above), "Abroad the Regal Banners Fly" is one of the most famous and important hymns of the Holy Cross and the Redeemer's passion. It was once sung at Vespers during the Liturgy of the Hours of Passiontide, on the feast of the Holy Cross and on Good Friday when the Eucharist was brought for communion from its repository (now a time of silence). Since the fourteenth century, it has known some fifty translations into English alone.

Abroad the regal banners fly,
Now shines the cross' mystery;
Upon it Life did death endure,
And yet by death did life procure.

Who, wounded with a direful spear,
Did, purposely to wash us clear
From stain of sin, pour out a flood
Of precious Water mixed with Blood.

That which the Prophet-King of old
Hath in mysterious verse foretold,
Is now accomplished, whilst we see
God ruling nations from a Tree.

O lovely and refulgent Tree,
Adorned with purpled majesty;
Culled from a worthy stock, to bear
Those Limbs which sanctified were.

Blest Tree, whose happy branches bore
The wealth that did the world restore;
The beam that did that Body weigh
Which raised up hell's expected prey.

Hail, Cross, of hopes the most sublime!
Now in this mournful Passion time,
Improve religious souls in grace,
The sins of criminals efface.

Blest Trinity, salvation's spring,
May every soul Thy praises sing;
To those Thou grantest conquest by
The holy Cross, rewards apply. Amen.

The Wandering Jew

This universal medieval legend has taken many forms. The basic story is of a man, the cobbler Ahasuerus according to some, who witnessed the Way of the Cross, and refused Christ a resting place at his door: "Get off! Away with you!" To this Jesus replied, "Truly I go away, and quickly, but tarry thou til I come again." With that the cobbler was condemned to wander the earth 'til Christ's return. In various national stories his reoccurring appearances are recounted, with imaginative embellishments.

Stations of the Cross

The Stations commemorate the stops along the *Via Dolorosa* (Lt: Way of Sorrow), Jesus' journey of about a mile from Pilate's court to Calvary. Mary, the mother of Jesus, is believed to have often retraced the sorrowful way her Son made on Good Friday. (Scriptures from *The Jerusalem Bible.*)

1. **Jesus is condemned to death**
   Yes, God loved the world so much that he gave his only Son, so that everyone who believes in him may not be lost but may have eternal life. Jn 3.16

2. **Jesus bears his cross**
   If anyone wants to be a follower of mine, let him renounce himself and take up his cross every day and follow me. Lk 9.23

3. **Jesus falls the first time**
   We had all gone astray like sheep, each taking his own way, and Yahweh burdened him with the sins of all of us. Is 53.6

4. **Jesus meets his mother**
   All you who pass this way, look and see: is any sorrow like the sorrow that afflicts me? Lam 1.12

5. **Simon of Cyrene helps Jesus carry his cross**
   I tell you solemnly, in so far as you did this to one of the least of these brothers of mine, you did it to me. Mt 25.40

6. **Veronica wipes the face of Jesus**
   To have seen me is to have seen the Father. Jn 14.9

7. **Jesus falls a second time**
   Come to me, all you who labour and are overburdened, and I will give you rest. Mt 11.28

8. **Jesus meets the women of Jerusalem**
   Daughters of Jerusalem, do not weep for me, weep rather for yourselves and for your children. Lk 23.28

9. **Jesus falls a third time**
   Everyone who exalts himself will be humbled, and the man who humbles himself will be exalted. Lk 14.11

10. **Jesus is stripped of his garments**
    None of you can be my disciple unless he gives up all his possessions. Lk 14.33

11. **Jesus is nailed to the cross**
    I have come from heaven, not to do my own will, but to do the will of the one who sent me. Jn 6.38

12. **Jesus dies on the cross**
    He became as men are; and being as all men are, he was humbler yet, even to accepting death, death on a cross. Phil 2.7–8

13. **Jesus is taken down from the cross**
    Was it not ordained that the Christ should suffer and so enter into his glory? Lk 24.26

14. **Jesus is placed in the tomb**
    Unless a wheat grain falls on the ground and dies, it remains only a single grain; but if it dies, it yields a rich harvest. Jn 12.24

Christ's Passion in Christian Art

Ecce Homo (Lt: Behold, the man)

A name given to the Good Friday pictures of Jesus, crowned with thorns and presented to the crowds by Pilate: "Behold the man" (Jn 19.5). See especially Correggio, Durer, Poussin, Rembrandt, Reni, Titian, Van Dyck.

Crucifixion Group

Donatello's famous bronze work surmounts the main altar of the basilica of St. Anthony in Padua, which houses the tomb of the famous Franciscan preacher.

Pieta

The "13th station"; artistic representation of the dead Christ in his mother's arms. The Roman virtue of love and reverence for parents/children was *pietas* (piety); see Pius Aeneas, who rescued his father from Troy when it was burning, and Antoninus the Pius who had his adoptive father Hadrian deified. (The most famous *Pieta* is Michelangelo's, in St. Peter's Basilica in Rome.)

Michelangelo and the Image Asleep

Michelangelo, says Irving Stone in *The Agony and the Ecstasy*, always supervised the cutting of his own blocks of marble from the quarries at Carrara. He did this in part because he believed that the sculpture he envisioned lay trapped inside the stone, and his task as sculptor was to remove the excess stone to reveal the *Pieta* or the *David* that lay within.

DEVOTION TO THE INFANT OF PRAGUE

This is the name of a devotion that has evolved from the gift of an eighteen-inch wooden statue of the child Jesus. The figure's left hand holds a globe surmounted by a cross and its right hand is poised in blessing. It represents both the Kingship of Christ and Holy Childhood. It gained ecclesiastical approval from the Bishop of Prague in 1655.

Infant of Prague

"About the middle of the seventeenth century the community of Discalced Carmelite Fathers in Prague found itself reduced to a state of extreme want. A certain pious benefactress had great faith in the miraculous powers of a beautiful waxen Image of the Infant Jesus given her by her mother who had brought it from Spain. Desiring to aid the Fathers in their distress, she presented them with this statue, saying: "As long as you honor this Image, you shall never want." The words proved prophetic. The Image was given a place of honor in the oratory and the community flourished. When the monastery was pillaged and the statue lost, the Fathers, when able to return, were forced to live in dire poverty until the Image, found after a long search, was restored to its rightful place. So many were the favors obtained through this Image that it was decide to place it in the church that the faithful might share in the blessings which the Divine Infant dispensed with such liberality. They came in great numbers to pray at the shrine and countless were the favors granted and even miracles worked on their behalf. The devotion soon spread beyond the limits of Prague to all Europe and thence to all parts of the world. It has continued to increase in popularity so that today thousands are obtaining favors of all kinds by reason of their devotion to the Infant Jesus of Prague."

Devotions II—
Veneration of
Saints and
Heroes

Adoration and Veneration

1. *Latria*—Supreme worship due God alone
2. *Dulia*—Veneration given to saints
3. *Hyperdulia*—Higher veneration given to Mary

Catholic Veneration of Saints*

Liturgically

1. Annually, according to the universal liturgical calendar, with feast days, sometimes including special readings (departing from the seasonal cycle) and references in the three presidential prayers.
2. Annually (and similarly), in the Liturgy of the Hours (which includes an office of Readings which includes a brief biography plus a reading by or about the saint on the feast day).
3. Daily, in the Eucharist prayer.

Popularly

4. The Litany of the Saints.
5. Traditional public devotions and novenas.
6. Private devotions, including asking saints' intercessions (see "Patrons"), and using specific prayers that saints have used—prayers that have been preserved.

"All holy men and women of God, intercede for us"

DEVOTION TO MARY

Mary in the Bible

See favorite Marian symbols and images, which include references to the Scriptures in which they are rooted.

---

*The *Acta Sanctorum* (Acts of the Saints) The monumental collection of saints' lives, initiated by the Bollandists, a group named after the seventeenth century Jesuit, Jean Bolland. The *Lives of the Saints,* arranged according to the liturgical calendar, now consists of almost seventy volumes, and is growing.

The Seven Words of Mary
The Scriptures record Mary speaking seven times

1. "How can this be since I do not know man?" **Lk 1.34**
   Response to the Annunciation.
2. "I am the servant of the Lord. Let it be done to me as you say."
   Lk 1.38
   Acceptance of her vocation.
3. "Mary entered Zechariah's house and greeted Elizabeth." **Lk 1.40**
   The Visitation: Mary the Christ-bearer and guest.
4. "My being proclaims the greatness of the Lord. . . ." **Lk 1.46f**
   Joyful reflection on God's fidelity, the *Magnificat.*
5. "Why have you done this to us?" **Lk 2.48**
   The finding of the child Jesus in the temple.
6. "They have no more wine." **Jn 2.3**
   Her intercession on behalf of the Cana wedding hosts.
7. "Do whatever he tells you." **Jn 2.5**
   Her instruction to those waiting on table at Cana wedding feast.

The House of Loreto

This is the *Santa Casa,* the reputed Nazareth house of Mary around which the town of Loretto grew. This is some 15 miles down the eastern coast of Italy from Ancona on the Adriatic Sea. The tradition behind it is that the house was "translated" around 1290 to Fiume, Illyria, and then shortly to Recanati and finally to property owners by a Lady Louretta by Ancona. There are *bas reliefs* of episodes in Mary's life in the chapel, and an image of the virgin carved by St. Luke, the story goes.

Seven Sorrows of Mary
1. Prophecy of Simeon
2. Flight into Egypt
3. Loss in the Temple
4. Meeting on the Way of the Cross
5. Crucifixion
6. Taking down from the Cross
7. Burial

Seven Joys of Mary
1. Annunciation
2. Visitation
3. Nativity
4. Epiphany
5. Presentation of Jesus
6. Finding in the Temple
7. Assumption

Mater Dolorosa
The *Mater Dolorosa* is not uncommon in Christian art. (Any mother who has lost a child is a "sorrowful mother" after *the* mother who lost her son, Jesus.)

Stabat Mater (Dolorosa) (Lt: the mournful mother stands)
An anonymous Latin poem, for private devotion originally, now a common Lenten hymn.

At the Cross her station keeping,
Stood the mournful Mother weeping,
    Close to Jesus to the last.
Through her heart His sorrow sharing,
All his bitter anguish bearing,
    Now at length the sword had passed.

Oh! how sad and sore distress'd
Was that Mother highly blest
    Of the sole-begotten One!
Christ above in torment hangs;
She beneath beholds the pangs
    Of her dying glorious Son.

Is there one who would not weep,
Whelm'd by miseries so deep
    Christ's dear Mother to behold?
Can the human heart refrain
From partaking in her pain,
    In that Mother's pain untold?

Bruised, derided, cursed, defiled,
She beheld her tender Child
    All with bloody scourges rent.
For the sins of His own nation.
Saw Him hang in desolation,
Till His spirit forth He sent.

O thou Mother! fount of love!
Touch my spirit from above,
    Make my heart with thine accord:
Make me feel as thou hast felt;
Make my soul to glow and melt
    With the love of Christ my Lord.

Holy Mother! pierce me through,
In my heart each wound renew
    Of my Saviour crucified,
Let me share with thee His pain,
Who for all my sins was slain,
    Who for me in torments died.

Let me mingle tears with thee,
Mourning Him who mourned for me
    All the days that I may live:
By the Cross with thee to stay;
There with thee to weep and pray,
    Is all I ask of thee to give.

Virgin of all virgins best,
Listen to my fond request;
    Let me share thy grief divine,
Let me, to my latest breath,
In my body bear the death
    Of that dying Son of thine.

Wounded with His every wound,
Steep my soul till it hath swooned
    In His very blood away;
Be to me, O Virgin, nigh,
Lest in flames I burn and die,
    In His awful Judgment-day.

Christ, when Thou shalt call me here
Be Thy Mother my defense;
    Be Thy Cross my victory;
While my body here decays,
May my soul Thy goodness praise,
    Safe in Paradise with Thee.

Mary in Catholic Teaching

Recent Marian Doctrines Defined
The Immaculate Conception
> Bull *Ineffabilis Deus;* Pope Pius IX, Dec. 8, 1854.

The Assumption
> Apostolic Constitution *Munificentissimus;* Pope Pius
> XII, Nov. 1, 1950.

Some Recent Church Teachings on Mary
Ecumenical Council
> The *Dogmatic Constitution on the Church,* Second
> Vatican Council (1962–1965): chapter VIII,
> "The Role of the Blessed Virgin Mary,
> Mother of God, in the Mystery of Christ and
> the Church."

American Bishops
> *Behold Your Mother,* A Pastoral Letter on the Blessed Virgin Mary;
> National Council of Catholic Bishops (Nov. 21, 1973).

Pope
> *On Evangelization in the Modern World,* Apostolic Exhortation of
> Pope Paul VI (Dec. 8, 1975): para. 84, "Mary, Star of Evangeliza-
> tion."
> *Marian Devotions,* Apostolic exhortation of Pope Paul VI (1974).

Holy Sleeping

The Basilica of the Dormition ("sleeping") on Mt. Zion, and the
Church of the Tomb, near Gethsemani, are two beloved Marian
shrines in the Holy Land. The Scriptures record that Jesus gave
his mother into John's keeping, and tradition has it that he took
her to Ephesus; at her death, the apostles helped John in preparing her tomb—a temporary place for all of us, but more so for
her as things happened. Today, after crossing the Kidron Brook
at the foot of Mt. Olivet, the Church of the Tomb is the first
monument one finds. Shared since 1757 by Greeks, Armenians,
Syrians, Copts, and Abyssinians, it is venerated as a holy place
also by Moslems, who have long honored Mary.

Mary in Catholic Tradition

In Private Prayer

The four most ancient and venerable Marian prayers:

1. Hail, Mary
2. Hail, Holy Queen

3. *Memorare* ("Remember . . .")
4. *Angelus* ("The Angel . . .")

In the Liturgy

1. Honorable mention in the Eucharistic prayer
2. Choice of allusion in Penitential Rite
3. Reference in the Nicene Creed
4. Option of four specifically Marian prefaces
5. Feasts kept on the universal Roman calendar
6. Allowance for votive Masses of the Blessed Virgin on Saturdays or other weekdays with no other feast
7. Availability of three common Masses for the Blessed Virgin, a seasonal Mass for Advent, Christmas, and Easter
8. Availability of dozens of Scripture readings to provide appropriate text and to harmonize the occasion with the liturgical season.

Holy Mary, Mother of God

Mary's title "Mother of God" was canonized in 431 by the Council of Ephesus which, in defending Mary's divine maternity, was clarifying Christ's true nature. A man named Nestorius, the bishop of Constantinople, maintained that there were two distinct persons in the Incarnate Christ, one human and the other divine. True faith, on the other hand, believed in a "hypostatic" union of the two natures in the one person of Jesus of Nazareth, and thus could say, as believers still do, that God was born of Mary, that he was crucified, that he died. Even after the bishops of the whole Church clarified the truth and condemned the heresy, Nestorius and his followers continued to teach and preach in error, causing a confusion among the faithful which contributed to the success of Islam in the seventh century. "Nestorianism" too remained, developed a whole theology, spread through Asia Minor, and migrated to Persia. To this day, a Nestorian Church survives, namely "Assyrian Christians."

Titles

See the Litany of the Blessed Virgin and "Masses Honoring Mary.

a. Mother of God (Gk: *Theotokos,* "God-bearer") Mary's oldest title, celebrated on the January first solemnity.
b. Our Lady. "Notre Dame," corresponds with Italian "Madonna" and its equivalent in every language of Christendom.
c. The Immaculate Conception. Under this title, Mary is national patroness of the United States.

Principle Apparitions of the Blessed Virgin Mary

Banneux, near Liege, Belgium
Eight times in 1933 to eleven-year-old peasant girl Mariette Beco as the Virgin of the Poor.

Beauraing, Belgium
Thirty-three times in 1932–3 to five children.

Fatima, Portugal
Six times in 1917 to three children; Immaculate Heart, Our Lady of the Rosary.

Guadalupe, Mexico
Four times in 1531 to Juan Diego.

Our Lady of Guadalupe

Knock, Ireland
With figures of St. Joseph and St. John the Apostle to fifteen people in 1879.

LaSalette, France
To two children in 1846 as sorrowing and weeping figure.

Lourdes, France
Eighteen times in 1858 to fourteen-year-old Bernadette Soubirous as the Immaculate Conception.

Our Lady of the Miraculous Medal, France
Three times in 1830 to Catherine Laboure.

"The Five First Saturdays"

Devotion to the Immaculate Heart of Mary on the first Saturdays of five successive months originated in the revelations of Mary at Fatima. Mary told three shepherd children through a series of apparitions (May 13–Oct. 13, 1917) that she desired frequent recitation of the rosary and penance done for sinners. She predicted World War II, the rise of communism and Church persecution. She promised the conversion of Russia and peace for mankind if her wishes were followed. In particular, at the third apparition (July 13, 1917) she requested that Russia be consecrated to her Immaculate Heart, and that all Catholics receive communion in reparation for sin on the first Saturday of each month. In May of 1982, Pope John Paul II, in union with all the bishops of the world, consecrated the world to the Immaculate Heart of Mary, although Russia was not specifically mentioned. (It was Our Lady of Fatima whom Pope John Paul II credited when he survived the attempt on his life in 1981.)

The Secret of Fatima

A most thorough and apparently accurate account of this story, and the larger Fatima story, is in a 1983 book called *The Sun Danced at Fatima* by Rev. Joseph Pelletier. Although published without imprimatur, it is extolled by Bishop John Wright in its preface. According to this book, it was on July 13, 1917, that Fatima's most striking revelations were received by the three children. That apparition is divided in three parts, the first being a vision of hell; the second, a prediction of World War II, a world famine of punishment, a persecution of the Church, a request for the consecration of Russia to Mary's Immaculate Heart, a request for communions of reparation, and promises of Russia's conversion and world peace. The third part is unknown.

This all became public knowledge only in 1942. It hadn't been until about 1940 that one of the children, now grown, Sr. Lucia, transcribed this information (in her memoirs). She entrusted it to the bishop of Leira, Jose Alves Correia da Silva. In 1942, the apparitions' first two parts were revealed. Then Sr. Lucia committed the third part to writing and give it to Bishop Correia in a sealed envelop on June 17, 1944. Without reading it, he sealed it in another envelope and decided, in concert with Sr. Lucia, that it would not be published until her death, or in 1960—whichever came first.

Before either one came, the Bishop himself died (on December 4, 1957), but not before the Sacred Congregation for the Doctrine of the Faith requested photocopies of all Sr. Lucia's Fatima writings. Bishop Carreia sent that transcription of the third part of the July 13th apparition, the "Fatima Secret," to the Congregation, unopened. The word is that the pope at the time, Pius XII, did not open and read it, but that Pope John XXIII did, in 1960, whereupon the document was resealed and restored to Vatican archives, still a "secret." That's what's known, and the fact that it's short—on one sheet of paper—and written in Portuguese, and that it was for the pope, and that he decided not to reveal it. The allure and dramatics of this unrevealed part of the apparitions should not obscure the message of Fatima: God's call, through Mary, for conversion, reconciliation, prayer, and penance.

Popular Marian Devotions

Our Lady of the Snows

This devotion began on Rome's Esquiline Hill, in 352, and may be the oldest of Marian devotions. In the Eternal city, an elderly couple had an apparition of Mary one hot August night wherein she requested that a shrine be built on one of the city's celebrated hills. The next morning the city woke to find the Esquiline covered with snow. Today, St. Mary Major, "Church of St. Mary of the Snow," stands on this site as the largest and most important of all churches dedicated to the Blessed Mother. (In the United States, pilgrims can visit Our Lady of the Snows Shrine in Belleville, Illinois. Open year-around, the shrine includes meditative and devotional areas. It also is the site of an annual outdoor novena, celebrated during nine nights surrounding August 5th, the feast day of Our Lady of the Snows.)

Our Mother of Perpetual Help

This is the miraculous picture, icon-style, of the Madonna and Child. The original rests on the main altar of the shrine of the same name on *Via Merulana* in Rome. The five markings are names, or titles, in Greek. At the top: Mother (*Meter,* shortened to "MP"—*mu rho* in Greek) of God ("ThU"—*theta upsilon*). The marking over "M" is an old sign for the Holy Spirit, or redemption. The wavy line over "ThU" is an old indication for an abbreviation. Over the Christ child is "Jesus Christ." The angels are desig nated as the Archangels Michael (capital *mu* in Greek, "M" in English) and Gabriel (capital *gamma* in Greek, "G" in English).

A Bad Dream and a Good Mother

"Our Mother of Perpetual Help" originated in an episode, so says the legend, in young Jesus' life. One day the Christ Child was frightened by the terrifying vision of two angels showing him the instruments of the passion. He runs to his Mother for reassurance, almost losing his sandal on the way. Safely enfolded in her arms, his hands are turned palms down into his Mother's, illustrating that the graces of redemption are in her keeping.

The Story Behind the Picture

The odyssey of this picture is a story in itself. Explanations of its origin abound. One predictable legend has it that it was painted by St. Luke. Its creator and its age are in fact unknown. Some say it was venerated for centuries in Constantinople as a miraculous icon, and that it was destroyed by the Turks in 1453.

The story continues that a copy of that work was made in tempera on hard nutwood, 17x21 inches. It came from Crete, where it had been venerated, to Rome, in 1490. It was owned by a private family until a little girl of the household had an apparition in which the Blessed Mother told her that she wished to have the icon placed in a church, specifically "between my beloved church of St. Mary Major's and that of my beloved son, St. John of Lateran."

On March 27th, 1499, her request was fulfilled and the icon was exposed for veneration in the Church of St. Matthew. There it remained for three centuries, becoming a pilgrimage shrine for the Christian world. In 1789, the old church was demolished in a war, but the icon was saved by the Augustinian priests in charge of St. Matthew's. They took it with them to their new quarters in the city.

In 1855, the Redemptorist priests came to Rome and built a church in honor of their founder, St. Alphonsus, on the site of the old St. Matthew's. A Redemptorist priest recalled an old Augustinian of his youth telling of a miraculous picture in their chapel that had always been venerated in old St. Matthew's.

The Redemptorists petitioned Pope Pius IX to have the image placed in the church on the spot chosen by Our Lady herself. And the pope granting the request said: "It is our will that this picture of the Blessed Virgin be returned to the church between St. Mary Major's and St. John Lateran's." At the same time he commanded the Redemptorists to "make her known" all over the world.

On April 26, 1866, a solemn procession carried the miraculous Madonna to her chosen spot in the Church of St. Alphonsus Maria de Liguori, one of Mary's greatest lovers and defenders. Today the original painting reposes in Rome while millions of replicas bring her and her perpetual help to people everywhere.

Consecration to Mary

A devotional act promoted by St. Louis de Montfort (1673–1716) consisting of the entire gift of self to Jesus through Mary (as her "slave"), being a habitual attitude of dependence on her:

I, _____, faithless sinner, renew and ratify today in your hands the vows of my baptism; I renounce forever Satan, his pomps and works; and I give myself entirely to Jesus Christ, the Incarnate Wisdom, to carry my cross after Him all the days of my life, and to be more faithful to Him than I have ever been before.

In the presence of all the heavenly court I choose you this day for my mother and queen. I deliver and consecrate to you, as your slave, my body and soul, my goods, both interior and exterior, and even the value of all my good actions, past, present, and future; leaving to you the entire and full right of disposing of me, and all that belongs to me, without exception, according to your good pleasure, for the greater glory of God, in time and in eternity. Amen.

Marian Baptismal Names

Devotion to the Blessed Mother has inspired many baptismal names, whose bearers have Mary as their patron and a particular feastday—or any—as their Name's Day.

Mary is from the Hebrew Marah, Miryam, "bitter" (see Ruth 1.20). *Marah* is the Hebrew word for myrrh, an incense and perfume.)

Variations: Mara, Maria (Latin, Italian, Hungarian, German), Marie, Maretta, Marette, Marclla, Marictta, Marilla, Marilyn, Marla, Marya, Miriam, Muriel (Irish for "Star of the Sea"); Marianne ("Marian" in Italian) honors Mary and Ann.

Nicknames: Mame, Mamie, Mayme, May, Mari, Moll, Mollie, Molly, Polly

Translations
Bavarian—Marla
French—Marie, Manon, Manette, Maryse
Irish—Maire, Moira (Maura), Maureen
Slavic—Marya
Spanish—Maria, Marita, Mariquita

From Mary's many titles
Madonna—Italian for "My Lady"
Regina—Latin for queen (Mary's Queenship)
Virginia—honoring Mary's virginity

Male derivatives (from "servant of Mary"):
Gilmary, Gilmore, Melmore and Myles
(as are surnames Gilmartin, Kilmartin)

The *"Lamed Vav"*

The *lamed vav* are "the 36" righteous people, or *"tzaddikim,"* necessary in the world for God to keep mankind in existence. This famous legend from the Talmudic tradition is reminiscent of the Genesis account of Abraham dealing with God over the destruction of Sodom, which would have been spared for even ten righteous people in town. In the original legend, these humble, honorable, anonymous folk—whether shopkeeper, shoemaker or drayman, prince or pauper—would influence others to greater righteousness by their own example. In later tradition, they were ascribed miraculous power which a *tzaddik* would invoke in emergencies, rescuing a fellow man in danger. In the spirit of doing good secretly and without reward, however, they would then disappear, lest their identity be revealed.

ST. JOSEPH

For titles, see The Litany of St. Joseph; in art, he is often pictured: as a member of the Holy Family; holding Christ; with the tools of his carpenter trade; with a budding lily stalk.

Statue of Joseph's altar, St. Adrian's

The Joseph Legend of the Budding Staff of Lily

Zechariah the high priest told Mary that in a revelation he was instructed by an angel to bring together marriageable men and have each leave his staff in the temple overnight. The Lord's choice of a husband for Mary would be revealed through a sign. In the morning the staff of Joseph the carpenter was found blossomed, while the other suitors' were barren.

THE TWELVE APOSTLES

Their names are listed in four places. Some of them had two names, either a surname or a name given otherwise. Four were fishermen, one a tax collector, two sets of brothers (Simon/Andrew and James/John), two evangelists (Matthew, John). All were martyred except John. Judas Iscariot betrayed Jesus and was replaced in the Apostolic Church by Matthias Acts 1.21–26.

(Alpha-son of Alphaeus; Zlt-the Zealot; Isc-Iscariot; Jms-son of James)

MT. 10.2–4	MK 3.16–19	LK 6.12–19	ACTS 1.13
Simon	Simon	Simon	Peter
Andrew	James	Andrew	James
James	John	James	John
John	Andrew	John	Andrew
Philip	Philip	Philip	Philip
Bartholomew*	Bartholomew	Bartholomew	Thomas
Thomas	Matthew	Matthew	Bartholomew
Matthew	Thomas	Thomas	Matthew
James, Alph	James, Alph	James, Alph	James, Alph
Thaddaeus	Thaddaeus	Simon Zlt	Simon Zlt
Simon Zlt	Simon Zlt	Judas, Jms	Judas, Jms
Judas Isc	Judas Isc	Judas Isc	Matthias

Favored Apostles

Mentioned three times accompanying Jesus apart from the others (for the raising of Jairus' daughter, at the Transfiguration and during the agony in the garden) are Peter, James, and John.

THE APOSTLES IN THE SCRIPTURES

Peter

Andrew's brother Mt 4.18; Mk 1.16; Lk 5.1–11
From Bethsaida Jn 1.44
A fisherman Mt 4.18; Mk 1.16; Lk 5.1–11
Partner of James and John Lk 5.10
Called by Jesus Mt 4.19; Mk 1.17–18; Lk 5.11
Name changed from Simon Mt 16.16–18; Jn 1.41

St. Peter's
Cross

*Nathanael? (Jn 21.2)

Rebuked Jesus about suffering and was rebuked Mt 16.22–23; Mk 8.32–33

Walked on water, and sank Mt 14.28–29

Disputed with Jesus at Last Supper over foot washing Jn 13.5–10

Severed the ear of high priest's slave at Jesus' arrest Jn 18.10

Pledged his discipleship after which Jesus prophesied his denial
Lk 22.33–34

Denied Jesus Mt. 26.69–74; Mk 14.66–72; Lk 22.54–62

Given keys to the kingdom Mt 16.19

Gave answer (for disciples) to question "Who do you say I am?"
Mt 16.15-16; Mk 8.29; Lk 9.20

Approached by temple tax collectors about Jesus Mt 17.24–27

Present, with James and John, at raising of Jairus' daughter
Mk 5.37; Lk 8.51

Present, with James and John, for transfiguration Mt 17.1; Mk 9.2; Lk 9.28

Present, with James, John and Andrew, on Mt. of Olives for end times
and destruction of Jerusalem prophecy Mk 13.3

Present, with James and John, at the agony in the garden Mt 26.37;
Mk 14.33

Present, with six others, for resurrection appearance by the sea of
Galilee Jn 21.2

Told by Mary Magdalene about resurrection Mk 16.7

Ran to empty tomb Jn 20.2f

Repented and pledged love Jn 21.15–17

Charged by Jesus to lead the Church Lk 21.17; Jn 21.17

Supervised qualification for and election of Judas' replacement
Acts 1.15–26

First apostle to perform a miracle in Jesus' name Acts 3.1f

Later life: vague references Acts 12.17; 1 Cor. 1.12

"Apostle to the Jews" Gal 2.7

"Pillar of the Church" Gal 2.9

plus more than a dozen references to his apostolic ministry in Acts

Andrew

Peter's brother Lk 5.10

From Bethsaida Jn 1.44

A fisherman Lk 5.10

Originally the Baptist's disciple Jn 1.35–40

Called by Jesus Mt 4.18–19; Mk 1.16–17; Jn 1.35–40

Introduced Peter to Jesus Jn 1.40–42

Brought to Jesus boy with bread before multiplication Jn 6.8–9

Introduced, with Philip, some Greek believers to
Jesus Jn 12.21–22

Present on Mt. of Olives, with Peter, James, and John, for end-times
prophecy Mk 13.3

St. Andrew's
Cross ("Saltire")

James and John

Partners of Peter as fishermen **Lk 5.10**

Among first apostles, "fishers of men"
   Mt 4.21; Mk 1.19

(John) Called by Jesus **Jn 1.35–40?**

Nicknamed "Sons of Thunder" by Jesus **Mk 3.17**

(John) Scolded by Jesus for forbidding outsiders from
   exorcising **Lk 9.49–50**

Wanted to call down flames on Samaritan town
   inhospitable to Jesus **Lk 9.52–54**

Requested seats in heaven beside Jesus
   Mk 10.35–40; cf Mt 20.20–23

St. James' Cross

Present, with Peter, at raising of Jairus' daughter **Mk 5.37; Lk 8.51**

Present, with Peter, for transfiguration **Mt 17.1; Mk 9.2; Lk 9.28**

Present, with Peter and Andrew, on Mt. of Olives for end times and
   destruction of Jerusalem prophecy **Mk 13.3**

Present with Peter, at agony in the garden **Mt 26.37; Mk 14–33**

Their mother was present at crucifixion **Mt 27.56**

Witnessed Jesus' resurrection appearance by Sea of Galilee **Jn 21.2**

(John), with Peter, first healing in Jesus' name **Acts 3.1–11**

(John), with Peter, goes to Samaria on a mission **Acts 8.14**

"Pillars" of the Church **Gal 2.9**

(James) First apostle martyred; by Herod Antipas, A.D. 44 **Acts 12.2**

The "Beloved Disciple" *(John?)*

Reclined on Jesus' chest at last super **Jn 13.24–25**

Entrusted with care of Mary **Jn 19.26**

Told by Mary Magdalene (with Peter) of empty tomb **Jn 20.2**

Recognized Jesus on the shore **Jn 21.7**

Thomas *("Didymus"; Greek for twin)*

Encouraged disciples to accompany Jesus on return
   to Jerusalem **Jn 11.16**

Questioned Jesus in last discourse on where He was
   going **Jn 14.5**

Doubted Jesus' resurrection **Jn 20.25**

Made an act of faith in Jesus'
presence **Jn 20.26–28**

Witnessed Jesus' resurrection
   appearance at sea of
   Galilee **Jn 21.2**

Because you have seen me Thomas, you believe;
blessed are those who have not seen, and have
believed."

Matthew *("Levi", in Hebrew so-called by Mark and Luke)*

From Capernaum, in Galilee **Mk 2.1,14**
Son of Alphaeus **Mk 2.14**
A tax collector **Lk 5.27**
Called by Jesus (and left all) **Mk 9.9; Mk 2.14; Lk 5.28**
Hosted by Jesus for a meal with publicans and sinners **Mt 9.10; Mk 2.15;**
    Lk 5.29

Bartholomew *("Nathanael"?)*

Called by Jesus after Philip's introduction **Jn 1.43–51**
From Cana in Galilee **Jn 21.2**
Witnessed Jesus' resurrection appearance by sea of Galilee **Jn 21.2**

Philip

From Bethsaida **Jn 1.43**
Asked by Jesus to follow him **Jn 1.43**
Introduced by Nathanael to Jesus **Jn 1.45–46**
Advised Jesus of impossibility of feeding the multitude **Jn 6.5–7**
Introduced, with Andrew, some Greeks to Jesus **Jn 12.21–22**
Asked Jesus at Last Supper to "show us the Father" **Jn 14.9**

Simon *("the Zealot" in Luke and Acts)*

Judas *(Distinguished variously from Judas Iscariot)*

Asked Jesus why he revealed himself to them and not to the world
    Jn 14.22

James *(Son of Alphaeus)*

Brother of Matthew? (who was also "son of Alphaeus") **See Mk 2.14**

Judas Iscariot

Treasurer for the apostles **Jn 13.29**
Referred to prophetically by Jesus as a betrayer, a "devil" **Jn 6.70–71**
Advised Jesus that money spent for ointment could better be spent on
    the poor **Jn 12.5–6**
Induced by the devil to betray Jesus **Jn 13.2**
Conferred with high priests over betrayal of Jesus **Mt 26.14–16;**
    Mk 14.10–11; Lk 22.3–6
Revealed by Jesus at the Last Supper as the betrayer **Mk 26.20–25;**
    Mk 14.17–21; Lk 22.14, 21–23; Jn 13.26
Handed over Jesus **Mt 26.47–49; Mk 14.43–45; Lk 22.47–48; Jn 18.1–5**
Died **Mt 27.3–5**

Traditional Stories of the Apostles' Deaths

The twelve, plus Matthias, Luke, Mark, and Paul. Many of these stories have been retold, though some lack reliable support.

Andrew
Martyred in Patrae in 70; bound to a cross, he preached to his persecutors until he died. The X-shaped cross story arose in the Middle Ages. There is also unhistorical speculation that he was the first bishop of Byzantium (Constantinople).

Bartholomew
Martyred in Armenia in 44, by being flayed alive. He has been associated with the spread of gospel in Lycaonia, India, and Armenia.

James the Greater
Martyred in Jerusalem, by beheading. After his death in Palestine his body was put in a boat with sails set. The next day it reached the Spanish coast. According to another legend, it was his relics that were transferred to Spain, in a marble ship from Jerusalem where he was bishop. His body was discovered in 840 by a divine revelation to a Bishop Theodomirus, and a church was built at Compostella to enshrine it. Called *Mata-moros* (Moor-slayer) because he was believed to have come on a white steed to the aid of the Christians in their battle against the Moors.

James the Less
Martyred in Jerusalem. He was stoned to death, according to Josephus. A century later a tradition arose that he was taken to the pinnacle of the temple and ordered to dissuade the assembly from belief in Christ. He preached Christ instead, and so was hurled to the ground and stoned where he lay. Another tradition says he was clubbed with a fuller's pole.

John
Aristodemos, a priest of Diana, challenged him to drink a chalice of poison. John blessed it, whereupon a dragon-form of Satan flew from it; then he drank it without harm. In the Domitian persecution (96) he was immersed in boiling oil, but delivered unharmed he then was banished to the isle of Patmos, where it is said to have written the Book of Revelation. After his return to Ephesus he died a natural death.

Judas—*suicide*

Jude *(Thaddaeus)*
An apocryphal account says he evangelized in Persia, and was there shot to death with arrows.

Luke *(evangelist)*
An ancient source says he labored long in Greece and there died at the age of eighty-four (unmarried). Another tradition says he was martyred in Greece, by hanging on an olive tree.

Mark *(evangelist)*
Traditionally the evangelist of Alexandria, Egypt, and its first bishop. He was martyred there, during the reign of the emperor Trajan, after being dragged through its streets.

Matthew
Martyred in Nadabar. Preached for fifteen years in Judea, then took the gospel to Ethiopia, where he was slain by a sword.

Matthias
Stoned and then beheaded.

Paul
After he had converted one of Nero's favorite concubines he was beheaded at Rome (66), whereupon milk flowed from his veins. Tradition says the place of this martyrdom is now called *Tre Fontane,* and his body is buried where the Church of St. Paul outside the Walls stands.

Peter
Confuted Simon Magus, who was at Nero's court as a magician. Crucified in 66, and at his request head down because he deemed himself unworthy of a death the same as Christ's; his tomb is under the high altar of St. Peter's in Rome.

Philip
Probably preached the gospel in Phrygia, and died in Hierapolis, where his grave is now claimed to be.

Simon *(the Zealot)*
Evangelized in Egypt, and then Persia where he was martyred, along with Jude, some say.

Thomas
Martyred at Meliapour in south India. One account says he was run through with a lance at Coromandel in the East Indies. Spoken of in the apocryphal *Acts of St. Thomas.*

Burial Places of Apostles and Evangelists
Seven are buried in Rome:
> Bartholomew, in the church so-named, on the Tiber Island
> James the Less, in the Church of SS. Philip and James
> Jude
> Mathias, in St. Peter's
> Peter, in St. Peter's
> Philip
> Simon

Andrew at Amalfi (Naples)
James the Greater at St. Iago de Compostella in Spain
John at Ephesus
Matthew at Salerno (Naples)
Thomas at Ortona (Naples)
Mark the Evangelist at Venice
Luke the Evangelist at Padua

A laurel wreath represents victory, and also
eternity, since its leaves do not wilt

Nameless New Testament Personages Whom Tradition Has Named

Casper, Melchior, and Balthasar
The magi who brought the three gifts to the Christ Child.

Dismas
The good thief, who died in crucifixion with Christ, according to the
apocryphal *Gospel of Nicodemus*.

Gestas
The impenitent thief (see Dismas).

Ignatius
The child Jesus sat in the midst of the disciples as an example.

Joachim and Ann
Parents of the Blessed Virgin Mary.

John (apostle and evangelist) **The Beloved Disciple**
There is wide acceptance of the opinion that he is "the disciple Jesus loved," mentioned in the fourth Gospel on four occasions, all during or following Jesus' passion.

Longinus
The Roman soldier who lanced the crucified Christ, according to the apocryphal *Gospel of Nicodemus*. Stories of his spear were further told and embellished in the romance of King Arthur.

Mary Magdalen
The penitent woman who washed Jesus' feet with her tears and dried them with her hair (Lk 7.36f). Probably so-called because this episode is followed in Luke by a reference to a Mary Magdala "from whom seven devils had been cast." She has also been identified with the Mary of Mary and Martha (of Bethany), because of the story of this Mary also anointing Jesus' feet. **Jn 12.3**

Veronica
Tradition holds that a woman with this name wiped the face of Jesus on his way to Calvary.

True Face

The word "veronica" is the name given to the veil that tradition says was used to wipe the face of Jesus on his way of the cross. It is probably second only to the Holy Shroud among the *"Volto Santo"* (Holy Face) relics. "Veronica" is really the two Latin words, *vera* and *icon,* "true image," referring to the Sacred Face. Some say it was the centurian's wife, Seraphica, who did this work of mercy, and later discovered his face on the cloth. Other legends say the woman was Martha, and still others, Zacchaeus' wife, or the woman Christ healed of an issue of blood (Mk 5.25–32). No mention of an actual person named "Veronica" can be found earlier than the fifth century.

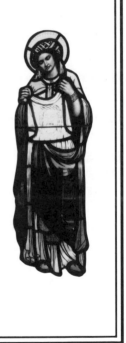

CHURCH FATHERS

Apostolic Fathers

First and second-century writers who associated personally with the apostles and whose writings reflect genuine apostolic teaching.

St. Clement (died about 97)
Bishop of Rome, third successor of St. Peter; author of the letter of the Church of Rome to the Church of Corinth *(Clement's First Letter)*.

St. Ignatius (about 50–107)
Bishop of Antioch, second successor of St. Peter in that See, by tradition a disciple of St. John; author of seven letters *(Ephesians, Magnesians, Trallians, Romans, Philadelphians, Smyrnaeans,* and *Polycarp, bishop of Smyrna)*.

St. Polycarp (69–155)
Bishop of Smyrna, disciple of St. John; author of a letter *(Philippians)*.

Author of *The Didache* (probably second century)
A Church manual and liturgical document discovered in 1873 at Constantinople containing the teaching of the twelve apostles (the priest's prayer while preparing the gifts is virtually verbatim from here, "Blessed are you, Lord, God of all creation . . .").

Author of *Epistle of Barnabas*

Other Early Christian Writers ("Sub-Apostolic")

St. Justin Martyr (100–165)
of Asia Minor, Rome; layman, apologist.

St. Irenaeus (130–202)
Bishop of Lyons, author of *Against Heresies,* an exposition of the faith.

St. Cyprian (210–258)
Bishop of Carthage, opposed Novatian heresy.

Fathers of the Church

Theologians and writers of the first eight centuries eminent in holiness and learning. They were such authoritative witnesses to the belief and teaching of the Church that their unanimous acceptance of doctrines as divinely revealed has been regarded as evidence that such doctrines were so received by the Church consistent with apostolic tradition and Sacred Scripture. Their unanimous rejection of doctrines branded the ideas as heretical. This is not to say all their writing is free of error in all respects.

The Four Main Prerogatives of the Church Fathers
Antiquity   Orthodoxy   Sanctity   Approval by the Church

Latin Fathers of the Church ("Four Great Fathers" appear in bold)

St. Ambrose (340–97), bishop of Milan

Arnobius (d. 327), apologist

St. Augustine (354–430), bishop of Hippo

St. Benedict (480–546), father of Western monasticism

St. Caesarius (470–542), archbishop of Arles

St. John Cassian (360–435), abbot

St. Celestine I (d. 432), pope

St. Cornelius (d. 253), pope

St. Cyprian (d. 258), bishop of Carthage

St. Damasus (d. 384), pope

St. Dionysius (d. 268), pope

St. Ennodius (473–521), bishop of Pavia

St. Eucherius (d. 449), bishop of Lyons

St. Fulgentius (468–533), bishop of Ruspe

St. Gregory of Elvira (died after 392)

St. Gregory (I) the Great (540–604), pope

St. Hilary (315–68), bishop of Poitiers

St. Innocent I (d. 417), pope

St. Irenaeus (130–200), bishop of Lyons

St. Isidore (560–636), archbishop of Seville

St. Jerome (343–420), priest, exegete, translator of the Vulgate

Lactantius Firmianus (240–320), apologist

St. Leo the Great (390–461), pope

Marius Mercator (early fifth century), Latin polemicist

Marius Victorinus (fourth century), Roman rhetorician

Minucius Felix (second or third century), apologist

Novation (200–62), the Schismatic

St. Optatus (fourth century), bishop of Mileve

St. Pacian (fourth century), bishop of Barcelona

St. Pamphilus (240–309), priest

St. Paulinus (353–431), bishop of Nola

St. Peter Chrysologus (400–50), archbishop of Ravenna

St. Phoebadius (d. 395), bishop of Agen

St. Prosper of Aquitaine (390–463), theologian

Rufinus (345–410), Latin translator of Greek theology

Salvian (400–80), priest

St. Siricius (334–99), pope

Tertullian (160–223), apologist, father of Latin theology

St. Vincent of Lerins (d. 450), priest and monk

Greek Fathers of the Church ("Four Great Fathers" appear in bold)

St. Anastasius Sinaita (d. 700), apologist, monk

St. Andrew of Crete (660–740), archbishop of Gortyna

Aphraates (fourth century), Syriac monk

St. Archelaus (d. 282), bishop of Cascar

St. Athanasius (c. 297–373), archbishop of Alexandria
Athenagoras (second century), apologist
St. Basil the Great (329–79), archbishop of Caesarea
St. Caesarius of Nazianzus (330–69)
St. Clement of Alexandria (150–215), theologian
St. Clement I of Rome (30–101), pope
St. Cyril (315–86), bishop of Jerusalem
St. Cyril (376–444), patriarch of Alexandria
Didymus the Blind (313–98), theologian
Diodore (d. 392), bishop of Tarsus
Dionysius the Pseudo-Areopagite (fifth century), mystical theologian
St. Dionysius the Great (190–264), archbishop of Alexandria
St. Epiphanius (315–403), bishop of Salamis
Eusebius (260–340), bishop of Caesarea
St. Eustathius (fourth century), bishop of Antioch
St. Firmillian (d. 268), bishop of Caesarea
Gennadius I (d. 471), patriarch of Constantinople
St. Germanus (634–733), patriarch of Constantinople
St. Gregory of Nazianzen (329–90), bishop of Sasima
St. Gregory of Nyssa (330–95)
St. Gregory Thaumaturgus (213–70), bishop of Neocaesarea
Hermas (second century), author of *The Shepherd*
St. Hippolytus (170–236), martyr
St. Ignatius (35–107), bishop of Antioch
St. Isidore of Pelusium (360–about 450), abbot
St. John Chrysostom (347–407), patriarch of Constantinople
St. John Climacus (579–649), monk
St. John Damascene (675–749), defender of sacred images
St. Julius I (d. 352), pope
St. Justin Martyr (100–65), apologist
St. Leontius of Byzantium (sixth century), theologian
St. Macarius the Great (300–90), monk
St. Maximus (580–662), abbot and confessor
St. Melito (d. 190), bishop of Sardis
St. Methodius (d. 311), bishop of Olympus
St. Nilus the Elder (d. 430), priest and monk
Origen (184–254), head of the Catechetical School of Alexandria
St. Polycarp (69–155), bishop of Smyrna
St. Proclus (d. 446), patriarch of Constantinople
St. Serapion (died after 362), bishop of Thmuis
St. Sophronius (560–638), patriarch of Jerusalem
Tatian the Assyrian (120–80), apologist and theologian
Theodore (350–428), bishop of Mopsuestia
Theodoret (393–458), bishop of Cyrrhus
St. Theophilus (second century), bishop of Antioch

DOCTORS OF THE CHURCH

"Doctor of the Church" is a title given since the Middle Ages to authors of eminent holiness and learning whose work has significantly enhanced the cause of Christ in his Church (which is not to say all their writing is free of error in all respects). Originally, the four Great Doctors of the Western Church were considered the Doctors of the Church. But the Church has officially added many more; there are thirty-two, including two women, Teresa of Avila and Catherine of Siena, named in 1970. All are saints.

Albert the Great (about 1200–1280)
Doctor Universalis, Doctor *Expertus;* Dominican; patron of natural scientists.

Alphonsus Liguori (1696–1787)
Patron of confessors, moralists; founded Redemptorists.

Ambrose (about 340–397)
Influenced a development of the Liturgy ("Ambrosian"); opponent of Arianism in the West; bishop of Milan.

Anselm (1033–1109)
Father of Scholasticism; archbishop of Canterbury.

Anthony of Padua (1195–1231)
Evangelical Doctor; Franciscan Friar.

Athanasius (about 297–373)
Father of Orthodoxy; main opponent of Arianism; bishop of Alexandria.

Augustine (354–430)
Doctor of Grace; bishop of Hippo.

Basil the Great (about 329–379)
Father of Monasticism in the East; one of three Cappadocian Fathers.

Bede the Venerable (about 673–735)
Father of English History; Benedictine priest.

Bernard (about 1090–1153)
Mellifluous Doctor (eloquent); Cistercian monk.

Bonaventure (about 1217–1274)
Seraphic Doctor; Franciscan theologian.

Catherine of Siena (about 1347–1380)
Second woman proclaimed Doctor (1970); mystic.

Cyril of Alexandria (about 376–444)
Patriarch; opponent of Nestorianism; contributor in Christology.

Cyril of Jerusalem (about 315–387)
Eastern opponent of Arianism; bishop.

Ephraem (about 306–373)
Deacon of Edessa; Harp of the Holy Spirit; Scripture exegete.

Francis de Sales (1567–1622)
Patron of Catholic writers, press; Counter-Reformation leader; bishop.

Gregory of Nazianzen (about 330–390)
The Christian Demosthenes; the Theologian (in the East); one of the three Cappadocian Fathers.

Gregory I, the Great (about 540–604)
Pope; defender of papal primacy; clerical, monastic reformer.

Hilary of Poitiers (about 315–368)
The Athanasius of the West; bishop.

Isidore of Seville (560–636)
Regarded most learned of his time; archbishop; theologian; historian.

Jerome (about 343–420)
Father of Biblical Science.

John Chrysostom (about 347–407)
The Greatest of the Greek Fathers; Golden-Tongued Orator; patron of preachers; bishop of Constantinople.

John Damascene (about 675–749)
Golden Speaker; Greek theologian.

John of the Cross (1542–1591)
Doctor of Mystical Theology; co-founder of Discalced Carmelites.

Lawrence of Brindisi (1559–1619)
Leading preacher in Counter-Reformation.

Leo I, the Great (400–461)
Pope; wrote against Nestorianism, Monophysitism, Manichaeism and Pelagianism.

Peter Canisius (1521–1597)
Counter-Reformation leader; Jesuit theologian.

Peter Chrysologus (about 400–450)
"Golden Worded"; bishop of Ravenna.

Peter Damian (1007–1072)
Reformer of Church and clerics; Benedictine.

Robert Bellarmine (1542–1621)
A champion of orthodoxy during and after Reformation; Jesuit.

Teresa of Avila (1515–1582)
First woman proclaimed Doctor (1970); Spanish Carmelite; mystic.

Thomas Aquinas (1125–1274)
Doctor *Communis;* Doctor *Angelicus;* The Great Synthesizer; patron of Catholic schools, education; Dominican philosopher and theologian.

St. Thomas Aquinas and St. Bonaventure, Doctors of the Church

TITLES OF SAINTS

Angel of the Schools: St. Thomas Aquinas (1225–1274)

Angelic Doctor: St. Thomas Aquinas
>Because of the greatness and purity of his work, his expositions seemingly beyond the human intellect's limit.

The Straw of a Genius

Thomas Aquinas died before he was fifty, but he left behind a towering monument of scholarship, and something greater. In 1273, he put aside his *Summa Theologica.* This work was destined to be a classic systematic exposition of theology—twenty-two volumes in translation—and has had enormous impact on Catholic theology and religion. In 1273 Brother Thomas left it unfinished saying, "All I have written seems to me like so much straw compared with what I have seen and what has been revealed to me." It was said of him, "His wonderful learning owes far less to his genius than to the effectiveness of his prayer."

Apostle among the Armenians: St. Gregory of Armenia (257–331)

Apostle of the Gauls: St. Denis (third century)

Apostle of Germany: St. Boniface (680–750); (originally Winifred, or Winfrith)

Apostles to the Slavs: Ss. Cyril and Methodius (ninth century)

Athanasius of the West: Hilary of Poitiers (about 315–368)

Beloved Disciple: St. John the Apostle (see e.g. Jn 13.23)

Beloved Physician: St. Luke, so-called by Paul (Col 4.14)

Bishop of Hippo: St. Augustine (354–430)

Black Pope: General of the Jesuits

Champions, The Seven Champions of Christendom: (A medieval designation of national patron saints): George of England, Andrew of Scotland, David of Wales, Patrick of Ireland, James of Spain, Denis of France, and Anthony of Italy

Christian Demosthenes: Gregory of Nazianzen (about 330–390)

Good Speaker

Demosthenes, the fourth-century B.C. Greek orator, once said of his rival Aeschines, "When you orate, they say, 'How well he speaks.' When I orate, they say, 'Let us march against Philip.' "

Desert Fathers: Ss. Anthony, Pachomius the Hermit, and Hilarion—The most noted fourth-century monks/hermits of Egypt from whom Christian monasticism evolved.

Divine, The: St. John the apostle, evangelist

Doctor

Divine Doctor: John Ruysbroek

Doctor *Angelicus:* St. Thomas Aquinas (1225–1274)

Doctor *Expertus*: St. Albert the Great (about 1200–1280)

Doctor of Grace: St. Augustine (354–430)

Doctor of Mystical Theology: St. John of the Cross (1542–1591)

Doctor Singularis: William of Occam (about 1347) scholastic, philosopher, Franciscan

Doctor Universalis: St. Albert the Great (about 1200–1280)

Ecstatic Doctor: Jean de Ruysbroek (1294–1381) mystic

Eloquent Doctor: Peter Aureolus, fourteenth century schoolman, archbishop of Aix

Evangelical Doctor: St. Anthony of Padua (1195–1231)

Illuminated Doctor: John Trauler (1294–1361), German mystic

Invincible Doctor: William of Occam

Irrefragable Doctor: Alexander of Hales (?–1245), English Franciscan

Mellifluous Doctor: St. Bernard (1091–1153) his writing being "a river of Paradise"

Seraphic Doctor: St. Bonaventure (1221–74)

Subtle Doctor: Duns Scotus (1265–1308), Scottish Franciscan

Dumb Ox: St. Thomas Aquinas (1224–74)

Because his tutor, St. Albert the Great, said, "The dumb ox will one day fill the world with his lowing."

Eagle of Divines: St. Thomas Aquinas

Father

Father of Biblical Sciences: St. Jerome (about 343–420)

Father of Church History: Eusebius of Caesaria (about 264–340)

Father of English History: Bede the Venerable (about 673–735)

Father in Faith/of the Faithful: Abraham (Rom 4; Gal 3.6–9)

Father of Monasticism in the East: St. Basil the Great (about 329–379)

Father of Moral Philosophy: St. Thomas Aquinas

Father of Musicians: Jubal (Gn 4.21)

Father of Orthodoxy: St. Athanasius (about 297–373)

Father of Scholasticism: St. Anselm (1033–1109)

Seraphic Father/Saint: St. Francis of Assisi

Last of the Fathers: St. Bernard (1091–1153), abbot of Clairvaux

Golden-tongued Orator: St. John Chrysostom (d. 407), Greek Father

Golden-tongued ("Chrysologus"): St. Peter, (d. about 449), bishop of Ravenna

Great (There are four saints so-called by the Church):

Basil the Great (about 329–379); Gregory the Great (about 540–604); Leo the Great (about 400–461); Albert the Great (about 1200–1280)

Greatest of the Greek Fathers: St. John Chrysostom

Great Synthesizer: St. Thomas Aquinas (1125–1274)

Hammer of the Arians: St. Hilary (d. 368), bishop of Poitiers

Harp of the Holy Spirit: St. Ephraem (about 306–373)

Holy Helpers, The Fourteen: George, Pantaleon, Denis, Eustace, Catherine, Blase, Vitus, Cyriacus, Giles, Barbara, Erasmus, Christopher, Achatius, Margaret

Grouping these saints, all martyred during the Church's early centuries, began in twelfth-century Germany, where saints are generally regarded as "helpers in need." They are venerated as a group because they are patrons of various nations and occupations, and of the victims of many common illnesses.

Ice (or Frost) Saints: Ss. Mamertus, Pancras, Servatius, and Boniface. Because their feast days fall in "black thorn winter" (the second week in May, between the 11th and 14th)

Illuminator, The: St. Gregory of Armenia (257–331) the apostle among the Armenians

Ireland: The Three Great Saints of: Patrick, Columba, Bridget

Lily of the Mohawks: Blessed Kateri Tekakwitha

Madonna: Mary ("my lady", Italian)

Maid of Orleans: St. Joan of Arc

Mata-moros (Moor slayer): St. James the greater, patron of Spain

Most Learned of his Day: St. Isidore of Seville

Myrrophores (Greek: myrrh bearers): the three Marys who visited Jesus' tomb (Mk 16.1)

Oracle of the Church: St. Bernard of Clairvaux

Pope of the Eucharist: Pope St. Pius X (1903–14)

Prince of the Church: a cardinal

Saint of Miracles: St. Anthony of Padua (1195–1231)

Spouse of Christ: St. Teresa of Avila (1515–821) "Spouse" is from the Latin *spondere,* to promise; hence, one who promises is a spouse.

Thaumaturgis (Gk: wonderworker; applied because of miracles worked): Gregory, bishop of Neo-Caesaria, Cappadocia (d. 270)
(*especially, but also:*)
Appollonius of Tyana, Cappadocia (3-98)
St. Bernard of Clairvaux (1091–1153), Thaumaturgis of the West
St. Filumena
St. Francis of Assisi (1182–1226)
St. Vincent de Paul (1576–1660): founder of the Sisters of Charity

Theologian, The (in the East): St. Gregory Nazianzen (329–390)

Weeping Saint: St. Swithin

Wonder-Worker of Padua: St. Anthony (1195–1231)

Worthies, The Nine (heroes often classed together):
From the Scriptures: Joshua, David, Judas Maccabaeus
From the Classics: Hector, Alexander, Julius Caesar
From the Romances: Arthur, Charlemagne, Godfrey of Bouillon

PRINCIPAL PATRONS

Not all of the following traditional patrons and patronesses (Lt: pater, father; see "pattern") have been included among the 173 saints of the revised Roman Missal. Herein are included saints' days according to the revised calendar. For the saint no longer so commemorated, the date of traditional observance according to the old calendar is included in parentheses.

ab-abbot   ap-apostle   aa-archangel   e-evangelist

Some fabled patronage were purely accidental. For example, St. Martin was the patron of "drunkards" because his feast day, November 11, coincided with the Roman Vinalia, or Feast of Bacchus. Times have changed, as have language, sensitivities and appreciation of what it means to be a patron. For a case in point, read below about Matt Talbot, patron of alcoholics.

Alcoholic Patrons

Matt Talbot (1856–1925) is a good example of why a person becomes a "patron." (He has not been called a "saint," but "venerable" which is one of the stages of the canonization process.) He was born of a poor family in Dublin and from age twelve had problems with drink. By the time he was twenty-eight it had progressed to the point that he begged for drinks. Deep in shame, and finding no one to buy him a drink, he took a pledge to the Sacred Heart one night to stop drinking. Realizing his sobriety depended on more than not drinking, Matt grew in holiness as he received daily Eucharist, prayed constantly, and practiced heroic personal penances.

Altar boys—John Berchmans, (Aug. 13)
Animals—Francis, Oct. 4
Animals, domestic—Ambrose, Nov. 30; Cornelius, Sept. 16
Archers—Sebastian
Architects/builders—Barbara, (Dec. 4); Thomas, ap, July 3
Armorers—Sebastian, Jan. 20
Armories—Lawrence, Aug. 10
Art—Catherine Bologna, (Mar. 9)
Artillerymen—Barbara, (Dec. 4)
Artists—Luke, Oct. 18; Michael, aa, Sept. 29
Astronomers—Dominic, Aug. 8
Athletes—Sebastian, Jan. 20
Authors—Francis de Sales, Jan. 29; Lucy, Dec. 13

Aviators—Joseph of Cupertino, (Sept. 18); Thérèsa of Lisieux Oct. 1;
Our Lady of Loretto, (Dec. 10)
Bakers—Elizabeth of Hungary, Nov. 17; Nicholas of Myra, Dec. 6;
Peter, ap, June 29
Bankers—Matthew, Sept. 21
Barbers—Cosmas and Damian, Sept. 26; Louis of France, Aug. 25
Barren women—Anthony of Padua, June 13; Felicity, Mar. 7
Basket-makers—Anthony, ab. Jan. 17
Beekeepers—Ambrose, Dec. 7; Bernard of Clairvaux, Aug. 20
Beggars—Elizabeth of Hungary, Nov. 17; Giles, (Sept. 1), Alexis, (July
17); Martin of Tours, Nov. 11
Blacksmiths—Dunstan, (May 19)
Blind—Dunstan, (May 19); Odilia, (Dec. 13); Raphael, Sept. 29

Patrons of the Blind

St. Dunstan is associated with work for the blind because of an
institution established during World War I at St. Dunstan's
House, Regent's Park, for the welfare and rehabilitation of
blinded soldiers (and later, civilians).

More inspirational is the story of St. Odilia who is said to have
been born blind and abandoned by her family. Raised in an Al-
sace convent, her sight was miraculously restored when she was
baptized as a twelve-year old. (She later became a Benedictine
abbess, dying around 720.)

St. Raphael, one of the three archangels mentioned by name in
the Bible, is another patron for the blind. The book of Tobit tells
the story of his miraculous intercessions. It was Raphael's instructions that Tobit's son followed in restoring his father's sight
(Tobit 11.7–14). (Legend has it he is the angel who moved the
waters of the healing pool in John 5.1–4.)

St. Lucy's patronage of the blind comes in part from her name,
which derives from *lux,* Latin for light. (Hence the ill-advised
custom of girls processing with candles on their heads: They
bring light. Tradition has it St. Lucy's persecutors put out her
eyes, which makes her patronage of the blind a natural.)

Bodily ills—Our Lady of Lourdes, Feb 11
Bookbinders—Peter Celestine, (May 19)
Booksellers—John, e. Dec. 27
Boyscouts—George, Apr. 23
Brewers—Boniface, June 5; Augustine, Aug. 28; Luke, Oct. 18;
Nicholas of Myra, Dec. 6

Bricklayers—Stephan, Dec. 26

Brides—Dorothy, (Feb. 6); Nicholas of Myra, Dec. 6

Builders—Vincent Ferrer, Apr. 5

Butchers—Anthony, ab, Jan. 17; Adrian, (Sept. 8); Luke, Oct. 18; Peter ap, June 29

Cab drivers—Fiacre, (Aug. 30)

Cabinet-makers—Anne, July 26

Cancer patients—Peregrine, (May 2)

Captives—Nicholas, Dec. 6

Carpenters—Joseph, Mar. 19; Thomas, July 3

Catholic action—Francis of Assisi, Oct. 4

Catholic writers/press—Francis de Sales, Jan. 24

Cattle—Cornelius, Sept. 16

Cavalrymen—George, Apr. 23

Charitable societies—Vincent de Paul

Children—Nicholas of Myra, Dec. 6; Pancras, May 12

Children's choir—Holy Innocents, Dec. 28

Chivalry—George, Apr. 23

Church universal—Joseph, Mar. 19

Clerics—Gabriel of the Sorrowful Mother, (Feb. 27)

Clockmakers—Peter, June 29

Clothworkers (fullers)—Severus

Comedians—Vitus, (June 15)

Communication workers—Gabriel, Sept. 29

Confessors—Alphonsus Liguori, Aug. 1; John Nepomucene (May 16)

Convulsion in children—Scholastica, Feb. 10

Cooks—Lawrence, Aug. 10; Martha, July 29

Coppersmiths—Benedict; July 11; Maurus, (Jan. 15)

Crops protection—Ansovinus, (Mar. 13)

Dairy workers—Brigid, July 23

Deaf—Francis de Sales, Jan. 24

Dentists—Apollonia, (Feb. 9)

Desperate situations—Jude Thaddeus, Oct. 28; Gregory of Neocaesarea, (Nov. 17)

Drapers—Ursula, (Oct. 21)

Druggists—Cosmas and Damian, Sept. 26; James the Less, ap. May 3

Dying—Joseph, Mar. 19; Barbara, (Dec. 4)

Ecology—Francis, Oct. 4

Elderly—Anthony of Padua, June 13

Emigrants—Francis Xavier Cabrini, Nov. 13

Engaged couples—Agnes, Jan. 21

Engineers—Joseph, Mar. 19; Ferdinand III, (May 30)

Expectant mothers—Margaret, (July 20); Raymond Nonnatus, (Aug. 31); Gerard Majella, (Oct. 16)

Eye trouble—Lucy, Dec. 13

Falsely accused—Raymond Nonnatus, (Aug. 31)

Family—Joseph, Mar. 19

Farmers—George, Apr. 23; Isidore, May 15

Firemen—Florian, (May 4)

Fire prevention—Catherine of Siena, Apr. 29; Barbara, (Dec. 4)

First communicants—Bl. Imelda, (May 12); Tarcisius (Aug. 15)

Fishermen—Andrew, Nov. 30

Florists—Dorothy, (Feb. 6); Thérèse of Lisieux, Oct. 1

Forest workers—John Gualbert, (July 12)

Founders—Barbara, (Dec. 4)

Foundlings—Holy Innocents, Dec. 28

Funeral directors—Joseph of Arimathea, (Mar. 17); Dismas, (Mar. 25)

Gardeners—Agnes, Jan. 21; Adalard, (Jan. 2); Dorothy, (Feb 6);
    Tryphon, (Nov. 10); Fiacre, (Aug. 30)

Geometricians—Thomas, ap. July 3

Glass workers—Luke, Oct. 18

Glaziers—Mark, Apr. 25

Goldsmiths—Dunstan, (May 19); Anastasius, (Sept. 7)

Grave diggers and graveyards—Anthony, ab, Jan. 17

Grace, those in need—Teresa of Avila, Oct. 15

Greetings—Valentine, (Feb. 14)

Grocers—Michael, aa, Sept. 29

Guardian angels—Raphael, aa, Sept. 29

Gunners—Barbara, (Dec. 4)

Hairdressers—Martin de Porres, Nov. 3

Handicapped—Giles (Sept. 1)

Happy death—Joseph, Mar. 19

Hatters—Severus of Ravenna, (Feb. 1); James the Less, ap. May 3

Haymakers—Gervase and Protase, (June 19)

Headaches—Teresa of Avila, Oct. 15

Heart ailments—John of God, Mar. 8

Hospitality—Julian, (Feb. 12)

Hospitals—Camillus de Lellis, July 14; John of God, Mar. 8; Jude Thad-
    deus, ap, Oct. 28

Housewives—Anne, July 26; Martha, July 29

Hunters—Hubert, (Nov. 3)

Huntsmen—Eustachius, Sept. 20

Innkeepers—Martin de Tours, Nov. 11; Amanda, (Feb. 6)

Interior souls—Joseph, Mar. 19

Invalids—Roch, (Aug. 16)

Ironmongers—Sebastian, Jan. 20

Jewelers—Eligius, (Dec. 1)

Journalists—Francis de Sales, Jan. 24

Jurists—Catherine of Alexandria, (Nov. 25); John Capistran, Oct. 23

Laborers—Isidore, May 15; James, July 25

Lawyers—Ivo, (June 17); Genesius, (Aug. 25)

Learning—Ambrose, Dec. 7; Acca, (Nov. 27)

Jude the Obscure

Finding the origin of St. Jude devotion is as hopeless as the cases for which he has become the patron. Like so many of the other apostles' lives, the details of his life are very obscure. The well-known devotion to him as the patron of hopeless or difficult cases may be rooted in the tradition that he was a close relative of Jesus, and that in childhood they were playmates. There is a Jude (or Judas in some translations) mentioned as Jesus' "brother" (relative) by Matthew (13.55), along with "James, Joseph and Simon." Some have taken this to be the St. Jude in question, hence a brother of James the Less who was the son of Alphaeus. This is a long way to go.

Devotion to him is of relatively recent vintage, in part owing to the similarity between his name and the betrayer's, Judas. It did, however, flourish in the fertile soil of the medieval mind, fertilized undoubtedly by an apparition of Christ to St. Bridget of Sweden, which is another story. In that one, the Lord directed Bridget to Jude: "In accordance with his surname, 'Thaddeus'— the amiable, the loving—he will show himself most willing to give help."

Artistically, Jude is sometimes pictured carrying the image of Jesus. The story behind that is that Abagaro, King of Edessa and also leprous, sent word to Jesus for him to come and cure him. Along with the request, the King sent an artist who was to return with a portrait of the Master. Impressed with his great faith, Jesus pressed into a cloth his image and gave it to Jude to take to the King, along with a cure. Abagaro was not only cured by Jude, but also, along with most of his subjects, converted to Christ.

Librarians—Jerome, Sept. 30
Locksmiths—Dunstan, (May 19)
Lost things—Anthony, ab, Jan. 17
Lovers—Raphael, aa Sept. 29
Maidens—Agnes, Jan. 21; Margaret, (July 20); Ursula, (Oct. 21)
Mailcarriers—Gabriel, Sept. 29
Marble workers—Clement I, (Nov. 23)
Mariners—Michael aa, Sept. 29; Nicholas of Tolentino, (Sept. 10)
Mentally ill—Dymphna, (May 15)
Merchants—Francis of Assisi, Oct. 4; Nicholas of Myra, Dec. 8
Metalworkers—Eligius, (Dec. 1)

St. Anthony and the Lost Manuscript

For a time in his life Brother Anthony lived in a friary in Montpellier, France, where he was a novice instructor. One of the novices was a restless and unhappy brother named Louis. Every hour away from teaching and prayer, Anthony spent in his cell working on a book of the psalms. It was a labor of love that had gone on for years, dedicated to anyone wanting to understand the psalms better. One afternoon he took a much needed respite from his work, but returned to find the manuscript gone. After a diligent search, it was left only for Anthony to pray.

At the same time it came to the attention of all in the friary that Brother Louis was gone too. What's more, an area farmer had seen him walking away from the monastery with a bundle under his arm. Anthony's prayer thus became more that Louis would find his vocation than that he would find his parchments. When he did pray that the book would be found and his life work salvaged, he compared his situation to a child loosing a toy.

Meanwhile, Louis was making his way to Paris to sell the work in his own name, and thus gain the fame and fortune he felt had eluded him in life. As he rested on the way on the bank of the river, a wild wind rose, churning the river into a frenzy. From its depths a monster came, advancing on Louis with a frightening aspect and a warning for him to restore the manuscript, lest he be destroyed. Frightened and repentant, Louis returned the work to Anthony, who counseled and tutored Louis in his vocation.

Anthony's intercession was credited with the find, and his prayer was requested throughout the monastery whenever anything was lost. His reputation spread throughout the area, especially later as he fulfilled a preaching vocation. He was a preacher of power, whose petition was heard—and always it was said, "This is the friar who finds lost objects."

Millers—Arnulph, (Aug. 15); Victor, (July 21)

Miners—Barbara, (Dec. 4)

Missions—Francis Xavier, Dec. 3; Thérèsa of Lisieux, Oct. 1; (Home)— Leonard of Port Maurice, (Nov. 26); (Negro)—Peter Claver, Sept. 9; Benedict the Moor, (Apr. 4)

Moral theologians—Alphonsus Liguori, Aug. 1

Mothers—Monica, Aug. 27; Ann, July 25

Motorcyclists—Our Lady of Grace, (May 31)

Motorists—Christopher, (July 25)
Mountaineers—Bernard of Menthon, (May 28)
Musicians—Cecilia, Nov. 22; Gregory the Great, Sept. 3; Paul, June 29

Musical Patron

St. Cecilia was a third-century Roman martyr. We are left with little more than enduring legends in learning about her life. While still a young girl, Cecilia dedicated her virginity to God. When forced by her family to marry, she converted her husband who also vowed celibacy. One legend tells of "pipes" played at her wedding. Although these pipes were probably the bagpipes common throughout Europe, ancient translations rendered the word "organ pipes." Consequently, St. Cecilia has often been portrayed by a pipe organ. Another legend calls her "the inventor of the organ," while another says an angel fell in love with her because of her musical skill. This heavenly visitant gave both her and her husband a crown of martyrdom, brought from heaven. With such ample fable and longstanding tradition, she is considered the patron of music and musicians.

Notaries—Mark, Apr. 25; Luke, Oct. 18
Nurses—Agatha, Feb. 5; Alexis (July 17); Camillus de Lellis, July 14; Raphael, Sept. 29; John of God, Mar. 8; Margaret, (July 20)
Orphans—Jerome Aemilian, (July 20)
Painters—John the Evangelist, Dec. 27; Luke, Oct. 18

St. Luke the Artist

Legend has it that Luke painted a portrait of the Blessed Mother, the icon of Our Lady of Czestochowa, also known as the Black Madonna. According to this tradition, he painted it on a board from the table St. Joseph built for the Holy Family. Historical studies, however, can only place the icon's origin between the 5th and 8th centuries. Today it can be seen at Poland's Jasna Gora monastery, where it has been a symbol of Polish spirituality and place of pilgrimage since 1382. It is said to have traveled from Palestine to Byzantium, Hungary and Ruthenia, and finally to have been brought to Poland by Ladislaus Opolczyk. (Other legends say that angels finished a picture of Christ that was outlined by St. Luke, and another, that he is the anonymous painter of Our Lady of Perpetual Help.

Pawnbrokers—Nicholas of Myra, Dec. 6

Peasants—Margaret, (July 20)

Penitents—Mary Magdalene, July 22

Pharmacists—Cosmas and Damian, Sept. 26

Philosophers—Catherine of Alexandria, (Nov. 25); Justin, June 1

Physicians—Cosmas and Damian, Sept. 26; Luke, Oct. 18; Pentaleone, (July 27); Raphael, Sept. 29

Pilgrims—Alexius (July 17); James, July 25

Evangelical Doctor, St. Anthony of Padua

Plague-stricken—Roch, (Aug. 16)

Plasterers—Bartholomew, Aug. 24

Poets—David, (Dec. 29); Cecilia, Nov. 22

Poisoning—Benedict, July 11

Policemen—Michael, Sept. 29

Poor—Lawrence, Aug. 10; Anthony of Padua, June 13

Porters—Christopher, (July 25)

Possessed, Bruno, Oct. 6; Denis, Oct. 9

Postal workers—Gabriel, Sept. 29

Potters—Sebastian, Jan. 20

Preachers—John Chrysostom, Sept. 13

Priests—Jean-Baptiste Vianney, Aug. 4; Paul, June 29

Printers—Augustine, Aug. 28; John the Evangelist, Dec. 27; Genesius, (Aug. 25); John of God, Mar. 8

Prisoners—Dismas, (Mar. 25); Barbara, (Dec. 4)

Prisoner Patron

Traditionally, the patron of prisoners is Dismas, the name tradition (and the apocryphal *Gospel of Nicodemus*) has given to the penitent thief who suffered crucifixion on the same day Jesus did.

Prisons—Joseph Cafasso, (June 23)

Publishers—John the Evangelist, Dec. 27; Francis de Sales, Jan. 29

Radiologists—Michael, aa, Sept. 29

Retreats—Ignatius Loyola, July 31

Rheumatism—James the Great, July 25

Saddlers—Crispin and Crispinian, (Oct. 25)

Sailors—Cuthbert, (Mar. 20); Erasmus, (June 2); Nicholas of Tolentino, (Sept. 10); Brendan, (May 16); Eulalia, (Feb. 12); Christopher, (July 25); Peter Gonzales, (Apr. 15)

Scholars—Brigid, July 23

Schools—Thomas Aquinas, Jan. 28

Schoolboys—Benedict, July 11; Lawrence, Aug. 10

Scientists—Albert the Great, Nov. 15

Sculptors—Luke, Oct. 18; Claude, (Nov. 8)

Secretaries—Genesius, (Aug. 25)

Seminarians—Charles Borromeo, Nov. 4

Servants, domestic—Zita, (Apr. 27); Martha, July 29

Shepherds—Cuthbert, (Mar. 20)

Shoemakers—Crispin and Crispinian, (Oct. 25)

Sick—Michael, Sept. 29; John of God, Mar. 8; Camillus de Lellis, July 14; Philomena, (Aug. 11)

Silversmiths—Andronicus, (Oct. 11)

Singers—Gregory, Sept. 3; Cecilia, Nov. 22

Singles—Andrew, Nov. 30

Skaters—Lidwina, (Apr. 14)

Skiers—Bernard of Menthon, (May 28)

Smiths—Eliquis, (Dec. 1)

Soldiers—George, Apr. 23; Adrian, (Sept. 8); Michael, aa, Sept. 29; Ignatius of Loyola, July 31; Sebastian, Jan. 20; Martin of Tours, Nov. 11; Joan of Arc, (May 30)

Sore throat—Blaise, Feb. 3

Spinsters—Catherine of Alexandria, (Nov. 25)

Stenographers—Genesius, (Aug. 25); Cassian, (Dec. 3)

Stonecutters—Clement, Nov. 23

Stonemasons—Stephan, Dec. 26; Barbara, (Dec. 4)

Students—Catherine of Alexandria, (Nov. 25); Jerome, Sept. 30; Thomas Aquinas, Jan. 28

Surgeons—Cosmas and Damian, Sept. 26

Swineherds—Anthony, June 13

Tailors—Boniface, June 5; Martin of Tours, Nov. 11; Homobonus, (Nov. 13)

Tanners—Crispin and Crispinian, (Oct. 25); Simon, (May 10); Lawrence, Aug. 10

Tax collectors—Matthew, Sept. 21

Teachers—Catherine of Alexandria, (Nov. 25); Gregory the Great, Sept. 3; Ursula, (Oct. 21); John the Baptist de La Salle, Apr. 7

Telegraph/Telephone/Television workers—Gabriel, aa, Sept. 29; Clare, Aug. 11

Television—St. Clare, Aug. 11
Tentmakers—Paul, June 29
Tertiaries—Louis of France, Aug. 25; Elizabeth of Hungary, Nov. 17
Theologians—Augustine, Aug. 28
Travelers—Christopher, (July 25); Julian, (Feb. 12); Gertrude, Nov. 16, Raphael, Sept. 29
Vocations—Alphonsus, Aug. 1
Watchmen—Peter of Alcantara, (Oct. 19)
Weavers—Paul the Hermit, (Jan. 15); Anastasius the Fuller, (Sept. 7); Anastasia, (Dec. 25)
Wheelwrights—Catherine of Alexandria, (Nov. 25)
Wine growers—Vincent, Jan. 22
Wine merchants—Amand, (Feb. 6)
Women in labor—Anne, July 26
Women's Army Corps—Genevieve, (Jan. 3)
Workers—Joseph, May 1
Yachtsmen—Adjutor, (Sept. 1)
Young girls—Agnes, Jan. 21
Youth—Aloysius Gonzaga, June 21; John Berchmans, (Aug. 13); Gabriel Possenti, (Feb. 27)

Mary and the Americas

This patroness of Mexico, with her appearance there in 1531, has also been declared patroness of Latin America (in 1910) and of the whole of the Americas (1945). Other devotions are still treasured, however, like Our Lady of Lujan in Argentina, Our Lady of Charity is Cuba, the Immaculate Conception in Brazil, and Our Lady of Sorrows in Ecuador.

Patron Saints of Countries

Argentina—Our Lady of Lujan
Amenia—Gregory Illuminator, (Oct. 1)
Australia—Francis Xavier, Nov. 13
Belgium—Joseph, Mar. 19

Bohemia—Wenceslaus, Sept. 28; Ludmilla, (Sept. 18); John Nepomucene, (May 16)

Borneo—Francis Xavier, Nov. 13

Brazil—Immaculate Conception, Dec. 8

Canada—Joseph, Mar. 19; Anne, July 26

Chile—James; Our Lady of Mt. Carmel, July 16

China—Joseph, Mar. 19

Colombia—Peter Claver, Sept. 9; Louis Bertrand, (Oct. 9)

Czechoslovakia—Wenceslaus, Sept. 28; John Nepomucene, (May 16); Procopius (July 8)

Denmark—Ansgar, Feb. 3; Canute, (Jan. 19)

Dominican Rep.—Our Lady of High Grace, (Apr. 4); Dominic, Aug. 8

East Indies—Thomas, ap, July 3

Ecuador—Sacred Heart

England—George, Apr. 23

Europe (co-patrons)—Benedict (July 11); Cyril and Methodius (Feb. 14)

St. Boniface,
Patron of Germany

Finland—Henry, July 13

France—Joan of Arc, (May 30); Denys, (Oct. 9)

Germany—Boniface, June 5

Greece—Nicholas of Myra, Dec. 6

Holland—Willibrord, (Nov. 7)

Hungary—Stephen, King, Aug. 16

India—Our Lady of Assumption, Aug. 15

Ireland—Patrick, Mar. 17; Brigid, Feb. 1; Columba (June 9)

Italy—Francis of Assisi, Oct. 4; Catherine of Siena, Apr. 29

Japan—Peter Baptist, (Feb. 5)

Lithuania—Casimir, Mar. 4; Cunegunda, (Mar. 3)

Mexico—Our Lady of Guadalupe, Dec. 12

Norway—Olaf, (July 29)

Paraguay—Our Lady of Assumption, Aug. 15

Philippines—Sacred Heart of Mary, (Aug. 22)

Poland—Casimir, Mar. 4

Portugal—Immaculate Conception, Dec. 8; Francis Borgia, (Oct. 10); Anthony of Padua, June 13

Russia—Andrew, Nov. 30; Nicholas, Dec. 6

Scotland—Andrew, Nov. 30

Slovakia—Our Lady of Sorrows, Sept. 15

Spain—James, May 3; Teresa, Oct. 15

Sweden—Bridget, July 23; Eric, (May 18)

Union of South Africa—Our Lady of Assumption, Aug. 15

United States—Immaculate Conception, Dec. 8

Uruguay—Our Lady of Lujan

Wales—David, (Mar. 1)

CANONIZATION

The Practice

Originally, only martyrs were so honored and "recommended" to the faithful, but by the fourth century there were added various forms of unbloody witness to Christ.

From St. Peter until the fourth century, all popes were referred to as saints (with a few minor and doubtful exceptions).

Local bishops would decide which candidates should have such honorable mention and a feast day on the liturgical calendar.

Over the years local bishops deferred the responsibility and privilege to the Bishop of Rome to review cases submitted and make the final decision. By the sixth century this became formalized to the point of inscribing names of the canonized on a roll of saints—the occasion being Boniface IV dedicating the Roman pantheon to St. Mary of the Martyrs.

It was not until 993 that a saint was formally and universally canonized in the way we know today. Pope John XV elevated Ulric of Augsburg (Germany) (890–973), renowned for his relief work among Germans devastated by the Magyar invasion.

It was Pope Alexander III (1159–81) who restricted the prerogative of canonization to the Holy See.

The Process

Changes in this process were announced in 1983, which included reducing the length of this process to ten years.

An interested party or group approaches their bishop. Working with the advocates of the candidate, he sends in a report on the person to the Congregation for the Causes of Saints.

"Venerable"
The congregation researches the candidate's virtues to verify if the person practiced virtue to a heroic degree, or died a martyr's death, and either does or does not recommend his/her cause. When the pope accepts the report the candidate is termed "venerable."

"Blessed"
This second (apostolic) process continues the first, which was initiated and accomplished in the Church proper (not the Curia). Now is a very lengthy process of scrutiny over the person's life, virtues, writings and reputation for holiness. Customarily two miracles must be credited to the candidate's intercession with God. The venerable candidate would then be "beatified" by the pope at a ceremony in St. Peter's basilica:

— declaration as a *beatus* (*beata,* f),
— unveiling of a photo or painting,
— recommendation to city/region/religious order for veneration.

"Saint"

The criteria has not always remained constant (for example, the strictest requirements regarding miracles), but canonization means being "raised to the full honors of the altar." In the ceremonies, the name of the saint is mentioned in the Eucharistic prayer of the Mass, and is usually accorded a triduum, often in another church in Rome.

Beatification allows veneration, canonization requires it. The beatified are not "recommended" to the whole Church, the canonized are.

Advocatus Dei (Advocate of God)

The Promotor of the Cause (or prosecuting attorney), authorized to examine virtues, reports miracles of one whose cause for beatification has been opened. Sometimes called Promoter of the Faith (*Promotor Fidei*), or "Devil's Advocate" (*Advocatus Diaboli*), because he is required to raise objections. Hence the use of the phrase for anyone fond of taking the unpopular side, as for the sake of argument.

Examples

St. Francis Xavier Cabrini
First American citizen declared a saint
1946—Canonized by Pope Pius XII

St. Elizabeth Ann Seton
First native-born American citizen to be canonized
1774—Born and baptized
1805—Joined the Catholic Church
1821—Died
1882—Church begins a study of her sanctity
1959—Declared venerable by Pope John XXIII
1963—Beatified by Pope John XXIII
1975—Canonized by Pope Paul VI

St. John Neumann
Third American canonized
1860—Died
1921—Declared venerable by Pope Benedict XV
1963—Beatified by Pope Paul VI
1977—Canonized by Pope Paul VI

Blessed Kateri Tekawitha
First American Indian, and American lay person, to be beatified
1680—Died
1932—The Church opens her cause for sanctity
1943—Declared venerable by Pope Pius XII
1980—Beatified by Pope John Paul II

St. John Neumann

This native of Bohemia was an immigrant to America in 1836 and was subsequently ordained. After serving in the New York Diocese, he was named in 1852 Bishop of Philadelphia. Throughout his life, he used his knowledge of eight languages, helping many immigrants in the United States. He organized the first system of parochial schools on a diocesan level. His feast day is January 5.

Korean Canonization

Andrew Kim, Paul Chong, and their companions were canonized on May 6, 1984, during Pope John Paul II's visit to Korea, making it the first canonization to take place outside Rome in modern Church history.

World War II Saints

In 1982, Father Maximilian Kolbe became the first victim of the Nazi concentration camps to be canonized. He was sent to Auschwitz after refusing involvement in the Nazi movement. He volunteered to take the place of a father of several children who was scheduled for execution at the death camp August 14, 1941. Another martyr, Fr. Titus Brandsma, O. Carm., was recently beatified. Fr. Titus, a native of the Netherlands, was arrested for urging newspaper editors to refuse to accept Nazi propaganda. While in concentration camps at Amersfoort and Dachau, he led prayers, heard confessions, and ministered to the sick and dying. He was executed July 26, 1942.

SAINTLY: SIGNS AND MEMORABILIA

Hagiography is the writing and study of the lives of the saints

Relics

Objects associated with saints:

1. **1st class:** Body, or part of
    for example, the tongue of St. Anthony, preserved at his shrine in Padua
2. **2nd class:** Part of clothing, or article used by
    for example, the celebrated Shroud of Turin, inherited by the Holy Father in 1983
3. **3rd class:** Any object touched to a first class relic.

Respecting these material things has been more or less popular since the early Church, varying according to era and culture. Mystique, exaggeration, and legend are common, and the Church is slow to offer official guarantees of authenticity; when it is established, she offers warm approbation. If a relic is notable in size, a bishop's permission is required for it to be kept in a private home.

The Great Relics

The three main relics of Christ's passion, preserved in St. Peter's and given special veneration during the Triduum.

1. Piece of the true cross
2. Point of the spear with which he was lanced
3. Veil offered by Veronica on the way of the cross

Shroud of Turin

The winding sheet of Jesus' burial (presumably). It was long venerated in Turin, Italy, where it was enshrined since 1578. Before that it was in France where a clear tradition of authenticity has been traced to the seventh century. It has produced a whole science, sindonology (Lt: *sindo*, shroud), dedicated to its study and theological interpretation. It is a strip of linen, fourteen feet three inches  long and three feet seven inches wide bearing the front and back imprints of a crucified human body. The stains of sweat and blood constitute a photographic phenomenon whose nature and preservation have not been explained naturally.

The Holy Coat of Treves (Trier, Germany)

Many legends have grown out of relics like the Last Supper chalice, the crucifixion cross and the seamless garment of which Christ was stripped (Jn 19.23,25). Of the latter, it is claimed that the Empress Helena (see true cross) discovered and preserved it in the fourth century, and further claimed by the cathedral of Treves, that it is now in their possession. (A sixth-century tablet as well as twelfth-century documents substantiate this.) A "Holy Coat of Argenteuil" makes a similar claim, with a story as likely, this one counting Charlemagne as its hero. This French city has a twelfth-century document mentioning the *"cappa pueri Jesu"* (garment of the Child Jesus). From this legend has arisen the story that the coat was woven by the Blessed Virgin Mary and that it grew with Jesus as he grew. Both relics are objects of popular pilgrimage.

AN EXTRAORDINARY GLOSSARY

Stigmata (Lt: *stigma,* the brand on a slave or criminal)
Marks on a body that correspond to some or all of the wounds of Christ; (marks of Jesus' passion and crucifixion, or, as in specific cases, the mark of the spear or the crown of thorns). No one must believe in stigmatism's divine origin, but it remains a special sign of oneness with Christ's sacrificial suffering (see St. Paul Gal 6.17) and is for some an aid to piety.

The first known stigmatic is Francis of Assisi, who developed bleeding sores on his palms. Others include Catherine of Siena, Nicholas of Ravenna, Anne Girling (foundress of an English sect of the Shakers, and—in our own day—Padre Pio and Theresa Neumann.

Odor of Sanctity

A pleasant odor emitted from a body of a saint, especially after death or disinterrment, was a common medieval belief and "evidence" of sanctity: a symbol of the fragrance of extraordinary virtue. E.g.: St. Francis' stigmata reportedly emitted a sweet perfume on occasion; the water in which the body of St. Theresa of Avila was bathed as she was prepared for burial retained a pleasing fragrance; for nine months a mysterious perfume arose from her grave. (Note the "aroma of Christ," 2 Cor 2.15.) In this case, the failure of the body of a saint to decay is a sign of the person's spirituality; a clear allusion to incorruptibility that is:

absolute: God, wholly unchangeable by nature;
natural: angels and souls, indestructible because of their basic spirituality.

Prolonged Abstinence

The miraculous survival without nourishment for many years. E.g.:

> Angela of Foligno, 12 years
> Catherine of Siena, about 8 years
> Elizabeth of Reute, over 15 years
> Lidwina, 28 years
> Catherine Racconigi, 10 years

This phenomenon is often associated with stigmatics who have lived a long time without food except the eucharist. In verifying this as supernatural the Church has rigorously scrutinized such fasting for its authenticity, including whether the person continues attending to customary responsibilities.

Liquefaction

Solids, like congealed blood, miraculously liquefying; reported about relics of some saints, like St. Januarius' blood.

The Blood of St. Januarius

This is a renowned relic of the Cathedral of Naples. Januarius was the bishop of Benevento, and was beheaded in 304 during the Diocletian persecution. The Cathedral still treasures his head and two vials of his blood. The solid red substance liquefies many times a year, usually after a time of prayer by the thousands of Neapolitans who flock to the Cathedral on those days, especially September 19, the saint's feast day. The cruets are removed from their silver case beneath the altar and exposed near the saint's head. This is a very famous liquefication, and has been recorded since 1329. A scientific explanation has never been adduced. Neapolitans believe that when the blood liquefies, it portends blessings for the city during the period ahead.

Oil of the Saints

Oily substances believed to flow from relics on graves of certain saints; referring also to the oil of their shrine lamps and water from sources near their graves. These substances are said to have curative powers for the faithful. For example:

1. St. Walburga, abbess of Heidenheim, Bavaria.
   After her death (A.D. 870) her body was brought to Eichstadt where beginning in 893 oil was noticed flowing periodically from her relics.
2. St. Nicholas of Myra
   In Bari, Italy, oil is seen to exude from the relics in his shrine.
3. St. Menas
   Oil has come from a holy well near his national shrine at Mareotis in the Libyan desert.

Ecstasy

Mystical enrapture of the body and soul.

Levitation

Floating above the ground, referred to in the life of St. Francis.

Locution

Supernatural communication to the sense of hearing.

Bilocation

The apparition of a saint in two different places at the same time, as in the appearance of St. Anthony at the same time in the pulpit and in a distant friary choir.

A GALLERY OF PAGAN GODS

The Twelve Major Deities ("Dii Majores")

	Greek	Latin
King	Zeus	Jupiter
Sun (and music)	Apollo	Apollo
War	Ares	Mars
Messenger	Hermes	Mercury
Sea	Poseidon	Neptune
Smith (artist)	Hephaistos	Vulcan
Queen	Hera	Juno
Tillage	Demeter	Ceres
Moon (and hunting)	Artemis	Diana
Wisdom (and weaving)	Athena	Minerva
Love, beauty	Aphrodite	Venus
Home life	Hestia	Vesta

Minor Deities ("Dii Minores")

Love	Eros	Cupid
Under world	Pluto	Pluto
Pluto's wife	Persephone	Prosepine
Time	Kronos	Saturn
Wife of Kronos/Saturn	Rhea	Cybele
Wine	Dionysus	Bacchus

The Day the Great Pan Died

"Great Pan is Dead" is what was heard by many, tradition says, at the moment of the crucifixion. This cry was to have swept over the ocean, as a sort of pagan version of the rendering of the temple veil, whereupon the oracles ceased for good. As well as the god of forest, flocks and pastures, Pan (Gk: all, everything) was the personification of the deity which imbued all of creation. (Elizabeth Barrett Browning has a poem entitled "Great Pan is Dead.")

Mythical Places and Things

Mt. Olympus	Dwelling (in Thessaly)
Ambrosia	Food
Nectar	Drink
Ichor	Blood
Tartarus	Place of the Titan's imprisonment after their fall
Elysian Fields	Heaven for mortals favored by the gods

According to one cosmogony

Chaos	Origins of heaven and earth
Heaven and Earth	Parents of the Titans (including Saturn and Rhea)
Saturn and Rhea	Parents of Jupiter
Atlas	a Titan, condemned to bear the heavens on his shoulders
Prometheus	a Titan, supervisor of man's creation

Scandinavian Deities

The Aesir—Their collective name

Odin—Chief

Sons

1. Thor (oldest), Thunder
2. Tiu, Wisdom
3. Balder, Sun, Light
4. Hermoder, Messenger
5. Vali (youngest)

Bragi—Poetry

Vidar—Silence

Hoder the Blind—Slayer of Balder

Hoenir—Present at creation, giving humans reason and motion

Odnir—Love, beauty; Freyja's husband

Loki—Mischief

Freyja—Odin's wife, Freyr's sister; Love, the dead (see "Friday")

Dwelling

Asgard ("Olympus"), in the center of the universe, accessible only by the rainbow bridge, and including many mansions and regions (Valhalla and Gladsheim, for example).

First Man and Woman

Ask and Embla, made by the gods from an ash tree.

Pagan Deity Patronage

Classical, Teutonic and Scandinavian included; for Classical deities, only the Roman name is given.

Air—Ariel, Elves (T)
Beauty and Charm—The Graces: Aglaia, Thalia and Euphrosyne
Caves, Caverns—Pixies (T)
Commerce—Mercury
Corn—Ceres
Dawn—Aurora
Eloquence—Mercury
Evening—Vesper
Fairies—various, Oberan in Shakespeare (Gk)
Fate—the Three: Parcae, Moirae and Keres (Gk)
Fields—Faunus
Fire—Vulcan, Vesta, Mulciber
Flowers—Flora
Gardens—Priapus: Vertummus and Pomona, his wife
Hills—Pixies, Trolls (There are also wood trolls and water trolls.)
Home Life—Vesta
House—Penates, Lares
Hunting—Diana
Justice—Themis; Astraea; Nemesis; The Furies (*Erimyes* in Greek the
    Avengers of Wrong; called *Eumenides,* "good tempered"):
    Tisiphone, Alecto and Megaera
Laughter—Momus
Love—Cupid
Marriage—Hyman
Medicine—Aesculapius
Memory—Mnemosyne
Morning—Aurora
Mountains—Oreads, Trolls
Ocean—Oceanides
Poetry and Music—Apollo; the Nine Muses; Calliope (Chief), Clio (his-
    tory and heroics), Euterpe (Dionesian music, double flute), Thalia
    (gaity, comedy, pastoral life), Melpomene (song, harmony, tragedy),
    Terpsichore (choral dance, song), Erato (erotic poetry, the lyre),
    Polyhymnia (inspired hymns), and Urania (astronomy and the celes-
    tial)
Rainbow—Iris
Rivers and Streams—Fluviales; Naiads, Nymphs
Sea—Neptune; Triton (his son); Nixies, Mermaids, Nereids
Shepherds, Flocks—Pan, Satyrs
Sleep and Dreams—Morpheus
Time—Saturn
Trees—Dryads, Wood-Trolls

War—Mars, Bellona, Thor
Wealth—Plutus
Wind—Aeolus
Wine—Bacchus
Wisdom—Minerva
Wrestling—Mercury
Youth—Hebe

Catholic Symbols

CROSS

The cross is the distinctive, though not exclusive, Christian symbol because it was the instrument of Christ's death.

The Forms of the Cross

Traditionally, these are the four basic forms of the cross:

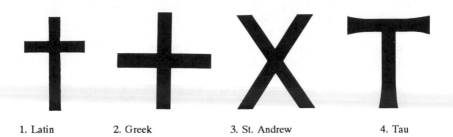

1. Latin	2. Greek	3. St. Andrew	4. Tau

1. Latin Cross; *Crux Immissa; Crux Ordinaria*
   Upright extending above transom.
2. Greek Cross; *Crux Immissa Quadrata*
   Used by the Red Cross.
3. St. Andrew's Cross; *Crux Decussata; Saltire*
   His martyrdom.
4. Tau Cross; *Crux Commissa;* St. Anthony's Cross
   Old Testament cross; prophecy, anticipation, advent.

Various Forms of the Cross

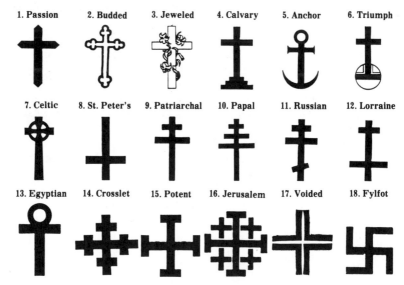

1. Passion 2. Budded 3. Jeweled 4. Calvary 5. Anchor 6. Triumph

7. Celtic 8. St. Peter's 9. Patriarchal 10. Papal 11. Russian 12. Lorraine

13. Egyptian 14. Crosslet 15. Potent 16. Jerusalem 17. Voided 18. Fylfot

1. **Passion Cross**
   Ends pointed, like the nails of the passion.
2. **Budded Cross**
   Trefoil ends (the Trinity); often topping a Christian flagpole.
3. **Crux Gemmata** (Jeweled Cross)
   Suggesting a living tree, flourishing with leaf and flower.
4. **Calvary Cross;** Graded Cross
   Steps (grises) represent faith, hope, and love (see 1 Cor 13.13).
5. **Anchor Cross** (See Heb 6.19)
   Seen in catacombs; Egyptian in origins; a concealed cross.
6. **Cross of Triumph;** Cross of Victory; Cross of Conquest
   The orb was originally a separate symbol, (though with verticle line running down from horizontal). The segments of the orb represented Asia, Africa, and Europe. In early Christian art, Christ was pictured holding this orb. Later it was altered to a ball with a cross upon it, to represent the sovereignty of the spiritual over the temporal.
7. **Celtic Cross;** Cross of Iona
   Taken by Columba to isle of Iona, sixth century; circle represents eternity.
8. **St. Peter's Cross**
   His martyrdom.
9. **Patriarchal Cross;** Archiepiscopal Cross
   Part of heraldic arms of an archbishop, carried before him in procession.
10. **Papal Cross;** Triple Cross of the Western Peoples
    (Two upper bars represent the two crucified with Jesus).
11. **Russian Cross;** Eastern Cross
    Cross of Russian Orthodox Church; (footrest either slant or straight); upper bar represents the inscription; the cross of early Christianity.
12. **Cross of the Lorraine**
    Lorriane was a medieval kingdom in Western Europe along the Moselle, Meuse and Rhine rivers.
13. **Egyptian Cross;** *Crux Ansata* ("having a handle")
    Key of the Nile *Ankh* ("life"); immortality; originally pagan.
14. **Cross Crosslet;** Holy Cross; German Cross
    (Four Latin crosses); evangelization.
15. **Potent Cross** (Fr. *potence,* crutch)
    (Four Tau crosses; each cross resembles the top of an old-fashioned crutch); healing.
16. **Jerusalem Cross;** Crusader's Cross
    (Four Tau and four Greek crosses); Christ's five wounds; evangelization (earth's four corners).
17. **Voided Cross;** Gammadia (four gammas)
18. **Fylfot Cross;** Swastika (Sanskrit: "good Fortune")
    Gammadion charm (Greek capital gammas), to dispel evil; Hitler Germany.

St. Helena and the True Cross

The Church used to speak of the "invention" of the cross, using the word in its original sense, "to come upon, to discover" (Lt: *invenire*). An inventer is a discoverer. The discovery of the true cross used to be celebrated on May 3: "The Invention of the Cross." According to tradition, the mother of Constantine, Helena, was the inventer. From Asia Minor, and an innkeeper's daughter, she entered a marriage with a Roman general, Constantius Chlorus, that ended in divorce. Her son Constantine became emperor in 306, and in 313 (after his vision at the Mulvian Bridge) issued the historic Edict of Milan that granted freedom of worship to Christians. His sixty-three-year-old mother gladly converted. The likes of the historian Eusebius document her devotion as a Christian.

According to tradition, Helena is credited with finding the true cross in 326. She engineered an arduous dig in the vicinity of the Holy Sepulchre and was allegedly rewarded with the buried remains of the three crosses used the day Christ died. This wood was declared to be wood of the true cross when a woman experienced a cure when it was applied to her. The Empress Helena enshrined the relics in a silver casket within a church built for the purpose on that spot, and delivered a portion of it to Rome as well.

St. Helena is depicted in art with various symbols of the crucifixion, and was commemorated by the Church on August 18. An incidental note: Because it was on this feast day that the Portuguese discovered an island in the south Atlantic in 1501, it was given her name. It was after a six-year exile on St. Helena's Island that Napoleon died in 1821.

"A Cruce Salus": "Salvation (comes) from the Cross."

The Wood of the Cross

The crucifixion has been a most fertile soil for the growth of legends and customs, as they germinate in the mystique of the cross. One says that the Savior's cross was constructed from four different woods: palm, cedar, cypress, and olive, representing the four corners of the earth. Here are some others.

The Quaking Aspen

The leaf of the aspen trembles, it is said, because of the tree's horror and shame. It is the tree that furnished the wood for the Lord's cross. As a matter of fact, the leaf stem of the "trembling poplar" is flat, which gives the tree a unique sound in a slight breeze.

The Legend of the Dogwood Tree

In the days before the crucifixion of Christ, legend has it, the dogwood tree matched the oak in stature and strength. Because of these qualities, it was chosen to provide the wood of the cross. This cruel purpose greatly distressed the noble dogwood, a sympathy Jesus sensed. The one pitied, pitied another, as Jesus smiled upon the tree. He transformed it into a slender, twisted shrub, only so that it could never again be used ignobly. Escaping destruction, the dogwood would be cherished as a reminder of the Savior's sacrifice. Furthermore, he designed its blossoms to be in the form of a cross, with two long petals and two short, each bearing nail prints, brown with rust and stained with blood. At the flower's center he enshrined an image of his crown of thorns.

"Holly Wood"

Holly has had a host of holy associations. There are stories about its Christmas symbolism. There is also the story that the holly, like the dogwood, was once a full-sized tree, but now allowed to grow no larger than a shrub, for its role in the crucifixion. In this story, holly's stature is deemed a punishment, whereas dogwood's is called a protection, and a sign of our Savior's sacrifice.

San Damiano Cross

This is the cross which St. Francis was praying before when the Lord commissioned him to "rebuild the Church." (The original hangs in *Santa Chiarra*—St. Claire—Church in Assisi, Italy.) It is an "icon" cross because of the style of the image of Jesus—and others—that it includes. With its various images, it teaches more fully the meaning of the crucifixion.

Jesus—Both wounded and strong, regal and suffering. Note halo, color contrasts, Jesus' prominence.

Major Witnesses—These second largest figures are: the Blessed Mother and the Beloved Disciple, Mary and John, on the left; and on the right, Mary Magdalene, Mary, mother of James (wife of Cleopas—Mk 15.40), and the centurion of Mark's Gospel ("Truly this is the Son of God"), with an onlooker at his shoulder. His hand gesture, a classic position of Christian witness, is a traditional sign for "I am speaking."

Minor Witnesses—Longinus, the soldier who pierced Jesus' side (Jn 19.34) is the smaller figure below Mary, holding the spear and standing beneath the droplets of precious blood. (In some art, he is shown with the blood dropping in his eye, which was then healed, so says one tradition, of its blindness.) The miniature opposite is "Stephaton" (faulty derivation from the Greek word for sponge), whom Umbrian art pairs with Longinus as the soldier who offered Jesus the vinegar-soaked sponge **Jn 19.28–30.**

Six Angels—They marvel at this event at each end of the crossbar, their hands representing awe, discussion, and invitation.

Umbrian Patrons—The six bottom figures, typical of this Umbrian art form, are the area's patrons: Ss. John, Michael, Rufino, John the Baptist, Peter, and Paul.

Rooster—At Jesus' left calf, representing Peter's denial **Jn 18.25.**

Resurrection/Ascension—Represented at the top: Jesus in royal garb, brandishing the cross like a scepter, welcomed by ten angels, alive by the power of God (right hand).

Franciscan   Glory   Adorned   Quadrate   Coptic   Maltese

St. Chad's   St. Julian's   St. James'   Chain   Paternoster   Canterbury

Patee   Patee Formee   Alisee Patee   Patee Fitched   Patee Fitched (foot)   Crosslet fitched

Barbee   Bottony   Cercelee   Clechee   Millrine   Moline

Fitchy   Fleuree   Fleurette   Entrailed   Mascly   Frettee

Trononnee   Aiguisee   Patonce   Avellaine   Four Ermine spots   Four Pheons

Crenelle   Ragulee   Wavy   Nebulee   Demi sarcelled   Degraded

Bezant   Lambeau   Fimbriated   Cantonee   Triparted   Parted and Fretty

395

Old Testament Figures

Adam—spade, pickaxe, apple
Eve—spindle, distaff
Cain—plow, ox goad, yoke
Abel—shepherd's staff and lamb
Noah—ark, dove with olive branch, vine
Abraham—altar, stars
Isaac—bundles of wood in the form of a cross
Jacob—ladder, sun and full moon encircled with twelve stars (Jacob, wife and twelve sons)
Joseph—multicolored coat, star, sheaf of wheat, Egyptian column, scepter and chain
Moses—tablets of stone, basket of bullrushes, burning bush, rod and serpent, rays of light from brown, water from rock
David—young lion, sling, seventy-five stones, head of Goliath, crown, horn of oil, tower, key
Solomon—temple
Isaiah—saw (traditional means of his death)
Jeremiah—stone (reputed means of his death)
Ezekiel—a closed gate (4.3)
Elijah—burning chariot
Daniel—ram with four horns (8.8)

The Trinity

Equilateral triangle
Three circles
Interwoven triangle and circle
Two interwoven triangles
Two triangles and a circle

Trefoil (with triangle)
Triquetra (with circle, triangle)
Shield
Three fishes
Shamrock etc.

The Father

Hand of God (*Manus Dei*) (Ps 98.1)
Souls of the Righteous (in hand)(Wis 3.1)
All-Seeing Eye

Creator's Star
Two Yods
Etc.

Jesus

Agnus Dei Is 53.7; Jn 1.29; Rv 5.6f
Branch Zec 3.8; Jer 23.5
Butterfly
Cornerstone Eph 2.20; 1 Pt 2.6
Cross and Orb
Crown Jas 1.12; 1 Pt 5.4; Rv 2.10 3.11
Crucifix
Daystar 2 Pt 1.19
Door Jn 10.9
Fish (with rebus)
Fountain Zec 13.1
Good Shepherd Jn 10–11
Lion Rv 5.5
Ox Mt 11.30
Rock 1 Cor 10.4; Ps 18.2; Ex 17.6; Mt 7.24; Mt 16.18
Scepter
Serpent of Brass Jn 3.14
Star Nm 24.17; Rv 22.16
Sun Mal 4.2
Tree of Jesse Is 11
Vine Jn 15.1

See also Myth and Folklore listing, Christological Titles, and Litany of the Holy Name of Jesus.

Jesus' Three-fold Office
Priest—alb, chasuble, stole
Prophet—long robe
King—jeweled crown

The Passion

Agony in the Garden
chalice and rising cross Lk 22.42
Betrayal
lantern Jn 18.3, torch Jn 18.3,
    sword and staff crossed, purse,
    kiss, Peter's sword (with
    Malchus' ear), rope
Trial and Condemnation
pillar, two scourges, scarlet robe
    and reed, crown of thorns, basin
    and ewer (vase-shaped pitcher),
    reed, rooster crowing
Crucifixion
Latin cross, five wounds, INRI
    scroll, ladder, hammer and
    nails, vinegar-gall, reed and
    hyssop, seamless coat, veiled
    sun and moon, passion
    flower, pierced heart, stigmata
    (wounds) in hands
Descent from the Cross/Burial
ladder and sheet, pincers, myrrh and
aloes, shroud, tomb

Agony in the Garden

The Holy Spirit

Descending dove, flame, seven lamps, scroll with seven gifts, mystic star (seven points)

Angels

Michael—shield with symbol of Trinity
Raphael—staff, pouch, fish
Gabriel—fleur-de-lys

The Blessed Virgin

Often holding a rosary (St. Dominic; Lourdes and Fatima apparitions)

As the Virgin
With flowering tresses (Virginity)

As Queen of Heaven and Earth (Glorified Madonna)
Crowned with twelve stars (Rv 12.1), with scepter, orb with cross, robed and surrounded by angels, crescent moon underfoot

As Mother of Sorrows (Lt: *Mater Dolorosa*)
Older, seated, clothed in mourning, as in the pieta, head draped, heart pierced

In her Immaculate Conception
With the crescent moon underfoot

As Our Lady of Mercy
With arms extended, spreading out a mantle gathering sinners

As Mother of God
With snake underfoot Gn 3.15

*See "passion flower" in Glossary

398

Mysteries of the Rosary
Joyful—green leaves or white rosettes
Sorrowful—thorns or red rosettes
Glorious—roses or gold rosettes

Midnight Blue, Lifeblood Red

In traditional Eastern Orthodox art, Mary's robe is often a midnight blue, since she is the wise virgin, wrapped in deepest night, anxiously awaiting the bridegroom's coming. (Legend has it that she laid her blue cloak on a rosemary plant to let it dry, thus transmitting the lovely blue color to that flower. Another version, linking her to the rosemary, has it that she hid behind a rosemary bush when she fled with the infant Jesus to Egypt.) If not in blue, she is robed in bloody red, since the mother of the crucified is also mother of the living, robed in the risen Spirit and Christ's own lifeblood, giving birth as queen to royal children, the children of God.

Other Marian Symbols
(See also the Litany of the Blessed Virgin)

Apple
Ark of the Covenant
   Lk 1 and 2 Sm 6
Balsam
Book of Wisdom
Closed Gate
Crescent Moon **Rv 12**
Crown of Twelve Stars **Rv 12**
Cypress
Enclosed garden **Sg 4**
Fleur-de-Lys
Flowering Almond **Nm 17.1–8**
Gilly Flower
Hawthorne
Lily (of the King)
Lily of the Valley

Myrtle
Olive
Palm
Pierced Heart **Lk 2.35**
Rod of Jesse
Rose **Sg 2.1; Sir 24.18**
Sealed Book
Sealed Fountain **Sg 4**
Snake-encircled Globe
Snow-Drop
Speculum (mirror)
Star ("Miriam")
Starry Crown **Rv 12**
Sun and Moon **Rv 12**
Tower of David **Sg 4**
Woman treading serpent

Apostles' Symbols

Including Matthias and Paul. (See Scriptures of the Apostles, as well as stories of their deaths, which symbols often reflect)

Andrew
X-shaped (saltire) cross; pictured as an old man with long white hair and beard, holding the Gospel and leaning on a saltire

Bartholomew
Knife (flayed alive)

James the Great (of Compostella)
Scallop shell (because the Spanish coast was said to abound in them); pilgrim's staff (as a patron of pilgrims); gourd bottle

James the Less
Fuller's pole (struck in the head)

John
Chalice and serpent (attempt to poison him)

Judas Iscariot
Bag (he held the common purse, from which he would help himself, Jn 12.6)

Jude
Club, staff, carpenter's square (his trade)

Matthew
Hatchet, halberd, purse (occupation: tax collector); pictured as a bearded old man, accompanied by an angel dictating the Gospel

Matthias
Battleax

Crossed Keys

Paul
Sword, open Bible (the new Law he preached); pictured short, bald with a bushy beard

Peter
Key (authority given by Christ); cock (betrayal, Mt 26.75); pictured as a bald old man with flowing beard, clad in white mantle and blue tunic, holding Scripture

Philip
Staff, surmounted with a cross (upon which he was suspended by the neck from a pillar); a basket of loaves, alluding to his part in the multiplication of the loaves, Jn 6.5–7

Simon
Saw; fish (occupation)

Thomas
Lance

> ## *Quo Vadis?*
>
> As Peter was fleeing Rome during Nero's persecution, the story goes, he met Christ going to Rome. "*Quo vadis?*", Peter asked him (Latin for "Where are you going?"). Christ replied, "I am coming to be crucified again." Peter, ashamed, took this as a rebuke, and returned to Rome. He was crucified on a cross planted in the earth upside down. This legendary question was used by the polish Henryk Sienkiewicz as the title for a novel (1895) on the life of the early Christians in Rome during Nero's persecution.

The Church

Ship Mt 8.23–27	House on a rock	Flock
Crowned woman	Hill	Wheat and tares
Ark of the covenant	Leaven	Drag net
Vine	Mustard seed	Ark Mt 24.37–39;
Woman and the dragon	Candlestick	Heb 11.7; 1 Pt 3.20;
Bride of Christ	Vineyard	2 Pt 2.5

Sacraments

Baptism
Shell with water, baptismal font, font with dove, running water

Confirmation
Dove, lamp with oil, bishop's staff/mitre

Eucharist
Host/chalice, wheat/grapes, bread/wine, basket of loaves, wine, flowing water, vineyard, pelican

Reconciliation
Keys, scourge, closed door

Anointing of the Sick
Olive branch

Marriage
Strands tied in a knot, linked rings

Holy Orders
Keys, chalice, host, book, stole

Denominations

Symbols associated with selected churches

1. The nine crosses of the Episcopal Church shield commemorates the nine original dioceses represented at the First General Convention (1789).
2. The well-known emblem of Martin Luther consists of a black cross on a red heart against the Marian rose on a heavenly blue background within a gold circle (symbolizing eternity). Luther adopted it as his own coat of arms to express his trust in God: "The Christian's heart/is resting on roses/E'en while beneath the cross/it reposes."
3. The cross and flame of the Methodist Church.
4. A recently designed Presbyterian logo incorporates cross, open book, dove and flames (representing the burning bush and Pentecost).

LITURGICAL FEASTS AND SEASONS

Annunciation
Budding fleur-de-lys, lily, dove, two interlocked circles.

Presentation
Fifteen Steps

Ascension
Elijahs' fiery chariot, broken chain, open gates, clouds, palms of victory, birds flying homeward, fish net, bail and cross

Pentecost
Descending dove, flames, beehive, Blessed Virgin, any symbol of the Church (ark, for example), censor, circle, city, fish net, lighthouse, mountain, rock

Trinity Sunday
Triangle, three interlocked circles/fish, shamrock, hand, dove, *chi-rho*

Corpus Christi
Pelican, altar bread, chalice, fish, grapes, peacock feeding on grapes, vine, wheat, wine

Assumption
Empty tomb, lily, palm and two lilies crossed, clouds, crown, angels

Seven Sorrows
Heart pierced with seven swords, Marian monogram

All Saints
Sheaf of wheat, crown, symbols of beatitudes, rayed *Manus Dei (souls of the just in the hand of God)*

Soul Cakes

Doughnuts, "soul cakes," are a special November food. Their circular form symbolizes the cycle of life, death and rebirth: a seed springs to life, grows, matures, produces its seed-bearing fruit, and dies and rises again as its seeds spring to life again, germinate, and emerge, closing the circle of life.

Christ the King
Crown, stole, sheaf of wheat, sceptor, throne, ball and cross

Advent/Christmas

Advent
Empty throne, dew falling from heaven, rising sun, fleece, anchor of hope, violet color, O Antiphons, scroll of prophecy.

Biblical Christmas Tree

The story of the Jesse tree—or rather its inspiration—is Isaiah's prophecy, "There shall come forth a shoot from the stump of Jesse." (Is 11.1) Jesse is King David's father and, so, an ancestor in Jesus' family line (the House of David). Tradition has taken Isaiah's suggestion of Jesus' "family tree," decorating it with ornaments or pictures representing various ancestors (like Noah, Jacob, Moses, Ruth, Jesse himself, and David, of course). Jesus' spiritual heritage is thus illustrated, and celebrated.

Immaculate Conception
Shield with Marian monogram or symbol, Mary treading a serpent, moon

Christmas
Crib, star, two interlocked circles, Trinity, tree, lambs, angels, trumpet, Holy Family symbols, three steps, candles, crook, throne, shepherds, hand of God, dove, hawthorn, glastonberry thorn in blossom

Holy Innocents
Lily buds, sword, palms, hoops and halos

Epiphany
Three crowns, three gifts, wisemen, five-pointed star

Holy Name
Chalice, tablets of stone, Jesus' name/monogram

Purification
Candles, sword, two drinking doves

Christmas Symbols

Most Christmas symbols' significance is obvious; others, although commonplace, have deeper meaning not immediately apparent, and stories no longer remembered, like:

Candy Cane
It's the shepherd's crook, representing the nativity's first witnesses. Its alternating white and red stripes represent the Lord's purity and sacrifice, even as the same colors do liturgically, as his feasts are celebrated through the year. Its lively peppermint flavor stands for the royal gift of spice. Finally, like the Body of Christ itself, the candy cane is given to be broken and shared.

Christmas Holly
Its bright green leaves and red berries, well into the cold season, make holly right for Christmas, but its symbolism is much deeper. For the early Christian it was not only reminiscent of Moses' burning bush, but prophetic as well: in the face of Christmas sentimentality, it foretells, with its prickly points and drops of blood-like berries, Christ's crown of thorns. According to ancient legend, its berries were once yellow, but were stained permanently red by Christ's blood, since it was used to fashion the Savior's crown of thorns. (Maybe this is the reason for the superstition that holly, if brought into the house before Christmas Eve, would provoke family fights.) Holly's symbolic roots go deeper still, into the subsoil of the Roman culture. They would send holly, in a gesture of friendliness and good will, to friends during the mid-winter feasts. Later, Northern Europeans hung it on doors as a symbol of shelter for the wood spirits.

Poinsettia

This plant, native to Central America, is named after Dr. Joel Roberts Poinsett, U.S. Ambassador to Mexico in the early 1800s, because he introduced it to the United States. Some ascribe its popularity at Christmastime to its star-like, red bracts, thought to resemble the Star of Bethlehem.

St. Boniface and the Christmas Tree

St. Boniface was an eighth-century missionary (praised by Pope Gregory II) who brought Christianity to Germany. Returning to Germany later, he found paganism still alive—and the eldest son of the chieftain Gundhar being readied for sacrifice to the gods. It was Christmas Eve. The place was under the giant oak tree, sacred to their patron Thor. Boniface, in order to prove these gods powerless, felled the tree with the stroke of an ax, to the astonishment of the onlookers. When he was then asked for the Word of God, Boniface pointed to a nearby evergreen and proclaimed, "This is the word, and this is the counsel. Not a drop of blood shall fall tonight, for this is the birth-night of the Saint Christ, Son of the All-Father and Savior of the world. This little tree, a young child of the forest, shall be a home tree tonight. It is the wood of peace, for your houses are built of fir. It is the sign of endless life, for its branches are ever green. See how it points toward Heaven. Let this be called the tree of the Christ-child; gather about it, not in the wild woods but in your homes; there it will shelter no deeds of blood, but loving gifts and lights of kindness."

Martin Luther and the Christmas Tree

A popular legend with many is how Martin Luther was inspired during a Christmas Eve walk with the beauty of the star-lit night sky. To reproduce this celestial wonder, and to commemorate Christ's birth under the starry Bethlehem sky, he brought a fir tree to his home, decorated it with candles, and arranged beneath it the nativity scene. There is little interest in—or evidence of—the history behind this story. It is beloved. It is also an interesting collaboration of St. Boniface (the tree), St. Francis (the nativity scene) and Martin Luther.

Lenten Season

Lent

Fish, money bag and incense, praying hands, cross, violet color, lamp and oil, pitcher, two scourges, saltire, pretzel

Palm Sunday

Palms

Holy Thursday
Chalice and Eucharistic symbols, oil containers (Chrism liturgy)

Good Friday
Latin cross, crown of thorns and passion symbols, Hot Cross Buns

Hot Cross Buns

Hot cross buns, a European staple on Good Friday, are made of sweet, spiced dough with icing shaped in the form of a cross. They were commonly distributed to the poor, and even considered a blessing against sickness and house fires. In some locales, they were baked and distributed the day before Ash Wednesday, a kind of last celebration before the fast. One example of the doggerel verse is:

> Hot cross buns. Hot cross buns.
> One a penny, two a penny.
> > Hot cross buns.
> If your daughter' won't eat them,
> Give them to your son.
> But if you have one
> > of those little elves,
> Then you must
> > eat them all yourselves.

Another tradition, believe it or not, is that the buns were to be made of dough kneaded for the altar host, and marked, accordingly, with the cross. They were then to keep mold-resistant for twelve months:

> Good Friday comes this month:
> > the old woman runs
> With one-a-penny, two-a-penny
> > "hot cross buns."
> Whose virtue is,
> > if you believe what's said,
> They'll not grow moldy
> > like the common bread.

With such a characteristic, and with such a holy association, this humble bun qualified as a charm against evil, according to some, and was superstitiously hung in the house.

Easter Season

Why wouldn't the season most powerful in faith be also the most prolific in symbol?

Resurrection Gardens

"Unless a grain of wheat falls in the earth to die, it remains but a single grain. But if it dies, it rises to produce abundantly," says St. John (12.24). There is an old paschal custom of tucking red-dyed eggs into sprouting seedlings. The "Easter grass"—ryegrass or wheat—is started early and kept moist in a bowl of perlite. Come the Pasch, a few of the dyed eggs are nestled in, reminders of the baptized "who have washed their robes white in the blood of the Lamb" (Rev 7.14). Like the egg itself, a believer can open into the white and gold of risen life. (Boiling the eggs good and long in a container stuffed with yellow onion skins gives them a beautiful bloody, mahogany color. Tying tiny ferns and flowers to the egg with thread before boiling gives it a tracery effect. Eggs can be rubbed with butter for a shine.)

The Proud Lily

There is much lily lore. It would be enough for it to be a spring flower, representing life's renewal and the spirit's rebirth. But there is more. According to legend, the lily lost its self-respect on the night of Christ's agony in the garden: the other flowers bowed their heads in sorrow in Christ's presence, but not the lily. How could it, being the most fragrant and beautiful flower in the Garden (according to its own estimation)? Upon Christ's display of humility, however, the lily belatedly hung its head in shame, and has humbly remained so ever since. (As a matter of fact, our Easter lily is not native to Palestine, but was imported in the 1880s from Bermuda. "Croft's Lily" is grown mainly in the Pacific Northwest and California.)

Easter Caskets

Eggs . . . Not only do they symbolize spring's rebirth, but also Christ's resurrection, representing his tomb: the hard, cold casket from which new life finally and triumphantly broke forth. The Roman proverb *Omne vivum ex ovo* ("All life comes from an egg") took on a new, religious significance.

Lent's Over

In Germany, eggs became part of the Easter decoration and celebration in the nineteenth century. If it was not its tempting symbolism that gave the egg a place in the Church, it was simply the food that it was: Eggs were prohibited during Lent, and allowed again at Easter; so, at very least, they symbolized the end of the fast!

Colored Eggs

According to a Ukrainian folk tale, a poor peddler went to the marketplace to sell a basket of eggs one day. He encountered a crowd  mocking a man who staggered as he carried a heavy cross on which he was about to be crucified. Running to his aid, the peddler left the basket by the roadside. Upon his return, he found the eggs wondrously transformed with exquisite designs of bright colors. The man was Christ; the peddler, Simon of Cyrene. And the eggs were to become the symbol of rebirth for all mankind. Even today in the Ukraine, decorating "*pysanky*," as the native eggs are called, is a treasured craft and custom.

Gilding the lily is always unnecessary, but gilding the egg is almost essential at Easter, bringing beauty and added significance to one of nature's fruits. Literal gilding—with actual gold leaf— was the privilege of the wealthy and none was more extravagant than the great nineteenth-century goldsmith Peter Carl Faberge who gilded eggs for Czar Alexander III of Russia. Plainer folks merely dyed their eggs. Boiling them with certain materials produced special effects—spinach leaves or *anemone* petals for green, gorse blossom for yellow, logwood chips for deep purple and the fluid of the *cochineal,* a scale insect of tropical America, for scarlet.

Easter Bunnies

Though it's now a secular symbol, the rabbit was originally a religious symbol for the pagans. It begins with the legend of "Eastre" (Easter), the European goddess of spring. While this season of rebirth erupted with abundant new life, Eastre's pet bird would lay eggs in baskets and hide them in unlikely places. On a whim, Eastre transformed her bird into a rabbit but its egg-laying ways remained unchanged from its feathered past! Whether fowl or hare, Eastre's pet and its profligate produce represented abundant new life and earth reborn. Even back to the sixteenth century, there is reference to an egg-laying rabbit.

Easter Baskets

Easter baskets have become a fixture, and presume eggs and candy. Originally, however, it was not that way. The baskets held fresh, whole foods. In a day when reliance on the soil and its produce was more immediate and apparent, folks would bring this stuff or life as an analogy of Easter's new life. So in the beginning, "Easter baskets" were a more graphic life-sign, and were brought for blessing on Easter Saturday. In the days when the new water was blessed at Holy Saturday's morning service, holy water too added to the spiritual significance of nature's food and life.

408

SACRED MONOGRAMS/ABBREVIATIONS

The use of certain groups of letters, derived from Greek and Latin words, as symbols of our Lord Jesus Christ was instituted in the early days of the Christian Church. Many monograms are based on Greek words.

A and Ω *(Alpha and Omega)*
The first and last letters of the Greek alphabet, signifying the early Church the eternity and the infinity of God (Rv 1.8, 11; 22.12); symbolizing Christ who is the beginning and the end

AM—
Lt: *Ave Maria* (Hail Mary)

A. M. D. G.
Ad Majorem Dei Gloriam (For the Greater Glory of God), see mottoes

AMGPDT
Lt: *Ave Maria, gratia plena, Dominus tecum* (Hail Mary, full of grace, the Lord is with you)

AMR
Lt: *Ave Maria, Regina* (Hail Mary, Queen)

BVM
Blessed Virgin Mary

D. G.
Lt. *Deo Gratia* (By the grace of God)

D. O. M.
Lt: *Datur omnibus mori* (It is destined that all die)

D. O. M.
Lt: *Deo Optimo Maximo* (To God who is the Best and the Greatest), see mottoes

D. V.
Lt: *Deo Volente* (God willing; by God's will)

ICHTHYS

An acronym meaning "fish" in Greek.

From the many titles of Jesus, three emerged as the favorites of believers: Christ (Gk: "anointed"), Son of God, and Savior. These three would easily combine, becoming a creed and a prayer (see the Jesus Prayer). In Greek, the holy name of Jesus, plus these three titles, would read: *Iesous Christos Theou Yos Soter* (Jesus Christ, Son of God, Savior).

The initial letters of these five words form the Greek word *"ichthys,"* or "fish" in English. For this reason, Christ is often pictured as a fish, a rebus (a pictorial representation of a word) which became an early Christian secret symbol for the Redeemer, and for his followers.

IHS (or IHC)

First three letters of the name/title of Jesus Christ in Greek capital letters: IHCOUC (the older form of the Greek sigma, S, resembling our C). In art, St. Ignatius Loyloa is sometimes pictures with this monogram, alluding to his fabled miraculous knowledge of the Trinity. As IHS it has various interpretations:

1. *Iesus (Jesus) Hemeteros Soter* (Gk: Jesus our Savior), common early Christian Greek inscription;
2. *Iesus (Jesus) Hominum Salvator* (Lt: Jesus Savior of Man), common Latin phrase on early Christian monuments; popularized by St. Bernadine of Siena in the fourteenth century;
3. *In Hac Salus* (Lt: Safety in this i.e., cross);
4. *In Hoc Signo (Vinces)*; "In this Sign (you will conquer)," from the vision and promise received by Constantine before his victory at the Mulvian Bridge (313);
5. I have suffered.

ICXC

Iota sigma; first/last letters of "Jesus Christ" in Greek (IHCOYC XPIC-TOC)

IES

Iota eta sigma; same as IHS, but in lower case: first three letters of "Jesus" in Greek

INI

Lt: *In nomine Jesu* (In the name of Jesus); often used at the close of letters

INRI

Latin abbreviation of *Iesus Nazarenus Rex Iudaeorum* (Jesus of Nazareth, King of the Jews) over Jesus' cross (Jn 19.19). (A slightly-curved horizontal line over the letters indicates abbreviation.)

410

In This Sign

There is a well known story of Constantine's vision of the cross. In the year 312, this pagan leader was marching on Rome to engage Maxentius. At the Mulvian Bridge over the Tiber, he met the foe who stood between him and Rome. The night before the Battle of *Saxa Rubra* in a dream he saw a luminous cross and heard the words *"In hoc signo (crucis) vinces,"* "In this sign you will conquer." He determined to become a Christian immediately, whereupon he inscribed the sign and motto on his soldiers' shields. On October 28, 312, there occurred one of the decisive military engagements of history, in which Maxentius lost the battle, and his life. The West was Constantine's. The Christian God, he believed, had given him the victory. Christianity was given legal equality with any religion in the Roman Empire. The age of persecution was over.

Because of this story, some interpret the Greek letters *iota, eta, sigma* (IHS the first three letters of the name Jesus in Greek) to be Latin *"ihs"* *(In hoc signo)*. That's probably better than the attempted English version of *ihs*, "I have suffered."

The story itself has been called a standing legend, for there are other such "cross and victory" stories, with interchangeable parts. In a Spanish version the hero is Don Alonzo, and the battle is against the Moors at Ourique in 1139. In a vision of the crucifix in the eastern sky, the crucified Christ promised the Christian king a total victory.

In Denmark it is told on Waldermar II. It was a victory over the Estonians (1219) that was promised by the sturdy old vision. The Dannebrog (**brog,** cloth), the Danish national flag, is a white cross on a red field.

IX
Iota chi, initial letters of "Jesus Christ" in Greek.

JMJ
Jesus Mary Joseph

M, Maria, Mariam
Mary

NIKA
Gk: "Victor" or "Conquers" (usually combined with ICXC)

U.I.O.G.D.
Lt: *Ut in omnibs Glorificetur Deus* (That God may be glorified in all things), St. Benedict's admonition to followers

XP
Greek letters (capitalized) *chi* and *rho;* shaped like an X and P, they are equivalent to *CH* and *R* in Latin or English. It is a monogram for Christ, being the first two Greek letters of the word. Hence called the *Chi Rho* ("Key Row"). Also called a *chrisma* (Gk: ointment). Arranged artistically in a variety of ways. This abbreviation or monogram also explains the origin of "Xmas," another expression of the ubiquitous *chi rho.*

NUMBERS AND THEIR SIGNIFICANCE

In many cases in the Scriptures, a number is used not so much for its numerical value ("literally"), but because of its symbolic meaning and the associations it has ("figuratively"). Sometimes the use of a number serves both purposes. (Any number squared emphasizes its significance.) Three, five, and nine have been called mystical.

One
Unity; refers to God.

Three
Numerical signature of the Trinity. The classic "three symbolism" reflects the old adage, *omne trinum est perfectum* "everything in threes is perfect". Man's three elements (body, soul, spirit), theological virtues (see the three altar steps), elements of faith, evangelical counsels, notable duties, sons of Noah, angels that visited Abraham, branches of the vine of butler's dream, baskets of the baker's dream, cities, witnesses, companies of soldiers, arrows, darts, sons, years, days, months, rows of stones, pillars, cubits, prayers, Hebrew children, days of Jonah in fish's belly, days of Jesus in tomb, times which God's voice was heard acknowledging his son, three-fold punishments, blessings, denials, Peter's confessions, personages at Transfiguration, favored disciples, days of Saul's blindness, temptation of Jesus, men who came seeking Peter, etc.

Four

Numerical signature of nature (four seasons) and creation (four corners of the earth). Evangelists, Latin/Greek fathers, rivers of paradise (Pison, Gihon, Tigris, Euphrates), beasts of the Apocalypse, living creatures of Ezekiel, horsemen of the Apocalypse (conquest, war, pestilence, death), cardinal virtues, last things, Gospel versions, winds of heaven, soldiers at foot of cross, virgin daughters of St. Philip, etc.

Six (Seven minus one) The imperfect number, being one short of seven.

Seven (Three plus four) The perfect number, signature of totality, the first of the symbolic numbers. Every seventh day is a Sabbath, every seventh year a sabbatical year, every seventh sabbatical year is followed by a Jubilee year. There are seven weeks between Passover and Pentecost, the Passover and Tabernacle feasts last seven days, during which time twice-seven lambs are offered daily. Also: days of creation, days of the week, patriarchs, Jacob's years of service, ears of corn/oxen in Pharaoh's dream, trumpets of Jericho, baths of Naamen, penitential psalms, Jewish festivals, gifts of the Holy Spirit, works of mercy, joys/sorrows of Mary, last words on the cross, deacons in the apostolic Church, churches of Asia Minor, lamps, spirits before the throne of God, candlesticks/stars/trumpets of Revelation, seals on the Book of Life, sacraments, great councils of the early Church, champions of Christendom, deadly sins, cardinal virtues, seas, ages of man, star in the Pleiades (supposed by the ancients to be heaven), etc.

Eight

Regeneration, baptism, completion. An octagonal baptismal font, people saved in the ark, beatitudes, the time of circumcision, sons of Jesse, etc.

Nine

The number of mystery; the trinity of trinities, the perfect plural (thrice three, which is the perfect unity.) Choirs of angels, the nine crosses.

Ten

The complete number, signifying order; worldly power; any number multiplied by 10 (or 10s) is the highest possible, commandments, plagues of Egypt faithful disciples, wicked brothers of Joseph, sons of Haman, servants of Joshua, virgins, lepers, pieces of silver, etc.

Twelve (Three times four) The universal number, signature of God's people; maturity; totality; the Book of Revelation has much imagery built around this number. Sons of Jacob, tribes of Israel, apostles, stones of the altar, pillars, months, signs of the zodiac minor prophets, sibyls, gates of Jerusalem, fruits of the Tree of Life (Rv 22), men and stones of Joshua, oxen/bullocks/lambs/goats of the sacrifice, cities, princes of Israel, baskets of bread at the feast of the 500, thrones, legions of angels, stars in the woman's crown, foundations of the Holy City, etc.

Fifteen
Signifying ascent, progression, steps of the temple, the gradual psalms, mysteries of the rosary.

Forty
Indicates one generation; also a great many; a long time; Biblical number for trial, testing, waiting; represents the Church militant. The days of the flood, years of Israel's wandering, days of Moses on Mt. Sinai, days of Elijah's fasting, days of Nineveh's probation, days of Jesus' post-resurrection ministry.

The Rainy Saint

This is the story of a man who was canonized by popular tradition. Legend has it that a ninth-century Bishop of Winchester, Swithin, desired to be buried not inside, but outside, in the cathedral's churchyard, so the "sweet rain of heaven might fall upon his grave." So it was. But upon his canonization the good monks determined to honor his sainthood (if not his wishes) by enshrining this body in the choir. And so they did, on July 15th. It forthwith began to rain, and continued for forty days, Biblically enough, until the monks gathered that the saint was averse to their desire and reversed their position and his.

This story has given birth to the saying, "If it rains on St. Swithin's Day, there will be rain for forty days." This story has also given birth to a Scottish version (St. Martin Bullions, July 4), French (St. Gervais; and St. Medard, June 8) and Flemish (St. Godelieve). In any event (or locale): "The Weeping Saint", because of this watery folklore. To this day "St. Swithin" betokens forty day's rain or dry weather.

Fifty (Seven times seven plus one) Pentecost (Gk: *pentekoste,* the fiftieth day): Easter's jubilee octave ($7 \times 7+1$); fulfillment of divine promise.

One hundred (Alone or as multiple) Plenitude. Jesus spoke of a hundredfold harvest, hundredfold reward.

Six Sixty-Six
Perfect imperfection, falling three times short of seven. In Rv 13.18 called a man (a beast), meaning, possibly, a set of men, or an institution headed by a man or a group of men. It seems to mean a name, the letters of which, when regarded as numerals, total 666. In both Hebrew and Greek, letters are used for numbers, the value corresponding to the place of the alphabet; by adding up the number-values in a word, a name or

word may be obtained. St. Ireneus figured *Lateinos* (L-30, a-1, t-300, e-5, i-10, n-50, o-70, s-200), Eganthos, and Teitan; others have figured popes (Leo X), emperors, generals (Napoleon), religious reformers (Knox, Luther). Dr. Kepler equated A with 100, B with 101, etc., and figured "Hitler." The most common interpretation is Nero Caesar, determined by using the Hebrew consonants for that name along with their traditional number values (N-50, R-200, W-6, N-50, Q-100, S-60, R-200).

One Thousand
An indefinitely large number; too large to be counted; eternity ("with the Lord, a day can mean a thousand years, and a thousand years is like a day," 2 Pet 3.8).

144,000
The Church militant (Rv 7.4; 14.1). The number in the Church, (the New Israel, the first fruits of the gospel) at any given moment, representing a totality, which is derived by adding up the traditional twelve tribes of Israel, with each digit magnified one thousand times. (Or similarly: 12×12×1000).

CREATURES OF MYTH AND FABLE

Basilisk (Cockatrice)
A winged reptile from classical and European mythology with a hornlike growth on its rooster head and the body of a reptile, it is hatched from an egg laid on a dunghill. It was said to repel serpents and possess a glance lethal for man. Contact with its body would split a rock. To slay it one had to look into a mirror in order to reflect its venom . . . all provided the slayer saw the creatures before it saw him. (The mirror is the gospel.)

Centaur
Pagan personification of man's evil inclinations. A mythical creature in the form of a horse with human head, arms, and chest. (Can be found on many ancient fonts symbolizing the baptismal transformation of the old Adam into the new Man.)

Chimera
Fright; destruction. A fire-breathing monster of Greek mythology with the head and chest of a woman, forepaws of a lion, body of a goat, and tail of a dragon.

Griffin
Human/divine natures; also omnipotence/omniscience. A monster from Greek mythology with a lion's body and an eagle's head and wings and sometimes a serpent's tail. He drew the chariot of the sun.

Harpy
Evil; rapacity. A fabled monster with woman's head and bust, and vulture's body.

Hydra
The cancerous nature of sin and heresy. A venomous serpent of Greek mythology which sprouted two extra heads whenever one was cut off.

Remora
Jesus, protector of the Church. According to ancient folklore a little fish of disproportionate strength, able to adhere itself to ship's keel and prevent its rolling or pitching even in the most violent storm.

Satyr
The children of evil. A fabled monster with human head and goat legs.

Wyvern
A medieval winged monster with a dragon's head, two legs with clawed feet, and a barbed tail tied in a knot.

GENERAL GLOSSARY OF COMMON SYMBOLS

Something visible with hidden meaning "cast into" (Gk: em, in; ballein, to cast; hence "emblems")

Acorn—latent strength, potential greatness
Agate—health and long life, (June)
Almond—the favor of God (Nm 17.8), Mary
Alpha and omega—See Sacred Monograms/Abbreviations
Altar—Christ, Eucharist, sacrifice, Abraham, worship, God's presence; two-Cain and Abel
Amethyst—repentance, sincerity; (February)
Anniversaries—Fanciful names representing worth, durability and common symbolism; being material suitable for gifts on those occasions:

1st—Cotton (Wedding)		
2nd—Paper	12th—Silk; Fine Linen	30th—Pearl
3rd—Leather	15th—Crystal	40th—Ruby
5th—Wood	20th—China	50th—Gold
7th—Wool	25th—Silver	75th—Diamond
10th—Tin		

Ant—religious industry (Prov 6.6), frugality, foresight
Anchor—Christ, hope (Heb 6.19), salvation, the annunciation; St. Clement of Rome, cast into the sea while bound to an anchor; Nicholas of Bari, patron of sailors
Ape—levity, lust, cruelty, fraud
Apple—original sin, Eve, capital sins (seven on tree of knowledge)
Arch—triumph; broken-untimely death
Argent—In heraldry, the tincture (color) silver
Ark—Church, Mary, Noah
Ark of the covenant—Mary, presence of God (Ex 25)

416

Arm—might, protection

Armor—security, resistance to evil

Arrows—fortune, persecution, martyrdom, St. Edmund, St. Sebastian, St. Ursula

Ashes—repentance, grief

Aspergillum—purity, holiness

Ass—humility, patience, service, peace, burden bearing (See Mt 21.1f); St. Anthony of Padua

The Ass's Stripe

This beast was honored by Christ, tradition says, for his triumphant ride into Jerusalem. The dark stripe running down its back, and crossed by another at its shoulders, was bestowed by Jesus, prophetic of the crucifixion, as an honorable badge for its part in redemption.

Aureola (Lt: *corna,* wreath, halo of gold; from *aurum,* gold)—an elongated nimbus surrounding entire body, signifying the holiness of Jesus in glory; often seen with Madonna and child. Traditionally, its use has signified the heavenly reward over and above the beatific visions itself for the conquerors of the enemies of human salvation: virgins, for victory over the flesh (Rv 14.4); martyrs, for victory over the world (Mt 5.11–12); faithful teachers of the truth, for victory over the devil, the father of lies (Dn 12.3; Mt 5.19). See halo.

Azure—in heraldry, the tincture (color) blue

Bag of money—almsgiving, the betrayal

Balances—justice

Ball and cross—power of Christ encircling world, Church's mission

Balsam—Mary

Banner—victory, the resurrection

Basin and ewer—passion (see Pilate); service

Bat—night, desolation, death

Bay (wreath)—death, grief

Bear—self-restraint, solitary life, martyrdom, Satan

Sweet Talk

The story is told that when John Chrysostom was an infant, bees came to light on his lips, prophesying his sweet speech. The same story is told of Plato, Sophocles, Pindar, and St. Ambrose. Hence a beehive is Ambrose's symbol.

Beaver—The sacrifice of all that interferes with the spiritual quest. It was believed that the beaver has a sack with a treasured medicinal fluid in it. When endangered, however, it would sacrifice this treasure by biting it off, thereby avoiding further pursuit.

Bees—resurrection, tireless activity, chastity, fertility; hive—the faithful, eloquence; St. John Chrysostom, St. Ambrose, St. Bernard, St. Isidore

Bell—call to worship

Birch—authority

Birds—the faithful; caged—soul in body; released—soul flight at death (Ps 123.7)

Black—death, mourning, despair; Benedictines, Augustinians, Jesuits, Cowley Fathers; formerly used at funeral liturgies

Black and white—humility, purity of life

Black over white—Dominicans

Blood—death, redemption, martyrdom, sacrifice

Bloodstone—courage, (March)

Boar—ferocity, sensuality

Blue—firmament, heaven, heavenly love, fidelity, wisdom, truth, Mary

Book—priest's/deacon's teaching power, prophet, wisdom, revelation; open—book of life (Phil 4.3); St. Anne

Brazen serpent—Jesus

Bread—Eucharist, Jesus; loaf in hand, St. Anthony

Briars—sin, temptation, cares of the world

Bridge—Christ

Brown—renunciation of the world, spiritual death, degradation

Budding rod—St. Joseph

Bullock—sacrifice, atonement

Burning bush unconsumed—Mary's virginity; with stone tablets—Old Law given to Moses (Ex 3.2)

Butterfly—resurrection

Camal—submission

Candle—Christ (Jn 1.9), human life, resurrection, baptism, burning—baptismal sonship

Candle, Paschal—five incense grains: five wounds

Candlestick, seven-branched (menorah)—Old Testament

Cat—cruelty, self-indulgence, witchcraft

Caterpillar—earthly man

Cedar tree—steadfastness in the faith, prosperity, longevity

Censer—worship, prayer, priesthood

Chain—slavery, imprisonment, might

Chalice—eucharist, worship, faith, Gethsemane; St. John the evangelist

Chariot, fiery—Elijah

Chrism—baptism, confirmation, orders, anointing

Chrysolite—antidote to madness, (September)

Circle—perfection, eternity, wholeness

City on a hill—Church, Mary

When a "C" is Not a "C"

Those who read music know of the "C" that may appear after the clef sign. It is commonly thought, even by some musicians, that this designation for 4/4 time stands for "common." Not true. This C is not even a C. The most common time, in the morning of music, was "perfect" time, having three beats to the bar. This trinity of beats was considered analogous to the three persons of the Trinity. Naturally—or symbolically—a complete circle, with the connotations of God's completeness and perfection, was used as its sign. 4/4 time, on the other hand, was not perfect and complete, and so its symbol was an incomplete circle . . . the "C" that is not a "C".

Cloak—love, righteousness
Cloud—divine presence, covenant
Clover leaf—Trinity, St. Patrick

St. Patrick's Shamrock

The mysteries of the faith are difficult to teach. Legend has it that St. Patrick helped himself to explain the Trinity to the king's two daughters by using a shamrock. Its three leaflets on one stem represent the three persons in one God. Some say the occasion was his sermon to Laoghaire, chief of the Irish clans who had come to seize the saint for daring to ignite the Easter fire on the Hill of Slane.

Columbine— Spirit's seven gifts
Corn ears—Eucharist
Cornelian—contentment, (July)
Cornerstone—Jesus
Cornucopia—God's providence, liberality, thanksgiving
Corona—see halo
Crescent (sickle) moon—Mary, purity
Crocodile—hypocrisy
Crosier (*baculum pastorale*)—episcopal authority
Cross—atonement, redemption, Christ, Christianity
Crow—the devil's temptings; (the call "caw, caw" likened to "*cras, cras*", "tomorrow, tomorrow", the temptation to procrastination); bad luck (like ravens and owls)

Crown (tiara)—saints in heaven (Rv 2.10; 4.4), victory; of 12 stars—Mary (Rv 12.1)

Cypress—immortality, death, grief, heaven

Daisy—innocence, youth

Dates—the faithful

Diamond—purity, happiness, innocence, (April)

Dice (three-throw of 18)—great reward

Dog—fidelity, loyalty, orthodoxy, watchfulness; at the feet of Ss. Bernard, Benignus, Wendelin; licking the wounds of St. Rock; carrying burning torch by St. Dominic

Dolphin—baptism, love, society, Jesus bearing the souls to heaven

Dove—Holy Spirit (Mt 3.16), gifts of the Spirit (Rv 5.12), the soul, peace, humility, divine inspiration, enlightenment, creation; on a vine—souls in Christ; carrying a ring St. Agnes; on the shoulder of St. David; at the ear of Ss. Dunstan and Gregory; bringing chrism to St. Remigius

Door—Jesus (Jn 10.9), salvation

Dragon—a winged crocodile, with serpent's tail; sometimes the same as a serpent. As a metaphor of evil and paganism, see Rev 7.9 and Ps 91.13 ("the saints shall trample the dragon underfoot")

Duck (over church doors)—enter quietly and pray

Eagle—Christians and their flight to God, Jesus, baptism, St. John, the Gospel, Ss. John the evangelist, Augustine, Gregory the Great, Prisca

Earthen vessels—mortality, humanity (Is 64.8)

Easterly direction—To symbolize a deceased's belief in the resurrection, and their journey to Christ, bodies traditionally have been buried with feet to the east.

Egg—resurrection, hope, creation, spring

Elephant—chastity (because it was thought to be without passion), the fall of man (because it was thought to be without knee joints so, if it fell, it needed help to get up)

Emerald—life, growth, hope, success in love (May)

Escallop—baptism, pilgrimage

Evergreen—immortality

Eye—the Trinity (Prv 22.12; Ps 33.18; 1 Pt 3.23), God's omniscience

Fig tree—fruitfulness, faithfulness

Fish—Jesus, Christians, baptism, Eucharist; St. Peter; see Monograms

Fleur-de-lys—This ancient and beautiful symbol, thought to derive from the iris, is a heraldic device representing a lily. A classic symbol of Mary (also the Trinity), it has varied greatly in style through various periods and countries.

Fire—spirit, Pentecost, martyrdom, fervor, temperance (Ps 65.10)

Fountain—salvation, grace (Is 12.3)

Fox—deceit, trickery, lust, cruelty, wisdom. (There is folklore saying it would bury itself in sand with only its red tongue showing. Birds, attempting to consume the apparent delicacy, would be quickly dispatched.)

Frankincense—"true", "pure" incense—Old Testament priesthood

Frog—resurrection (reappearing after winter hibernation)

Fruit—fruits of the Holy Spirit; St. Dorothea

Garden, enclosed—Mary (Sg 4.12)

Gargoyle—evil exorcised by the gospel

Garnet—constancy; (January)

Gate, closed—chastity, Mary, Ezekiel (4.3)

Gladiolus—the incarnation

Globe—the world of God's creation

Goat—sacrifice, fraud, Old Testament, lust, cruelty

Gold—royalty, wealth, providence, glory

Grapes—Eucharist, Church

Grapevine—Eucharist, autumn

Gray—ashes, humility, mourning; Franciscans (dark brown if the reformed branch)

Green—hope, growth, increase, life, immortality, fidelity; used on Sundays in Ordinary Time

Gridiron—martyrdom; St. Lawrence

Gules—in heraldry, the tincture (color) red

Halo—Holiness of Persons of the Trinity, angels and saints. The following words are sometimes used interchangeably, although they are technically distinguishable:

> **Halo**—Gk: originally a circular threshing floor; the luminous circle around the sun or moon when mist refracts the light, hence a circle or disk.
>
> **Nimbus**—Gk: cloud; an aura.
>
> **Aureole**—Lt, Gk: golden, gold: a radiance; see heaven
>
> **Corona**—Lt: crown; white or colored circle or concentric circles of light wreathing the sun or moon.

Three forms:—

> 1) *Vesica piscis*—Lt: bladder, fish; so, "fish form," The oval glow or ornamentation that twelfth-century artists commonly used to frame pictures of Mary and of Christ. It symbolized the fish (see "*ichthus*", for fish significance). Also called "aureole", an elliptical halo of light.
>
> **2) Circular (halo);**
>
> **3) Radiated, star-like.**

Developments:

> 1) with **rays** diverging triangularly, for Diety;
>
> 2) with a **cross**, for Jesus;
>
> 3) with **a circle** of stars, for Mary;
>
> 4) **encircled with rays**, including quatrefoils (an ornament with four lobes radiating from a common center) for other personages.

Christians began using the halo as a symbol of holiness and the soul's immortality about A.D. 400. A thousand years prior, however, it already existed as a popular symbol in Indian, Egyptian, Greek, and Asian cultures.

Hand—God the Father (Prv 1.24, Sir 10.4, 2 Mc 7.31); protection, creativity, possession; often emerging from a cloud (mystery) and in the Latin form (thumb and first two fingers extended; see Benedictions, with human figures within—God involved with man whom he protects (Ps 139.10; Is 49.2); with 3-rayed halo (*nimbus*)—holiness of the Trinity; open and above—blessing.

Harp—David, praise; St. Alfred, St. Cecilia

Hare—Christians haste to receive grace and the Kingdom

Hart (see. hind)—solitude, purity of life, piety, religious desire (Ps 42.1), Ss. Hubert, Julian, Eustace

Hawk—watchfulness, predaciousness

Hawthorne—Jesus' birth; good hope (end of winter, beginning of Spring)

Heart—love, devotion; with arrows through—St. Augustine, St. Theresa; flaming (charity)—St. Augustine

Hen and chickens—God's providence (Mt 23.37).

Heron—resistance to the ugliness of sin and heresy (because it is said to abhor all dead and decaying things)

Holly—Jesus' birth, Mary's love, resurrection, immortality, foresight

Honey (with milk)—promised land, purity, sweetness

Horn (empty)—vow of poverty, horn of salvation

Horse—courage, generosity, war; ridden—conqueror (Jer 22.4); Ss. Martin, Maurice, George, Victor, Leon

Hourglass—end of time, death

Hyacinth—peace; might

Ichthys—see halo; also Monograms

Idol—apostasy, the world

Incense—faithful's prayer (Ps 115.2; 141.2), thanksgiving

Ivory tower—Mary

Ivy—memory, fidelity, eternal life (because it remains continually green); wreath—conviviality

Keys—penance; St. Peter (Mt 16.19); priesthood; David (Is 22.22);papal authority (saltire—wise, one gold, one silver); entrance into kingdom

Knife—martyrdom, sacrifice; St. Bartholomew

Lamb—Christ (Jn 1.29); suffering servant; with banner—resurrection with cross—suffering Christ; three-rayed for holiness, and reclining to signify the wounded Christ; meekness, an apostle, a believer (Jn 10.1–16); Ss. Agnes, Genevieve, Catherine, Regina; carrying one—John the Baptist

Lamp—Word of God (Ps 119.105), saints, human soul, knowledge; with oil pitcher—a virgin; seven—Holy spirit (Rv 4.5); sanctuary—the Real Presence

Lantern—betrayal by Judas

Laurel—victory, good news; wreath—artistic achievement

Lightning—divine justice, God's power and majesty

Lily—innocence, Mary, Joseph; Easter—the resurrection, immortality; buds—Holy Innocents, serenity, trust (Mt 6.29); the annunciation, Gabriel

Lily of the Valley—humility

Lion—Jesus (lion of Judah), strength, fortitude, royalty, Samson, Satan (1 Pt 5.8), Ss. David, Mark, Jerome

Lizard—the transforming power of the gospel, healer of spiritual blindness (because it was believed of old that when the lizard is old and blind, he can regain his sight by stretching his head toward the rising sun)

Loaf—charity to the poor; Ss. Philip the apostle, Osyth, Joanna, Nicholas, Godfrey

Magpie—bad luck

Mandala (a circular design radiating outward from a center point; nature's examples include a tree's cross section and flowers opening out)—wholeness, organic oneness, healing, growth, all finding their source in the life-giving center, the "still point of the turning world" (*Burnt Norton*, T.S. Elliot); see the mandala in the Jesus of the Eucharist.

Marigold—Mary

Mistletoe—immortality

Moon—Mary in her Immaculate Conception ("Who is she that comes forth as the morning rising, fair as the moon," Sgs). Often crescent, under her feet, (". . . a woman clothed with the sun and the moon under her feet," Rev. 12.1); purity; eclipsed at the crucifixion, on one side of the cross, opposite the sun; in creation and judgment scenes. Used in one of its forms:

1) new (or invisible)
2) crescent, or waxing (with horns upward);
3) decrescent, or waning (with horns sinister, or leftward);
4) first, last quarter, or half moon;
5) gibbous, or more than half
6) full.

Mountain—Church, prayer, aspiration

Myrrh—Epiphany, mortification; in vases on the heads of the Myrrophores (the three Marys who visited the sepulcer with myrrh and spices, Mk 16.1)

Myrtle—virginity

Nails—passion; three—evangelical counsels

Net, fisherman's—Church

Nimbus—see halo

Nymphs—temptation, worldly pleasure

Oak—strength, mercy, virtue; wreath—hospitality

Oil—healing, confirmation, anointing

Olive—peace (Gn 8.11), prosperity, healing, harmony, winter

Olive branch—peace, end of God's wrath (Gn 8.11); gesture of conciliation; see eagle (U.S. symbol) clutching arrows (power) and olive branch (peace)

Olive tree—Gethsemane

Opal—hope, (October)

Organ—see harp

Orange blossom—virginity

Orpheus—Christ; Christian teaching; compelling grace. (The ancient Roman myth of Orpheus, who made such beautiful music that even wild animals were tamed and trees swayed in harmony, has long been applied to Jesus, whose immortal teachings and amazing grace can harmonize man's sinful passions.)

Otter—Christ's descent among the dead

Owl—mourning, desolation, wisdom, bad luck (like ravens and crows); a "funeral bird" (screeching before bad weather)

Ox—patience (Mt 11.30), fortitude, sacrifice priesthood; Ss. Luke, Frideswide, Leonard, Sylvester, Medard, Julietta, Blandina

Palm—victory (Ps 92.12), resurrection, triumph; tree—Joseph, destiny of the just (Ps 92.13)

Pansy—the Trinity, meekness

Panther—grace (In ancient folklore, the panther was said to have a sweet smelling breath, pleasing to all animals except the dragon. The sweet aroma of Jesus' grace attracts the faithful and repels Satan and evil ones.)

Partridge—Satan (There was a saying that the partridge seeks to gather the young of other birds. This is one of the many symbols adapted by St. Jerome.)

Passion Flower—Jesus' passion (central column: column of the scourging; ovary: hammer; three styles: nails; five stamens: wounds; tendrils: whips; rays within the flower forming a nimbus: Jesus divinity and power; leaf shape: spear; ten petals: the ten apostles, minus traitorous Judas and faithful John, who never abandoned Jesus; said to stay open three days, representing the burial/Jesus' three days in the tomb, and also Jesus' three-year ministry; white tint: purity; blue tint: heaven

Peacock—the resurrection (see story)

Pelican—Jesus, Eucharist, charity (see story)

Phoenix—the resurrection (see story)

Pillar—scourging of Jesus, passion

Plough—work, diligence

Poinsettia—star of Bethlehem; red: love of Christ

Pomegranate—resurrection, Church unity, fertility

Potter's wheel— life and its shaping by the Lord

Pulpit—Word of God

Purple—sorrow, penitence, preparation; used during seasons of Advent and Lent

Purpure—in heraldry, the tincture (color) purple

Pyramid—Holy Family's flight into Egypt

Quail—divine providence (Ex 16.12–13)

Quill—divine inspiration

Rain—grace, divine impartiality (Mt 5.45)

Rainbow—peace between God and man, hope, covenant of God's fidelity

Rake—St. Barnabas, because his feast is June 11, the time of the hay harvest

Ram—Daniel

Raven—restlessness, Noah; death (because their sense of smell enables to locate from afar dead and decaying bodies); the indifferent and unrepentant sinner (the raven did not return to the ark of Noah); with owls and crows, bad luck (swallows and storks being good luck); divine providence (alluding to the ravens which fed Elijah); in St. Oswald's hand with a ring in its mouth; at the feet of St. Augustine; bringing St. Paul the Hermit a loaf of bread

Rays (emanations)—Holy Spirit, God's activity and presence, grace; from a dove—guidance of Holy Spirit

Red—sacrifice, particularly the sacrifice of the life (blood), charity, zeal, Holy Spirit; used on commemorations of our Lord's passion, and of the apostles and martyrs for the faith; Pentecost and liturgies honoring Holy Spirit; sandy red, see yellowish

Reed—passion

Ring—marriage, (although now a common part of the wedding ceremony, it is not part of the sacrament); St. Catherine of Siena

Spouse's Ring—Worn on the third finger, left hand (the third finger of the right hand signifying engagement); the common symbol of permanence. The "ringfinger ring" indicates love and affection (it once was believed that a nerve, or a vein of blood, ran from this finger to the heart). A ring on the index finger symbolizes a haughty, bold spirit, while one on the middle finger, prudence, dignity and discretion.

Nun's Ring—Worn on the third finger right hand, plain gold assumed on the day of her profession.

Bishop's Ring—Worn on the third finger right hand; gold; formerly kissed by one on bended knee out of respect for the office; formerly with a stone: sapphire (cardinal), amethyst (bishop, abbot), cameo, emerald or ruby (pope).

Ring of the Fisherman—Bestowed on a pope on the occasion of his election; a seal (inscribed with St. Peter fishing from a boat) used for sealing papal documents. At his death it is ceremoniously broken by the papal chamberlain.

Robe, white—baptismal innocence

Rock—Christ (1 Cor 10.4), church, St. Peter, stability; Jeremiah (his martyrdom)

Rood (screen)—gates of heaven

Rose—love, one without peer, messianic; of Sharon—Jesus (Sg 2.1); mystic—Mary; red—martyrdom; white—purity, incorruption; in St. Dorothea's basket; in the hands or caps of Ss. Casilda, Elizabeth of Portugal, Rose of Viterbo; being scattered by St. Theresa of Lisieux; in a crown on Ss. Rosalia, Angelus, Rose of Lima, Ascylus and Victoria;

when placed over a confessional (sixteenth-century origin) a rose refers to the sacramental seal (see story).

Rose (color)—subdued joy, relieved repentance; formerly used on *Gaudete* Sunday (third of Advent) and *Laetare* Sunday (fourth of Lent)

Rooster—watchfulness, vigilance, call to prayer; with flopping wings—mortification (1 Cor 9.27); with palm near or held in his bill—victory gained; on tomb—resurrection; on tower—preaching office; when fighting—Christians; Peter's denial (Mk 14.27)

Sable—in heraldry, the tincture (color) black

Salamander—the graced Christian resisting temptation (because this lizard-like reptile was thought to be resistant to fire)

Salt—wisdom

Sapphire—heavenly reward, truth

Sardonyx—conjugal felicity, (August)

Saw—martyrdom; St. Joseph

Scales—judgment, justice (Lv 19.36) Ss. Joseph, Michael

Scepter—majestic authority, messianic

Scorpion—Satin, sin, rebuke, remorse

Scroll—Pentateuch, prophets, petition

Scythe (sickle)—death, end of the world

Serpent—Satin, sin, original sin, wisdom (Mt 10.16); bruised—Mary; with staff—Moses and Aaron; brazen on a cross—crucifixion (Jn 3.14–15); Ss. Cecilia, Euphemia, Patrick; (There is an opposite serpent symbolism, surprisingly: see story.

Shamrock—Trinity; St. Patrick

Sheaf—abundance, providence

Ship—Church

Shell—John the Baptist

Shepherd—Christ (Jn 10.11): care, protection (often carrying a lamb)

Shield—faith, protection

Shovel—man's labor

Silver—chastity, eloquence

Skeleton (skull)—death: a *"memento mori,"* a reminder of the inevitability of death ("remember that you must die")

Snow—purity

Spear—martyrdom

Sphinx—(A fabled creature with a woman's head and chest and a lion's body, feet, and tail)—silence; mystery; Egypt

Spider—patience

Squirrel—Christian attitude in the face of eternity; anticipation

Staff—the Good Shepherd (Jn 10.11), apostle, bishop

Stag—Jesus' power (in ancient folklore the stag with his breath could kill the serpent or dragon); drinking—baptism; Ss. Aidan, Eustace, Hubert; see Ps 42

Star—David, house of Jesus' family; 6 pointed—Creator's star, the six days of creation; the six in the Pleiades—heaven, according to the ancients; "day-star, morning star"—Christ (2 Pt 1.19; Rv 22.16), the faithful Christians (Rv 2.26–28), Lucifer (IS 14.12); Ss. Bruno, Dominic

Steps to the altar, the three—faith, hope and charity

Stole—reconciliation, priesthood

Stone—St. Stephan

Stork—filial piety, birth, good luck (like swallows)

Sun—Jesus, overcoming sin in death; New Testament (Mal 4.2); with moon and twelve stars—Jacob, wife and sons (Gn 37.9–11); Mary

Sunflower—obedience (sunflower looks to the sun from dawn to dusk, see Ps 122.2)

Swallow—resurrection (It was believed by some to sleep in the water all winter and emerge in spring); good luck (like the stork)

Swine—impurity, filth, unbelievers, abomination

Sword—fortitude, war, justice, might; Spiritus Gladius (sword of the Spirit) God's word; flaming—explosion from Eden

Tabernacle—Old Testament worship

Tablets—the Law

Tear drops—Mary's seven sorrows

Temple—God's dwelling place

Tetramorph (*Ez 10:4 headed creature with eight wings, fiery wheels underneath*)—the four evangelists

Thorns—sorrow, passion, atonement

Thistle—original sin

Tiger—cruelty, treachery, martyrdom

Topaz—in heraldry, the tincture (color) gold; fidelity (November)

Torch—the Word of God, enlightenment, fervor

Tower—strength, God, defense; with three windows, St. Barbara

Tree—life (Gn 2.9), faith

Trefoil—(design with three leaf-like parts)—Trinity

Triangle—the Trinity

Trumpet—judgment day, resurrection, call to worship

Turquoise—prosperity, (December)

Unicorn—Christ

Vase (pottery)—man

Veil—modesty, flight from the world

Vert—In heraldry, the tincture (color) green

Vesica pisces— see halo

Vine—Jesus, Christian life

Vine and branches—Christ and the Church (Jn 15.5)

Violet—humility; see purple

Volcano—God's retribution

Vulture—evil

Water—grace, divine life

Water lily—love

Weather vane—instability

Well—the Word of God, refreshment

Whale—Satan

Wheat—Eucharist; with tares—the faithful and the wicked (Mt 13.24–30); summer

Whip—repentance, penance

White—purity, simplicity, candor, truth, hope, innocence, virginity, joy; used on all occasions of the joyful and glorious mysteries of our Lord (e.g. Christmas and Easter), of Mary (e.g. Annunciation), of angels, and of saints who were not martyrs; traditionally worn on celebrations honoring John the Baptist, the Chair of Peter, and the Conversion of St. Paul; as the color of a habit—reformed branch of the Benedictines, Cistercians, Praemonstratensians, the Order of the Holy Cross

White over brown—Carmelites

Willow—grief, death

Wine—Eucharist

Wine press—God's wrath, Jesus (Rv 19.15–16), joy

Wings—a divine mission, human aspiration

Wolf—Satan, false prophet (Mt 7.15), hypocrisy, famine, cruelty, lust, tribe of Benjamin

Yellow—infidelity, deceit, treason

Yellowish—treason; Cain and Judas are often shown in ancient art with yellowish or sandy red (or "cane" colored) beards (hence "Judas-colored" means fiery red)

Yew—immortality

Yoke—redemption, slavery, meekness

Word and
Phrase Origins

Words and Phrases with a Biblical Origin or Allusion

Abomination of Desolation
An abominable thing, an idol, a pollution. Quoting Jesus Mt 24.15.

Abraham's Bosom
The rest of the blessed in death, alluding to Lk 16.22, and the custom of a friend reclining on one's bosom, as John on Jesus'.

Abyss. A Great Abyss Fixed
An unsurmountable barrier, alluding to Lazarus and Dives, Lk 16.26.

Adam's Ale
Water; the only drink in Eden.

Adam's Apple
The remnant of Adam's sin, a piece of the forbidden fruit stuck in his throat.

The Adversary ("Opponent")
The devil 1 Pet 5.8

Agur's Wish
"Give me neither poverty nor riches" Prov 30.8.

Ahithophel
A treacherous counselor and friend. This man was David's advisor, but joined the revolt of Absolom, advising him "like the oracle of God"See 2 Sam 16.20–23.

All Things to All Men
Indispensable; the effort to relate to all. What St. Paul said of himself 1 Cor 9.22.

Alpha and Omega
The beginning and the end. A biblical reference to a divine title being actually the first and last letters of the Greek alphabet. (Rv 1.8)

Apple of One's Eye
Something/someone precious. Quoting Ps 17.8.

Armageddon
A slaughter, or great battle. According to Rv (16.16), the site of the last great battle on Judgment Day. Geographically, the mountainous district near Megiddo.

Ashes to Ashes, Dust to Dust
Complete finality. An old English burial service phrase, alluding to the creation of human beings out of clay (Gn 2.7). See also "Remember man that you are dust . . . ."

Babel
All-out confusion, unintelligibility. Allusion to the confusion of tongues at Babel Gn 11.

Balm: Is There No Balm in Gilead?
Where is consolation? (Jer 8.22), balm being comfort.

Benjamin
The youngest, a favorite. Allusion to Jacob's youngest of this name **Gn 35.18.**

Benjamin's Portion (or mess)
The largest. Allusion to Joseph's banquet for his brothers in Egypt (and Benjamin's share being five times the others) **Gn 43.34.**

Beulah Land
A paradise, "promised land," far away dream-come-true land. Is 62.4 reference to Israel called not "Forsaken" but "Espoused" (Beulah in Hebrew).

Bird: A Little Bird Told Me
Sir 10.20, a caution against speaking privately what one would not want known publicly.

Birthright: To Sell Your Birthright for a Mess of Pottage
To exchange one's heritage for a trifle. Alluding to Esau selling his for Jacob's pottage **Gn 25.29–34.**

Blind Leading the Blind
Allusion to Mt 15.14, Jesus confronting the pharisees.

Bosom Friend
In 2 Sm 12.3 Nathan tells David a parable in which he describes a poor man's ewe lamb in those terms; see also Lazarus on Abraham's bosom **Lk 16.22** and John on Jesus' **Jn 13.25.**

Bowing the Knee to Rimmon
Temporizing; knowingly doing wrong in order to save face. Allusion to 2 Kgs 5.18: Naaman the Syrian getting Elisha's permission to worship Rimmon when with his master.

Bread: Ask for Bread and Receive a Stone
Spoken of a rebuff, a denied request. From Mt 7.9 where Jesus teaches about the power of prayer.

Bread: Break Bread
Eat together. Typical scriptural language for the Eucharist (for example, **Acts 20.7).**

Bread: Cast Your Bread upon the Water
". . . after a long time you may find it again." (Sir 11.1) Be adventuresome, take a chance, be generous, don't expect immediate recognition. (The waters of the ocean sometimes bear lost treasures to the shore.)

Bricks: To Make Bricks Without Straw
Trying to do a job without ability or materials. Allusion to Hebrew forced labor under Egyptian taskmasters **Ex 5.6–14.**

Build on Sand
Working with poor planning or unsure beginning. From a parable of Jesus **Mt 7.26.**

Burden: Bear the Burden and Heat of the Day
To do all the hard work; the complaint of those in Jesus' parable who got paid no more than those who came on at the eleventh hour **Mt 20.12–old translation.**

Cain: The Curse (brand, mark) of Cain
Said of one with nowhere to go, or no place to call his own. The stigma of murder. Blood guilt that cannot be expiated. Allusion to God's judgment after Cain murdered Abel **Gn 4.11–12, 15.**

Calf: Kill the Fatted Calf
Let's celebrate. To welcome with the best. Allusion to Prodigal Son parable **Lk 15.30.**

Charity: Charity Begins at Home
In 1 Tm 5.4 Paul teaches about the true piety for widow's children.

Citizens of No Mean City
A recommendation because of background. Quoting Paul who referred to Tarsus as he solicited a hearing in Jerusalem **Acts 21.39.**

Clay Feet
A surprising flaw in one esteemed. From the clay feet of the image in Nebuchadnezzar's dream **(Dn 2.31,32)** and an allusion to the standard composition of ancient idols.

Cloud of Witnesses
Quoting the *Letter to the Hebrew's* reference (12.1) to the witness of the faith of the ancients.

Coals: Heap Burning Coals on One's Head
Using kindness to melt another's animosity; turning the other cheek; repaying good for evil: an effective reproach **Prv 25.21,22; also Rm 12.20.**

Come to Pass
Happen. A phrase made popular by old translations of Christ's words regarding what would happen before the end **Mt 24.6.**

Cover a Multitude of Sins
A compensating virtue; a pleasing cover of good over the bad that you can't see. Quoting St. Peter when he spoke of love, the ultimate virtue **1 Pt 4.8.**

Crumbs from the Rich Man's Table
A pittance for the poor. A phrase from a parable of Christ: all that Lazarus said he wanted from Dives **Lk 16.21.**

Cup: Let this Cup Pass Away
May I not have to go through this. From Christ's Agony in the Garden Mt 26.39.

Cup: My Cup Runneth Over
I am richly blessed Ps 23.5,6.

Dan; from Dan to Beersheba
From one end (of the Kingdom) to the other. Coast to coast. All over. These two cities were the farthest north and south in Israel.

Dead: Let the Dead Bury the Dead
Against temporizing. Let bygones be bygones. Break with the past. Quoting Mt 8.22: the conditions for following Jesus.

Delilah: There is No Leaping from
Delilah's Lap into Abraham's Bosom
That is to say one cannot live and die in grave sin and expect salvation. Referring to the lovely betrayer of Samson (Jdg 16), and to the patriarch whose bosom represented reward and rest see Lk 16.22.

De Profundis (Lt: Out of the depths)
Said of a bitter cry. First Latin words of Ps 130; common in burial services.

Doubting Thomas
A skeptic. Thomas doubted when told of the resurrected Christ Jn 20.25–29.

Eat, Drink, and Be Merry
In Sir 8.15 it is pessimistically recommended to enjoy life while we have it, since this is the best we can do in the world. In Is 22.13, in another context, there is a similar phrase, with the added "tomorrow we shall die."

Eleventh Hour
Just in time. An allusion to the Day Laborers parable Mt 20.1–16, and the ones hired last.

Entertain an Angel Unawares
Encountering a virtual saint; surprised by virtue. From a biblical exhortation on hospitality Heb 13.2.

Eye for an Eye, Tooth for a Tooth
The *Lex Talionis* (Law of reciprocal punishment in kind) Dt 19.21.

Eye of a Needle
A difficult task, if not a human impossibility. From Mt 19.24: "It's easier for a camel to pass through . . ."

Flesh: Remembering the Fleshpots of Egypt
Fantasizing over, glorifying the (perceived) good things of the past when they are no longer available Ex 16.3

Fly in the Ointment
A little thing that spoils everything, or at least detracts from its attractiveness Sir 10.1

Forbidden Fruit
Anything stolen, but especially illicit love. Alluding to the fruit stolen by Adam and Eve in the Garden.

Fruit: By Their Fruits You Shall Know Them
(A Tree Is Known by Its Fruits)
Judging by one's actions, not words; results, not intentions. From Mt 12.33 where Jesus exposes the pharisees' legalistic, externalized perversion of religion.

Gall and Wormwood
Extremely distasteful, a bitter pill. Quoting Lam 3.18, 19.

Gird Your Loins
Roll up your sleeves; hitch up your figurative belt for vigorous action. Common biblical exhortation See 1 Kgs 18.46; Job 38.3; Jer 1.17; 1 Pt 1.13.

Giving: There Is More Joy in Giving than in Receiving
Words of Jesus, although not in the Gospel. Paul ends his farewell address to the elders of Ephesus by recalling these words of Jesus Acts 20.35.

Giving up the Ghost
Death. Expression used by Job (Jb 14.10) according to King James Version, by the Psalmist (Ps 31.6; Lk 23.46); and by John for Jesus' death (Jn 19.30), for example.

Gladden: To Gladden the Hearts of Men
Allusion to Ps 104.15; the purpose of the gift of wine.

Glory: In His Glory
In one's natural, truest element; Jesus was seen in his glory only in transfiguration (Mk 9:2–10). Used of those who are at their best, in their natural habitat, doing their destiny.

Goads: To Kick against the Goads
Competing against odds, especially authority or fate, or in Saul's case grace (Acts 9.5). This line, following "I am Jesus whom you are persecuting", is no longer included in good modern translations because it was never found in the Greek or in the best Latin manuscripts.

Good Samaritan
A good neighbor, helper of the distressed. Alluding to Jesus' parable involving the priest, the Levite, and the Samaritan Lk 10.30–35.

Grapes of Wrath
Potential recipients of just punishment; used by Steinbeck as the title of a novel and occurring in the first stanza of the *Battle Hymn of the Republic*. Allusion to the winepress image of Rv 14.19–20 which teaches about the harvest of the earth and the impending doom of the ungodly.

Greater Love than this No One Has

From Jesus' last discourse (Jn 15.13), where he teaches about the extent to which love will take the followers: martyrdom for the beloved; applied to the unbloody martyrdom of unrecognized service, especially when *agape* (sacrificial/divine love) and *philia* ("brotherly" love) are united in one person.

Green Wood: If They Do These Things in the Green Wood, What Will Happen in the Dry?

If the innocent (green wood) suffers so, what will come of the wicked (dry wood)? Quoting Jesus meeting the Jerusalem women on the way of the cross Lk 23.31.

Handwriting on the Wall

The all but obvious being revealed. The announcement of the imminent fulfillment of some doom. At Belshazzar's party (Dn 5) it was right there on the wall, "Your days are numbered."

Hewers of Wood and Drawers of Water

Drudges; humble workers. Quoting Dt 29.11 where Moses, in his final discourse, is summoning all Israel, from least to greatest, to a renewal of the Covenant. In Jos 9.21 it is also used as a phrase for the slaves of the community.

House Built on Rock

Someone or something with a sure foundation. Allusion to Jesus' parable on the practice of religion Mt 7.24.

House Divided

When some said that Jesus was casting out devils by the power of the prince of devils (Lk 11.14f), he said that Satan in that case would be divided against himself, and such a house divided falls; but his kingdom lasts.

Howling Wilderness

Suggesting dreariness and savagery (wind and wild beasts). From Moses' song of deliverance Dt 32.10.

Jacob's Ladder

Steps that are high and steep; the flaw in a stocking where only the ladder-like weft is left; also "jacob" for a ladder. An allusion to the ladder of Jacob's dream on which God's messengers were going up and down Gn 28.12.

Jeremiad

A doleful complaint, lamentation. Jeremiah contains warnings of disaster for Israel that reveals his own inner conflicts and personal feelings about God and his job Jer 15.10–21; 18.18–23; 20.7–18.

Jericho
Used to give a specific name to an indefinite place. Allusion to the "Stay in Jericho until your Beards Grow Back" story in 2 Sm 10.1–5 (in other words, "stay away for awhile").

Jeroboam
One who is of great promise, but who ends up a perversion. Allusion to the mighty man of valor "who made Israel sin" 1 Kgs 11.28; 14.16.

Jeroboam, Rehoboam
Wine bottles, about five quarts and about three quarts. The first King of Israel and the first King of Judah. Association?

Jesse Tree
A genealogical tree, sometimes taking the form of a vine (sometimes arising from Jesse himself, recumbent), or a branched candlestick, tracing ancestry of Jesus. (If in a window, a "Jesse window"). From Is 11.1, ". . . a shoot from the stump of Jesse."

Jezebel: A Painted Jezebel
A depraved and seductive person. A flaunting woman; bold in manner and morally loose. About ninth-century B.C. Phonician wife of King Ahab of Israel who fostered worship of other gods in Israel and who arranged the murder of Naboth 1 Kgs 16.31–32; 18.1–19.3; 21; 2 Kgs 9.7–37.

Job
Personification of patience, poverty. Book of Job.

Job's Comforter
An ineffectual empathizer or pretender who only worsens the situation. Job's friends concluded that he must have somehow caused his own grief Jb 16.2

Jonathan's Arrows
A warning, not meant to hurt. Allusion to 1 Sm 20.18f and the story of the arrows Jonathan shot to signal to David according to a prearranged code

Jordon: Bathing Seven Times in the Jordon
A remedy; an action (sacramental), not necessarily understood, and not therapeutic in itself, but efficacious. Alluding to the directions Elisha gave Naaman the Syrian to heal his leprosy 2 Kgs 5.1–27.

Jordon: Crossing Jordon; Jordan Passed
Dying. Like the pagan river Styx, the Jordon formed the boundary of the Promised Land, and crossing it ended the journey in the wilderness ("the world") Jos 1.1f.

Joseph
One unsuccessfully seduced, unwavering in continency. Allusion to the wife of Potiphar (the pharaoh) trying to seduce Joseph Gn 39.

Jot or Tittle: Not One Jot or Tittle
The absolute minimum, the smallest possible amount or degree. Alluding to Jesus referring to letters of the Law which would not pass away until they were fulfilled Mt 5.18. In old translation, "the smallest letter" (see *New American Bible*) was more literally rendered "jot," which is from Latin *jota*, which is from the Greek *iota*, which is the ninth—and smallest—letter of the Greek alphabet. Hence the saying "not one iota." "Tittle" is rendered "part of a letter" because it is an old name for the so-called diacritics used in Hebrew that furnished a vowel sound for a word; hence, not even a letter.

Kedar's Tents
This world; nomadic existence. Allustion to Ps 120.5, the cry of one so dwelling; Kedar being a son of Ismael (Gn 25.15) and a nomad.

Kill the Fatted Calf
Prepare to celebrate! Especially, warm hospitality for a homecoming. The prodigal son's father gave these instructions upon his son's return Lk 15.

Kiss of Judas
Pretended affection; betrayal. An obvious reference to Judas and Jesus Mt 26.49.

Labor of Love
Work engaged in because of affection for, or desire to please, another. Probably alluding to St. Paul (1 Thes 1.3) and the *Letter to The Hebrews* (6.10) where the believers are commended for the way they live.

Laborer Is Worth His Wage
Be fair. With these words (Lk 10.7), Jesus assured the seventy-two he was sending on mission that they could "stay in one house eating and drinking what they have . . .".

Land of the Living
Life. A phrase Jeremiah used in quoting his enemy's evil intents (Jer 11.19). Also Ps 27.13, meaning *while still here* "I shall see the Lord's bounty."

Land of (flowing with) Milk and Honey
Paradisal; heaven. In Ex 3.8 this was the phrase used to describe the destiny of the enslaved Hebrews whom Moses was called to lead. See Joel 3.18.

Laodicean
One indifferent about religion, because the Christians of that city of the Apocalypse were Rv 3.14–18.

Lazar
Victim of a repulsive disease; any poor beggar. From Lazarus, the leper laid daily at the rich man's gate, cured by Jesus Lk 16.19–25.

Legion: My Name Is Legion.
Many; hydra-headed; more than one would want or guess. It was the name given by the Gerasene demoniac in **Mk 5.9.**

Leopard Changing Its Spots
An impossibility. This is how Jeremiah described the ability of disgraced Jerusalem to change from evil to good **Jer 13.23.**

Light: To Hide Your Light Under a Bushel Basket
Modesty, to the point of "depriving" others. Concealing abilities or merit. From Christ's Sermon on the Mount, **Mt 5.15.**

Lines Have Fallen to Me in Pleasant Places, The
My portion, destiny, is good. Quoting Ps 16.6, meaning the lines drawn for the portion of a tribe.

Lion Shall Lie Down with the Lamb, The
Harmony. Quoting Is 65.25 and the prophesy of a new world.

Lip Service
Just talk. From Jesus' discussions with the pharisees **Mt 15.8 See Is 19.13.**

Live By the Sword, Die By the Sword
Harm set, harm get. Jesus' use is recorded in Mt 26.52, when he was being arrested and a follower drew a sword.

Loaves: With an Eye to Loaves and Fish
Poor motive. Camouflaged desire for material gain. Allusion to Jesus teaching and feeding the multitude, and his knowledge of their motive **Jn 6.26.**

Lord of Creation
Man. An allusion to the divine gift to man of dominion in the world, **Gn 1.28–29.**

Lord Loves a Cheerful Giver, The
So saith Paul **(2 Cor 9.7)** as he teaches stewardship and generosity.

Love of Money Is the Root of All Evil, The
According to Paul, **1 Tm 6.10.**

Magdalene
A reformatory for prostitutes. Allusion to the great sinner of Lk 8.1–3, Mary of Magdala, out of whom Jesus cast seven devils.

Magnificat
Any hymn of praise; deriving from Mary's: "My soul magnifies (*magnificat*) the Lord. . . ." **Lk 1.46f.**

Mammon of Righteousness
Money. An old translation of Lk 16.9, where Jesus is counseling on the right use of this world's goods.

Man Proposes, God Disposes
Ancient proverb; Scriptural version, **Prov 16.9.**

438

Many Are Called but Few Are Chosen
A warning about the need for ongoing conversion and growth, especially in the face of apathy and self-assurance; being the last line of Jesus' Wedding Banquet parable Mt 22.1–14.

Mark of the Beast
Anything so designated is branded evil, unorthodox, from Rv (16.2; 19.20) and the references to the personification or focus of evil in the world.

Maudlin
Sickeningly sentimental; from Mary Magdalene (Lk 8.1–3), whose face and eyes according to some ancient artists had that kind of look.

Miserere (or misericord)
The underside of a folding choir stall seat, so-called because in its folded-up position it is comfortable for the aged in a kneeling position. Named from the Latin title (first word) of Ps 51, David's prayer of repentance.

Money (love of), the Root of All Evil
See Love.

Mouths: Out of the Mouths of Babes
. . . the greatest wisdom comes, which, according to Ps 8.2 and Mt 21.16, is praise.

Naboth's Vineyard
A vulnerable holding; another's possession that one could take. Ahab did take Naboth's 1 Kgs 21.

Name: Their Name Lives on
Popular memorial saying. From the famous Praise of the Ancestors in Sirach 44.14.

Nazareth: Can anything Good Come from Nazareth?
A not very indirect put-down; doubting greatness because of humble origin, as Nathanael did of Christ Jn 1.46.

New Jerusalem
Paradise; heaven. Allusion to John's vision of the new creation Rv 21.

New Wine in New Skins
Brand new, not a re-make. In Mt 9.17 Jesus expounds on the need for a recreated spirit, not just a remodeled religion.

Nimrod
A distinguished, daring hunter. Nimrod was "a stout hunter before the Lord" Gn 10.9.

No Respecter of Persons
Indiscriminate, ignoring distinctions. Quoting St. Peter (Acts 10.34 old translation) explaining that God doesn't play favorites.

No Rest for the Wicked
Isaiah's observation (*"Nemo malus felix"*, *"No bad man is happy"*).

Nothing New under the Sun ("Nil novi sub sole")
From Ecclesiastes 1.9, "That which has been is that which shall be, and that which has been done is that which shall be done; there is nothing new under the sun."

Numbered: Your Days Are Numbered
Doom saying. What Daniel saw in the handwriting on the wall Dn 5.26.

Nunc Dimittis: To Receive One's. . . . to Sing One's. . . .
Leave taking: permission to, satisfaction at. From the opening words of Simeon on the occasion of the presentation of the child Jesus, "Now you may dismiss your servant. . . ." (*nunc dimittis*) Lk 2.29f.

Olive Branches
A lighthearted term for one's children. The psalmist (128.3) calls them that, and the wife a fruitful vine.

Ox: Thou Shalt Not Muzzle the Ox that Treadeth Out the Corn
Do not begrudge a laborer his little compensations. Quoting Dt 25.4 and applying it to the laborer and the privileges that could be allowed him in the circumstances and byproducts of his work. Paul's use: 1 Cor 9.9; 1 Tim 5.18.

Patience of Job
Maximum longsuffering and forbearance. From the Book of Job, though no particular line in it speaks exactly those words of old Job.

Patmos
A hermitage; exile. In Rv 1.9 it says John was retired/exiled there.

Pearls: Casting Pearls Before Swine
Giving what is precious to the unappreciative; to waste. Allusion to Mt 7.6 where Jesus acknowledges that the Good News will not be accepted by all, and that responsibility for this belongs to the one who "tramples it underfoot."

Philistine
A boorish, uncultured person. Israelite neighbor and long standing enemy. Their name came to be used because they believed in Canaanite religion and because they stole the Ark of the Covenant.

Physical, Heal Thyself
The advice, recorded by St. Luke (4.23), for those who should take the advice they give ("*Medice, cura te ipsum*").

Plough; Put One's Hand to the Plough
Commencing in earnest. Quoting Lk 9.62, where Jesus preaches the cost of discipleship, and the temptation to temporize.

Poor as Job
The man dispossessed through the devil's testings Book of Job.

Poor as Lazarus
A beggar by this name laid daily at the gate of the rich Dives Lk 16.19–25.

Potters' Field

A cemetery for the poor. Originally the land in the infamous Valley of Hinnom (Gehenna) called Aceldama (Field of Blood, Acts 1.19) bought with Judas' betrayal money (Mt 27.7) as a cemetery for foreigners. "Potters' " possibly because it was once used for clay; or because it was where potsherds were discarded (see Jer 19.1f), the land being good for nothing else.

Prodigal Son

The wastrel who returns, repentant, after dissipation; from the great parable of such a one by which Jesus taught about the nature of his Father. Lk 15.

Promised Land

The place of one's dreams, referring originally to Canaan, promised to Abraham by God Ex 12.25; Dt 9.28.

Prophet Is Not Without Honor, Except in His Native Place, A

Admiration and fame is greater the farther one is from home. Proverbial in the Scriptures See Mt 13.57; Mk 6.6.

Race: The Race Is Not to the Swift, nor the Battle to the Strong

Adapting Sir 9.11, the pessimistic original.

Raise Cain

Raise a ruckus, make noise, cause trouble: Cain, Abel's brother and the first murderer (Gn 4), being a euphemism for the devil.

Reed: A Bruised Reed

Unstable, in a weakened condition, untrustworthy. Allusion to Egypt as an ally for the Jews against Assyria 2 Ks 18.21; Is 36.6.

Reed Shaken in the Wind

One who goes where the wind goes. Jesus said John the Baptist was not one (Mt 11.7), but was a man with firm conviction.

Remember Man that You Are Dust, and to Dust You Shall Return

An Ash Wednesday warning See Gn 3.19 and Ez 28.18.

Render unto Caesar What Is Caesar's (and unto God what is God's).

Quoting Jesus allowing the just claims of the state; from a discussion on tribute to the emperor Mk 12.17.

Return to One's Vomit

Backsliding; return to sin. 2 Pt 2.22, citing a dog's disgusting habit. See also Prv 26.11.

Right Mind: In One's Right Mind

Sane; serenity following agitation. This is how the townsfolk found a demoniac whom Jesus had exorcised Mk 5.15—old translation.

Root of the Matter

Basic issue; quintessence. Job (19.29); wondered if the problem's cause was within him.

Sabbatical
Time allowed a teacher/professor that is free from teaching for the sake of future study or travel; from the practice of leaving land fallow every seventh year Ex 23.10, Lv 25.2–7; dt 15.1–11.

Sackcloth and Ashes
Penitence, strictly speaking. Common Scripturally; see Mt 11.21.

St. Peter's Fingers
The fingers of a thief ("a thief has a fish hook on every finger"), alluding to the fish Peter caught that had a coin in its mouth Mt 17.24–27.

St. Stephen's Loaves
Stones. Allusion to the stoning of St. Stephan Acts 7.54–60.

Salt: Covenant of Salt
An unbreakable bond. From 2 Chr 13.5, referring to God's covenant with Israel, salt being a symbol of incorruption and perpetuity.

Salt of the Earth
Good people, for their sanctifying effect on others, "preservers of civilization." Used by Jesus of disciples, Mt 5.13, in the Sermon on the Mount.

Samson
An exceptionally strong person. Referring to the Hebrew hero in Judges 13–16.

Sanctum Sanctorum
A private place, holy ground, intimacy; Lt: holy of holies, properly the inner chamber of the Jewish temple entered only by the high priest on the high feast of Atonement.

(Is) Saul also among the Prophets?
Of one who now espouses a cause or idea he hitherto assailed. In 1 Sm 10.12 it tells of the origin of this proverb. It might have been used of another Saul (or is it Paul?) in Acts 9.21.

Scapegoat
An innocent one bearing responsibility for the guilty; one paying the price for another. From the Old Testament Atonement ritual (Lv 16): two goats were brought to the temple: one was sacrificed to the Lord, the other "heard" the confession of the high priest and was taken into the wilderness with the transferred sins of the people.

See How the Land Lies
To check out; make preliminary investigations; to test the water. An old translation of Nm 13.16 ("reconnoiter"), where Moses is readying to enter Canaan.

Semitic
Pertaining to the Jews. Of the descendants of Shem, the eldest son of Noah (Gn 10), that is, the Hebrews, Arabs, Assyrians, Aramaeans, and others.

Seventy is the Sum of Our Years, or Eighty if We Are Strong
Our alloted span, our natural life. Frequently used scripturally as in Ps 90.10.

Shake the Dust Off Your Feet
Leave an unhospitable place; implying judgment, or at least determination and finality. Alluding to Jesus' advice to disciples in the event they were not received well Mk 6.11; Lk 9.5.

Sheep: To Separate the Sheep from the Goats
The good from the bad; alluding to Last Judgment, Mt 25.32.

Shibboleth
A catchword, slogan or test word; the criterion for distinguishing insiders. Differences in the pronunciation of this word's initial sound betrayed rival tribal affinities and became the basis for discovering and exterminating outsiders Jgs 12.4–6.

Simony
Buying and selling sacred things and Church offices. From the magician Simon Magus' offer to buy the power to bestow the Holy Spirit Acts 8.18.

Skin: By the Skin of One's Teeth
Just barely. Job thus described his hold on life 19.20.

Slow to Anger
Equable, as Nehemiah describes God 9.17.

Sounding Brass (or tinkling cymbal)
Noisy gong, clanging cymbal. A lot of talk; words without sense. Allusion to a traditional translation of 1 Cor 13.1, Paul's description of a loveless person.

Sow: As You Sow, So Shall You Reap
An old translation of Gal 6.7.

Sow the Wind, Reap the Whirlwind
Causing trouble, and getting more than you bargained for; starting something you can't finish. So Hosea fumes (8.7) about Israel's perversity.

Spare the Rod and Spoil the Child
It's folly to allow childish faults to go unreproved. A version of Prv 13.24.

Spirit: The Spirit Is Willing but the Flesh Is Weak.
Good idea, poor execution. The will, but no power. It is the caution of Jesus from Mt 26.41, human nature being what it is.

Stars in their Courses
Destiny. Alluding to Jdg 5.20: the enemy of Sisera in battle.

Still, Small Voice
Conscience; an insight after a lot of huffing and puffing. Allusion to 1 Kgs 19.12, the voice Elijah finally heard after the earthquake and the fire.

Stolen Sweets Are Always Sweeter
Illegality charms, making such ill-gotten gains more palatable. An old translation of an Old Testament proverb **Prv 9.17.**

Stone: To Cast the First Stone
To lead in fault finding. Quoting Jesus' defense of the woman caught in adultery **Jn 8.7.**

Straight and Narrow
Path of virtue. Probably alluding to Mt 7.14 where Jesus describes the path to eternal life.

Strain: To Strain the Gnat and Swallow the Camel
Fussing about peccadilloes while committing serious offenses. Not allowing a small point all the while blithely accepting a difficult one. From Mt 23.24, and the practice of straining wine. In this instance Jesus is criticizing the pharisees.

Stranger in a Strange Land
A foreigner, or feeling like one. This is an allusion to the explanation Moses gave for the name ("Gershom") he bestowed on his son born in Midian when he was taking refuge there from the pharaoh **Ex 2.22.**

Strength: To Go from Strength to Strength
To improve work, reputation, and so on; so the psalmist proclaims the progress of the just **Ps 84.8.**

Suffer Fools Gladly
Because you know that at least you are wise; be patient. Quoting one old translation of 1 Cor 11.19, where Paul acknowledges factions in the community, and teaches that the good will stand out by contrast.

Sun: Don't Let the Sun Go Down on Your Anger
Quoting **Eph 4.26.**

Sweat: By the Sweat of Your Brow
By hard manual labor. The injunction of God to Adam after the fall **Gn 3.19.**

Sweating Blood
Anxiety, if not anguish. From Christ's experience in the garden the night before his death **Lk 22.44.**

Swords: To Beat Swords Into Ploughshares
Changing from war mongering to peace seeking. Quoting **Is 2.4; see Mi 4.3.**

Taking Your Life In Your Hands
Risking your life. A common Scriptural expression; for example, Jephthah **Jgs 12.3,** David **1 Sm 19.5,** Job **Job 13.14.**

Talent
Gift, ability. Reference to Jesus' parable of Mt 25.14–30; this was the name of a weight or piece of money in the ancient world (Gk: *talanthon*, a balance).

Teeth Set on Edge
Grating; experience difficulty or revulsion. When Jeremiah (31.29) and Ezekiel (18.2) teach about the consequences of sin and our personal responsibility for it they quote a proverb with this line.

Tell It Not in Gath
Don't publicize this, lest my enemies rejoice. Don't tell anybody or they'll laugh at me. Quoting David (2 Sm 1.20) lamenting the death of Saul, aware that the Philistines (in Gath) would rejoice.

Thirty Pieces of Silver
Blood money, a bribe. Judas Iscariot's payment for betraying Christ Mt 27.3.

Thorn in the Flesh
In Nm 33.55, the Lord used this phrase in describing for Moses the inhabitants of Canaan should they be allowed to remain after the Hebrews took over. However, the line usually alludes to St. Paul's reference to some personal cross of his 2 Cor 12.7.

Tongue, a Double-edged Sword
When words wound, as in an argument cutting both ways, addressing both the pro and the con. Alluding to Heb 4.12 describing the Word of God. Also Rv 1.16 and the sword out of the mouth of the Son of Man with one edge to convict, the other to redeem.

Touch-Me-Not.
Name given to an *impatiens* plant, from the post-resurrection words of the Lord to Mary Magdalene in Jn 20.17. *(Noli me tangere—NO-lee may TAN-ger-ray).*

Tried and Found Wanting
Or "weighed in the balance . . .". Tested and proven false. Translations of a line from Daniel's interpretation of Belshazzar's dream Dn 5.27.

Turn the Other Cheek
Advice against retaliation, and an allusion to Jesus' mandate to love the enemy Lk 6.29.

Twinkling of an Eye, In the
Quickly. So St. Paul describes how quickly the bodies of believers who are alive at the end of the world will be changed 1 Cor 15.52.

Uriah: Letter of Uriah
A treacherous missive; a death warrant in the guise of a friendly letter. Alluding to the letter by David to General Joab that Uriah should be sent to the front 2 Sm 11.15.

Vanity of Vanities, All Is Vanity
The opening words of the book of Ecclesiastes, *"Vanitas vanitatum, omnis vanitas* ("vanity" being fruitlessness; the sense being, "everything man does is in vain").

Voice Crying in the Wilderness
Prophetic voice, precursive word and warning. John the Evangelist thus described John the Baptizer 1.23.

Wages of Sin is Death, The
Sin results in death. So Paul teaches in Rom 6.23.

Wars and Rumors of Wars
Bad news. In Mt 24.6 Jesus cautions that these are not signs of an immanent end.

Washing One's Hands
To back out of; to disdain responsibility after initial involvement. An allusion to Pilate with Jesus on his hands Mt 27.24.

Way of All Flesh
To die, including demise and burial. A common Scriptural phrase See Jos 23.14; 1 Kgs 2.2.

Weathercock
A person always changing his mind; one not living up to his own words. A weather vane in the form of a rooster; it was a medieval tradition to adorn church steeples with this symbol of St. Peter. An allusion to St. Peter's denial of Christ after Christ predicted it Mt 26.31f.

Widow's Cruse
Any small supply that—managed well, or merely spent—becomes adequate and apparently inexhaustible. From Elisha's miracle with the cruse (or cruet) of oil in 2 Kgs 4.1–7.

Widow's Mite
A small amount at great sacrifice. The offering praised by Christ in Mk 12.42.

Wine: Good Wine Gladdens a Person's Heart.
This Latin phrase (*Bonum vinum laetificat cor hominis*) makes a proverb of Psalm 104.15, "Wine (God's bountiful favors) that maketh glad the heart of man" See also Jgs 9.13.

Wings of the Wind
Swiftly. Alluding to Ps 18.10 describing omnipresence, divine mobility.

Wisdom of Solomon
Proverbial wisdom; great wisdom. Referring to the Hebrew King of the Old Testament. See Solomon's prayer for wisdom (Wis 9.1–12). Jesus recalled that the Queen of the South came to hear the wisdom of Solomon, and that "something greater than Solomon is here." Lk 11.31.

Wise as Serpents, Gentle as Doves
Quoting Jesus (Mt 10.16) in his mission to the twelve, a modern translation renders "clever" and "innocent" as these two virtues that are not mutually exclusive.

Youth Renewed like the Eagle's
From Ps 103.5, and the ancient belief that every ten years an eagle would fly into the "fiery regions," thence to the ocean depths, and rising, molted, to a new life.

Words and Phrases with a Church Origin or Allusion

Bartholomew Pig
An obese person. One of the principal attractions at the St. Bartholomew Fair was the pig, roasted whole and served up hot.

Braid: To Braid St. Catherine's Tresses
Living as a virgin.

Bead
A prayer (A. S. *i-bed, biddan*). Prayers in some forms, were counted or "told" (kept track of) using a string of bean-like articles. Eventually, each was called a bead (a "prayer"), the whole device a string of beads (or a rosary) and, by association, any little bean-shaped article a "bead."

Bean: He's Found a Bean in the Cake
He got lucky; he won something; he came into unexpected good fortune. An allusion to the cake of Twelfth Night in which a bean is hidden, awaiting a finder who thereby becomes Twelfth Night King.

Bell, Book, and Candle
Used in connection with a reprimand in terms of rejection, closing a case. It has overtones of laying down or upholding the law, and originated in an ancient ceremonial excommunication in which the bell was rung, the book closed, and the candle extinguished.

Catherine Wheel
A firework, twirled by its explosions; because of its shape, which was the instrument of her martyrdom.

Catherine-wheel Window
A circular window, like a rose window, because of the method of St. Catherine's torture and death.

Cloistered
Reclused; withdrawn from the world. A cloister is the covered walk, usually around three sides of a quadrangle of a monastery.

Cruet
Salt, pepper and mustard containers. Specifically, the containers for water and wine to be used at Eucharist.

Carnival
Shrovetide, originally; the little season before Lent ending on Shove Tuesday: a time of merriment and excess before the spartan season of Lent; good eating before the abstinence. Through It: *carnevale,* from Lt: *carnilevanem* (*carnem*, flesh; *levare*, to lift), to remove meat.

Devil's Advocate *(Advocatus Diaboli)*
The person fond of taking the opposing view in any discussion, for the sake of argument. From the role of Promoter of the Cause ("Devil's Advocate") in the canonization process.

Ex Cathedra (Lt: from the chair)
Authoritative; a dogmatic assertion, self-sufficient mandate. From the papal pronouncement made "from the chair" of St. Peter's successors (that is, authoritative and binding) which fulfills certain criteria and is binding for the universal Church.

Filbert
The nut, so called because it is ripe by August 20, the feast day of St. Philibert, a seventh-century abbot.

Good-bye
Contraction of "God be with you." (Like adieu, Fr: *a' Dieu,* "I commend you to God".)

Grange
A national farm organization. From Lt: *granum* (granary), the monastery's farm and its corn storage; derivatively, a lone farm or house attached to a monastery on which rent was paid in grain; more loosely, a country house on the grand side.

Magnificat: To correct *Magnificat* before one has learned *Te Deum*
Presumptuous criticism; performing above station (The former being more difficult than the latter).

Magnificat: To sing the *Magnificat* at Matins
Doing things in the wrong order. *Magnificat* is a Vespers (evening) and not a Matins (morning) canticle.

Martin
A bird of the swallow family, maybe associated with St. Martin (and the goose legend), or maybe because it comes upon the scene (for some) in March (the Martian month) and departs around Martinmas (November 11).

Martinmas: His Martinmas will come, as it does to every hog.
Death is inevitable. November and St. Martin's tide was prime time for butchering among the Anglo-Saxons.

Mumpsimus
That's what a person is who knows he's wrong but refuses to change, stubbornly adhering to error (which is also called a "mumpsimus"). This because of *sumpsimus,* a word in the Latin Mass meaning "we have received" (which is beside the point). Centuries ago, a certain aged priest would mumble "mumpsimus" for *sumpsimus,* and a certain young priest would correct him, without effect. Furthermore, in some kind of justice, what made the wrong one a mumpsimus made the right one a sumpsimus, or one who officiously insists on using a technically correct term or form instead of what's popular but incorrect. So there.

448

Odour: (He died) in the Odour of Sanctity
As a saint. Because it was believed in the Middle Ages that a pleasant odour was given off by the body of a saint at death (or disinterment, in the event of the remains were being moved).

Orientation: Oriented
Referring generally to getting one's bearings, learning the ropes. From the custom of facing the east (orient) in prayer, already a practice before Christ. Christianized as (1) the direction to Israel, where Christ lived on earth, and (2) the direction of the sunrise, and the east whence he will come to judge the living and the dead.

Poor as a Church Mouse
Where could a mouse find even a crumb in a building with no cupboard or pantry?

Red-letter Day
Lucky day, memorable. On calendars, in daybooks, and so on, saints' days and holidays were printed in red ink (days which have special prayers in liturgical books).

Repenter Curls
A woman's tresses. A repentant Mary Magdalene washed Jesus' feet with tears and dried them with her hair.

Robbing Peter to Pay Paul
Debt shifting; borrowing money from one to pay off another; impoverishing one Church to improve another. Commonly referring to an English fable: property of St. Peter's Abbey Church, Westminster, was used to help defray repair expenses on St. Paul Cathedral, London (about 1560); however the phrase was used prior to this date.

Rose *Sub Rosa* (Lt: under the rose). See Rose

Rubric
Law, directive, heading. Lt: *rubrica,* red ochre, the color in which the Romans wrote laws (rubrics), while court edicts were posted on white. In Church books, directions, titles, and such were printed in red.

St. Anthony's Fire
The pestilential disease *erysipelas* ("the sacred fire"), because of the cures experienced in the eleventh-century plague through the intercession of St. Anthony.

St. Anthony's Pig ("Tantony Pig")
The runt of the litter, and one that becomes a pet is so-called because proctors of a St. Anthony's hospital would protect pigs that were unfit for food by tying bells around them. Hence St. Anthony, the fourth-century founder of a society of ascetics, is the patron of swineherds and often pictured with a little pig at his side.

St. Bernard Passes
Two passes in the Alps into Italy, the Great St. Bernard from Switzerland and the Little St. Bernard from France. Because on the Great Pass stands the great hospice of St. Bernard of Menthon (923–1008).

St. Bernard Dogs
Bred and trained by the Augustinian Canons which staffed the hospice of St. Bernard in Switzerland's Great St. Bernard Pass for tracking and helping snowbound travellers.

St. Crispin's Holiday
Monday, for those whose work week begins on Tuesday. Because Monday is the day off for a shoemaker, whose patron saint is Crispin, the shoemaker.

St. Cuthbert's Duck
The eider duck, because its breeding grounds are in the Farne Islands, which is also locale of that saint and legends about him.

St. Dunstan and Blindness
Associated because of a World War I era institution for the blind at St. Dunstan's House, Regents Park; for the care and rehabilitation of blinded soldiers, and later for all.

St. Elmo's Fire
The "corposant" (Port: *corpo santo;* body, holy), or fire ball sometimes seen around masts and rigging of ships in a storm. A brush discharge, electrically speaking; a luminous electrical field, reddish when positive, bluish when negative. There is no such saint. Perhaps the name is a corruption of Anselm of Lucca, or Erasmus (patron saint of Neapolitan sailors), or Helena (sister of Castor and Pollux, the twins whose names are also associated with the corposant).

St. Francis' Distemper
Poverty, impecuniosity, because of the Franciscan's vows of poverty, and the rule which disallowed carrying money.

St. Lawrence: Fiery Tears of St. Lawrence
A name for the shooting stars of the prolific perseid meteor shower at its height between August 11 and 13. Legend has it that ever since A.D. 258, when he was burned to death on Aug. 10, the deacon Lawrence weeps from his place in heaven over the cruelty of humanity, and his tears glisten through the dark sky like drops of gold.

St. Martin's Beads
Trinket jewelry. St. Martin-le-Grand once had a reputation as a place for imitation jewelry.

St. Monday
Any Monday, facetiously so-called by those who take a long weekend by making it a holiday (or holyday); when idle workmen spend Saturday's paycheck in amusement or dissipation.

St. Vitus' Dance
Chorea, the disease. In Medieval Germany it was believed that an annual dance around a statue of St. Vitus on his feast day (June 15) would secure the gift of good health for that year. The near mania that evolved came to be compared to, if not confused with, the symptoms of chorea, and vice versa, with the saint himself becoming an intercessor for those with the disease.

Sunday Saint
A practicing Church person and church goer who doesn't practice faith the other six days.

Supererogation; Works of Supererogation
Service beyond the call of duty. An archaic term theologians gave to things done but not enjoined on believers. (Lt: *super,* above; *erogare,* to pay out.)

Sinecure (Lt: *sine cure,* without cure/care)
Salary and position with responsibility. A benefice with salary but no pastoral duties.

Scot-free
Exempt from payment, penalty or punishment. A Scot (from early Saxon silver coin "*sceat*") was an ancient Anglo-Saxon tax levied to support the clergy. The payment, originally in corn, was made on St. Martin's (November 11).

Sic transit gloria mundi
Old phrase addressed to a newly-elected pope on the occasion of his enthronement: "so passes the glory of the world."

Tawdry
Corrupted from St. Audrey, which is in turn a corruption of Etheldrida. Originally referring to the ostentatious low-quality lace and jewelry at the annual St. Audrey fair in the isle of Ely.

Tiffany
A sheer, woven fabric like gauze, originally silken. A corruption of "theophany" (Gk: *Theos,* God; *ephainein,* to show), a divine manifestation (an epiphany); applied to the material because it was a common costume fabric for the Twelfth Night (Epiphany) revels.

Index

*Story
**Picture

Impediments to marriage, 270
Imprimatur, 69
In articulo mortis, 91
In extremis, 91
Incarnation, the (charts), 149
Incense, 282**
Incorruptibility, 88
Indian Summer, 312
Individualism (chart), 176
Indulgences, 101
Indult, 195
Infant of Prague, the, 338
Infidel, 66
Infiorata, 325
In Hoc Signo, 411*
INI, 410
Initiation, 240–242
In Memoriam, 94
In petto, 195
INRI, 169, 171*, 397, 410
Insignia, 203–204
Institution, of the Eucharist, 255
Intercession; in the Mass, 254–255;
    stories about, 372*
Interdict, 268
Interregnum, 190
In this sign, 411*
Intinction, 247
Intuitive prayer, 75
Invalidation, 272
Invocation, 77
Invocation gesture, 264
Irish: blessing, 55; saints, 366; harp
    in art, 55**
Isaiah, 36, 131**, 396
Islam, (chart), 111; 188
Israel (chart), 111; (map), 145; name,
    140; tribes, 144–145; Kingdoms,
    145; national stories, 124*, 126–
    137*, 146*
"Ite, missa est," 180
Itinerarium, 77
IX, 411

JMJ, 411
James and John, 351, 353
Jehovah, 139
Jerome and the Lion, 114*
Jerusalem, 140 ("Zion"), 141 (map),
    165; church of, 215
Jesse Tree, 403*, 436
Jesuits, 212
Jesus Prayer, the, 9
Jesus prays, 73
Jesus teaches prayer, 73

Jew, see Israel
Jewish calendar, 320–321
Joachim and Ann, 310, 357
John XXIII, Pope, 199, 219
John and James, 351, 353
John, apostle (picture/symbol), 159,
    358
John the Baptist, 161; feast of, 292;
    309
John Paul II, Pope, 193, 201, 202,
    204, 222
Joining the Church, 240–242
Joseph, picture, 22; Legend of the
    Budding Staff, 350**; day of
    week, 291; St. Joseph Day, 324;
    statue, 350
Journeys of Paul (maps), 181–182
Joys, Seven of Mary, 14, 15
Jubilee Year, the, 320
Judah, 140, 145
Judaism (charts), 111, 123
Judas, 354, 355, 356*
Jude, St., 371
Judges stories, 129*
Judgment, in Scripture, 90, 91
Julian Calendar, 288
Julian the Apostate, 67*
Juniper, the, 244*
Justice; divine, 59
Justin, martyr, 248, 359

Kerygma, 177, 180
Kergymatic sermons in Acts, 180
Keys symbol, 128**, 190**, 196**,
    400**, 422
Kingdom of God, 96
Kings of Israel stories, 130–131*
Kings, the three, 49*, 61**–62*, 357
Kneeling, 264
Knights of the Holy Sepulchre, 168
Knights of St. Gregory, 168
Koinonia, 177
Koran, the, 116
Kyrie, eleison, 256

Lack of form (in marriage), 272
Laetare Sunday, 271, 295, 298
Lamb of God, the, 155, 157**,
    249**, 397, 422
Lamed Vav, the, 350*
Land of Milk and Honey, 140, 437
Languages of a Catholic tradition,
    256
Languages of the Bible, 116, 256
Last Blessing, the, 91

Consecration to, 349; shrines, 314, 343

Mary Magdalen, 358

Mas (suffix), 293

Mass: word translated, 180; access prayers, 249; changes in, 248; structure and parts of, 58, 249; of the Presanctified, 300; of the Resurrection, 92; fruits of the, 254

Matins, 278

Matrimony, Sacrament, 239, 240; elements of, 270; end of, 272; of the Mystery of Jesus, 302; Marian, 303

Mater Dolorosa, 342, 398

Matthew (picture/symbol), 159**, 354, 356

Maundy Thursday, 300

May Day, 307*

Mea culpa, 6, 256

Meal Prayers, 9–10

Meal Scenes in Luke, 167

Medals, 286

Meditation, 75

Memorare, the, 15, 344

Memorials, list, 303–314

Mendicants, 210

Menorah (the (shield), 127**, 144, 321** (picture), 418

Mesopotamia (map), 123

Meteors, 184*

Metropolitan, 187

Michaelmas Day, 100*, 292, 319

Michelangelo, 128, 169, 197, 337*

Midsummer Day, 309*

Millennialism, 107 (diagrams), 108

Millennium, the, 107

Minister, title, 276

Minor orders, 273

Miracles of Jesus, the 164

Miraculous Medal, the, 345

Miraculous medals, 286

Missal, 248, 260

Mission of the Church, the, 177

Missionary journeys of Paul, the, 181; (map), 182

Missions, California, 210

Miter and crosier, 185**, 203**, 195**

Mizpah Blessing, the, 36

Mohammed, see Moslem

Monastery, 209–210, 235

Monastics, 209–210

Monk, 208–210, 244*

Monograms, sacred, 409–412

Monsignor, title, 276

Monstrance, 257, 259**, 327**

Month's Mind, 94

Months, names, and dedication, 290

Montserrat, 221

Moon, 71*, 293*, 423

Moral virtues, 58, 68

Morality, in Scripture, 90

Mordecai Day, 321

Morning Offering, the, 9, 333

Morning Prayer, 278: canticles, 279; structure and elements of, 279

Mortal Sin, 87; elements of, 87

Moses, 128, 245, 396

Moses' final blessing, 37

Moslems, 222 (chart) (map), 189

Mosque, 222

Mother of God, 344

Mother of Perpetual Help, Our, 347*, 348*

Mothers' Day, 271

Mothers' Patrons, 272

Motherhouse, 235

Motivation, 180*

Mottoes, 201–202

Motu Proprio, 195

Mount Zion and Moriah, 140

Ms. Wisdom, 137*

Music emblem, 419

My Breastplate Prayer (St. Patrick), 29

Mystery of faith, the three-fold, 63

Mysteries of Christianity, the chief, 63

Mystical rose symbol, 22

Myth/folklore symbols, 386–388, 415–416

Names: of God, 137–139; of Christ, 18; of the Chosen People, 140; of the Promised Land, 140; of popes, 191–193; changed, 244; of months, 290; of days, 291; Marian, 349

Naming after saints, 243, 349

Narthex, 232

Nathanael, 354

Nationalities within ancient Christianity, 215

Nativity, 149; relics, 382

Nativity scenes, 61**, 148*, 405*

Nave, 232

Nazareth years, the, 161*

Neophytes, 242

sion foretold, 168; Passion symbols, 397
Passover, the, 321; picture, 166**, story*, 167, in the Triduum, 300
Pastor, title, 275, 276
Paten, 259
Patriarch, 186; of the West, 193, 216
Patriarchs, the Seven, 140
Patriarchal stories; the 7, 140; sanctuaries, 142
Patriarchates, the 5 (map), 188
Patron saints, 367–377
Paul, conversion experience picture, 181**; death, 356
Paul's journeys, 181–182
Pauline Privilege, 272
Peace Prayer of St. Francis, the, 28
Peacock symbolism, 95**, 424
Pectoral cross, 203
Peculium, 72
Pelican symbolism, 329, 424
Penance, new rite outline, 267
Penance; see Reconciliation
Penitential observance of Lent, 80
Pentecost, feast of, 292, 301; Jewish, 321
Perjury, 89
Perpetual adoration, 326
Perpetual Help, Our Lady of, 347**
Persecution; stories, 184*; the Ten Great, 184, 401*
Persian Empire, the (map), 133
Peter, 191; faith development, 351–352; death, 356, 400, 401*
Peter's Pence, 197
Petition, see intercession, 74
Philip, 354, 356, 400
Phoenix symbolism, 96, 424
Phrases/words of Scriptural origin, 430–447
Phrase/words of Church origin, 447–451
Pieta, 337
Pike, symbol, 398*
Pilate, 170*, 171*, 335
Pilgrim, 247*
Pilgrimage, 222–223
Pius X, Pope St., 191, 247, 331, 366
Pius XII, Pope, 191, 330
Plenary indulgence, 101
Poems and songs in the Old Testament, 34–36
Pomegranate, symbol, 177, 424
Pontiff, 193
Pontificate, 190

Poor Clares, 376
Pope, 185, 190–198; first/twentieth century, 191; names, 191–192; titles, 185, 192–193; distinctive popes, 191; correspondence to, 193; ring, 204; coffin, 198; election, 190; papal statements, 194–196; coat of arms, 200; crown, 204
Populations of religious/denominations, 111
Postures, liturgical, 263–264
Poverty, 72*, 205
Prague, the Infant of, 338*
Praises, the Divine, 88
Prayer, 73–78, kinds of, 74–77: of Jesus, 2, 58; motive for, 78; object of, 78; teachings by Jesus, 73; Jesus prays, 73; "rule of praying", 78; from the New Testament, 41–49; from the Old Testament, 31–36; Pauline gratitude, 46–47; at the foot of the Altar, 228**; of the faithful, 248, 254; after Mass, 6; of the Liturgy of the Hours, 278–279; to St. Michael, 6; before a crucifix, 10; before meals, 9; prayer of self-offering, 30; to the Holy Spirit, 11–12; to the Guardian Angel, 10; liturgical, 238; posture, 264; devotional, 324–388
Prayerful greetings, 45–46
Preachers, 276
Preaching, 253
Precepts of the Church, the, 70 71
Precious Blood of Jesus Litany, the, 19–20; day of week, 291
Prefigurations in the Old Testament, 149–154
Prelate, 276
Premonstratensians, 210
Presbyter, 277
Presence, the Real, 246
Presentation of Christ, the, 151, 284*
Presentations to Catechumens
Preternatural gifts, 86
Pretzels, 264
Priest, 205, 272, 277
Primate, 187, 193
Primus inter pars, 192
Prince of the Apostles, the, 192
Principles of devotional prayer, 324
Prior, 277
Priory, 235, 275

466

Roman Canon, the, 255
Roman Empire, the (maps), 189
Romanesque, 225
Rome, Church of, 215
Roots, Christian (chart), 123
Rosary, the, 12–15, 58, 101, 345, 399
Rose, liturgically, 263; symbolically, 426; Rose of Paradise, the, 86*; Rose symbol, 425; Rose, the Golden, 298; Roses, Mothers' Day, 271; Roses from heaven, 97*
Ruskin Blessing, the, 56

Sabbath breaking, 71
Sabbatical year, 320, 442
Sabbatine (Saturday) Privilege, 207
Sacrament: basic concept, 238; defined, 238, 240; listed, 239
Sacraments of the Church, the, 239, 240, 246–247, 265–267, 272–277
Sacraments, symbols of, 401
Sacramentals, principal, 280–286
Sacramental Seal, the, 266
Sacramentary, the, 248, 254
Sacred College, the, 187
Sacred Heart, consecration to and enthronement of the, 331, 332–333; devotion to, 330–333; promises of Our Lord, 331; encyclical on, 330; Sacred Heart, the illustration, 330**; Sacred Heart, Litany of the, 16; Sacred Heart, the Great Promise, 91
Sacred places, 219–222
Sacred monograms/abbreviations, 409–412
Sacred vessels, 257
Sacrifice, 246
Sacrificial giving, 82
Sacrilege, 88
Sacristan, 257
Sacristy, 233, 257
Saints: Agnes, 304; Aidan, 280*; Alphonsus, 348; Ambrose, 8, 79; Anacletus, 191; Andrew, 390, 400; Anne, 208, 271, 272, 310; Anthony, 75, 88, 372, 374; Augustine, 8, 10, 12, 64, 79, (prayers), 30; Barbara, 92**; Bartholomew, 2, 69, 400; Basil, 23, 209; Bellarmine, 178; Benedict, 209, 275; Bernadette, 110; Bernard, 13, 15, 209; Bernadine, 18*; Blaise, 324; Bonaventure, 88; Boniface, 377, 404*; Bridget, 272; Bruno, 209;

Catherine, 382; Cecilia, 373; Celestine, 192; Christopher, 318; Chong and Companions, 380; Clare, 376; Clement, 191; Colomba, 289*; Crispin, 450; Cyprian, 359; Cyril and Methodius, 214; Distaff, 304; Dominic, 211; Dorothea, 97; Dunstan, 104, 368, 450; Elizabeth Ann Seton, 379; Evaristus, 191; Francis of Assisi, 72, 211, 382, 383, 394, (Peace Prayer), 28, (Canticle to Brother Sun), 28–29; Francis Xavier, 212, 379; Gabriel, 99; George, 106; Gertrude, 247; Giles, 208; Helena, 392*; Hubert, 66; Ignatius, 30, 185, 212, 326, 359; Irenaus, 359; James, 400; Januarius, 383; Jerome, 114; Joachim, 310; John Chrysostom, 365, 417; John Eudes, 330; John Lateran, 348; John Neumann, 326, 379–380; John of the Cross, 212; John the Apostle, 159**, 358; John the Baptist, 309*; Joseph, 85, (Litany), 22–23, (death), 350; Joseph of Arimathea, 358*; Jude, 371, 400; Justin Martyr, 359; Kateri Tekawitha, 379; Andrew Kim and Companions, 380; Lawrence, 184; Linus, 191; Luke, 159**, 323; Margaret Mary, 91, 110, 333 (Promises to), 91, 110, 331; Margaret of Scotland, 272; Mark, 159**, 167*; Martin, 83, 221, 275, 319; Mary Major, 348; Matthew, 159**, 348, 400; Matthias, 400; Maximilian Kölbe, 380; Methodius, 214; Nicholas, 315; Nicholas of Ravenna, 382; Odilia, 368; Pachomius, 209; Patrice, 64, 100, 261, (Breastplate Prayer), 29; Paul (Blessings), 47–48, (Gratitude Prayers), 46–47, 400; Peregrine, 265; Peter, 191, 400; Peter Damien, 278; Philip, 400; Pius X, 191, 247; Polycarp, 359; Raphael, 368; Robert, 209; Roch, 270; Stephen, 184; Swithin, 414; Teresa of Avila, 212, 383; Thérèse of Lisieux, 213; Thomas the Apostle, 226, 400; Thomas Aquinas, 114, 327–329, 364–365;

Wonders of the world, the, 125
Woods of the cross, the, 393*
Word of God, 246
Words/phrases of Scriptural origin, 430–447; of Church origin, 447–451
Works of *supererogation*, the, 70, 451
Works of Mercy, the, 83
World religions major, (chart), 111; western, 110
Worship, three dimensions, 246
Wort, St. John's, 309
Worthies, the Nine, 366
Wounded Healer, A, 270*

Writers, early Christian, 359

"Xmas"
XP, 412**
Yahweh, 138, 139 (chart)
YHWH, 138, 139

Yawning, legend, 103
Year numbering, 289
Yoke symbol, 428

Zechariah's Canticle, 39
Zion, 141, 253
Zucchetto, 204